AF479037

ROBERT
HOULE

RED IS BEAUTIFUL

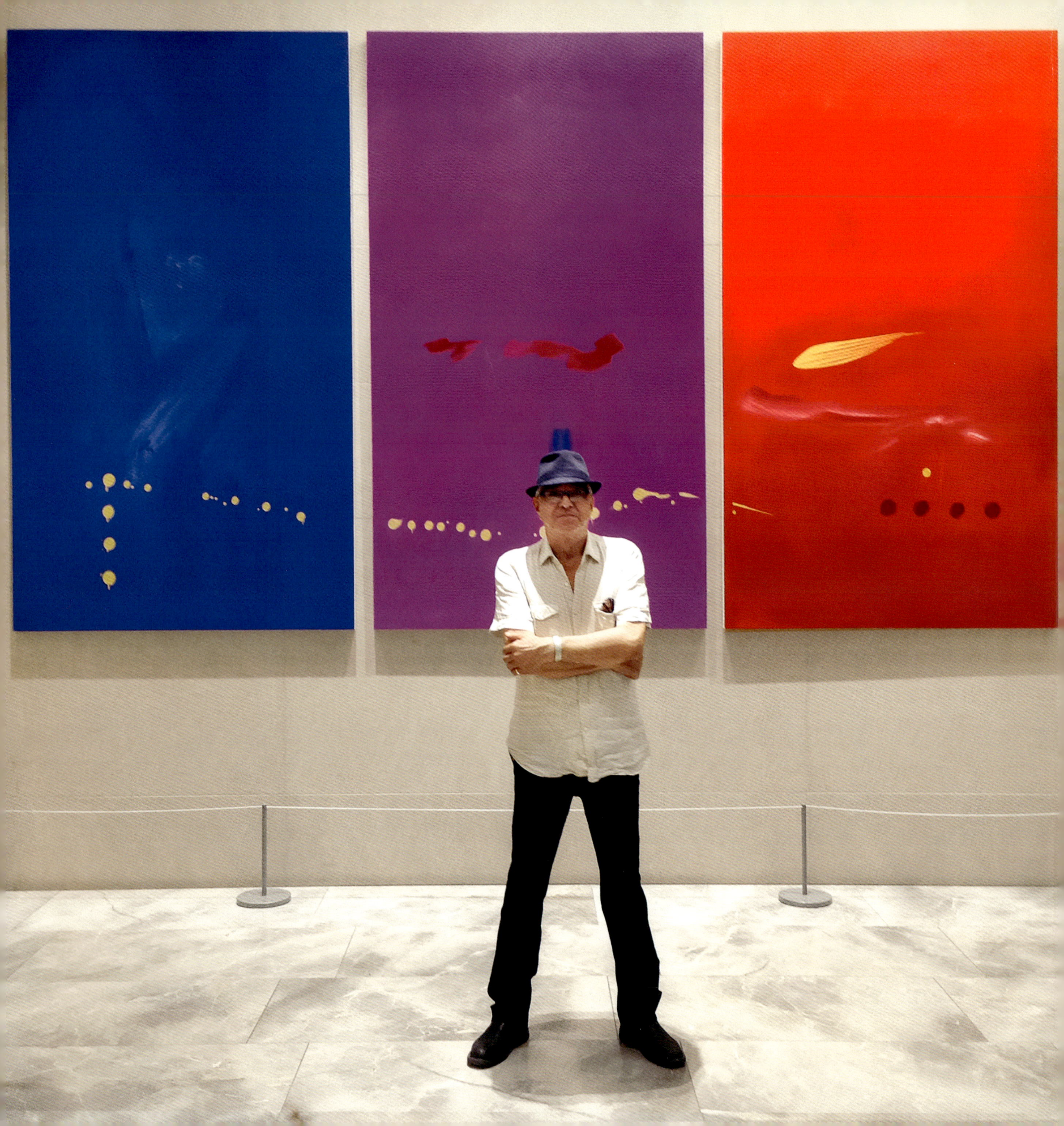

ROBERT HOULE

RED IS BEAUTIFUL

Edited by
Wanda Nanibush

Art Gallery of Ontario

DelMonico Books • D.A.P.
New York

Table of Contents

Opposite title page:
Robert Houle with *Colours of Love* in the lobby of 1 Bedford Street, Toronto, after the work was installed on August 17, 2015. Image courtesy of Barry Ace.

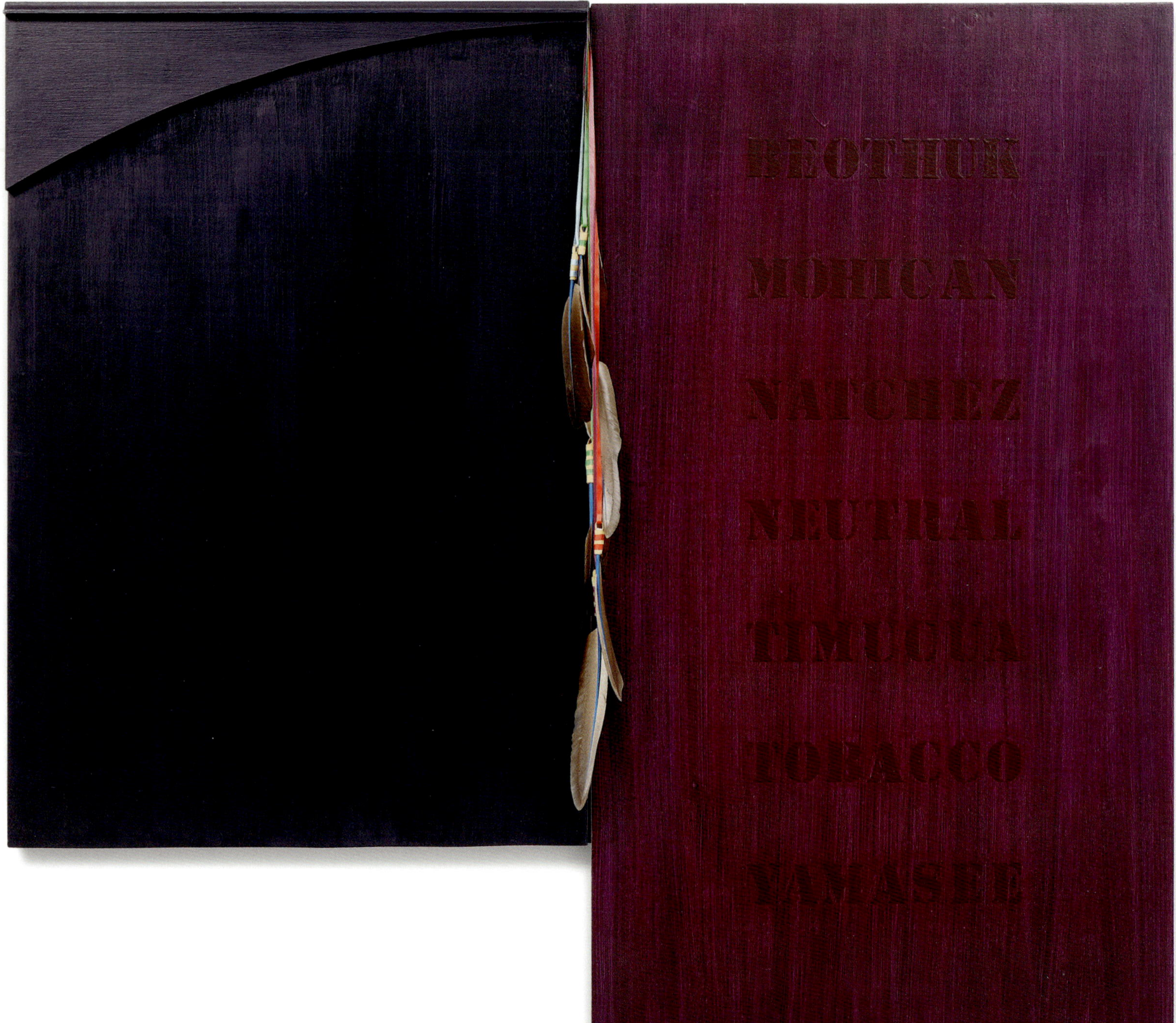
BEOTHUK
MOHICAN
NATCHEZ
NEUTRAL
TIMUCUA
TOBACCO
YAMASEE

Director's Foreword
Stephan Jost

Over his fifty-year career, Robert Houle has continuously challenged our understanding of Western and First Nations art history. By channelling his early interest in Abstract Expressionism and the expansive possibilities of colour through the lens of Indigenous explorations of spirituality, geometry, and abstraction, he established a dazzling new visual language. He has used his skills as a master colourist and his critical insights to tell new and necessary stories about sovereignty and the ongoing history of Indigenous Peoples on this land.

Robert Houle: Red is Beautiful is the Art Gallery of Ontario's first major retrospective of Houle's paintings, drawings, and installations. Expertly curated by Wanda Nanibush, the AGO's Curator of Indigenous Art, this exhibition showcases a remarkable range of work produced between 1970 and 2021, illuminating Houle's technical and aesthetic talents and incisive explorations of such urgent themes as war, resistance, and sovereignty.

We are tremendously grateful to the individuals and organizations whose generosity was integral in mounting *Robert Houle: Red is Beautiful*. These include our Supporting Sponsor, CIBC, and our Contributing Sponsor, McCarthy Tétrault LLP. We also appreciate the generous support of Cecily & Robert Bradshaw, The Delaney Family Foundation, Gerald Sheff & Shanitha Kachan, and David Staines & Noreen Taylor. Thanks as well to our Media Partner, blogTO, and our government partner, the Canada Council for the Arts.

This remarkable show would not have been possible without the efforts of Project Manager Katarina Veljovic, Interpretive Planner Nadia Abraham, and Administrative

Opposite page:
Robert Houle, *In Memoriam*, 1987. Oil, feathers, leather, and ribbon on plywood, 137.2 × 151.9 × 9 cm. Art Gallery of Ontario, gift of Vanessa, Britney, and Nelson Niedzielski, 2000. 2000/1196.

Assistant Chloé Wittes. Many thanks are also due to Jim Shedden, Manager of Publishing, and his department, along with designer Sébastien Aubin, and Lucas Elke and his associates at Type A Print Inc., for realizing a beautiful accompanying publication. Additionally, I would like to thank staff across all areas of our museum, including Production Manager Malene Hjørngaard and Production Assistant Evelyn Quinn, as well as exhibition designers Aleksandra Grzywaczewska and Theodora Doulamis.

We are very appreciative of all the contributors who shared their profound insights and personal reflections about Houle and his work: Ron Benner, Stephen Borys, Mark Cheetham, Alanaise Onichin Ferguson, Jamelie Hassan, Faye HeavyShield, David Penney, Duke Redbird, Gerald Vizenor, and Kay WalkingStick. We are also obliged to Michael Bell, Mark A. Cheetham, and Jessica L. Horton, who graciously gave us permission to include excerpts of their superlative texts in our publication.

We thank the lenders who have generously shared works for this exhibition: Barry Ace and Earl Truelove; Agnes Etherington Art Centre, Queen's University; Art Gallery of Hamilton; Canada Council Art Bank; Canadian Museum of History; Carleton University Art Gallery; Deborah Chansonneuve; City of Toronto Art Collection, MOCCA Collection; Comsatec Inc.; Confederation Centre of the Arts; Norm Dumontier; Paul Gardner; Robert Houle; Indigenous Art Centre, Crown-Indigenous Relations and Northern Affairs Canada; MacKenzie Art Gallery; David McIntosh; McMichael Canadian Art Collection; Museum London; Wanda Nanibush; National Gallery of Canada; National Museum of the American Indian, Smithsonian Institution; Brian Norton; a private collector; Osler, Hoskin & Harcourt LLP; Remai Modern; The Robert McLaughlin Gallery; Royal Bank of Canada Art Collection; Royal Ontario Museum; Amy Smart; Stephen B. Smart; Sylvia and Michael Smith; Melvin Thompson and Harvey Bouchard; Thunder Bay Art Gallery; Christopher Varley and Sandra Shaul; Grant Wedge and Bob Crouch; David Andrew Welling; and Winnipeg Art Gallery.

On a personal note, I would like to thank Robert for his generosity and courage. This exhibition and publication pay tribute to his career as a political and creative leader—a legacy he remains committed to as both an artist and an activist.

Stephan Jost
Michael and Sonja Koerner Director, and CEO
Art Gallery of Ontario

Curator's Preface
Wanda Nanibush

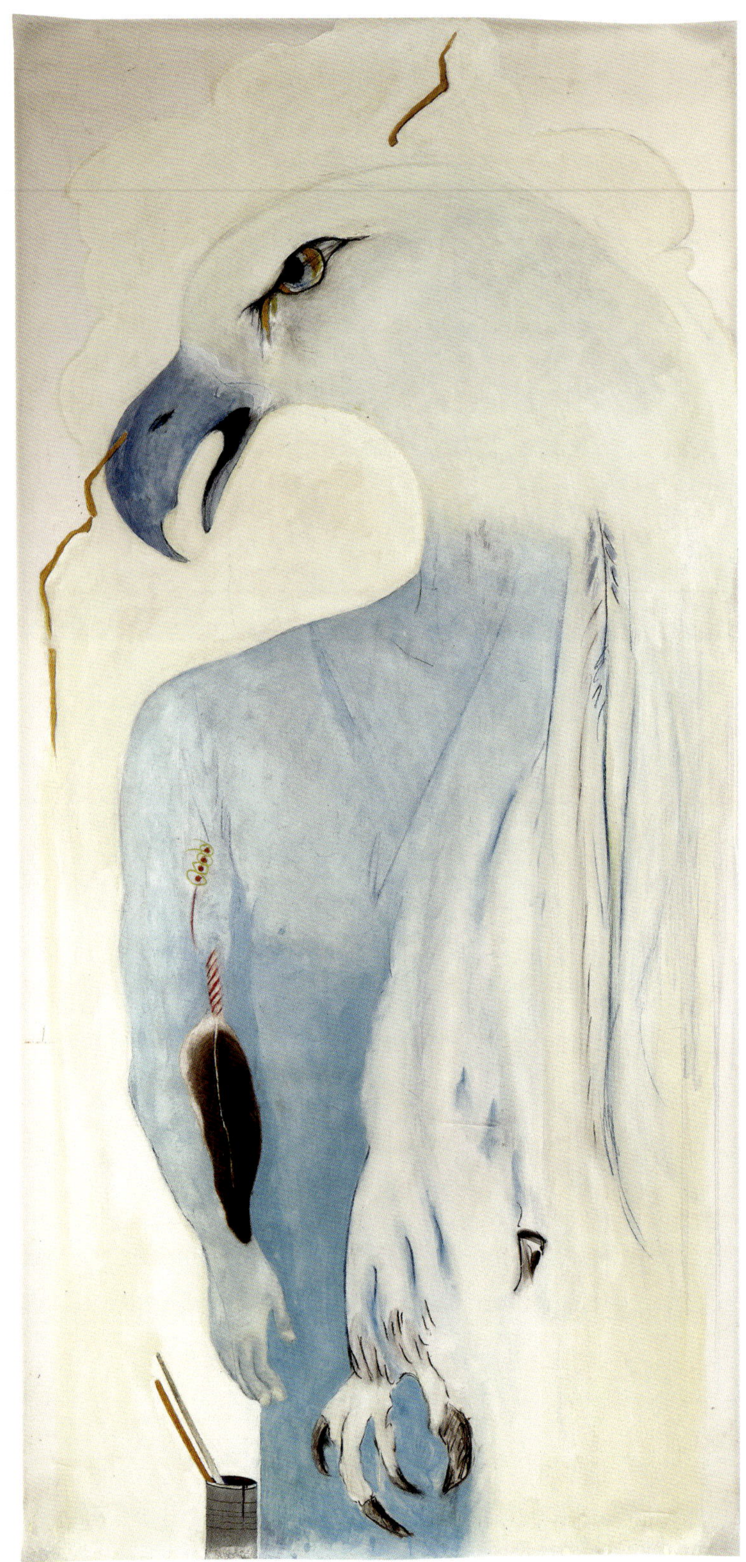

It is with immense gratitude that I thank Robert Houle for his time, trust, and knowledge working on this exhibition.

Saulteaux Anishinaabe artist Robert Houle (b. 1947) is one of the most influential First Nations figures to break into the contemporary art world. The first major retrospective of his work, *Robert Houle: Red is Beautiful* celebrates this singular artist's avant-garde career, which spans the years 1970 to 2021. A citizen of Sandy Bay First Nation in Northern Manitoba, Robert went from residential school to art college to museum boardrooms and made his mark on the global stage as an artist, curator, and writer.

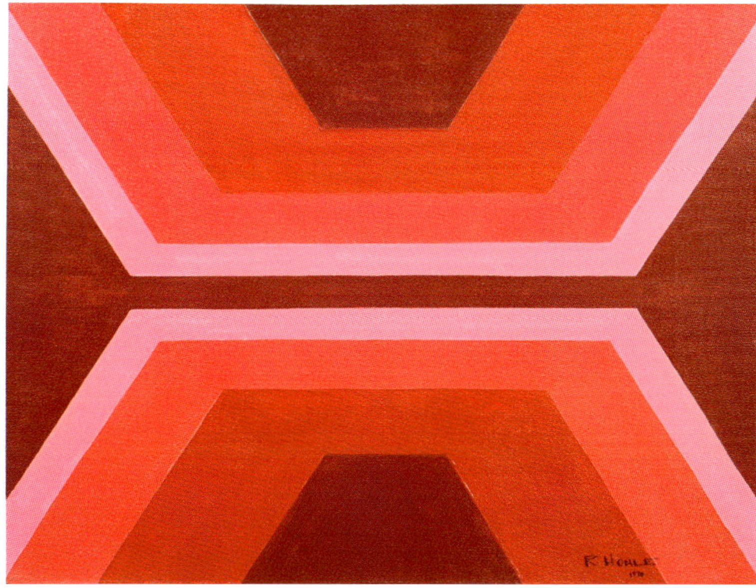

The exhibition is named *Red is Beautiful*, which is the title of the first work Robert sold to a museum: the painting was bought by the Museum of History (then the Museum of Man) in 1970. For many artists, an institutional purchase marks the beginning of their professional careers. At the time, Robert was still in Montreal, where he was studying art history and arts education at McGill University.

Robert produced *Red is Beautiful* (1970) during his early period (1970–1983), a time when he was exploring the work of Abstract Expressionists such as Jackson Pollock, Mark Rothko, and Jasper Johns; he was drawn to the way artists like Barnett Newman strove to understand the spiritual aspect of abstraction. While Robert was also interested in the work of Kazimir Malevich and Piet Mondrian, as an artist from a culture that deeply values women and one who learned from many feminist teachers, he found Mondrian's strict geometric approach too masculinist. He turned instead to the sacred geometry of First Nations art, which offered a new visual language outside the patriarchal renderings of the West. Robert brought an older Indigenous abstract tradition to this history and, by combining the two, emerged as a new voice in modern abstraction, one who values immediacy, gesture, the spiritual qualities of colour, the earth, and the sacred. His work challenged audience expectations of what First Nations art could be, and the first exhibitions he curated initiated a new discourse about contemporary First Nations art. Robert stayed independent, apart from the trends and stereotypical cultural performances of the day.

These early years marked a time of increasing public resistance by Indigenous Peoples against the strictures and laws of colonialism, against settler incursions into our lands. There were calls for Native control of education and child welfare; there were treaty negotiations, land-rights cases, protests against mining and logging, and

Opposite page:
Robert Houle, *Transforming BlueThunder*, 2021. Oil on mylar, 222.25 × 106.68 cm. Courtesy of the artist.

Above:
Robert Houle, *Red is Beautiful*, 1970. Acrylic on canvas, 45.5 × 61 cm. Musée canadien de l'histoire / Canadian Museum of History. V-F-174.

assertions of fishing and hunting rights. The '70s also saw a strong renaissance in the theatrical and visual arts, the emergence of the American Indian / Red Power movement, and the development of national Indigenous leadership. Concomitantly, spiritual practices that had been vilified in the church and boarding schools and banned until 1951 had returned in full force. Young folks were coming out of residential schools and travelling the country to seek cultural knowledge from Elders and knowledge keepers. Artists were using Western tools to produce creations from within Dene, Anishinaabe, Blackfoot, and other First Nations paradigms. Robert was at the centre of this vibrant, exciting, and hope-filled moment.

Those threads of cultural renaissance and political resistance are also embedded in the meanings of *Red is Beautiful*. After centuries full of policies that perpetuated cultural genocide and assimilation, artists were central to the positioning of our cultures in a positive light. The title also emphasizes the significance of the colour red for Robert, who is both a modernist colourist who works in oils and a Saulteaux man who knows his language and was raised in the Sun Dance ceremonies.

This exhibition consists of more than 100 works, including *Kanata, Parfleches for the Last Supper, Premises for Self Rule, Muhnedobe uhyahyuk [Where the gods are present]*, and *Paris/Ojibwa*. These iconic selections centre Indigenous perspectives on capital-H history while acknowledging the colonial manoeuvres of the state. Works such as *Kanehsatake, The Pines, Ipperwash, Innu Parfleche*, and *Warrior Lances for Temagami* highlight Robert's subtle and consistent attention to land defenders across Turtle Island (North America), and the state-sanctioned actions that curtail their capacity to exercise their sovereignty. Robert's large-scale paintings and installations also challenge the ways First Nation names like Pontiac and Apache have been commercially appropriated in the service of capitalism and warfare. Instead, he focuses on Pontiac's active resistance, memorializing the Odawa chief's actions and name.

As one of the first artists to capture his personal experience of the residential school system, Robert has exhibited great bravery by bringing this era into sharp relief. *Sandy Bay* (1998–1999) is a monumental work, capturing his emotional turmoil in remembering the trauma of being torn from his home. The five panels move from documentary photographs to colour fields, as he himself moved from representation to using colour and gesture to abstractly express his internal insight and pain. After 2008, Robert began to deal with the physical and sexual abuse he survived, memories of which were triggered by the government apology.[1] *Sandy Bay Indian Residential School series* (2010–2012) is a faux schoolroom installation where he distills and names his experiences, and ultimately enacts a letting go. Robert, a masterful colourist who understands the spiritual qualities of different hues, shows how the act of painting can be healing.

Robert's powerful portraits of shamans feel like an assertion of their power and presence. Though the residential schools attempted to eradicate belief in shamanic power, those efforts ultimately failed—the shaman continues to hold a vital role in contemporary Anishinaabe life. Always, Robert turns toward the spiritual power of the ancient ones in providing a new vision for an Indigenous future that holds the complexity of contemporary First Nations identity in its grasp. Robert has given us a path forward full of colour, light, and sovereignty.

1 In 2008, Prime Minister Stephen Harper issued a formal apology on behalf of the Government of Canada for its complicity in the residential school system.

I Am the Redman

Duke Redbird

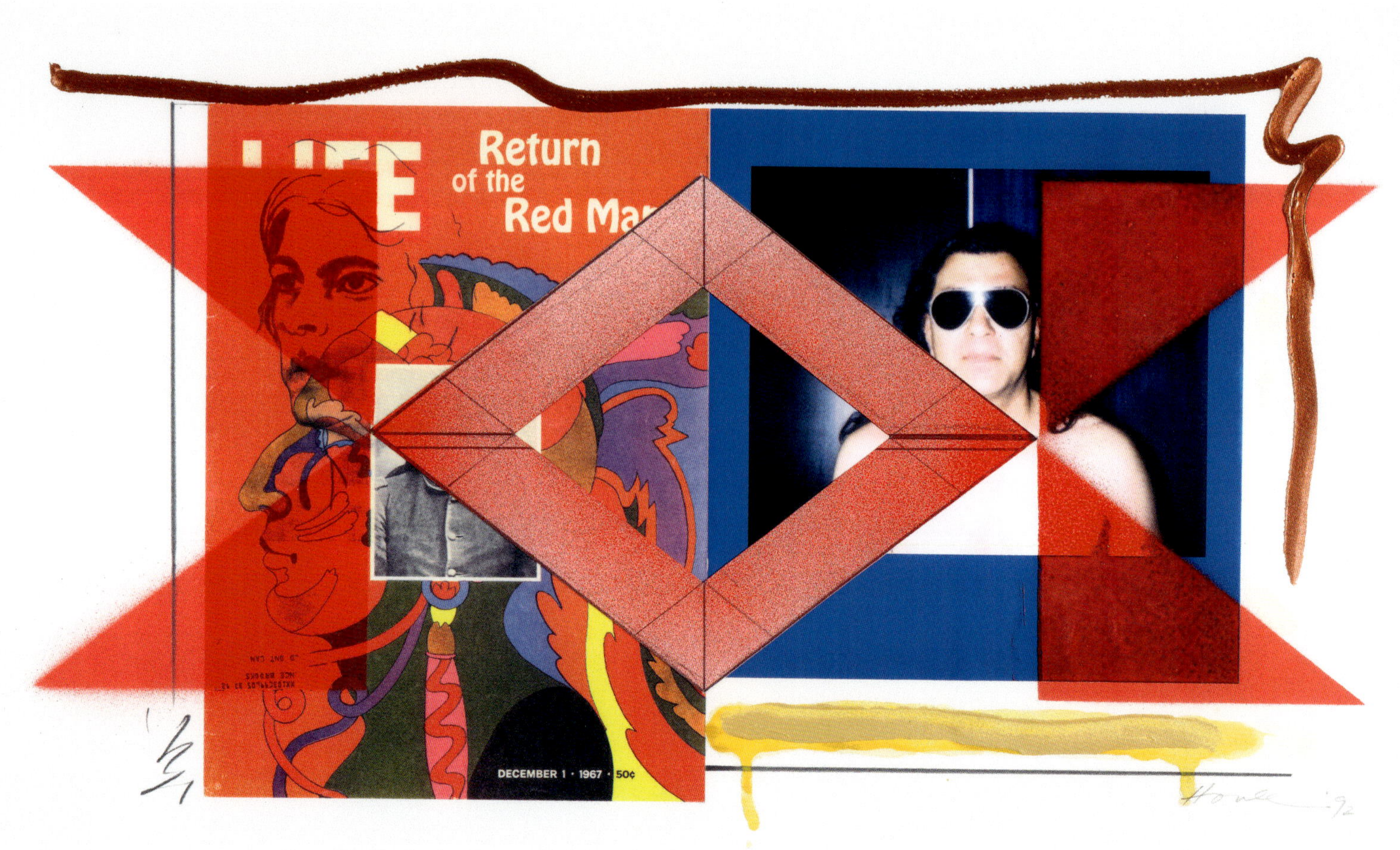

Robert Houle, *Return of the Red Man #1*, 1992. Polaroid photo, tape, paint, and magazine, 45.72 × 76.2 cm. Collection of Stephen B. Smart.

Louis Riel was born on October 22, 1844, and was unjustly executed for treason forty-one years later, on November 16, 1885. He had fought for Indigenous self-determination; a few months before his death, in a moment of reflection, he made this statement: "My people will sleep for one hundred years, but when they awake, it will be the artists who give them their spirit back." He meant that we cannot win our freedom through bullets, but we will win self-determination through art.

Riel's prophecy began to materialize during the first half of the twentieth century with the birth of two iconic Indigenous artists—Daphne Odjig in 1919 and Norval Morrisseau in 1932—who have become known as the "Grandmother" and "Grandfather" of Indigenous art in Canada. Later in the twentieth century, the birth of Robert Houle in 1947 would complete the prophetic vision attributed to Louis Riel.

I wish to then proclaim Robert Houle as the "Father" of contemporary art practised by Indigenous creators who are now recognized by the art world at large. It was Houle who first posited that Indigenous art did not only belong in the category of folk art; rather, it could be favourably compared to the finest creations at the forefront of the broader modern and contemporary art scenes.

The 1960s Red Power movement emboldened a generation of Indigenous youth across the United States and Canada, emphasizing the desire for Indigenous sovereignty and governance. Houle took this notion of Red Power and adapted it into his latest exhibition, *Red is Beautiful*, through his considerable talent as an artist and his extraordinary ability to curate this idea into reality. As a tribute to his work, I offer a poem I wrote called "I Am the Redman."

I am the Redman:
Son of the forest, mountain, and lake.
What use have I of the asphalt?
What use have I of the brick and concrete?
What use have I of the automobile?
Think you these gifts divine,
that I should be humbly grateful?

I am the Redman:
Son of the tree, hill, and stream.
What use have I of china and crystal?
What use have I of diamonds and gold?
What use have I of money?
Think you these from heaven sent,
that I should be eager to accept?

I am the Redman:
Son of the earth, water, and sky.
What use have I of silk and velvet?
What use have I of nylon and plastic?
What use have I of your ideologies?
Think you these are holy and sacred,
that I should kneel in awe?

I am the Redman:
Child of my Mother, the Earth.
I embrace All My Relations
And delight in the knowledge
That on the spectrum of life's reality
Red is Beautiful.

Parfleche in Motion: Robert Houle at Les Deux Magots

Gerald Vizenor

Robert Houle was a research artist at the Canada Council for the Arts International Residency Program in Paris when we first met about fifteen years ago. He was there to review the drawings of the Natchez in French Louisiana by Eugène Delacroix, and to envision the presence of the Ojibwe, related to the Mississauga, who were chaperoned by the painter George Catlin to pose as romantic warriors, mount traditional dances, mock battle with bows and arrows, and defer to Louis Philippe and the royals at Saint-Cloud on the River Seine.

Joëlle Rostkowski, the prominent scholar and translator of Native American[1] art and literature, invited me to meet Robert and Nelcya Delanoë for the first time over dinner at her homey apartment on Rue de l'Université. Joëlle and Nicolas Rostkowski are the proprietors of the Galerie Orenda in Paris. Nelcya is an author, a translator, and a notable professor at Université Paris Nanterre.

Joëlle, Nelcya, and Robert met with me a few days later at Les Deux Magots on Place Saint-Germain-des-Prés. The café conversation was casual, courteous, sometimes ironic, and always with generous humour and personal accounts of the extraordinary creative spirit, original styles, and reach of Native American art and literature. Robert gestured at times with the Saulteaux language, and together we told stories about guardian curators of traditional native art, the inadequate translations of native nicknames as surnames, the semblance of solitary forbearance as opposed to communal scenes, in the portraiture and early photographic images of natives, the concept of *transmotion*, or visionary motion in art and literature, and blue horses in native ledger art, and we naturally teased with ironic mercy the arrogance of cultural anthropology.

Les Deux Magots is a marvellous place to gather over herb omelettes, pastries, and dry white wine, and review the café's display of unusual fashions. The two elevated statues of mandarin traders have heard literary schemes, the inauguration of existentialism, resistance strategies during the wars, private favours and the secrets of cabals, and many other conventions for more than a century, but not much about the aesthetic sway of native art and literature.

Our cautious reveals and lighthearted hearsay were entirely natural in the liberal café culture and in the context of memorable tributes to so many eminent artists and authors: Simone de Beauvoir, Jean-Paul Sartre, Pablo Picasso, Albert Camus, James Joyce, Richard Wright, James Baldwin, Robert Houle, and Gerald Vizenor.

Robert related that afternoon that he carried a sketchbook and imagined the Ojibwe on the bridges and boulevards and outlined scenes of their presence in Paris. Later, in an essay for the installation *Paris/Ojibwa*, he wrote, "I recall drawing the Pont au Change early in the morning before the crowds had arrived and by the time I finished, American tourists were videotaping me and just being generally curious." The Pont au Change over the River Seine connects Le Marais to Île de la Cité.

The "four elegiac paintings in the installation are a pictorial representation of abstracted shapes and forms that leave traces of time, of paint and colour," Robert wrote in a publication produced by the Canadian Cultural Centre Paris. "The painted figures, a shaman, a warrior, a dancer and a healer become abstract monochromatic icons whose indigenous roots connect to the landscape in each painting. Together they are a poetic, symbolic, transatlantic return home through the magic of art, the spiritual aspect of memory."[2]

Robert was acquainted with "Dernière rencontre, ou comment Baudelaire, George Sand et Delacroix s'éprirent des Indiens du pentre Catlin," an essay by Nelcya Delanoë[3] and, referencing this text, he questioned, "Were North American Indians created with a false authenticity by using *en vrais trompe l'oeil?* The knowledge about us, even today is minimal and fictional,"[4] or literally an optical illusion.

Diane Camurat pointed out in "The American Indian in the Great War: Real and Imagined" that "Catlin offered the eternal romantic image he had of the American Indians" and "contributed a great deal towards creating what would become the visual stereotype of the Noble Indian."[5]

George Catlin revealed that he painted romantic scenes of the "wildest" tribes and later, as an entrepreneur, he promoted portrayals of the noble savage in concert with the natural world and traditions in the very ruins of civilization. "I have immersed myself in the midst of thousands and tens of thousands of these knights of the forest; whose whole lives are lives of chivalry, and whose daily feats, with their naked limbs, might vie with those of the Grecian youths in the beautiful rivalry of the Olympian games," wrote Catlin in *Letters and Notes on the Manners, Customs, and Condition of the North American Indians.*[6]

Prosper Mérimée published the novella *Carmen* in 1845, the same year that Catlin presented the Ojibwe troupe from three colonial fur trade empires to the citizens of Paris. Andrew Jackson, the seventh president of the

United States and the unpardonable enemy of native culture and sovereignty, died that same year, and in one more national arena of chance, irony, and contradictions, Frederick Douglass, the great liberal orator and abolitionist, published *A Narrative of the Life of Frederick Douglass, an American Slave* in Boston.

Robert asked about my research and writing, and that led to a serious discussion about the absence of natives in history and the thousands of natives from Canada and the United States who served as soldiers in the First World War in France. More than forty Native Americans had either enlisted or were drafted from the White Earth Reservation in Minnesota, and two of my relatives, Ignatius and Lawrence Vizenor, faced the enemy in deadly combat; that narrative of chance was the mainstay of my historical novel *Blue Ravens.*[7] Private Ignatius Vizenor was killed in action at Montbréhain near the Hindenburg Line on Tuesday, October 8, 1918. On the very same morning, his brother Corporal Lawrence Vizenor was decorated for bravery at Bois du Fays. Months after our meeting at Les Deux Magots, Nicolas and Joëlle provided the transportation and generously assisted me in locating the actual combat scenes of death and courage of my relatives.

Robert is a maestro of good cheer, and he marks the creative headway of a native presence in artistic portrayals and cultural liberty. That afternoon he related scenes about native art with a buoyant creative spirit, and that singular vitality was present in every thought, comment, and story. Yet the character of our lively conversations about native art and literature, about the royal encounter of natives more than a century ago, the concept of *transmotion* in native ledger art, and native teases was ironic because we are each related, as heirs of the fur trade, to the actual dire history and literary traces of colonial empires. Only merciful storiers would denounce the massacre of totemic animals over more than three centuries, and that afternoon at Les Deux Magots we were the fugitive heirs of the fur trade in the grace of native art and literature.

In 2010, Wanda Nanibush, the distinguished native scholar and art curator, invited Robert and me to discuss art and literature as part of Pine Tree Talks, a lecture series at Trent University in Peterborough, Ontario. Robert recounted in a gentle voice some of his experiences of separation, loneliness, and severity as a student at Sandy Bay Indian Residential School. The frightful conditions of bodily, mental, and sexual abuses of native children in churchy residential schools managed by the government have been the unbearable memories of more than a hundred thousand native people. For over a century and in more than 130 residential schools, native children could not easily find a way to reveal the burdens of sexual abuse, overcome the political evasions of the government and the cultural conceit and avoidance of the public, or even find a trustworthy person to ease the torment of memory and bear the curse of sexual predators.

The series of "new drawings, oil stick on paper" were not like "any of [Houle's] previous work," observed David McIntosh in *Robert Houle, enuhmo andúhyaun (the road home)*, the catalogue of an exhibition at the University of Manitoba. "I remember being overwhelmed by their garish colour palette: gaudy turquoise, muddy brown, unrepentant black. The drawing style was equally shocking and uncharacteristic, mixes of slashes and

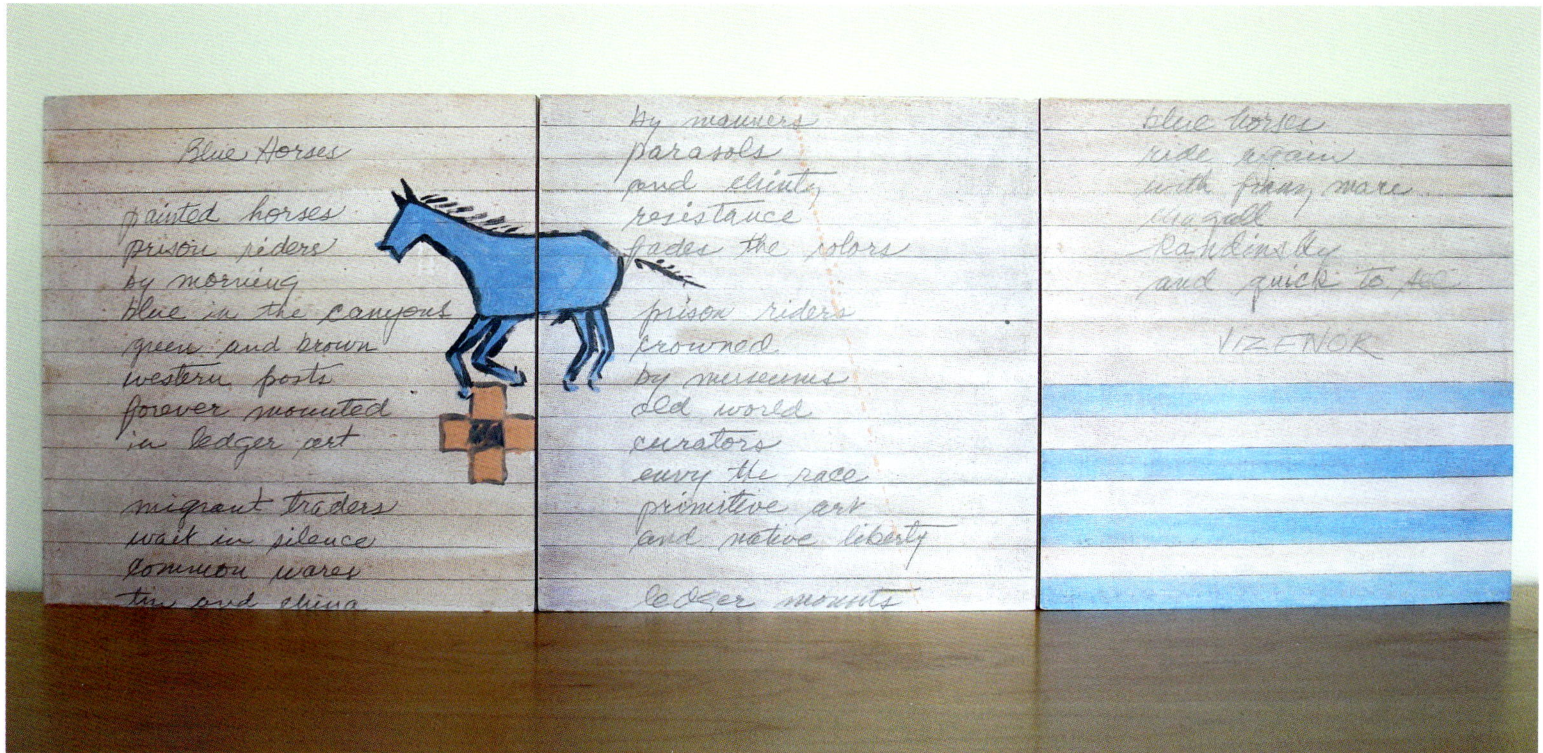

broad renderings, visceral and assured, figurative and gestural simultaneously." Robert portrayed "residential school experiences from over fifty years ago" and depicted "the school playground; beds in the dormitory; and religious figures."[8]

McIntosh pointed out that Robert "confronted and overcame, in his words, the 'fear and shame' of his residential school experience that he had held inside since he was a young boy." Robert had been "physically, spiritually and sexually abused during his elementary school years by the Sisters of Saint Joseph of Saint-Hyacinthe and the lay brothers of the Oblates of Mary Immaculate."

The drawings created a "sense of movement, of transitional spaces." The six "drawings of the school playground" depicted "almost the same landscape" but the position and perspective change with each one, "concluding with *the fear*, in which a black figure, a predator, appears. Similarly, there are eight drawings of beds in the dormitory, each drawn from a different position and perspective, concluding with *night predator*, in which a dark figure crouches behind a bed."[9] The sombre scenes of a boarding school were in motion, or *transmotion*: the visionary motion of abstract portrayals in native art and literature.[10]

Robert allowed the publisher to reproduce one parfleche painting from the series *Parfleches for the Last Supper* for the

FIG. 1
Robert Houle, *Blue Horses*, 2010. Acrylic on canvas, 3 parts: each 40.6 × 40.6 cm. Collection of Gerald Vizenor.

dust jacket of my novel *Father Meme.*[11] Robert "imagined the twelve disciples coming to that final meal with Jesus, each carrying a parfleche and opening it for the others to see," he told MaryLou Driedger, a former columnist for the *Winnipeg Free Press.* "I took a chance mixing two diametrically opposed ideologies for the first time."[12] The parfleche on the cover of *Father Meme* is number five, Philip the Apostle, embodied as two floating yellow crosses on a red background with porcupine quills in a wave of motion.

The narrator of the novel, once an altar boy, was betrayed by Father Meme at the Indian Mission Church of the Snow. "The Benedictine Monks at Saint John's Abbey first touched my heart with choral music, and then the priest silenced me by his greedy touch and sexual abuse. My heart was bright, light, truly at peace, and my body soared above the nave in the magical turns of light, the reds and blues of the stained church windows. I was twelve years old at the time, a lonesome altar boy converted that late summer morning by the glorious sound of Gregorian chants.

"I never again experienced that moment of ethereal rhythm. That perfect sensation of deliverance comes to me now in dreams, and with some humor, a sense of eternal peace, but only after so many years. Saint John's Abbey Church could have been my landmark of sacred remembrance. Father Meme ruined the virtue of that ecstasy. My memories of that time were obstructed by the shame of his sexual perversions."[13]

Robert created five concise black and white drawings for my book *Favor of Crows: New and Collected Haiku.*[14] A single crow in natural motion is about to land on the title page, two crows are perched on a bare branch in the first chapter of spring haiku, crows gather in the summer chapter, a spider in the autumn scenes, and a stand of seven birch trees in the last haiku scenes of winter. The concise drawings and imagistic poems came together as a native presence in the visionary motion of art and literature.

Robert read my poem "Blue Horses" in *Almost Ashore: Collected Poems*[15] and created a triptych painting of the poem and an abstract blue horse in visionary motion over a yellow cross (fig. 1). The cursive lines of the poem were painted on three panels, and the blue horse was a ledger mount in memory of the native prisoners and ledger artists at Fort Marion in Florida. The beautiful triptych was presented in an ordinary plastic shopping bag as a surprise gift at the end of our special program with Wanda Nanibush at Trent University.

Honanistto, or Howling Wolf, was a political prisoner for three years at Fort Marion. The Southern Cheyenne warrior and artist created Native scenes of visionary motion in ledger books and named this work ledger art. The scenes were not simulations or realistic poses or copies. The blue horses were painted in natural motion, hooves in the air, rarely touching the ground, and other horses were painted with the coloured pencils provided to the prison artists at the time. Howling Wolf created these scenes of visionary motion several years before the birth of the German expressionist artist Franz Marc, who painted sensuous horses in hues of blue, and before the birth of Marc Chagall, who painted marvellous fiddlers and characters in visionary motion.[16]

Robert Houle might have painted abstract blue horses, envisioned winter counts, and created parfleches as a native ledger artist more than a century ago, and his abstract paintings of natural motion would have been collected as they are today for exhibitions in galleries and museums. I might have travelled with him and related trickster stories, mocked the federal agents and missionaries, and created imagistic dream songs a century ago, and gathered with other native people at summer events with totemic narratives of visionary motion. We are the heirs of the fur trade, and we might have convened in the past in the same way we do today: as a painter, a storier, and as native artists of *transmotion* and liberty.

1. All instances of "native" and "Native American" in this text have been preserved, reflecting the author's preferred terminology.
2. Robert Houle, "Paris/Ojibwa," Canadian Cultural Centre Paris, https://canada-culture.org/wp-content/uploads/2010/04/Artist-Statement-v2.pdf
3. Nelcya Delanoë, "Dernière rencontre, ou comment Baudelaire, George Sand et Delacroix s'éprirent des Indiens du peintre Catlin," in *Destins croisés: Cinq siècles de rencontres avec les Amérindiens*, ed. Albin Michel (Paris: Éditions UNESCO, 1992).
4. Houle, "Paris/Ojibwa."
5. Diane Camurat, "The American Indian in the Great War: Real and Imagined" (master's thesis, Institut Charles V of the University of Paris VII, 1993), http://www.gwpda.org/comment/camurat1.html
6. Sharon Fairchild, "George Sand and George Catlin—Masking Indian Realities," *Nineteenth-Century French Studies* 22:3 and 4 (Spring, Summer, 1994): 441.
7. Gerald Vizenor, *Blue Ravens* (Middletown , CT: Wesleyan University Press, 2014).
8. David McIntosh, *Robert Houle: enuhmo andúhyaun (the road home)* (Winnipeg: School of Art Gallery, University of Manitoba, 2012), http://openresearch.ocadu.ca/id/eprint/1409/1/McIntosh_Robert_2012.pdf
9. McIntosh, *Robert Houle*.
10. Gerald Vizenor, "Native Transmotion: Totemic Motion and Traces of Survivance" in *Native Provenance, The Betrayal of Cultural Creativity* (Lincoln: University of Nebraska Press, 2019) 37.
11. Gerald Vizenor, *Father Meme* (Albuquerque: University of New Mexico Press, 2008).
12. MaryLou Driedger, "Parfleches for the Last Supper," (blog post, November 9, 2014), https://maryloudriedger2.wordpress.com/2014/11/09/parfleches-for-the-last-supper/
13. Vizenor, *Father Meme*.
14. Gerald Vizenor, *Favor of Crows: New and Collected Haiku, Wesleyan University Press, 2014*.
15. Gerald Vizenor, *Almost Ashore: Selected Poems* (Cromer, United Kingdom: Salt Publishing, 2006) 25.
16. Gerald Vizenor, "Native Transmotion," *Fugitive Poses: Native American Scenes of Absence and Presence* (Lincoln: University of Nebraska Press, 1998) 178–179.

My uncle, the artist

Alanaise Onischin Ferguson

With contributions by Megan Davies

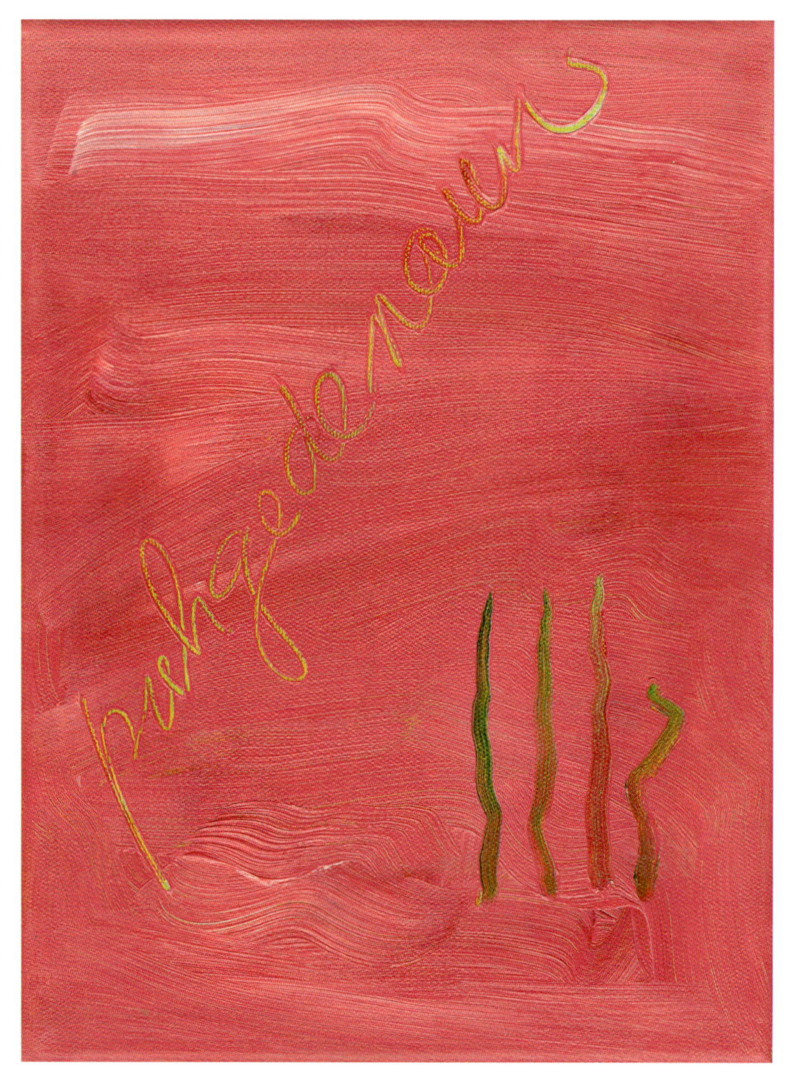

Introduction

I don't mind working with [a vivacious red] on a cloudy day—it brings out the heat [while painting].

—Robert Houle, 2015 Governor General's Awards video portrait[1]

My uncle Robert has been called an iconoclast—a title he earned thanks to his international reputation and the conceptual vigour of his paintings, installations, and writing. When particular aesthetics are ascribed to his works, they are often steeped in the academic traditions of art-history scholarship as well as Canadian and modernist art geneaologies. In contrast to these interdisciplinary discussions and lineages, my experience with my uncle's creations and their inherent Indigenous teachings and knowledge comes from the collected wisdom of our people. My essay draws on the Saulteaux scholarship transmitted among our family as we set our collective gaze on the exhibition *Robert Houle: Red is Beautiful* (2021). Our relative's artistic contributions are a multilayered site of healing and regeneration for our people.

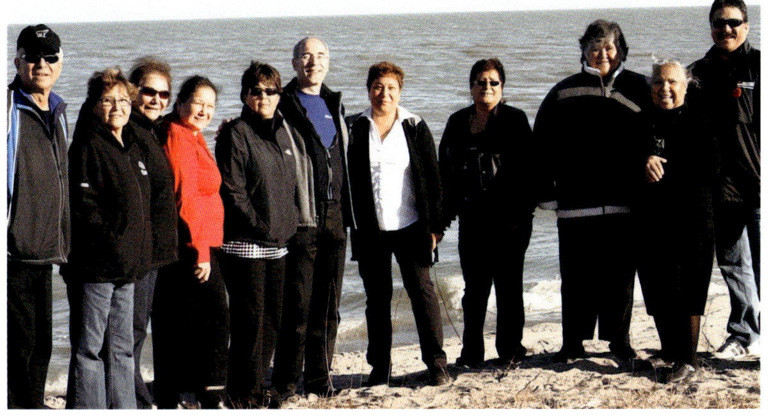

FIG. 1 (ABOVE)
Robert Houle with family, Sandy Bay First Nation, 2010, during the making of Shelley Niro's film *Robert's Paintings*. (From left to right: Robert Houle, Marilyn Beaulieu, Delores Roulette, Stella Bone, Kimberly McKay, Paul Gardner, Roberta Riglin, Sandra Beaulieu, Vivian Ferguson, Catherine Mousseau, Napoleon Houle.) Image courtesy of the artist.

Robert Houle was born in 1947 in Saint Boniface, Manitoba, and is the eldest of fifteen children (fig. 1). His parents are my grandparents; my late mother Vivienne, one year his junior, was his first reader and confidante since childhood. When my mother passed into the spirit world on November 25, 2017, Robert was preparing for the exhibition *Pahgedenaun* (figs. 2 and 4), the title of which is a Saulteaux verb meaning "to let (it) go" from one's mind. This monumental undertaking at the Carleton University Art Gallery brought together four bodies of work, all based on Robert's memories of attending Sandy Bay Residential School in the 1950s and '60s alongside his brothers and sisters. The school was strictly divided according to age and gender: he was forbidden to speak to his sisters if he saw them in the hallway. Robert's parents also attended Sandy Bay Residential School. Rooted in this shared family history, his artwork demonstrates the inherent powers of transformation and resilience among generations of our people as a result of their collective residential school experiences (fig. 3). My mother was scheduled to engage in a public dialogue with her brother at the CUAG's *Pahgedenaun* opening; their conversation would reveal sharp Saulteaux discourses representing the polyphonic voices of our people who survived this Canadian genocidal project. My mother's passing was sudden, and so I agreed to step into her very large shoes to provide a place of connection with my uncle, while he articulated the meanings of his memory drawings and paintings.

Robert arrived at the concept of *Pahgedenaun* after years of discussion with his family. I remember that my mother was filled with concern about Robert as he created these works. We prayed for our uncle. When we set our eyes on his drawings and paintings, we wept. This collection is a testimony to the survivance of our people and the strength

FIG. 2 (OPPOSITE PAGE)
Robert Houle, *people*, 2010, from *Sandy Bay Indian Residential School I*. Oil on canvas, 61 × 30.5 × 1.9 cm. Courtesy of the artist.

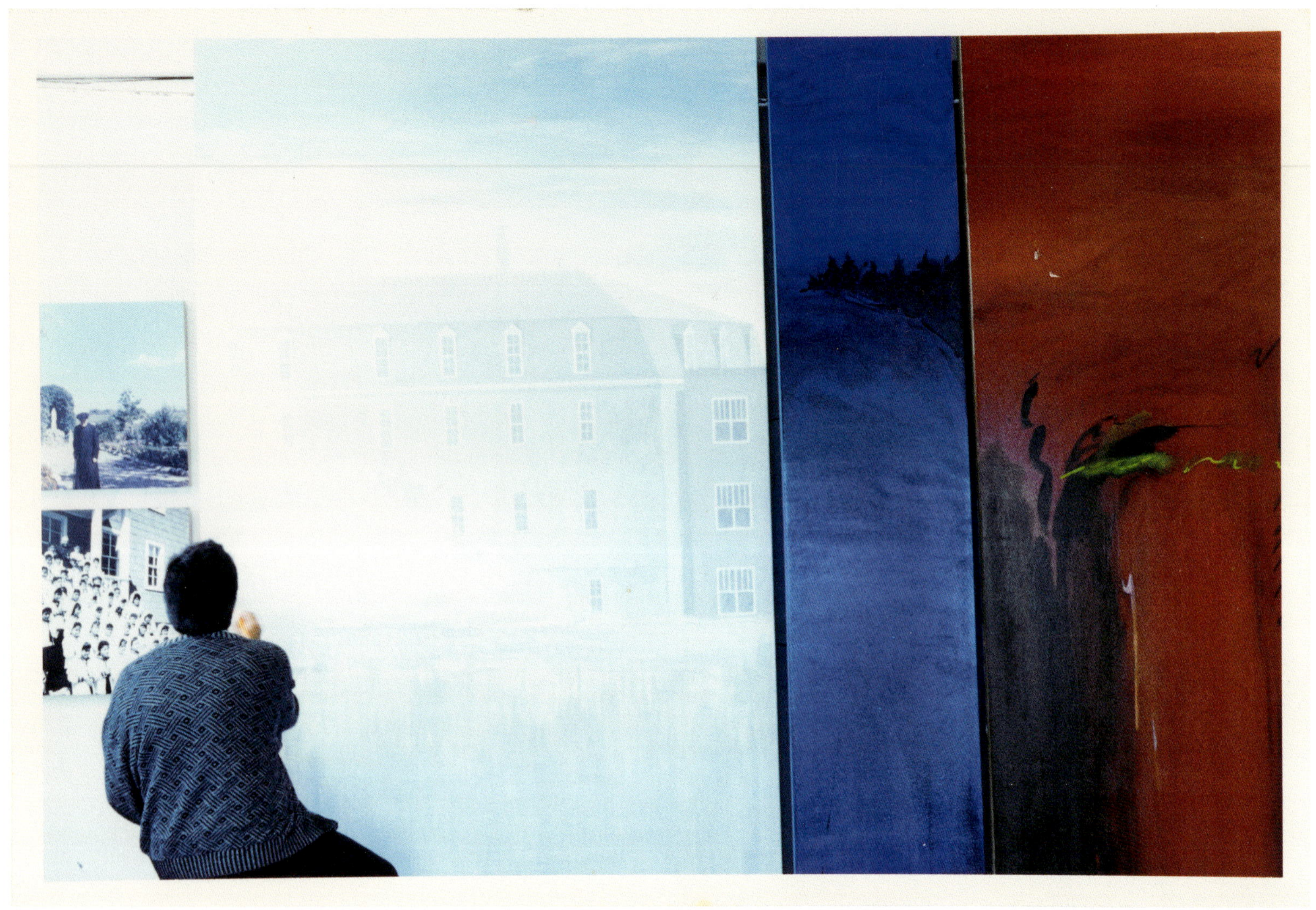

FIG. 3 (ABOVE)
Robert Houle painting *Sandy Bay* in his Spadina Avenue studio in 1999. Photographed by David Recollet. Image courtesy of the artist.

FIG. 4 (OPPOSITE)
Installation view of *Robert Houle: Pahgedenaun*, Carleton University Art Gallery, Ottawa, 2018. Photograph by Justin Wonnacott, courtesy Carleton University Art Gallery.

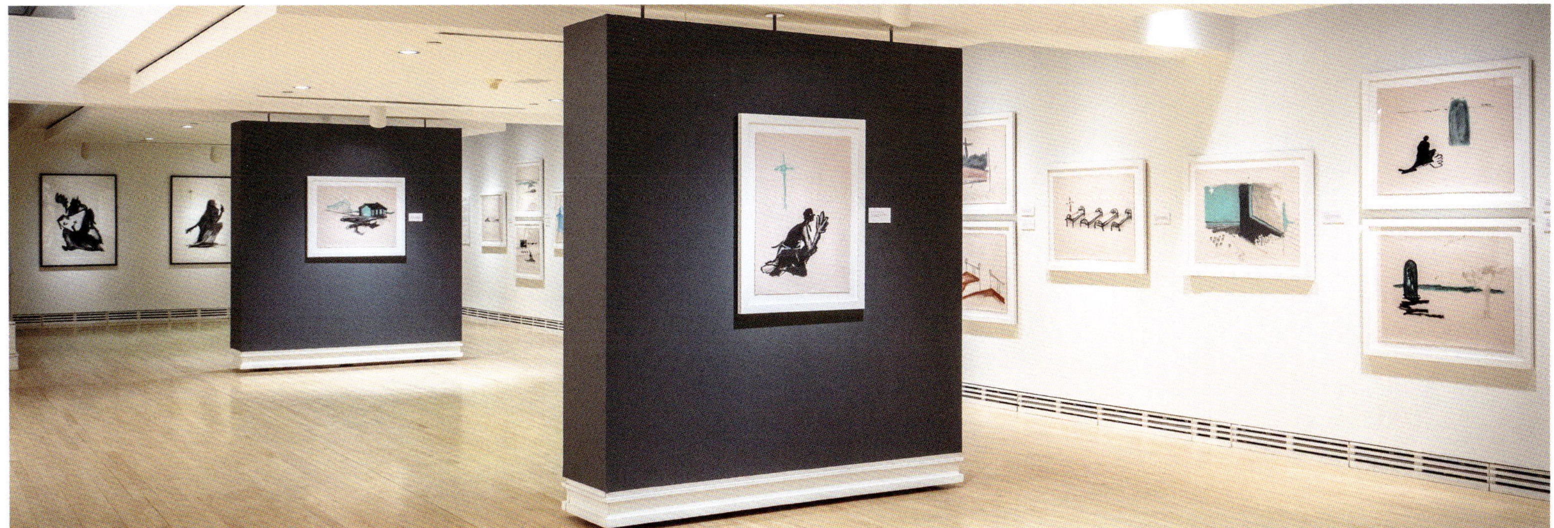

of spirit that runs through us. By creating a body of work addressing the memories of the residential school that two generations of our family endured, Robert demonstrated that he was able to truly take himself back. It is the most poignant act of personal sovereignty that I have witnessed among our people.

Two years before *Pahgedenaun* opened, Robert was awarded the 2015 Governor General's Award in Visual Arts. All of Robert's surviving sisters, as well as my son, who was fourteen at the time, travelled to Ottawa for this momentous occasion. Robert's professional accomplishments are a unifying force in our family; his art transcends generational lines, inspiring children to eavesdrop on their parents' phone calls and relatives to gather en masse at major events like this award ceremony. The Canada Council for the Arts celebrated my uncle's career by commissioning Canadian director Derreck Roemer to create a video portrait of his work for the occasion. In this short film, Robert discusses his piece *Kanata* (1992) as a retelling of Benjamin West's 1770 painting *The Death of General Wolfe*. I remember being struck by how he characterized the formation of Canada as a tripod: French, English, and First Nations. His allusion to this tripod of sovereign nations remains with me to this day—I use it here as a metaphorical structure to organize my thoughts around three themes: sovereignty, cultural appropriation, and protecting the sacred. In this discussion, I centre the voices of Robert and my family members, whose knowledge informed my selection of these themes.

My own area of expertise is in Indigenous ways of healing and well-being. Our family comes from a long line of medicine people, and my artistic expression is held within the practices of psychotherapy and teaching:
I am a researcher and scholar-practitioner in counselling psychology. For me, appreciating and learning from Robert's art is an ongoing process where a profound engagement with the emotional aspects of his creations precedes more fulsome knowledge and understanding of the context. Robert's works have continuity within the psyche, teaching and speaking across our collective

experiences through his fiery assertions of our people standing in our own lands. Throughout his career, he has prioritized the voices and experiences of Saulteaux peoples, weaving in our family knowledge and including our critical engagement with power structures, social placement, and Saulteaux linguistic integrity.

Sovereignty

Kiishiin kegoweeshaysik Anishinaabe maadayah.
— Alexander Mousseau (my great-grandfather and Robert's grandfather), 1948

If something is going to happen, our people will witness it.
— Robert Houle, 2015

I have vivid recollections of my mother speaking on the phone with Robert about his painting series *Premises for Self Rule* (1994). Their conversation, exclusively in Saulteaux, oscillated between solemnity and exuberance. Soon afterward, my mother explained to me that Robert's artistic process begins with Saulteaux language immersion before he code-switches, shifting his concepts and creations into English for his audience. The conceptual force of his paintings and installations is birthed in his Saulteaux language and his reverence for our worldview on sovereignty—unceded, unsurrendered, and matriarchal—is articulated through his resistance to our colonization. This makes Robert a rebel, but it was my grandmother who taught him how to fight. I see her critical posture of sovereignty in the work *Premises for Self Rule: Constitution Act, 1982* (1994; fig. 5). In his critical writing, Robert has asserted that we are the spiritual children of the ancient ones. In reflecting on this collective knowledge within our family, our most consistent teaching is that, as spiritual children, we are linked to the sacred circle of the land. We are also taught that the land gives birth just as a woman gives birth, and therefore our women are the rightful owners and stewards of the land. Robert challenges Eurocentric and patriarchal notions of land ownership in his creation process and the resulting political pieces by mobilizing our worldviews on sovereignty.

Shirley Madill has written that *Premises for Self Rule* represents Robert's entry into postmodernism through a mix of abstraction, appropriated photographs, and colonial text. The appropriated photograph in *Premises* is a postcard image of Niitsitapi (Blackfoot) women gathering in Fort Macleod, Alberta, published in 1907. The women in this photo have their backs turned to the camera, which reminds me of my grandmother's teachings—that our treaties have been broken and violated by the Crown, and furthermore, that our land was never surrendered because our women were not consulted for the treaties. These women refuse the authority of the camera, insisting that they never surrendered their sovereignty. My grandmother taught us that as Anishinaabekwe (Anishinaabe women), we never gave up our authority, that our power is sacred, and that our peoples' rights appear in early colonial legislation. In all five pieces of *Premises for Self Rule (Coming Home; Constitution Act, 1982; Treaty No. 1; Indian Act; British North America Act)*, another tripod emerges: appropriated legal text (colonial verification of our Aboriginal Rights and Title), vivid colour-field painting (the dreams our ancestors held for us), and visual memory cues for his audience (documentation of our people originally inhabiting the land and a tacit refusal to

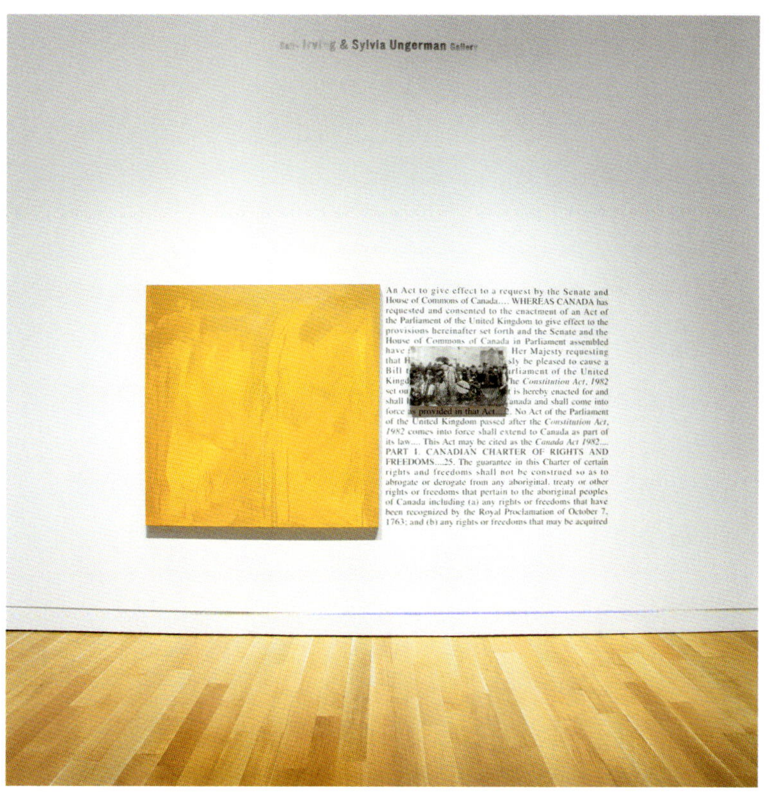

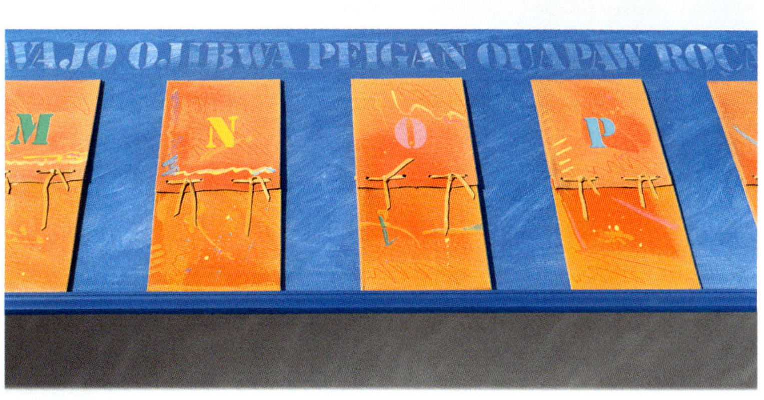

FIG. 5 (TOP)
Robert Houle, *Premises for Self Rule: Constitution Act, 1982*, 1994. Oil on canvas, photo emulsion on canvas, and laser-cut vinyl. Painting: 152.4 × 152.4 cm; photograph on canvas: 50 × 80 cm; laser-cut vinyl: 152.4 × 152.4 cm. Art Gallery of Ontario, purchased with funds from the Estate of Mary Eileen Ash, 2014. 2014/1.
Photo: Art Gallery of Ontario.

FIG. 6 (BOTTOM)
Robert Houle, *Everything you ever wanted to know about Indians from A to Z*, 1985.
Acrylic, rawhide, wood, and linen, 45.3 × 735 cm. Collection of the Winnipeg Art Gallery, acquired with funds from The Winnipeg Art Gallery Foundation Inc., G-89-1501 a-cc.
Photo: Ernest Mayer, courtesy of the Winnipeg Art Gallery.

surrender sovereignty). My uncle solidifies our Saulteaux conceptions of the land and of sovereignty through the interplay between text, colour, and memory cues.

Cultural Appropriation

If you are going to be an artist, paint only what you know.
— Gladys Houle (my grandmother and Robert's mother)

Our family tends to adopt a critically observant gaze to engage with the things that happen on our land. It ends up in our discourse through our humour and the ways we interrogate settler society's media and textual products. We assert our intellectual sovereignty through this oral scholarship that is largely unrecognized outside our own circles—until someone attempts to infiltrate our circles and lay claim to it. Gladys Houle is Robert's mother and my grandmother. Embedded in her statement about painting only what you know is a teaching about the dangers of cultural appropriation, long before that phrase first emerged in settler societies in the 1980s. Her teaching suggests that we respect one another's creative and sacred productions, a premise that goes back to our Saulteaux core values and the natural laws. Robert was encouraged to be a leader in our family and was chosen to hold many important roles, including sharing our cultural productions through his art.[2]

As one of two siblings in his family to relocate and live outside our ancestral territory, Robert represents the awe and respect our people hold for other First Nations' cultural productions. Robert has been in the presence of the Iroquois peoples throughout his life and work in Montreal, Ottawa, and then Toronto. In Ontario's capital, he explored Haudenosaunee topics and was immersed in the community's events and experiences, particularly those leading up to and during the Mohawk summer of 1990. Robert's kinship connections with the Haudenosaunee confederacy emerge through the ways he uses his own Saulteaux artistic and cultural knowledge to advocate for their campaigns against our mutual colonizers. My colleague Megan Davies was also deeply affected by the power of his advocacy and use of cultural productions during his 1992 exhibition *Hochelaga* at Galerie Articule, Montreal: "It really struck me, his support of Kanehsatake in Montreal in 1992, two years after the Oka Crisis. His work is fierce and brave and speaks to his tireless advocacy." Robert's work engages other sovereign nations to connect across cultures and broaden settler perspectives. These are the Saulteaux instructions we were given by our forebears.

Oneida is not flatware; Apache is not a helicopter; Pontiac is not a car.
— Robert Houle

Rallying against cultural appropriation requires perseverance and bravery to challenge the systemic disparities that marginalize and undervalue the cultural productions of our peoples. The gift of naming is a serious act of personal sovereignty and spiritual meaning for our peoples. Given the power and significance inherent in our names, it is no surprise that settler society has taken these terms and misappropriated them to label military vehicles, cars, and sports teams. Many of the works in this retrospective—including *I Stand, Pontiac, Blue Apache, Kekabishcoon Peenish Chipedahbung (I Will Stand in Your Path Till Dawn)*, and *Everything you ever wanted to know about Indians from A to Z* (fig. 6)—represent a return of the power to our names. In repatriating them, Robert acts on the values embedded in Gladys's teaching ("paint only what you know") by engaging in a familiar artistic form and rectifying settler society's violation of this teaching.

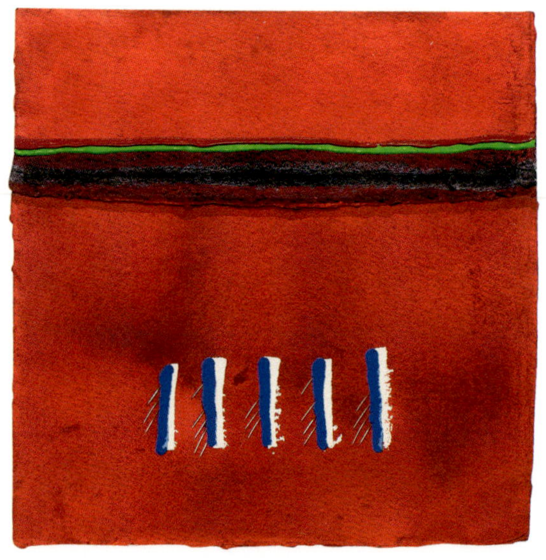

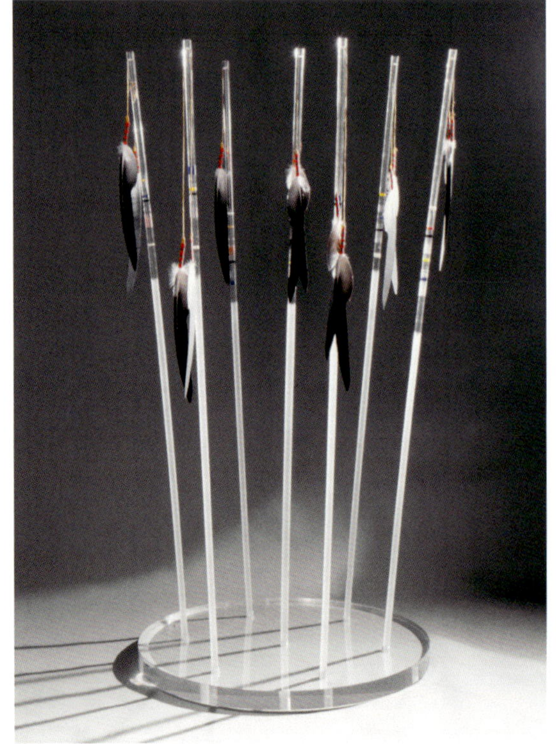

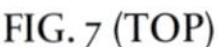

FIG. 7 (TOP)
Robert Houle, *Parfleche #6, Andrew*, 1983, from *Parfleches for the Last Supper*. Acrylic and porcupine quills on paper, 56 × 56 cm. Collection of the Winnipeg Art Gallery, gift of Mr. Carl T. Grant, Artvest Inc., G-86-465.
Photo: Serge Gumenyuk courtesy of the Winnipeg Art Gallery.

FIG. 8 (BOTTOM)
Robert Houle, *Warrior Lances for Temagami*, 1989. Mixed-media sculpture, base: 5 × 76.2 cm diameter, overall: 152.5 × 76.2 cm diameter. Indigenous Art Collection, Crown-Indigenous Relations and Northern Affairs Canada / Collection d'art autochtones, Relations Couronne-Autochtones et Affaires du Nord Canada.
Photo: Lawrence Cook.

Protecting the Sacred

Dreaming gave me the authenticity to say I am an artist.
— Robert Houle

As the first curator of Contemporary Indian Art at one of Canada's largest anthropological institutions, the National Museum of Man (now the Canadian Museum of History), Robert quickly developed a strategic vision to address cultural appropriation and its systemic disparities by removing numerous barriers. Though his tenure there was inflected with negativity, he nevertheless bravely worked toward these ends in his art, curation, and writing. Robert's experience at the museum was punctuated by macroaggressions and spiritually harmful confinement, including the sacrilegious treatment of our sacred belongings. This was a microcosm of the larger colonial project in which settlers and their institutions seek to subdue and remove our power within our own lands by extracting sacred objects and placing them in the past. The reckless opening of medicine bags by anthropologists as my uncle reacted in horror has been written about extensively; this had a huge impact on his decision to become an artist and change the art world. In several of his artistic pieces, this flashpoint experience became the catalyst for a creative reaction to the violation of our spiritual responsibilities to care for our belongings.

Robert has said *Parfleches for the Last Supper* (1983; fig. 7) was not inspired by any other artist or idea; it was his culture and history which connects to our instructions to protect the sacred. My mother said that they knew Uncle Robert had a gift of dreaming from an early age, and because it was a gift that came from the Creator, it had to be shared for everyone to enjoy. In all his works, Robert shares this gift while also protecting our culture. He uses materials to stand in for and represent that which should not be gazed at within the carceral system of a museum. In *Warrior Lances for Temagami* (1989; fig. 8), Robert chose high-quality photographs of eagle feathers in place of real feathers. I remember my mother pointing this out to me when the exhibition went up, as it was important to her that he did not actually use real eagle feathers at the top of the warrior lances. In *Parfleches for the Last Supper*, Robert's handmade paper parfleches, ceremonially closed with paint and porcupine quills, refute and repair the negligence of the anthropologists at the National Museum of Man. Robert's careful choices of materials serve as a teaching in the protection of the sacred when exhibiting and making public our cultural productions.

Conclusion

Don't do it unless you are going to do it with a good heart.
— Gladys Houle

Robert has done everything in his career with a good heart. Throughout his journey, his teachings around sovereignty, cultural appropriation, and protecting the sacred hold essential lessons about our peoples' survivance. I would like to thank him for the role his work has in the exaltation of our peoples' creations and art. Giitchii Miigwetch.

[1] Derreck Roember, "Robert Houle: Visual Artist and 2015 Canada Council Laureate," Canada Council, Mar. 24, 2015, YouTube video, 0:04:15, https://youtu.be/NNdigmKB7So.

[2] My mother kept a collection of publications, catalogues, flyers, and posters related to her brother's many artistic accomplishments. Many of these documents bear personal inscriptions addressed to my mother and me. While preparing to write this essay, I reviewed these documents, which included: *Hochelaga* (galerie articule, Montreal May 9 – June 7, 1992), *Memory Drawings* (Latcham Gallery, October 1 – November 12, 2016), *Path Breakers: The Eiteljorg Fellowship for Native American Fine Art* (2003), *Troubling Abstraction* (McMaster Museum of Art in collaboration with The Robert McLaughlin Gallery, September 7 – October 28, 2007), *Shaman Dream in Colour* (Kinsman Robinson Galleries, April 23 ¬– May 14, 2016), *Paris/Ojibwa* (Art Gallery of Peterborough, 2011), Shirley Madill's book *Robert Houle: Life & Work*, and an essay Robert wrote in the Summer 1991 issue of *C Magazine* entitled, "Sovereignty over Subjectivity." I also reviewed Shelley Niro's 2011 documentary, *Robert's Paintings* (V-Tape), which reminded me of the powerful impact that his work has on our family unity.

Selected Bibliography

Art Canada Institute. *Art Talk: Shirley Madill on the Rebel and Iconoclast Robert Houle.* n.d. Video, 0:17:26. https://www.aci-iac.ca/watch/art-talk-shirley-madill-on-the-rebel-and-iconoclast-robert-houle/

Art Gallery of Ontario. *Close Looking: Harris and Houle.* May 26, 2020. YouTube video, 0:27:36. https://www.youtube.com/watch?v=9c-hOIJD9N8

Cheetham, Mark A., Gerald McMaster, and Carol Podedworny, eds. *Troubling Abstraction: Robert Houle.* Hamilton: McMaster University Art Gallery and Oshawa: The Robert McLaughlin Gallery, 2007.

Collins, Curtis J. and Robert Houle. *Hochelaga: A Multi-Media Installation by Robert Houle.* Exhibition catalogue. Montreal: Galerie Articule, 1992.

Fox, Suzanne G., and Lucy R. Lippard, eds. *Path Breakers: The Eiteljorg Fellowship for Native American Fine Art.* Seattle: University of Washington Press, 2003.

Duncan, Chai, ed. Robert Houle's *Memory Drawings.* Exhibition catalogue. Stouffville, ON: Latcham Gallery, 2016.

Gardner, Paul, ed. *Robert Houle's Paris/Ojibwa.* Art Gallery of Peterborough: 2011.

Houle, Robert. "Sovereignty Over Subjectivity." In *C Magazine* (Summer 1991), 28–35.

Madill, Shirley. *Robert Houle: Life & Work*. Toronto: Art Canada Institute, 2018.

McIntosh, David, "Ge enahbundum nuh? Did you dream?" In *Robert Houle: Shaman Dream in Colour*. Toronto: Kinsman Robinson Galleries, 2016.

McIntosh, David, "uhpé guhnoodezowan (when I speak to myself)." In *Robert Houle: enuhmo andúhyaun (the road home)*. Winnipeg: School of Art Gallery, University of Manitoba, 2012.

Niro, Shelley, dir. *Robert's Paintings*. 2011: Turtle Night Productions. Video, colour, 52 min.

Robert & Me

Kay WalkingStick

Painting is a visual expression of ideas. Sometimes the ideas are clear: a memory, a story, or a history. Sometimes the ideas are more complex, layered, and philosophical but whatever is implied, the act of painting expresses visual content.

In the 1970s and 1980s, I was trying to express spiritual or historical thoughts, often together with emotional states through rather minimal geometric abstraction. So was Robert Houle. We shared the notion that non-figurative art could indeed express all sorts of spiritual states as well as emotive ones. Simply by looking and thinking about what one saw in our works, one could comprehend our ideas about human existence as well as the human condition. Or, at least, so we thought.

Robert and I did not live close to one another, nor did we know one another. That came later but nevertheless our goals were similar. We share a multivalent Christian upbringing. I come from a home in which God was constantly present. Robert grew up in schools in which God was always there and whether good or bad, rejected or accepted, that constant presence of ideas about God affects one's understanding of everything—including artmaking and the subjects that art embraces. Therefore, it is difficult to not deal with the mythic, the unknowable, in some way or other in one's work. Life and death, even the hereafter, become viable subjects. I was taught to talk to God and I suspect Robert was, too. Perhaps as a Shaman talks to the Spirit World—that is, directly.

Robert has made many diptychs, as I have. He has moved from strict abstraction to near figuration while I now paint landscapes, but neither of us has forsaken the need for meaningful content. Perhaps we are "soul siblings?" We are two painters who participate in the contemporary art world while contemplating our role here on earth as philosopher-artists. Robert and I have come to similar answers, although with quite different, but very painterly, solutions. We, like all artists, are the visual historians of our era.

a postcard from standoff.

Faye HeavyShield

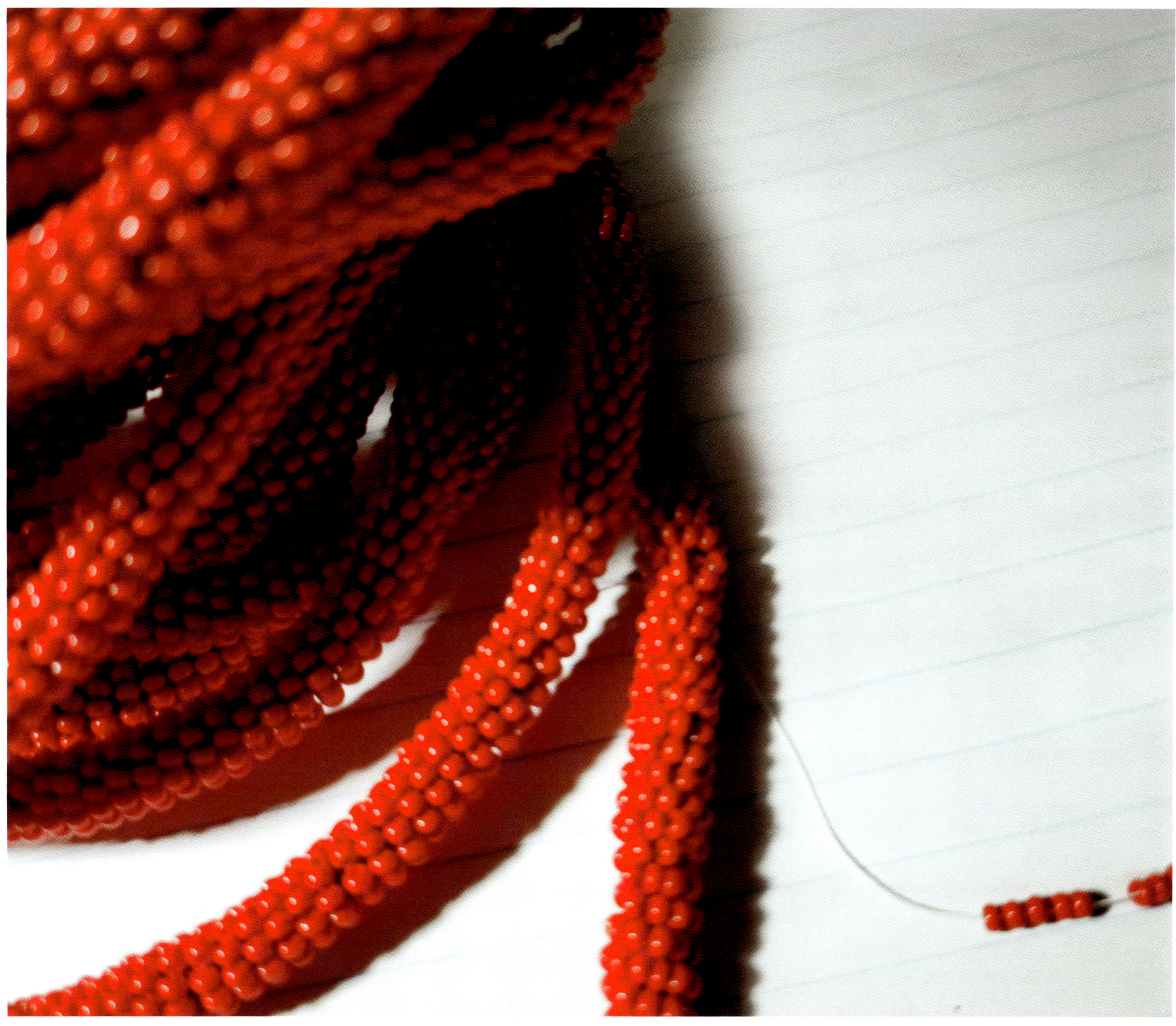

Friendships & Solidarity
Jamelie Hassan + Ron Benner

> *Date: Thu, September 26, 2019*
> *Subject: Re: Ron Benner's Cuitlacoche Corn Roast 2019 – Art Museum at the University of Toronto*
>
> *Hi Jamelie, Ron, apologies that we didn't make it but we're in Manitoba at the moment. Hope all went well and hope to see you both soon.*
> *Robert & Paul*[1]

Over the years, Ron and I made the drive from our home in London, Ontario, into Toronto, where we enjoyed meeting up with the local community of artists and friends at Ron's annual corn roast, hosted in connection with his garden on the University of Toronto campus. Sharing corn and updates in Ron's garden installations had become a yearly tradition. We missed Robert and his partner, Paul, during the 2019 event, and followed up with our friends upon their return to Toronto from Manitoba. Instead of our usual visit at the garden, we had the chance to host them at our home later that summer. Robert began his morning with the southern Ontario sunrise, the quiet calm interspersed with laughter as we exchanged stories over cappuccinos.

Since the beginning of our working relationship around the time of the Kanehsatake/Oka Crisis in the summer of 1990, Robert's projects have acted as an ethical and aesthetic compass in how we consider art and culture on Turtle Island. Robert's *Mohawk Summer* was originally installed in the windows of his second-floor studio on Queen Street West in downtown Toronto; these banners emblazoned with messages of sovereignty effectively blocked the light inside his space while the bold text faced out onto the street, reminding the public of the

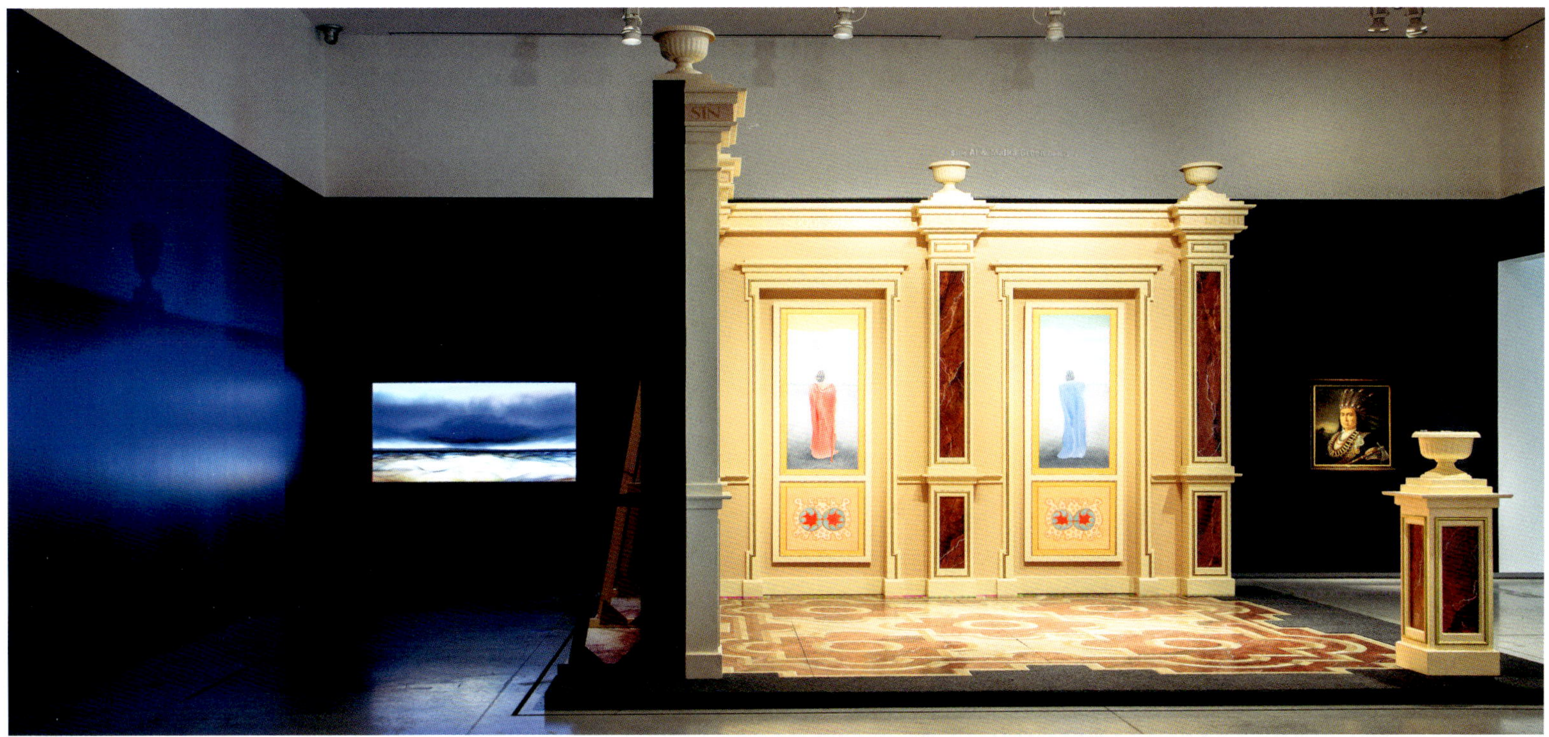

ongoing injustices of this conflict. These banners were later presented in *Okanata,* a group exhibition of forty artists (including Ron and myself) co-curated by Robert, Tom Hill, David General, at Workscene Gallery and A Space Gallery in Toronto. In the spring of 1992 the exhibition travelled to the Woodland Cultural Centre in Brantford, Ontario.

In 2016, with the critic and Islamic art historian Ruba Kana'an,[2] I coordinated the symposium *Home Ground: Canadian Perspectives* at the Aga Khan Museum in Toronto. This event represented an opportunity to hear from contemporary Canadian artists, critics, and curators as they discussed some of the issues raised in the exhibition *Home Ground: Contemporary Art from the Middle East,* curated by Suheyla Takesh from the Barjeel Art Foundation, Sharja, UAE. Issues related to the idea of home and the consequences of dislocation and migration are timely, provocative, and pertinent to the ongoing conversations many of us are having here in Canada and internationally. The question we posed in this symposium was whether the idea of home could be understood as what Edward Said might call "a creative act of affiliation."[3] The symposium's keynote speakers were Robert Houle and cultural critic Dot Tuer. Significantly, this was the first time that the Aga Khan Museum had included an Indigenous perspective in their program. In his keynote address, titled "Home Ground: A First Nations Perspective," Robert opened with this greeting: "Welcome to the traditional territory of the

FIG. 1
Robert Houle, *Paris/Ojibwa,* 2010. Installation view of *Toronto: Tributes + Tributaries, 1971–1989,* at the Art Gallery of Ontario, September 29, 2016 – May 22, 2017.
Photo: Art Gallery of Ontario.

Mississauga, to Paradise (as the Western Hemisphere was initially referred to during the Quattrocentro when Europeans began to arrive)."[4] For many in the audience that day, they were hearing an Indigenous land acknowledgement for the first time. In his keynote Robert traced a rich trajectory of his work encompassing Indigenous knowledge, history, and aesthetics. In March 2017, inspired by Robert's presentation, the AKM invited the Anishinaabe curator and critic Wanda Nanibush to give the keynote at the symposium *Rebel, Jester, Mystic, Poet*[5] Upon reflection, one recognizes that these symposia at the AKM are reminders of how cultural institutions bring together the public and the cultural community during grave and turbulent times in the world. To move forward in spirit of truth and reconciliation, it is necessary for Canadian institutions to address injustices and the violence of colonial histories in Canada and the Americas, and to engage community activists and socially engaged artists.

We reflect often on the different ways we came to understand the scope of Robert's work and advocacy. As the years passed, the intersections related to our work and research increased and our friendship deepened. There was the time we carried his paintings with us to present in the exhibition *Travelling Theory* held at the Jordan National Gallery of Fine Arts in Amman, Jordan.[6] Robert had planned to join us during the installation and opening of this first exhibition of contemporary Canadian art in the Arab world, but significant events in his life[3] did not permit him to make the journey.[7] We knew as we visited Petra, the rose-coloured city carved out of the cliff-faces, a trading centre of the ancient world, that Robert would have loved this archaeological site of the Nabateans. He would have understood these Indigenous peoples and how they had fought against imperial Rome, preferring to die of thirst rather than surrender to the Roman forces that blockaded the city.

In 2012, during a four-month stay in Paris,[8] Ron and I began our research on Eugène Delacroix and his travels to North Africa. This research took us to the Louvre archives where we examined the Delacroix materials held there. We asked, as we viewed the North African journals of Delacroix, to see the original Delacroix drawings that had inspired Robert's *Paris/Ojibwa* installation from 2010.[9] This multimedia installation brought so many elements together, innovatively transporting us to the Paris of 1845 when Delacroix created drawings of the Indigenous performers who had come to Europe. Seeing these performers had mesmerized George Sand to the extent that the author wrote a letter to her friend, the painter Delacroix, that he must return to Paris from his country home in Champrosy to witness this historic event,[10] and he wisely took her advice. Delacroix's few drawings done *in situ* and in haste became the entry point for Robert to take us into his elaborate and powerful *Paris/Ojibwa* (fig. 1).This counternarrative is revealed honouring the perspective of Maungwudaus and his Mississauga dance troupe who had journeyed so far from home. In this epic work, which visually and conceptually captivates the viewer, Robert sheds light on a remarkable story, and on an encounter that had largely been dismissed from the official record. The past, present, and future are painstakingly brought into our consciousness in such a way that we shall not allow ourselves to miss the urgent stories that unfold as we experience the work of Robert Houle.

— Jamelie Hassan, March 30, 2021

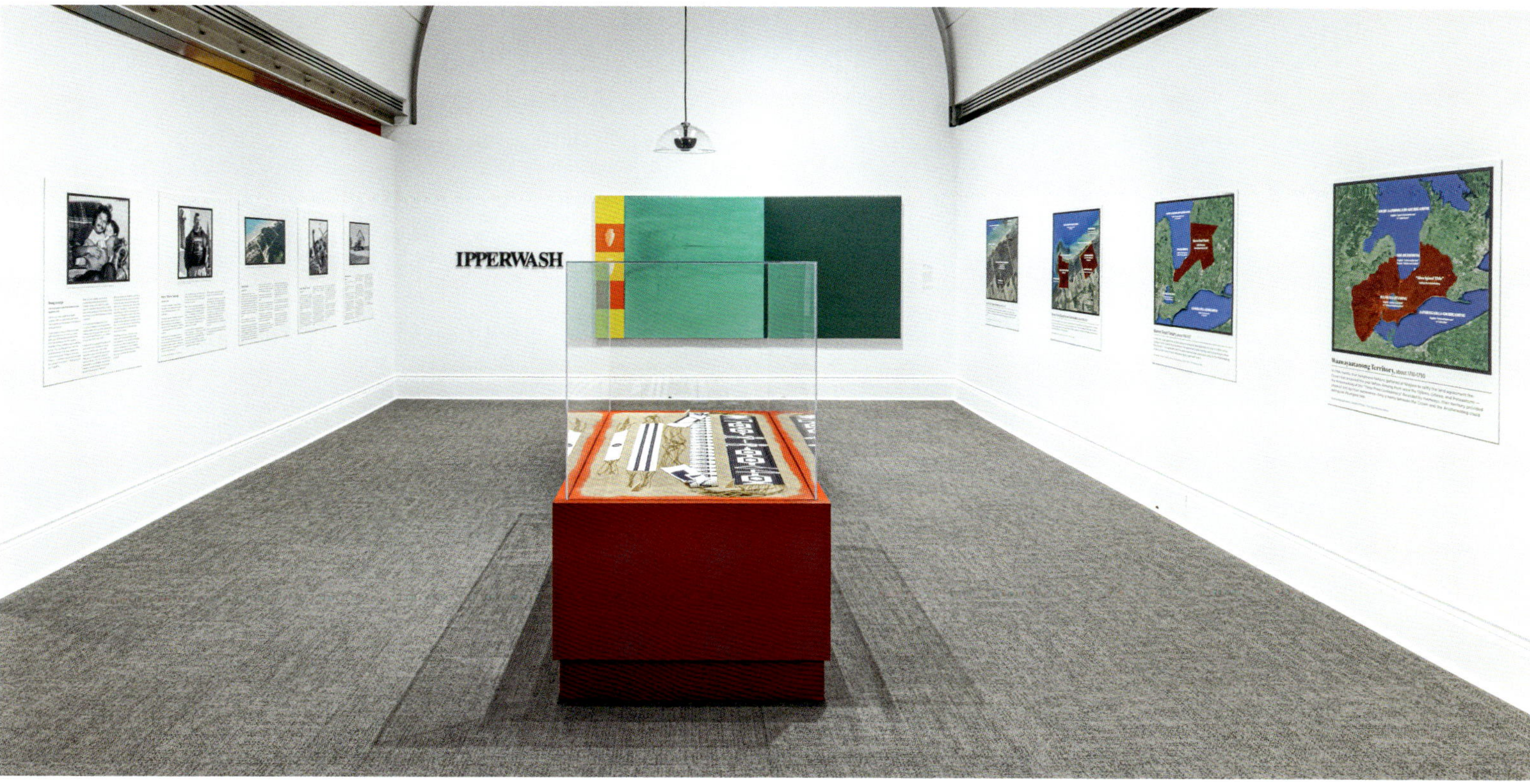

* * * * *

Since 1972 I have been installing work by other artists due to my involvement in artist-run centres and organizing independent cultural exchanges both nationally and internationally. In 2009, I began working as a part-time preparator at Museum London, in London, Ontario. The first time I installed a work by Robert Houle was in March 1992 at the Jordan National Gallery of Fine Arts for the exhibition *Travelling Theory*.[11] I had met Robert the previous summer in Kingston, Ontario, at a symposium organized by the Agnes Etherington Art Centre, celebrating the fiftieth anniversary of the Kingston Conference held at Queen's University in 1941.[12] We exchanged name tags. I became Robert and Robert became Ron. Later that year we were both involved in the *Okanata* exhibition, held in Toronto in solidarity with the Mohawks defending their land during the so-called Oka Crisis.

In 1997 and 1998 Robert and I were part of an Art Gallery of Ontario advisory circle on a proposal to revisit the 1927 National Gallery of Canada exhibition *Canadian West Coast Art: Native and Modern*, which travelled to the Art Gallery of Ontario in 1928. The purpose of the 1927 exhibition was, according to Eric Brown, then director of the National Gallery, "to mingle for the first time the art work of the Canadian West Coast tribes with that of our more sophisticated [*sic*] artists in an endeavour to

FIG. 2
Robert Houle, *Ipperwash*, 2000–2001. Installation view of *Gaawiin Ogiibagidenaawaasiiwaawan / They did not let it go* at Museum London in 2020–2021. Photo: © Toni Hafkenscheid.

analyse their relationships to one another, if such exist, and particularly to enable this primitive and interesting art to take a definite place as one of the most valuable of Canada's artistic productions."[13] The advisory circle's response to this statement by Brown and the revisiting of the exhibition involved an intense and heated debate. In my written contribution to the organizers, I stated the following concerning "relationships": "The recent confrontation between the Stony Point First Nation and the Ontario Provincial Police, which resulted in the death of Stony Point activist Dudley George and the conviction of OPP officer Deane of criminal negligence causing death, has affected everyone in the area. All my fellow advisors had followed these tragic events; I was making sure that the facts of Ipperwash were part of the public record at this round table. It is impossible for me not to think about First Nation issues and relationships." Robert ended his detailed and sophisticated written contribution by talking about Emily Carr's positive relationships with West Coast First Nations artists, and with the suggestion that the best course of action was to "perhaps create a new art history."[14]

Holding an artwork is a rare privilege offered to few and is a subjective experience which heightens one's perception and understanding of the work of art. In July 2020 I was asked by Museum London to install a new exhibition, *Gaawiin Ogiibagidenaawaasiiwaawan / They did not let it go* (fig. 2), co-curated by Summer Bressette and Monica Virtue.[15] The exhibition marked the twenty-fifth anniversary of the Ipperwash Crisis and featured only one contemporary artwork, Robert Houle's *Ipperwash* (2000–2001), from Museum London's permanent collection. Accompanying Robert's work were historical and contemporary elements including maps, wampum, interviews and testimonies, photographs and audio recordings of the waves of Lake Huron, and recorded police reports. As I installed Robert's artwork, so many *memories* of the crisis came flashing back to me. The first component was a dark green canvas. *The pines, ferns, and moss of the Lake Huron shoreline.* Next, a turquoise canvas. *Lake Huron on a sunny day.* Beside that, a vertical Masonite panel with squares of a cochineal-like red and a pale ochre yellow overlaid onto photographs of two projectile points. *Thousands of years old. Kettle Point chert. A hard, fine-grained, crystalline sedimentary rock found near Stony Point and Ipperwash. A 13,500-year-old history.* Finally, cast black metal letters—installed from right to left, "H-S-A-W-R-E-P-P-I." *Protesters holding up a mirror to reflect the sun's rays in the direction of the police. Premier Mike Harris saying, "I want the fucking Indians out of the park!"*[12] *Road trips to Ipperwash with Dan and Mary Lou Smoke. Meeting with Rose Manning and other Stony Point Elders. Court trials, racism, liars.* Today the expropriated land called Camp Ipperwash has been reclaimed by the Stony Point First Nation, and Robert Houle *has* created a new art history.

— Ron Benner, March 30, 2021

[1] Email from Robert Houle, found in the author's inbox as we began the writing of this text.

[2] Ruba Kana'an was Head of Education and Scholarly Programs at the Aga Khan Museum from 2011–2017.

[3] Edward Said, *The World, the Text, and the Critic* (Cambridge, MA: Harvard University Press, 1983.

[4] Robert Houle, "Home Ground: A First Nations Perspective," in *Asian Diasporic Visual Cultures and the Americas,* eds. Jamelie Hassan, and Ruba Kana'an. 2:3 (Fall 2016).

[5] Venetia Porter, Curator of Islamic Art and Contemporary Middle Eastern Art at the British Museum in London, was also a keynote speaker at this symposium.

[6] Curated by Fern Bayer and Jamelie Hassan. The title was inspired by the text "Traveling Theory" by Edward Said, in his book *The World, The Text and the Critic* (Cambridge: Harvard University Press, 1982). The exhibition included artists Ron Benner, Stan Denniston, Janice Gurney, Jamelie Hassan, Robert Houle, Lani Maestro, Robert McNealy, Marianne Nicolson, and David Tomas.

[7] Among Houle's commitments was his work curating the landmark exhibition *Land, Spirit, Power: First Nations at the National Gallery of Canada,* in Ottawa in 1992, alongside Diana Nemiroff and Charlotte Townsend-Gault.

[8] The author was awarded the Canada Council for the Arts artist in residency at the Cité Internationale des Arts in Paris in 2012.

[9] This installation was first presented at the Canadian Cultural Centre in Paris in 2010, then at the Art Gallery of Peterborough in 2011 and the Art Gallery of Windsor in 2012. Robert Houle presented the catalogue that documented *Paris/Ojibwa* to Ron at the Indigenous Curatorial Collective (then the Aboriginal Curatorial Collective) gathering at OCAD University in Toronto in 2011.

[10] Nelcya Delanoë, "Making the Past Dance" in *Paris/Ojibwa* (Peterborough: Art Gallery of Peterborough, 2011).

[11] See note 2.

[12] Revisiting the Kingston Artists' Conference at Queen's University in June 1991, organized by Michael Bell and Frances K. Smith. Jamelie Hassan and Robert Houle presented on the same panel on the subject of language and visual arts.

[13] Exhibition of Canadian West Coast Art: Native and Modern, December 1927, National Gallery of Canada, Ottawa. Introduction by Eric Brown, with an essay by Marius Barbeau. The participants in the AGO Roundtable included Anna Hudson, Matthew Teitelbaum, Dennis Reid, Judith Mastai, Robert Houle, Christos Dikeakos, Gerald McMaster, Brian Donnelly, Lynda Jessup, and Ron Benner.

[14] Written reflections and recommendations from Robert Houle submitted to the AGO meeting, 1998.

[15] The exhibition at Museum London opened to the public in September 2020.

[16] Quoted in testimony by Charles Warnick, former Ontario Provincial Attorney General, on Nov. 12, 2003. See Peter Edwards, *One Dead Indian: The Premier, the Police, and the Ipperwash Crisis,* McClelland & Stewart, 2003.

SACRED GEOMETRY

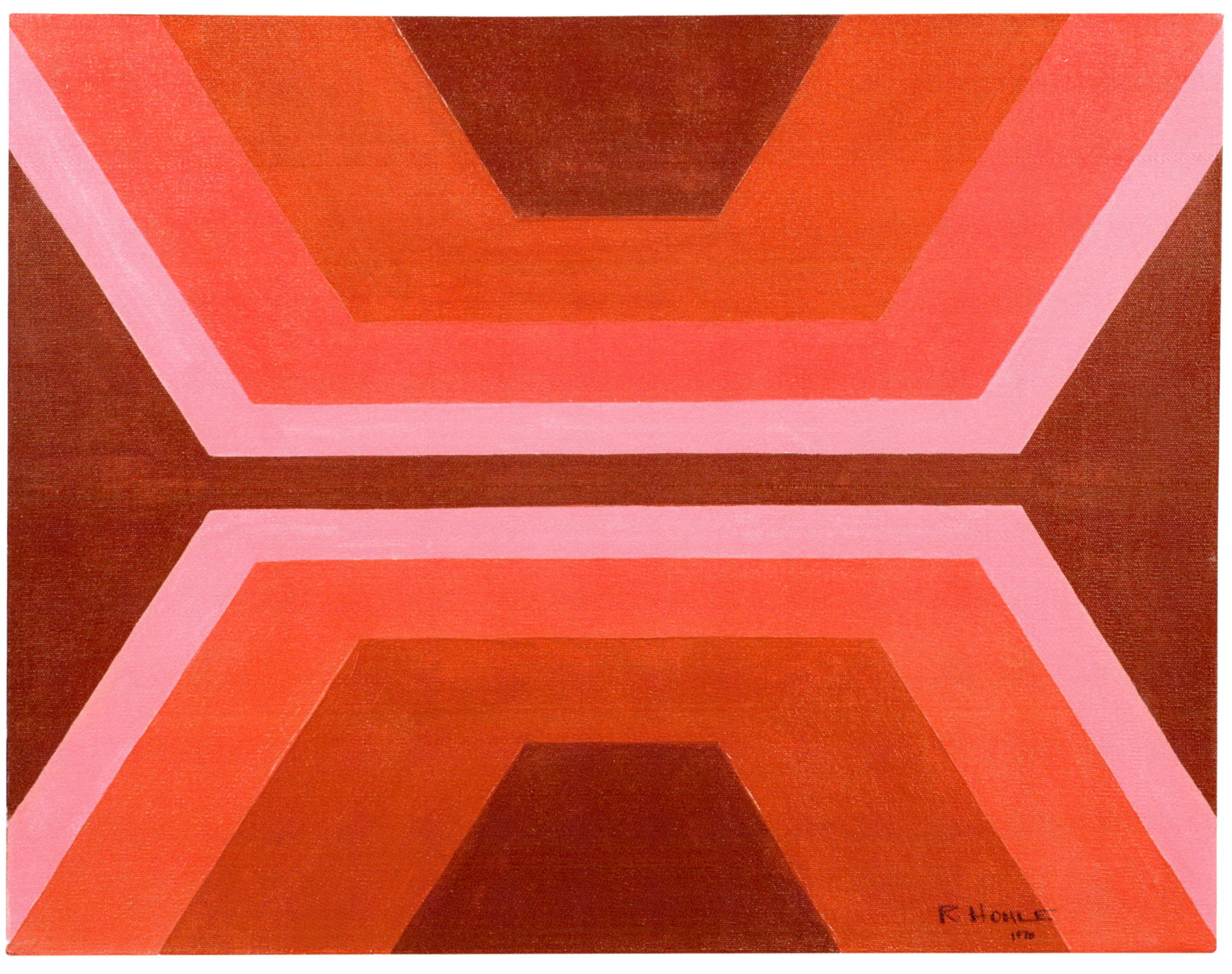

Red is Beautiful, 1970

Ojibway Blanket, 1983

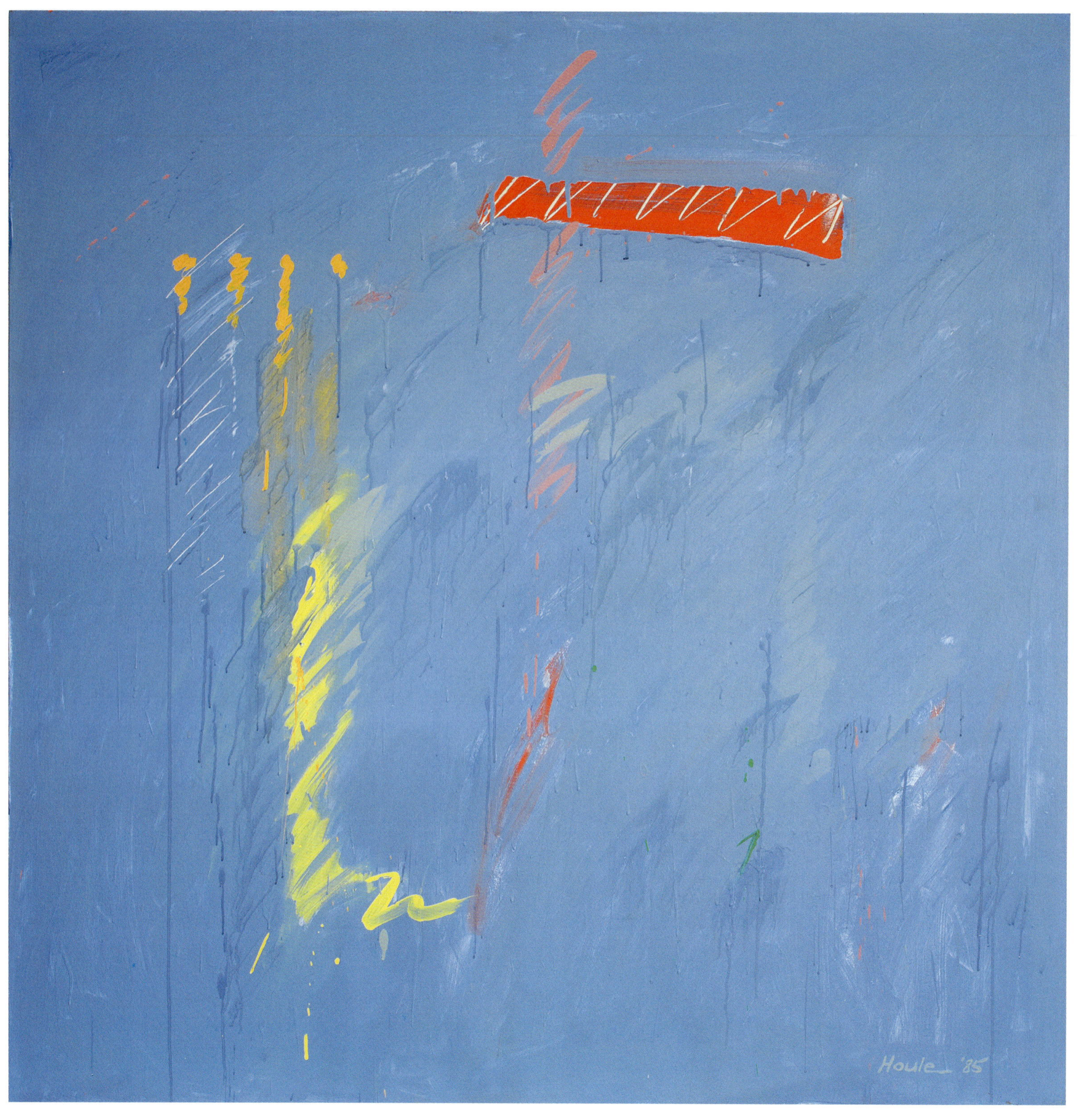

Idyllic Moments, 1985

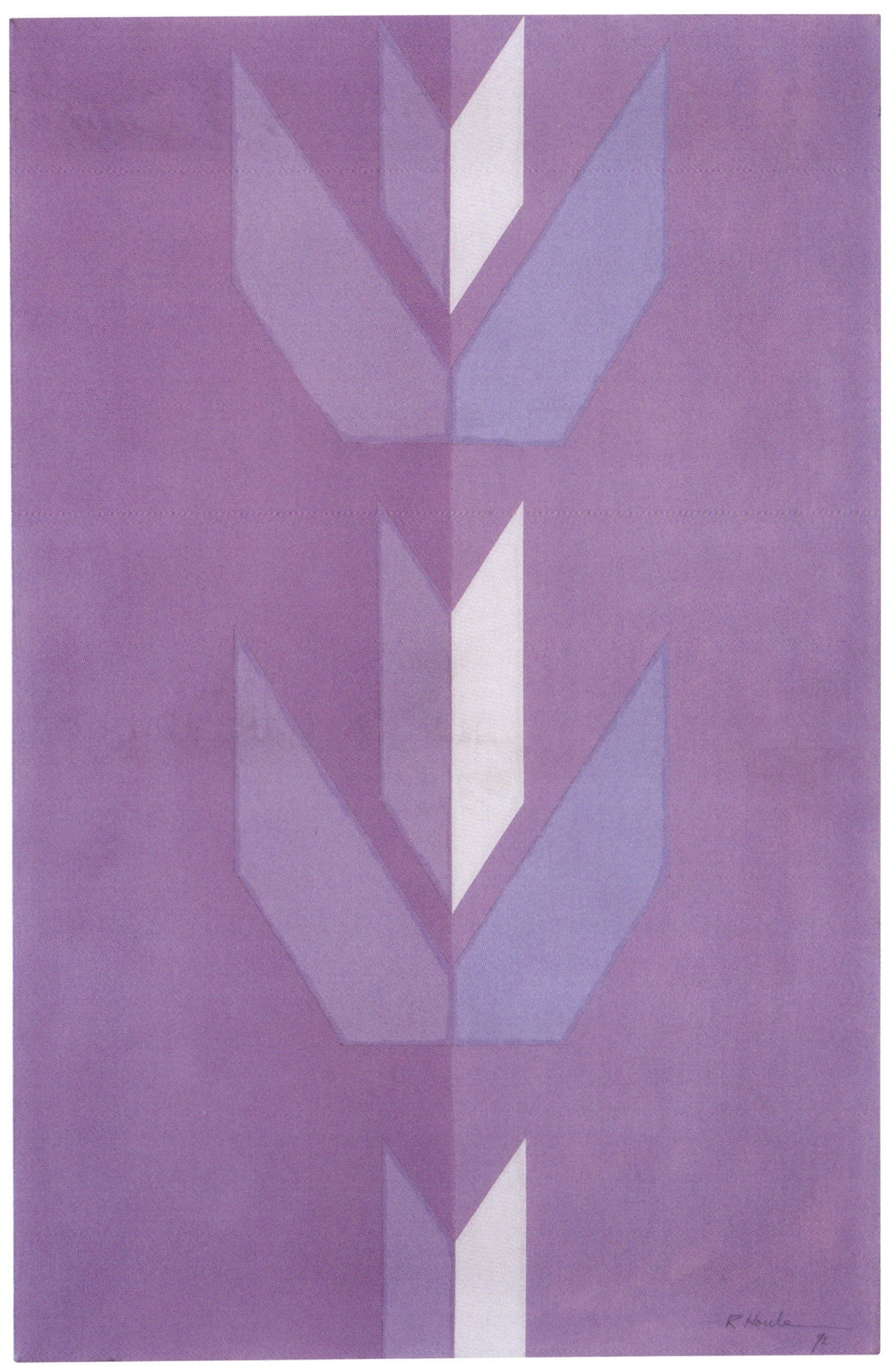

Ojibway Motif, #2, Purple Leaves Series, 1972

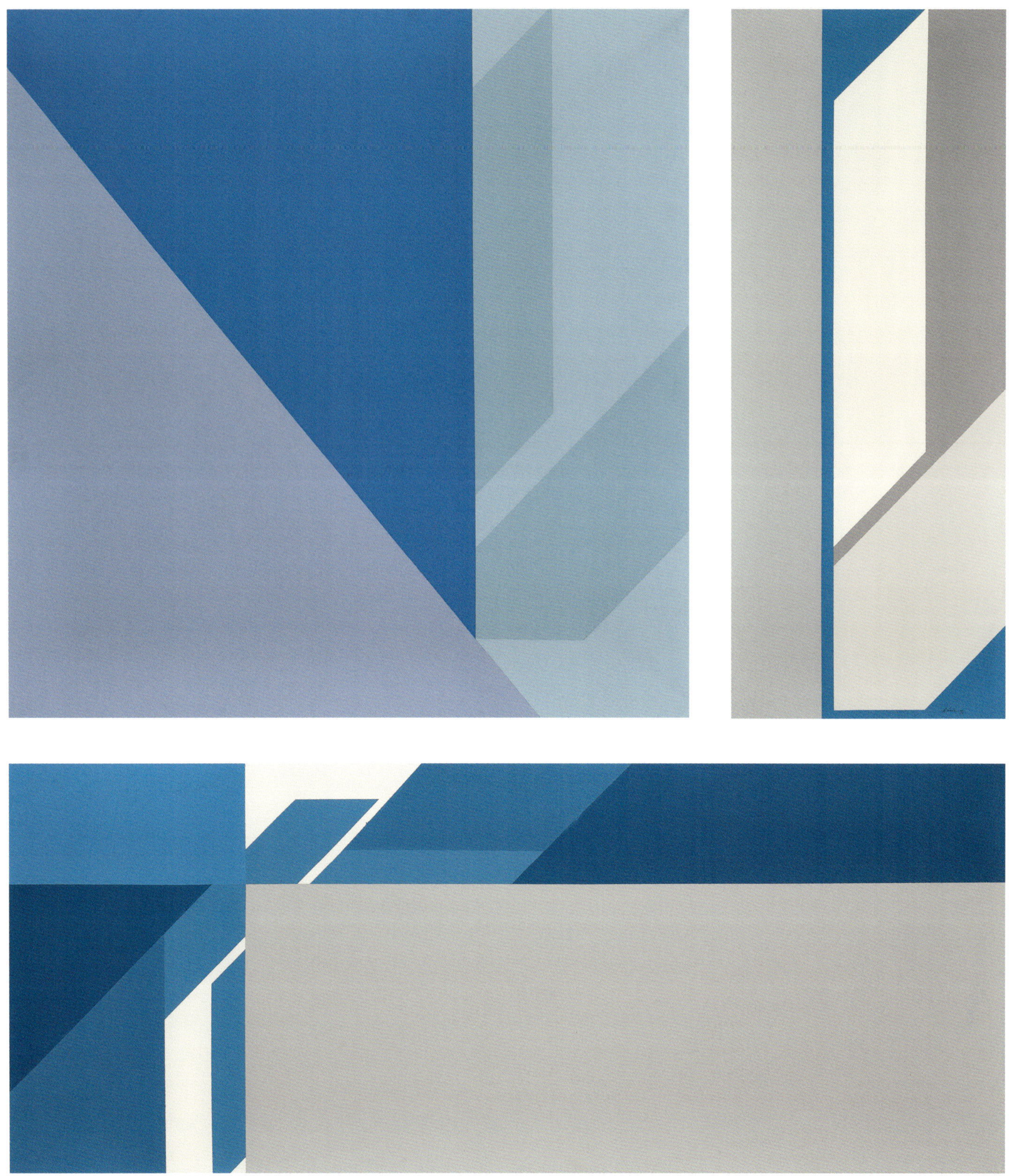

Love Poems, 1972
Games (top left), *The First Step* (top right), *The Stuff of Which Dreams Are Made* (bottom)

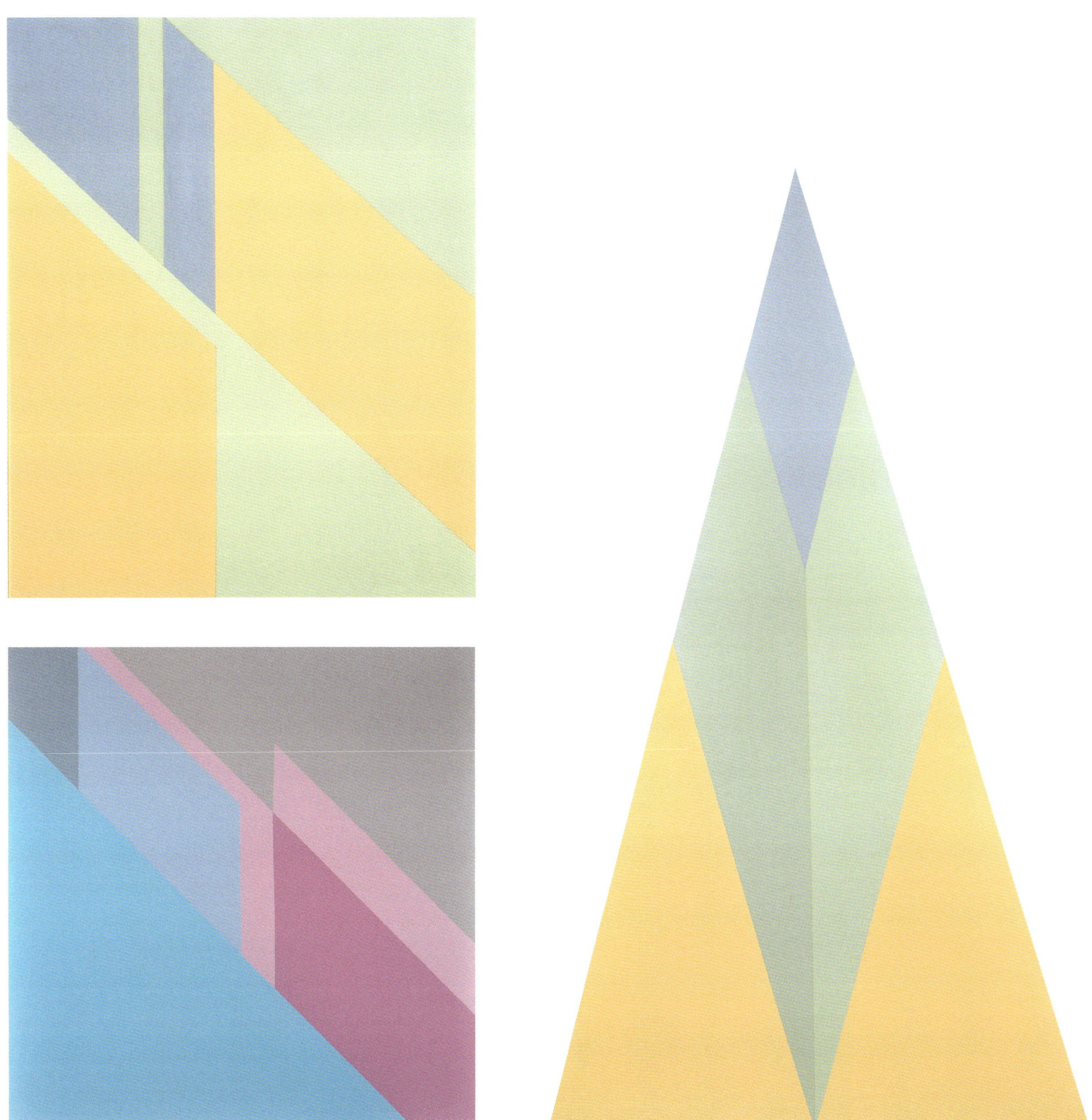

Love Poems, 1972
Parallel Lines (top left), *Epigram for the Shortest Distance* (bottom left), *Wigwam* (right)

The Transformative Abstraction of Robert Houle

Mark A. Cheetham

My sincere thanks to the McMaster University Art Gallery, to Robert Houle, and to curator Carol Podedworny.

Robert Houle has been a visionary since the beginning of his career as an artist, curator, and writer. It is painfully easy to be wrong about the future, yet twenty-five years ago in the catalogue for his pioneering exhibition *New Work by a New Generation,*[1] Houle foresaw directions from which profound change would come in First Nations art, his own, and that of others. He proclaimed the need to live in the present without forgetting specific histories and cultural traditions. His shibboleth was and remains: *mutual transformation*: "Native artists," he wrote in 1982, "are committed to involvement in the polemics of modern art.... Meaning ... derives from living in the twentieth century, where painting ranges from realism to abstraction and sculpture varies from shamanism to assemblage."[2] As if to enact in his text the complementary interchange between Indigenous and other modern art, Houle devoted about half his words to a discussion of how Jackson Pollock and Barnett Newman were transformed by their contacts with and respect for First Nations rituals and their material traces.[3] Still practising from what many in the art world see as (at least) a double disadvantage—working in Canada and being a First Nations artist, in other words, doubly vulnerable to marginalization—Houle has tenaciously, expansively, and, above all, generously insisted on reciprocity among the aesthetic and cultural specificities with which he engages. The forefathers of abstraction inform his work; he transforms them and the traditions of abstraction that he projects into the future.

It is a measure of the quality and success of Robert Houle's abstract work that it is effective on many planes. To appreciate fully his contributions in this genre, should we focus on the particularities of place and history elaborated in *Palisade I* and *II* (2001, 2007; page 60), or on the material and formal resonance we perceive in *Blue Apache* (2003–2004; page 141) or *Grandfather I* and *II* (2004)? We could examine his early engagements with Neoplasticism in *Diamond Composition* (1980; page 54) or reach beyond the confines of art's history to the often-tragic clash between indigenes and invaders in eighteenth-century North America, as Houle does with *Postscript* (2001) and *Palisade I* (2001), especially. Is it preferable to stay up close to his art or to step back to measure how much it is part of international attempts to revise the history of both Modernism and its epitome, abstraction? Ignoring the confines of grammar and rationality, to all these seeming disjunctions we are compelled to answer "yes." Three capacious frames of reference help us to place and assess Houle's abstraction, to appreciate the ways in which it is indeed "committed to involvement in the polemics of modern art": his purposeful interaction with earlier abstract art, his concomitant rejection of purity in abstraction, and his part in the turn toward a recognition of "discrepant" practices within Modernism, initiated by non-canonical practitioners and from officially peripheral places.

Houle is a serious student of abstraction. He was in Amsterdam in 1980, taking notes on key works by Mondrian, Malevich, and Newman at the Stedelijk Museum. *Diamond Composition* is a sophisticated homage to Mondrian and De Stijl; more, it is a harbinger of Houle's troubling of the corpus of abstract art. The diamond shape was Mondrian's famous solution to what he perceived in the second decade of the twentieth century as the problem of introducing diagonals into Neoplastic compositions, a practice adopted unproblematically in the regularly presented square format by his fellow traveller Theo van Doesburg. Mondrian's breakthrough in the lozenges was to recognize that their bordering limits are orthogonal at their junctions and yet potentially diagonal in their framing activity. Set a square on one corner point and you find the dynamism of oblique lines without having to unbalance what Mondrian held as the purity of upright rectilinear intersections within the frame.[4]

At first glance, Houle's *Diamond Composition* (page 54) is a respectful reflection of the order and tone of Neoplasticism. It is carefully designed, exquisitely executed, and trades in shades of grey favoured by Mondrian at this time. Yet many of its internal precincts are textured; specifically, they are inflected by insistent, four-stroke groupings of lines. Cool and collected as these markings may be, they also signal a revision of the master's priorities. Houle has remarked in conversation that he moved away from Mondrian at this time and toward Malevich's Suprematism work (fig. 1) that could be seen in abundance at the Stedelijk—if we may map such decisions in terms of white grandfather figures for the moment, a genealogy that Houle ultimately renders inadequate. *Diamond Composition*'s prominent black squares and rectangles suggest this change. Much as they look like Malevich's Suprematist forms, on their own, these simple elements do not depart from Mondrian's (later) vocabulary. It is the inclusion of what might appear to be innocent cross-hatchings that, in retrospect, alerts us to Houle's deviation from the transcendental and material pieties of Neoplasticism. Sometimes lines are just lines. If this were the case in

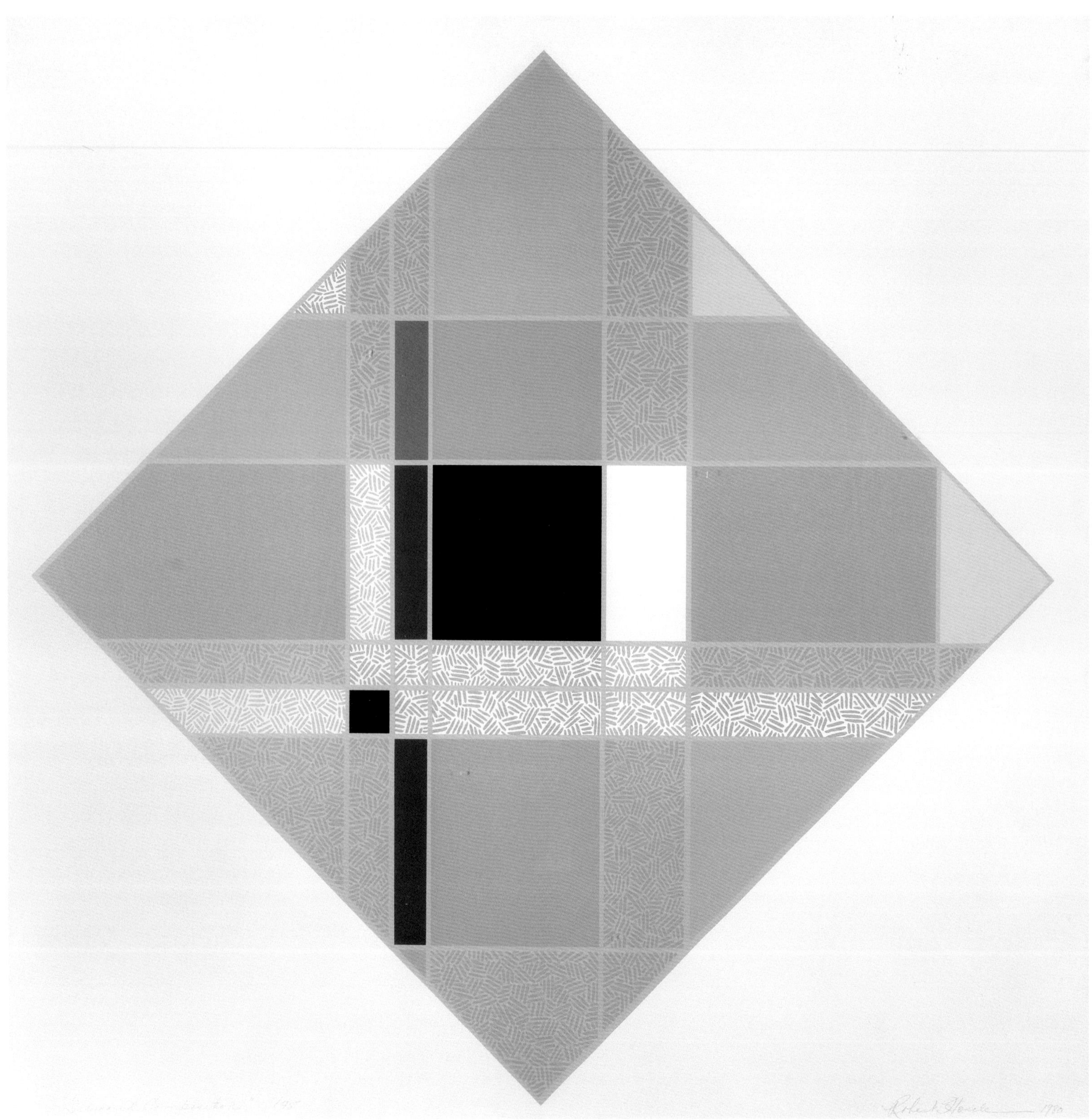

Diamond Composition, 1980

Diamond Composition or *Square No. 3* (1978; page 57), however, both works would still unsettle the careful surfaces of a Mondrian, at least visually. But these are not simple cross-hatchings set down only for tonal and surface effect. These strokes are intimations of porcupine quills—as well as memories of the parallel painted lines of eighteenth-century Innu garments and the linear indentations on ancient Iroquoian pottery—traces of commodities and techniques central to the decorative traditions of First Nations cultures. The quills prick our memories of a threatened past, a history with which Houle infects abstraction. Houle's stokes extend well beyond the surface to proclaim that abstraction can speak for history—his history.

It may seem inflammatory to claim that abstraction is like a body that may be infected. The description goes against much of the received wisdom about abstract art, especially that of Clement Greenberg's extraordinarily influential narrative of medium specificity and autonomy. Greenberg famously held that abstraction was the epitome of painting's evolution because it could be the most optically pure, that it required only colour and flatness. To infect the purity of abstraction within a composition and to suggest that the genre can have a narrative role beyond its frame is to challenge Greenberg's paradigms at the most fundamental levels. This rewriting of abstraction's history is justified, however, by the practice and theory of members of the avant-garde who invented the genre—Malevich especially—and by contemporary practitioners who have a relationship to this tradition, including Robert Houle.[5]

Kazimir Malevich's remarkable theory of the "additional element" is key to the revision in which Houle participates. In a series of texts from the early twentieth century and with his art movement, Suprematism, Malevich held that the ills of art could be cured by the homeopathic infusion of specific aesthetic antidotes. He diagnosed the needs of his students' work, then prescribed a treatment for the canvas, in the form of an additional or supplementary element. More often than not, this agent was a Suprematist form, such as a black square. Once administered, the transformative element would work within the composition to effect positive change toward what Malevich saw as a socially and spiritually superior art form. What Malevich ultimately bequeathed to the future was not Suprematism but rather a mechanism for constant change in the genre, an infection in the positive sense.

Houle's infection, his additional element, is the quill line introduced in *Diamond Composition*, *Square No. 3*, and *Punk Schtick* (1982). While contributing effectively to the formal effect of unity in the latter two works, the lines also move

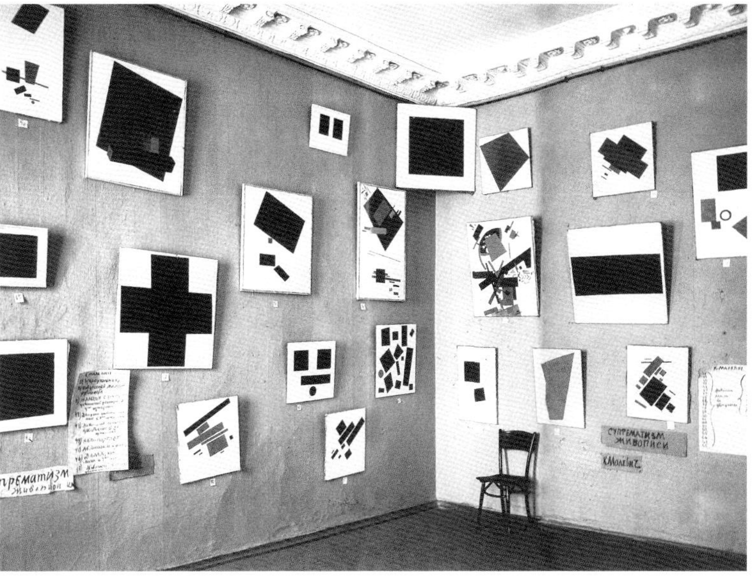

FIG. 1 (TOP)
Installation view of *0.10 – The Last Futurist Exhibition of Painting*, Petrograd, Winter 1915–1916, featuring Kazimir Malevich's *Black Square*.

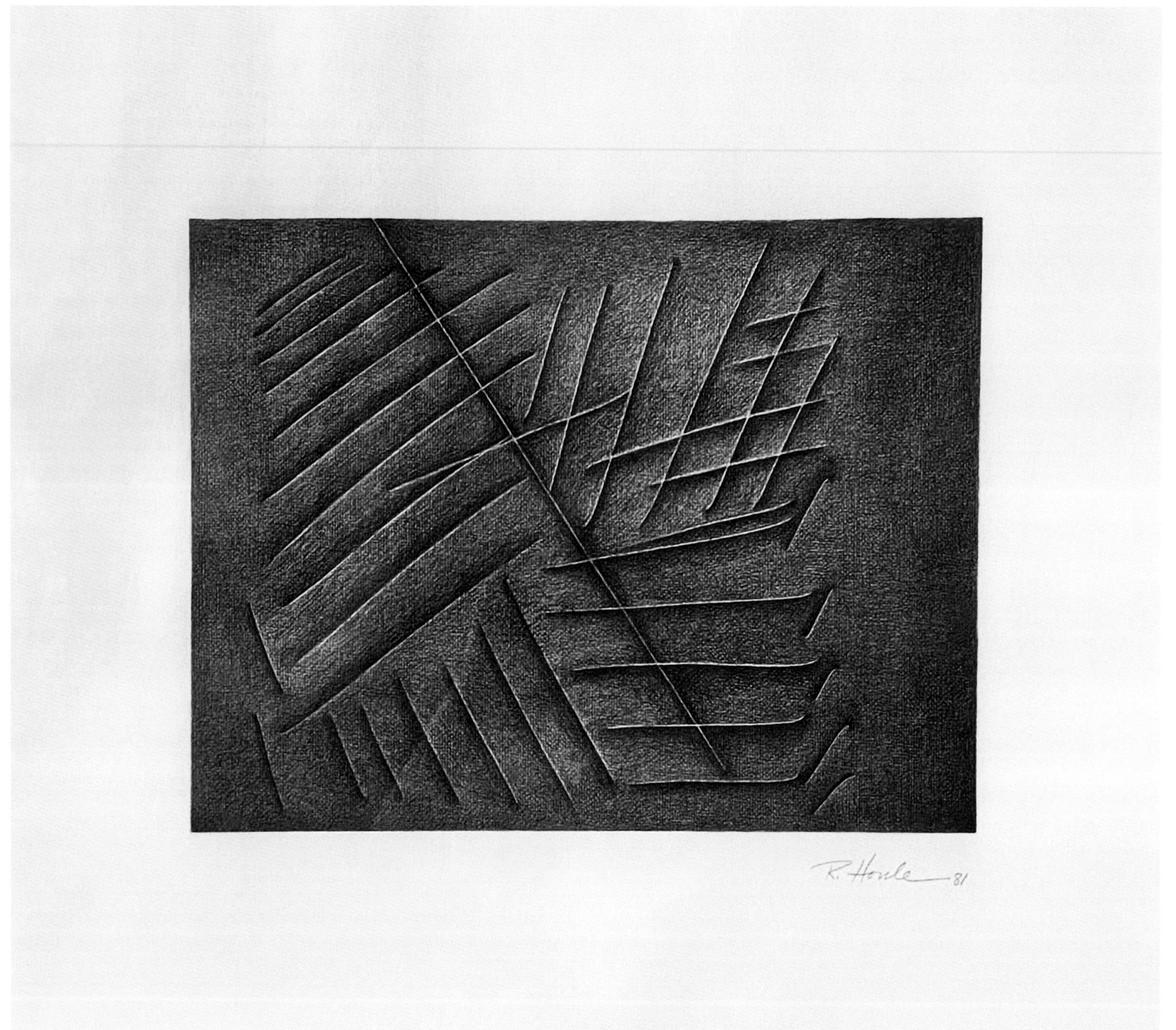

Cryptogram No. 2, 1981

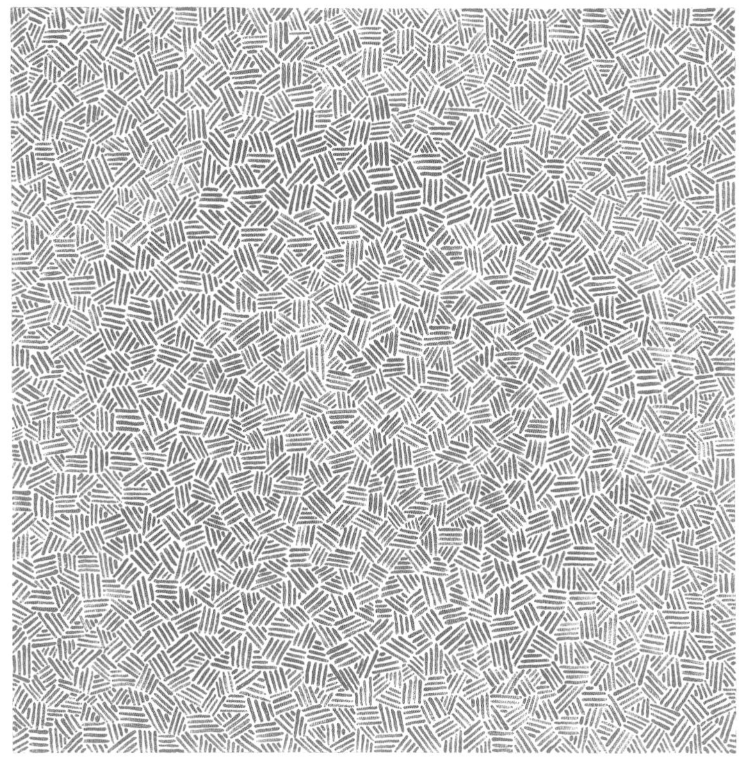

Square No. 3, 1978

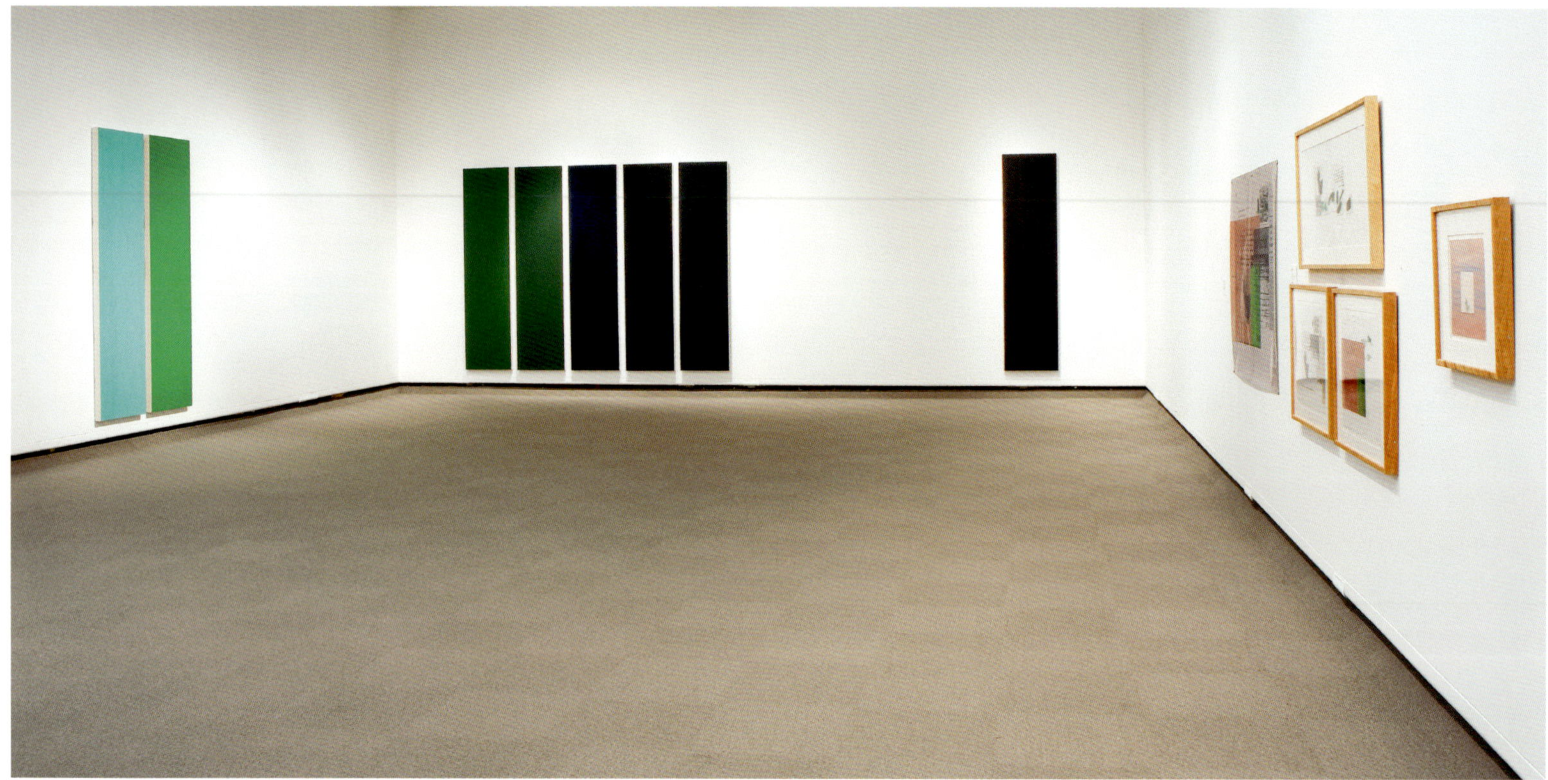

us past the concerns of composition by *alluding* to First Nations aesthetic practices—quillwork—and to a history of interaction with Western norms that rises to the surface here as tragically forgotten, just as quill embellishment has been lost beyond a small circle of practitioners. Both works subtly but confidently resist the isolation ward of formalism and they actively transform the efforts of their interlocutors. *Square No. 3* is reminiscent of Jasper Johns' so-called "Corpse + Mirror" works of the 1970s, which were an inspiration for Houle's experiments with cross-hatching, but again, Houle's reference to quills marks a different reflection on history. *Punk Schtick* alludes to Barnett Newman's three-dimensional works, those that are freestanding sculptures and those that attach to the wall, especially *The Wild* (1950). In a refracted manner, *Punk Schtick* even recalls the debt Newman proclaimed to West Coast First Nations' totem poles, and it reminds us that in the official history of Abstract Expressionism, Newman's outspoken affinity to these and other autochthonous practices is not as widely remembered as it should be. In Houle's abstraction, infection can lead to healing.

Nowhere do we see this beneficial effect more dramatically than in Houle's two versions of *Palisade*, the second of which was made for *Troubling Abstraction: Robert Houle*. In *Palisade I* (2001; fig. 2), his direct visual reference to Newman's three-part abstractions with their familiar zips, especially to the narrative effect of *Stations of the Cross* (1960; fig. 3),

FIG. 2
Robert Houle, *Palisade I*, 1999. Installation view of *To Be Reckoned With* at the MacKenzie Art Gallery in 2010. Oil on canvas, watercolour on paper, and lithographic print, installation dimensions variable (canvas panels are 244 × 61.2 cm each). Collection of the MacKenzie Art Gallery, purchased with the financial support of the Canada Council for the Arts Acquisition Assistance Program, 2000-001.
Photo: Don Hall, courtesy of the MacKenzie Art Gallery.

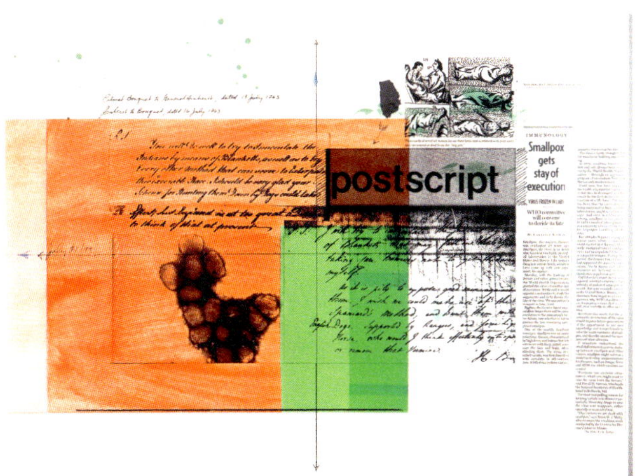

secures a place for Houle's abstraction within the heart of Modernism. But what Houle releases into this sometimes antiseptic progression of great Western artists and works is an art virus, one that keeps an appalling history in view. Just as he recalls quill work in some of his early abstractions, here the green and white vertical bands index the typical formal structure and memorial function of Amerindian wampum belts. On one level, the eight paintings in this series are analogous, handmade semiotic records of eight British garrisons captured in the conflicts of the mid-eighteenth century by First Nations warriors in the Great Lakes region during the period called Pontiac's Confederacy (1763–1766). Thanks to the texts about this history collaged in *Postscript* (fig. 4), which was integral to *Palisade I* and operates again here as a legend—both a key to understanding and a history—the apparent neutrality of abstraction in general as well as the Christian context of Newman's *Stations* are transformed.

Palisade I recalls the tactics of General Jeffrey Amherst—commander of the British military in North America during the Seven Years' War (1756–1763)—and his collaborator, Colonel Bouquet, specifically their diabolical plan to present smallpox-tainted blankets and a snuff box containing this infected cloth to a First Nations delegation during "peace" negotiations. A fragment of the green Hudson's Bay blanket used is abstracted in *Postscript*. Documentation from 1763 suggests that during Pontiac's resistance to the British, a specifically green and white wampum belt was used by the Odawa chief to signal First Nations' military strategy during such deliberations: "Pontiac's intended signal to his warriors to attack the occupants of Fort Detroit was to turn the wampum belt to show its green side."[6] Though Pontiac did not show

FIG. 3 (TOP)
Barnett Newman, *Twelfth Station*, 1965, from *Stations of the Cross*. Acrylic on canvas, 198.1 × 152.4 cm. National Gallery of Art, Washington, DC, collection of Robert and Jane Meyerhoff, 1986.65.12.

FIG. 4 (BOTTOM)
Robert Houle, *Postscript*, 1999. Lithographic print on paper, 121.9 × 163.2 cm. Collection of the MacKenzie Art Gallery, purchased with the financial support of the Canada Council for the Arts Acquisition Assistance Program. 2000-001-001.
Photo: Don Hall, courtesy of the MacKenzie Art Gallery.

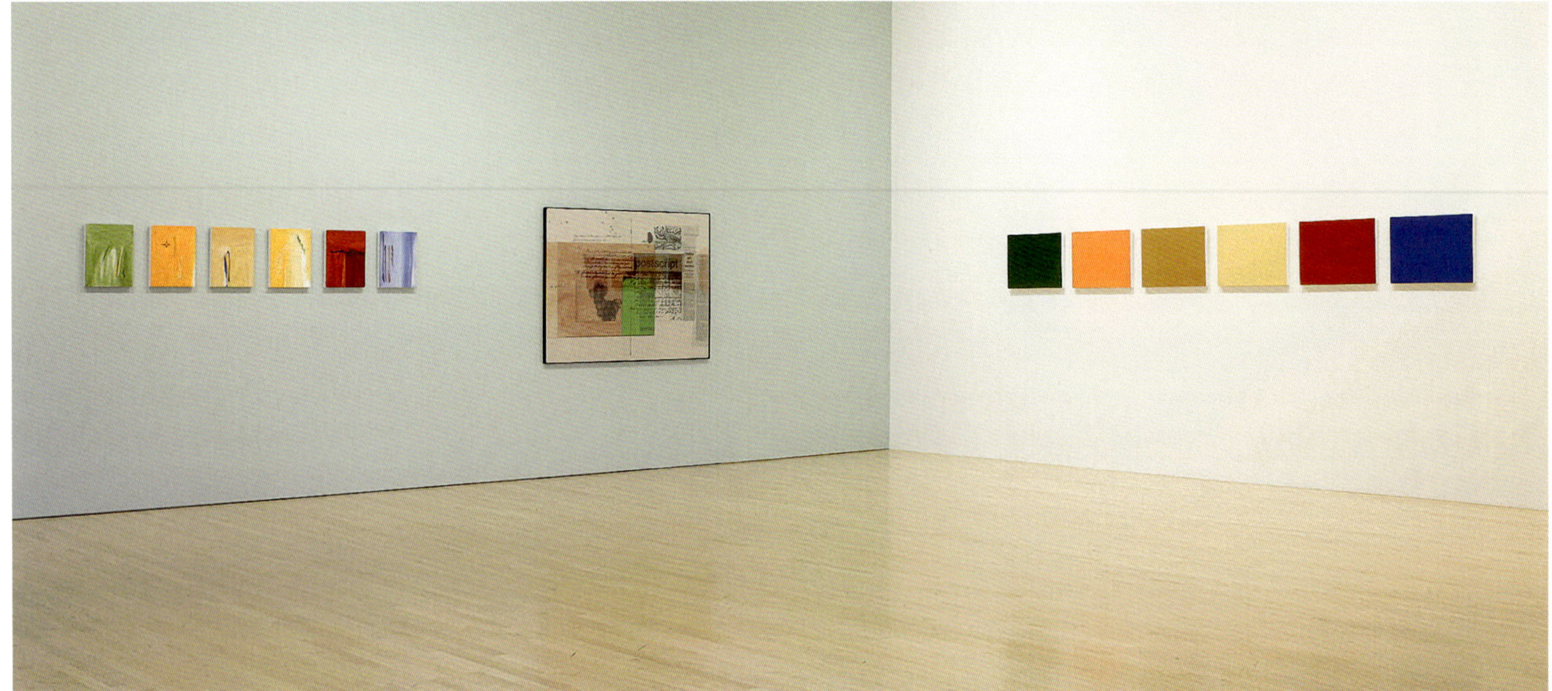

the green side at this time because his military intentions had been gleaned by the fort's defenders, the elements in Houle's installation move toward an ever darker green hue. But in showing the green side, as it were, Houle does not assail Newman. Houle's use of "infection" could not be more unlike that of the British military in the contexts he recalls. He knows that it was the First Nations that were attacked, in this case by germ warfare at Fort Pitt; what we have with the Newman-like *Palisade I* is another reminder of atrocity inscribed within the body of abstraction. As was the case for those actors in the eighteenth-century historical frame, both Newman's and Houle's works are transformed by this knowledge. In *Palisade I*, however, Houle employs this knowledge—his new additional element or "infection," in Malevich's sense—to transform Newman's legacy and extend its interaction with First Nations' history.

Palisade II (2007; fig. 5) is again a memorial, an homage to the Six Nations of the Haudenosaunee people, who, along with other groups, resisted the British during Pontiac's Confederacy. In six delicate studies that make reference to the medicine bags of each group and with six corresponding monochromes, Houle again uses an abstract painterly idiom to recall a history. The geographical deployment of these First Nations groups is recapitulated in the arrangement of these canvases: reading left to right (west to east) as we conventionally do, we see canvases for the Seneca (keepers of the "Western Door," and who sided with Pontiac as Houle notes), the Oneida, the Onondaga, the Tuscarora, the Cayuga, and finally the guardians of the "Eastern Door" of the collective territory, the Mohawk. *Postscript*, with its texts and abstract elements, functions once more as the didactic panel, as

FIG. 5
Robert Houle, *Palisade II*, 2007. Three-part installation consisting of twelve oils on canvases and one digital photographic print, installation dimensions variable. National Gallery of Canada, Ottawa, purchased 2008. Acc. # 42422.1-13. Photo: NGC.

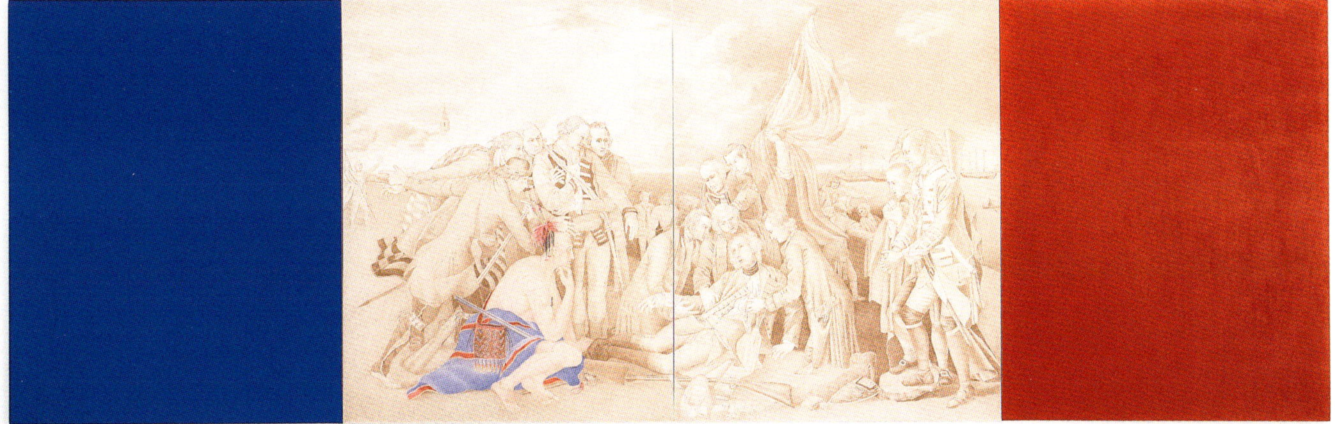

the historical conscience of abstract art. It is the hinge that joins *Palisade I* and *II*, linking Houle's concerns with the past and the active role that his infectious abstraction plays in the politics of the present.

Before turning again to individual works, let us step back and ask what part Robert Houle's abstraction plays in the far-reaching reconceptualization of Modernism that emerged in the 1960s. In a reflection on the meaning of "contemporary" in our thinking about art today, Terry Smith writes: "For more than two decades no one has articulated a successful generalization about contemporary art. First there have been fears of essentialism, followed by the sheer relief of having shaken off exclusivist theories, imposed historicisms, and grand narratives, and then, recently, delight in the simple-seeming pleasures of an open field."[7] On the one hand, scholars and artists alike seem tired of prescriptive definitions of what will count as significant contemporary art, the pronouncements that Greenberg was at first famous and later notorious for making. Few informed observers today are willing to identify progress or evolution in the visual arts, not because there is no change or because quality has necessarily fallen off, but because the goal-oriented model has become unacceptable in its reductiveness and cultural biases. One positive factor leading to the pluralism of the present is what Kobena Mercer describes as the augmented recognition throughout the art world of "the coexistence of different modernisms" in the twentieth century and up to our own time.[8] Mercer adeptly redeploys the ancient term "cosmopolitan" to describe an inclusive sense of

FIG. 6
Robert Houle, *Kanata*, 1992. Acrylic and conté crayon on canvas, 228.7 × 732 cm overall; panels: 228.7 × 183 cm each. National Gallery of Canada, Ottawa, purchased 1994. Acc. # 37479.1-4. Photo: NGC.

how Modernism can be reconstrued, with the result that its geography, materials, and especially producers have, for some,[9] come to be seen as much more diverse than in the canonical stories. Referring to such new and, until recently, largely forgotten practices of abstraction as "discrepant," Mercer argues that Modernism and abstraction have always been eclectic, as Houle's work shows.[10] From the "global turn" in exhibitions since the late 1980s to the pioneering scholarship of C.L.R. James, David Craven, or W. Jackson Rushing, what has changed is the realization of the many Modernist narratives and the ways in which these complex stories can help to rewrite our sense of recent art.

In Robert Houle's hands, an infected abstraction is the new history painting. From the Renaissance until its eclipse in the early twentieth century (a decline partially attributable to the transcendental and formal strains of abstraction), this genre was the acme of academic practice. One of its most acclaimed practitioners was the American Benjamin West, second president of the Royal Academy in London and creator of *The Death of General Wolfe* (1770; page 97), now a centrepiece in the National Gallery of Canada. Houle has recalled West's pictorial account of the British victory in North America—heavily laden as it is with emotion and eighteenth-century political spin—to great effect in his *Lost Tribes* (1990–1991) and *Kanata* (1992; fig. 6)[11] series. His revisions of the place of First Nations in the official history of this fraught period has been the focus of a study by Michael Bell.[12] What has not received sufficient analysis is the presence of abstract panels in this and other "history" paintings by Houle.

In *Kanata* (fig. 6), West's highly coloured and fantastical death scene is washed back to a faded sepia calm, to a sense of emotional remove that allows Houle to accentuate the mostly blue and red headdress and blanket of the First Nations warrior attending Wolfe's death throes. All the more vibrant in contrast to the framed scene are the blue and red monochromatic panels to the left and right that reinforce this palette. The National Gallery literature offers an allegorical explanation of the monochromes: the natives are caught between French and British military colours in the struggle to dominate North America. True enough, and tragically so. Another reading would see First Nations as inextricably bound to the British dominance celebrated by West's memorial to Wolfe, given that the red, white, and blue Union Jack is prominent in the painting. Either interpretation could, however, stem from Houle's treatment of West's drama alone. What do his dramatic monochromes add? A clue lies in his view, expressed in conversation, that his recent "Grandfather" works are "an abstraction of the parfleches."

Monochromes are the distillates of abstract painting. Presented in *Kanata* as frames for a revision of history, they can be thought of as abstract histories, as mute but powerful vehicles of emotion and reference. The radicality of the inclusion of these colour panels also reminds us that West, however much his most famous work relates a partial and hegemonic history, was himself a controversial innovator in this painting. This canvas was the cause of great disputation when exhibited in London in 1771. Even King George III initially advised against showing the protagonists of this colonial struggle in contemporary dress, preferring (in keeping with the taste of the time) to see a Greek, Roman, or

Biblical drama performed as an allegory of the present. By the same token, and in keeping with the principle of mutual transformation, *Kanata* is not "abstract" in the traditional, pure sense, but then Houle is not a traditional abstract artist. He demonstrates that abstraction can be much more than surface and much more than the transcendence of our earthly existence. It can be a powerful conveyance for the rewriting of history.

Robert Houle comes from a large and diverse family, aesthetically speaking. The genealogies apparent in his abstract works are productively mixed. We can see traces of grandfathers such as Malevich, Newman, and even Benjamin West. Especially when we look at his monochromes in *Troubling Abstraction: Robert Houle—Anishnabe* (1999), *Blue Apache* (2003–2004), and *Grandfather I* and *II* (2004)—we realize that the histories he conveys with these paintings are both sweeping in implication and intimate in effect. *Anishnabe* embraces a people, a First Nations group to which Houle belongs as a descendent and active member. Is it fanciful to construe the left-most panel in this tripartite unity as fluvial, making oblique reference with its watery surface to origin and belonging, to the "Saulteaux" or people of the river rapids, as French colonizers identified the Indigenous peoples around what is now Sault Ste. Marie, Ontario. Houle often insists that this origin—one of his own—inevitably bumps up against the languages of Europe, including abstraction, represented here by two uninflected monochromes. *Anishnabe* conveys Houle's double inheritance in colour and material.

Grandfather I and *II* make this double heritage explicit. We can think of them as family diptychs, abstract portraits of Houle's ancestry and of his present. In native tradition, Houle explains, a "grandfather" can refer to a stone from the earth. While he presents the pieces of slate that we see in the left panel of each of these works with the regularity of an abstract painting, they nonetheless retain the sense of native tradition and connection to the earth. Grandfathers survive, but through change and adaptation. The right-hand monochromes in *Grandfather I* and *II* are painted exemplars of a European and American lineage that also perdures through metamorphosis. *Grandfather I* and *II* are related in form but clearly individual. By making each element in this two-part work independent in size, material, colour, and spatial relationship to its partner, Houle can inflect their kinship with his usual sensitivity and sense of purpose, and in keeping with the principle and pattern of mutual transformation that he has established throughout his career.

Excerpt from the exhibition catalogue for Troubling Abstraction: Robert Houle *(McMaster University Art Gallery and The Robert McLaughlin Gallery, September 2007): 41–55.*

1 Norman Mackenzie Art Gallery, Regina, Saskatchewan, July 9 – August 29, 1982.

2 Robert Houle, "The Emergence of a New Aesthetic Tradition." In *New Work by a New Generation*, 2, 3. W. Jackson Rushing has given much of the institutional context for this emphasis in his Editor's Statement to the *Art Journal* special issue titled *Critical Issues in Recent Native American Art* 51:3 (Fall 1992): 6–14.

3 For a detailed discussion of these relationships, see W. Jackson Rushing, "Ritual and Myth: Native American Culture and Abstract Expressionism" in *The Spiritual in Art: Abstract Painting 1890–1985*, exh. cat. (Los Angeles: Los Angeles County Museum of Art, 1986), 273–295, and David Craven, "Abstract Expressionism and Third World Art: A Post-Colonial Approach to 'American' Art," *Oxford Art Journal*, 14:1 (1991), 44–66. Following Mikhail Bahktin, Craven calls for a "dialogical" understanding of the relationship between "AbEx" and its non-Western inspirations, a model wherein "an artwork is not a unified whole but rather an open-ended site of contestation wherein various cultural practices from different classes and ethnic groups are temporarily combined" (45).

4 See Mark A. Cheetham, *The Rhetoric of Purity: Essentialist Theory and the Advent of Abstract Painting* (New York: Cambridge University Press, 1991).

5 I have discussed the alternative history in detail in *Abstract Art Against Autonomy: Infection, Resistance, and Cure since the 1960s* (New York: Cambridge University Press, 2006).

6 Michael Bell, *Robert Houle's Palisade I*, exh. cat. (Ottawa: Carleton University Art Gallery, 2001), 8.

7 "Contemporary Art and Contemporaneity," in *Critical Inquiry* 32:4 (Summer 2006) 683.

8 Kobena Mercer, "Introduction" to *Cosmopolitan Modernisms*, ed. Kobena Mercer, 6–23 (Cambridge: inIVA/Mit Press, 2005), 10.

9 We may be cautiously optimistic in assessing this growing awareness of art that used to be below the limen of official approbation in the West, but at the same time, just as cautious when we see how slowly a new history of modernism is being told in the classroom. For example, a much-anticipated new textbook in the field—*Art since 1900: modernism, antimodernism, postmodernism* (2004), co-authored by four of the most influential writers in this field (Hal Foster, Rosalind Krauss, Yve-Alain Bois, and Benjamin H.D. Buchloh)—has been much criticized for its close adherence to the old canon of Modernism. Writing one of the extensive reviews of this publication in the June 2006 number of *The Art Bulletin*, an art-historical journal that styles itself the most important in the English-speaking world, Amelia Jones complains that "the work of non-white artists is ghettoized … into a handful of chronological segments," not all of which were even written by the four coauthors. "Others," she continues, "are clustered at the very end of the book, as if race has little or nothing to do with the visual arts until the 1990s. This has the effect of constraining the more general issue of the politics of racial and ethnic identity, which, I would argue, is structurally foundational to art since 1900 as well as art before that date" (378).

10 Mercer builds here on the anthropologist James Clifford's memorable phrase *from Routes: Travel and Translation in the Late Twentieth Century* (1997), for whom a "discrepant cosmopolitanism" is one that acknowledges the peculiarities and strains of a traveller's sometimes odd or strained circumstances precisely as a way to recalibrate our understanding of world citizenship. When we think of a "discrepant" abstract practice, we must now ask: "As opposed to what norm?" and "For whom?" See Kobena Mercer, ed. *Discrepant Abstraction* (Cambridge: inIVA/Mit Press, 2006).

10 Mercer builds here on the anthropologist James Clifford's memorable phrase from Routes: Travel and Translation in the Late Twentieth Century (1997), for whom a "discrepant cosmopolitanism" is one that acknowledges the peculiarities and strains of a traveller's sometimes odd or strained circumstances precisely as a way to recalibrate our understanding of world citizenship. When we think of a "discrepant" abstract practice, we must now ask: "As opposed to what norm?" and "For whom?" See Kobena Mercer, ed., Discrepant Abstraction (Cambridge , MA: inIVA/Mit Press, 2006).

11 The work was purchased by the National Gallery in 1994.

12 *KANATA: Robert Houle's HISTORIES*, exh. cat. (Ottawa: Carleton University Art Gallery, 1993).

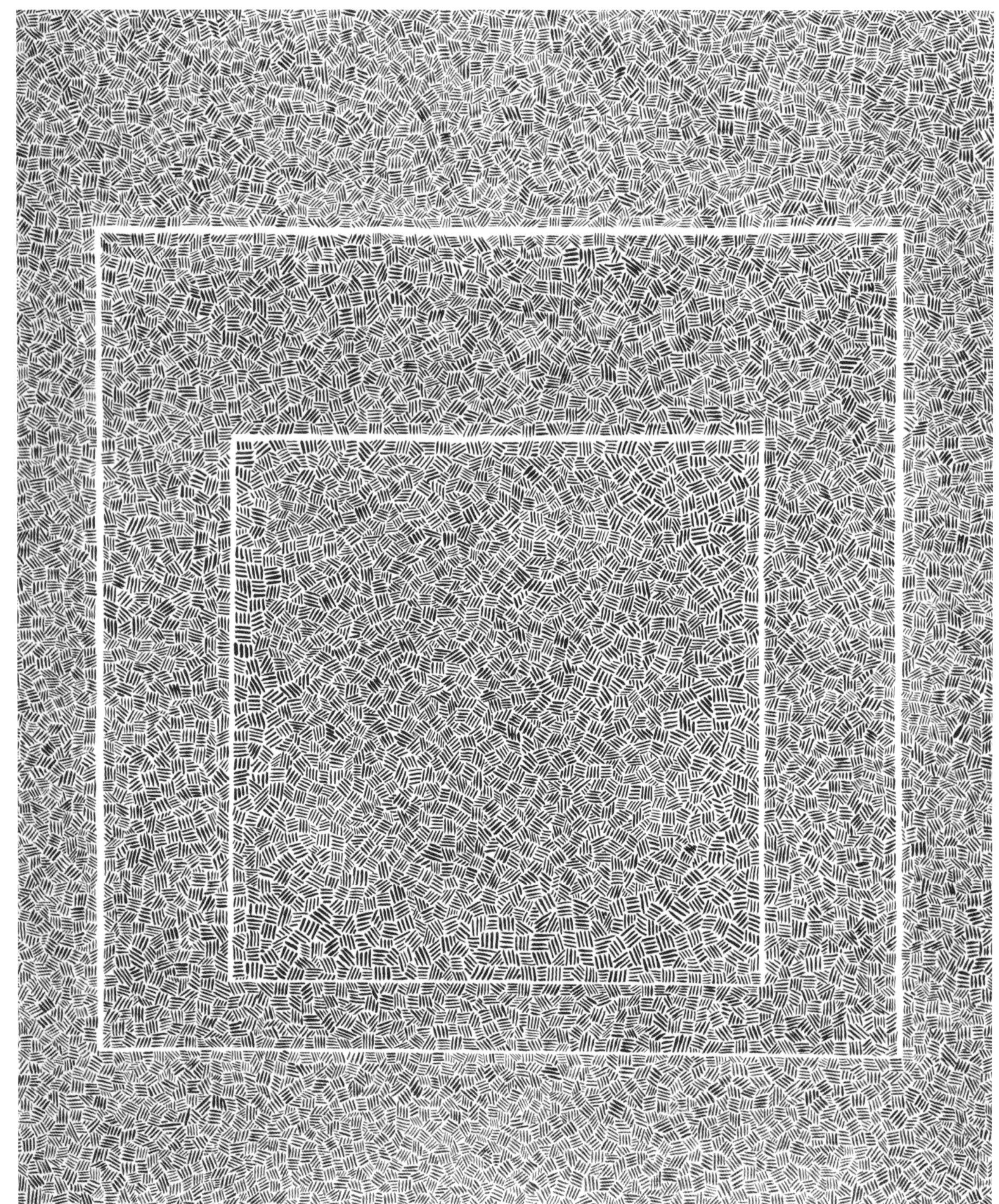

Square Homage to Albers, 1979

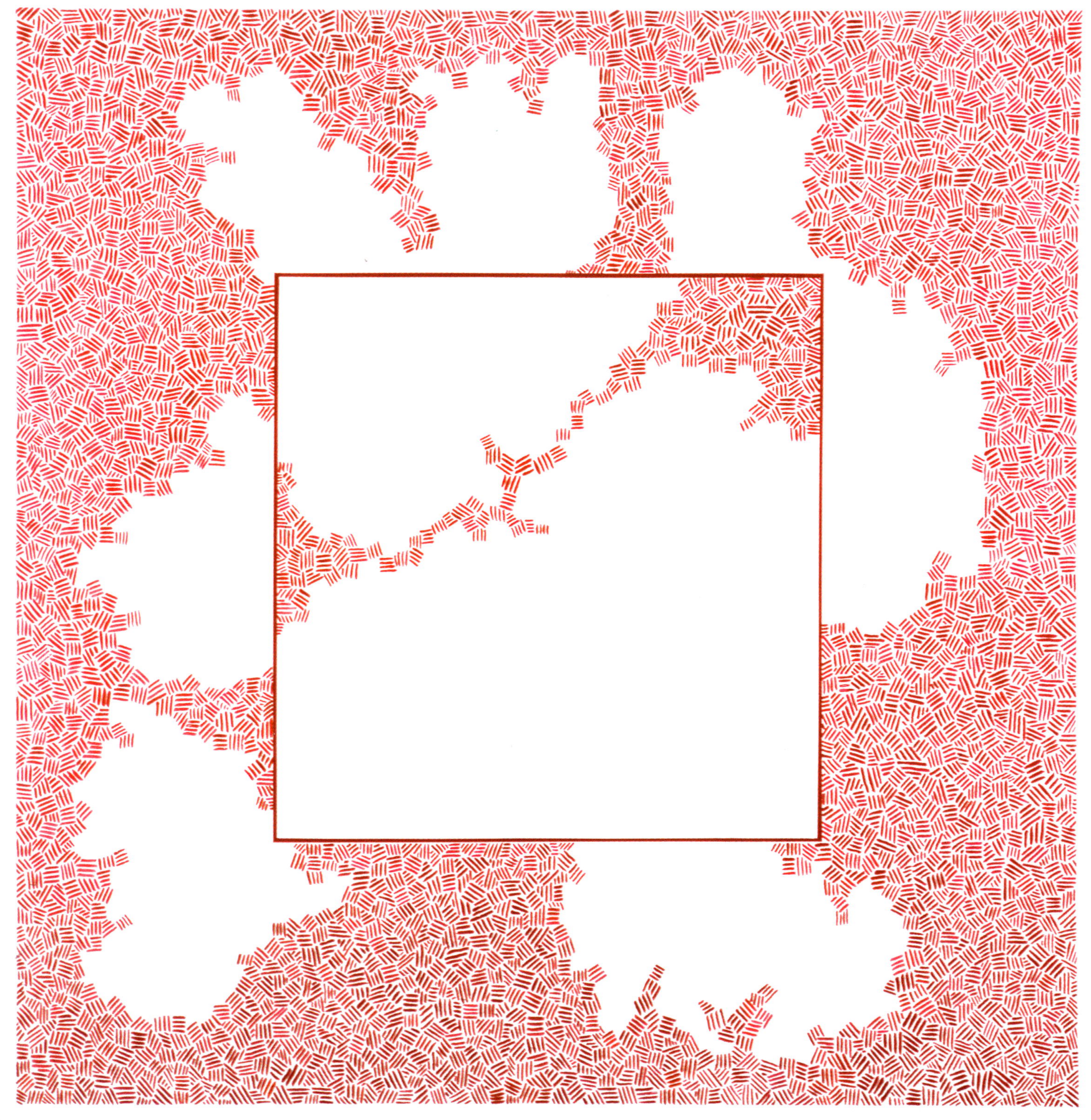

Square 4, 1980

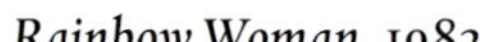

Rainbow Woman, 1982

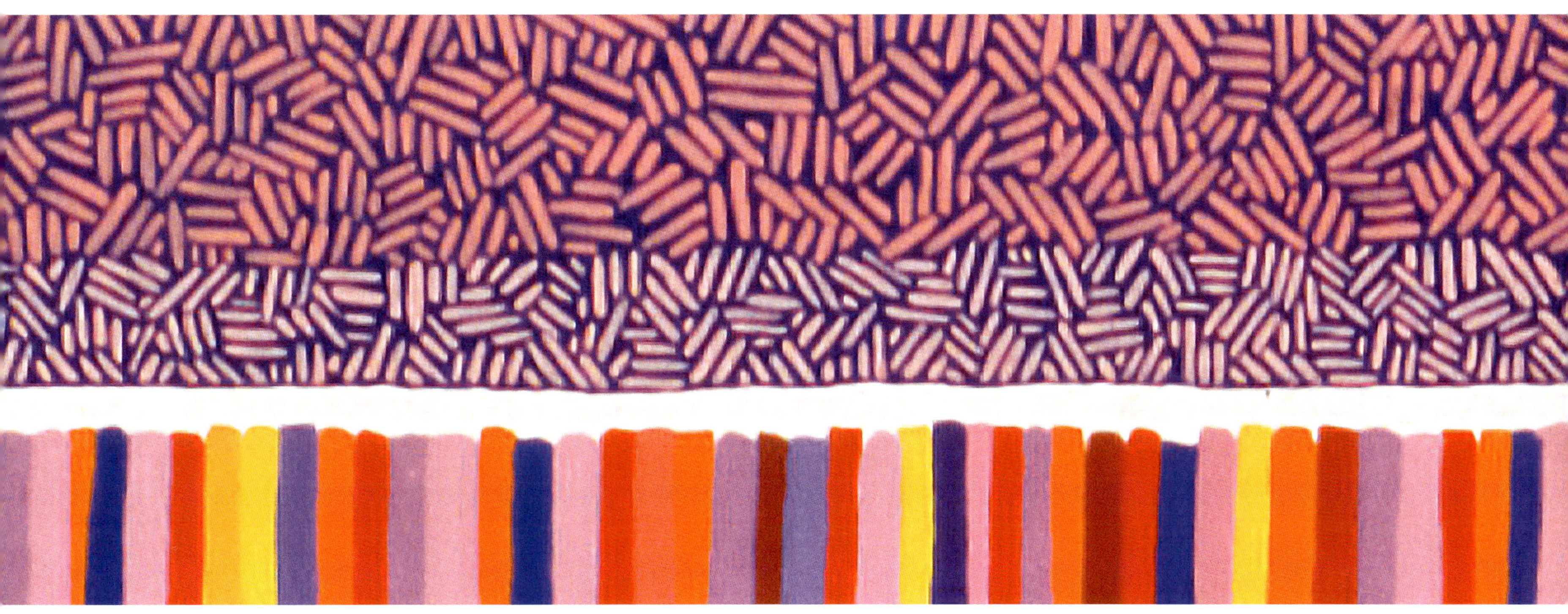

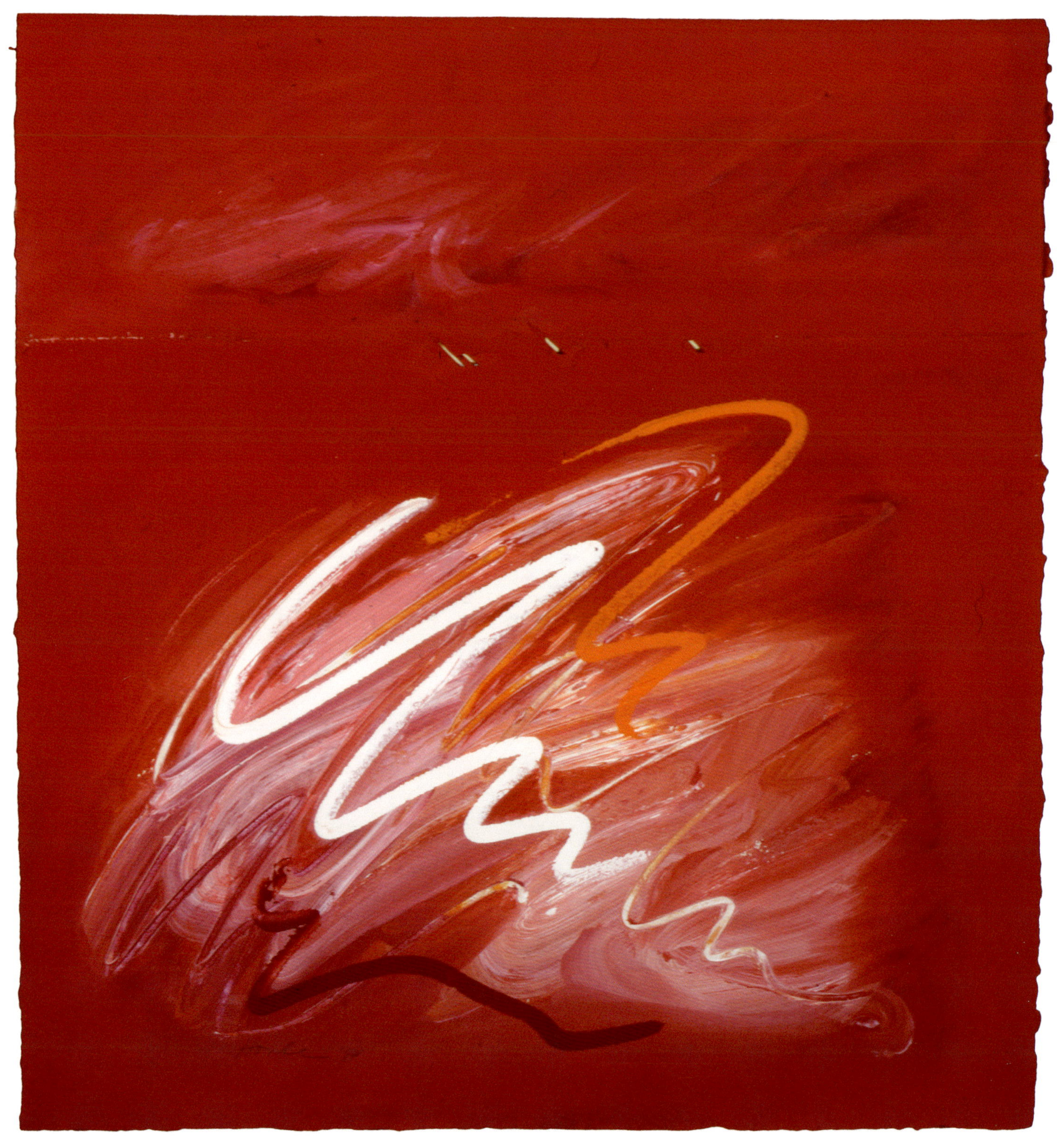

Parfleche II "H," 1984

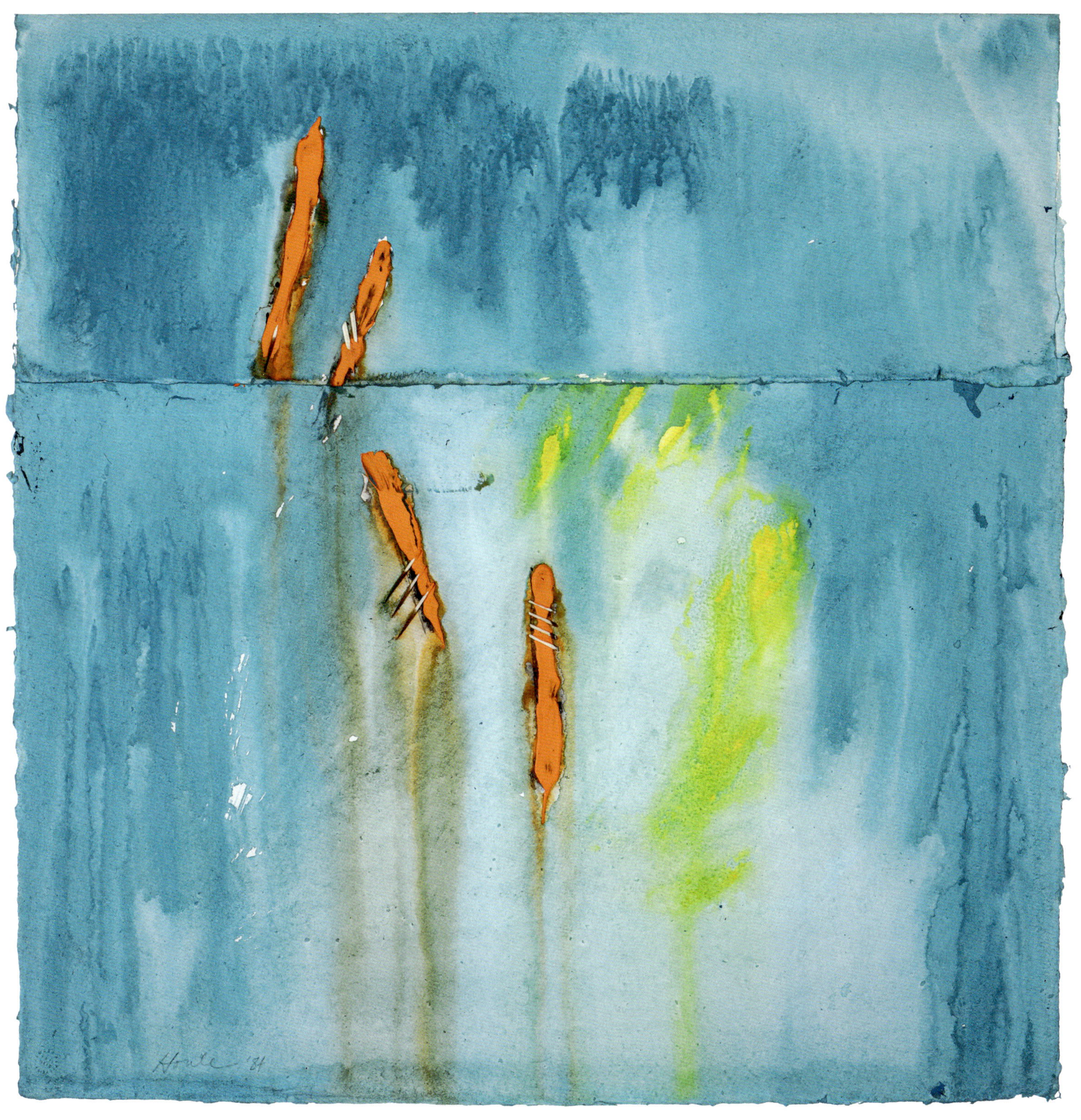

Parfleche II – C, 1984

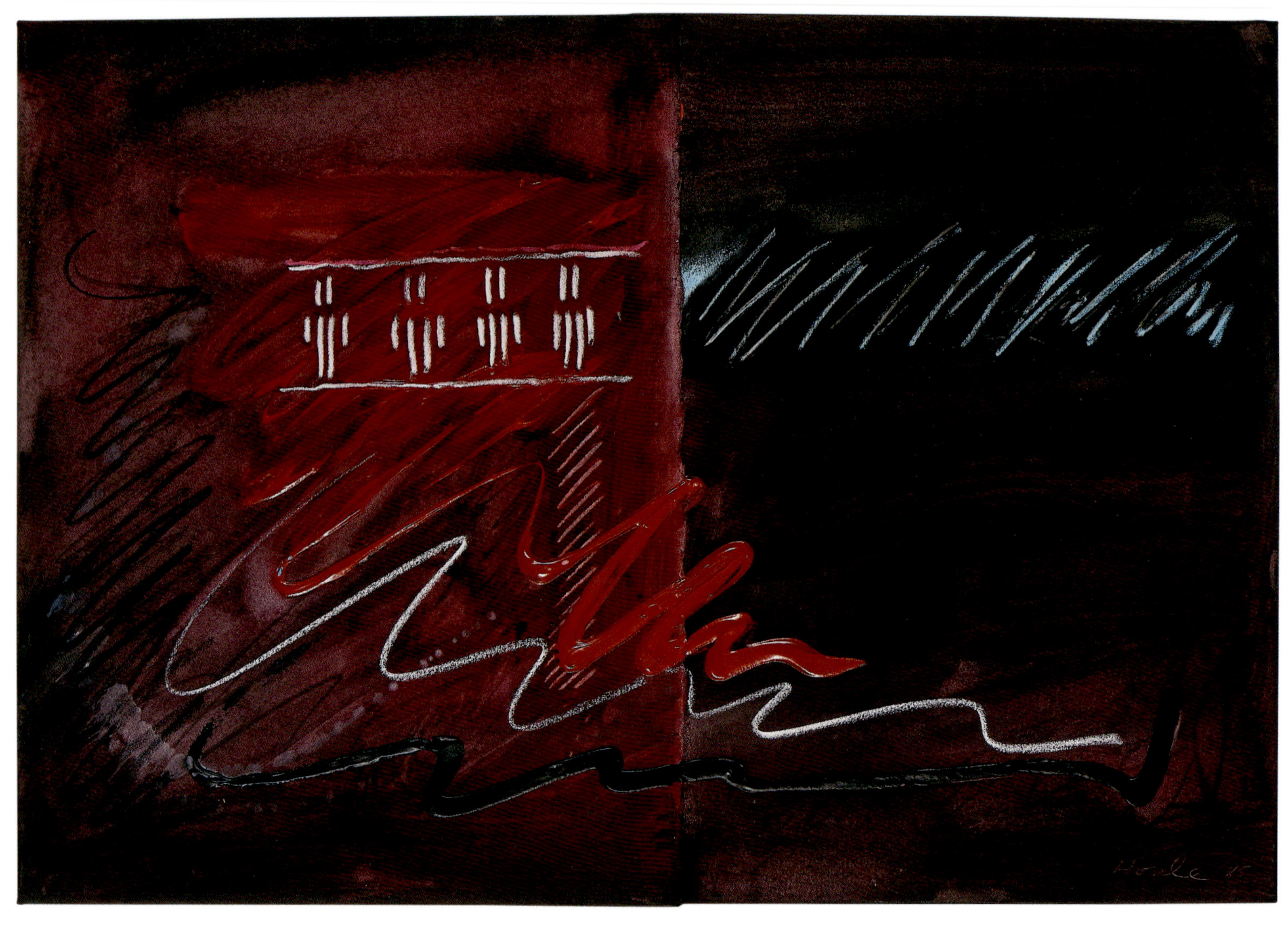

Parfleche II, 1985

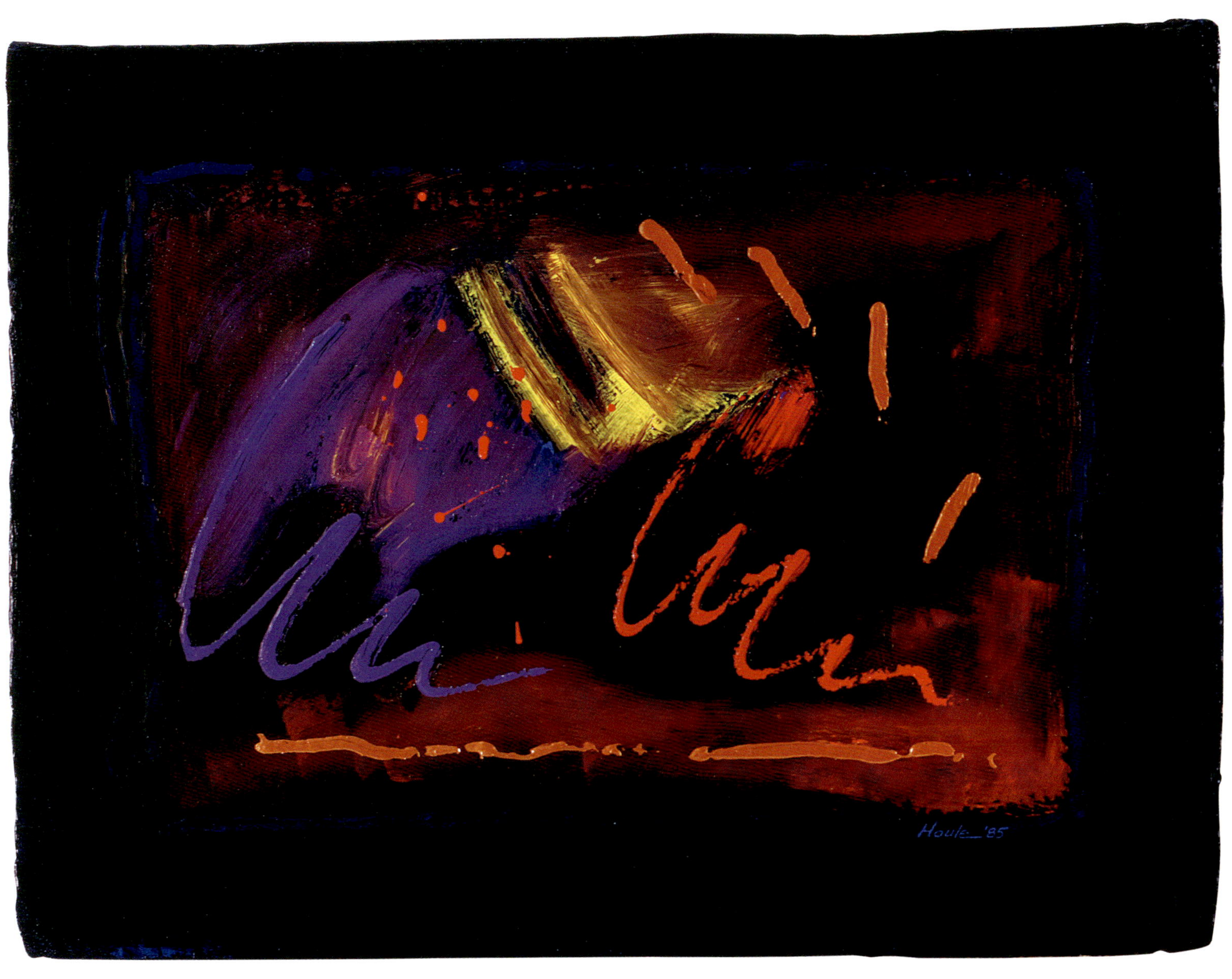

Parfleche III "A," 1985

THE SPIRITUAL LEGACY OF THE ANCIENT ONES

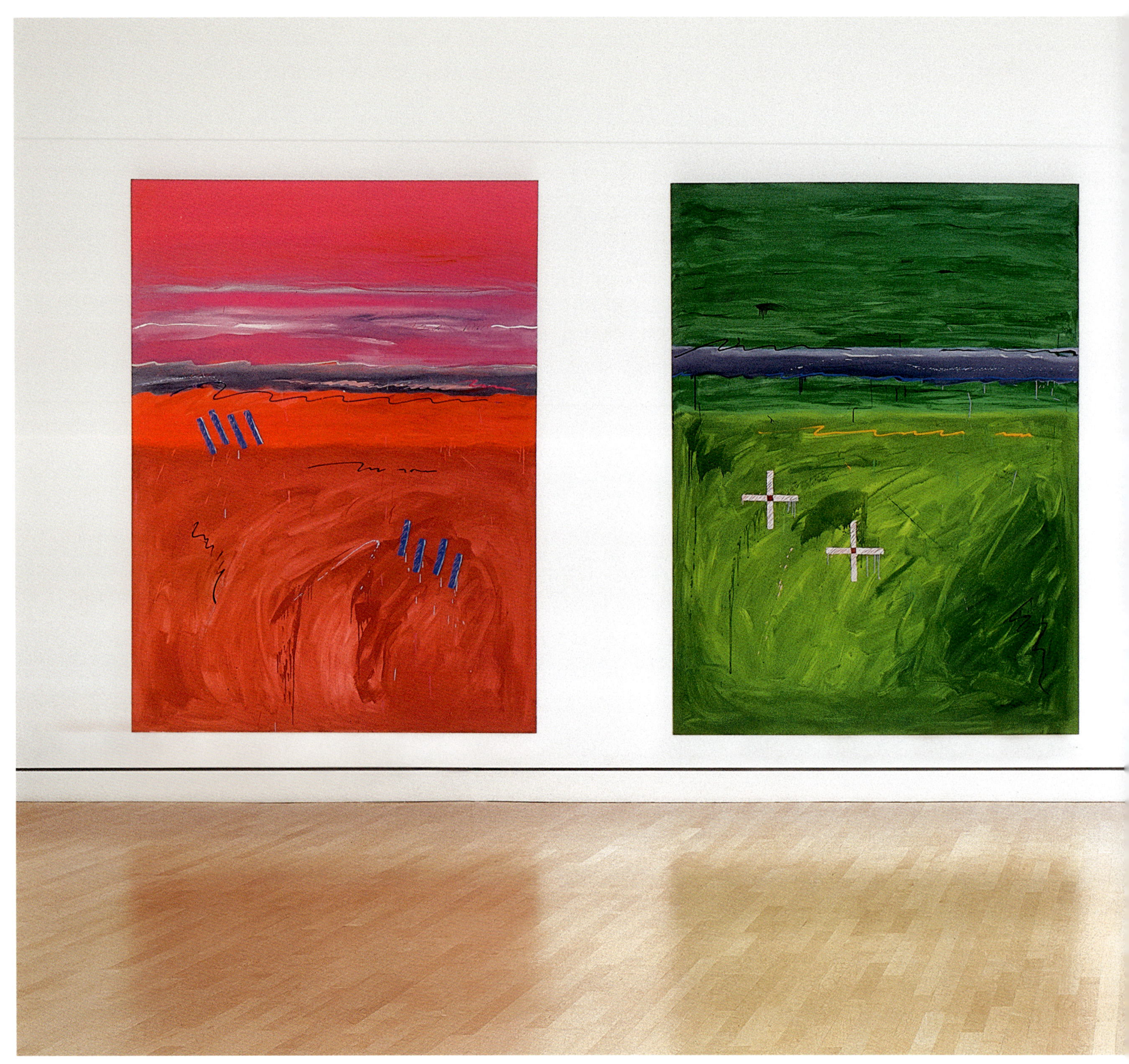

Muhnedobe uhyahyuk [Where the gods are present] (Matthew, Philip, Bartholomew, Thomas), 1989

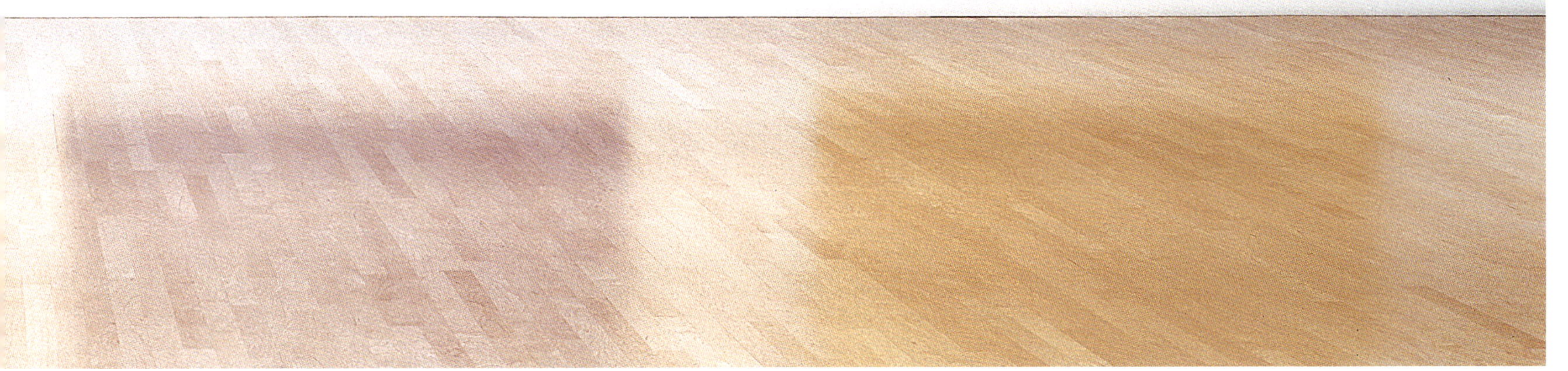

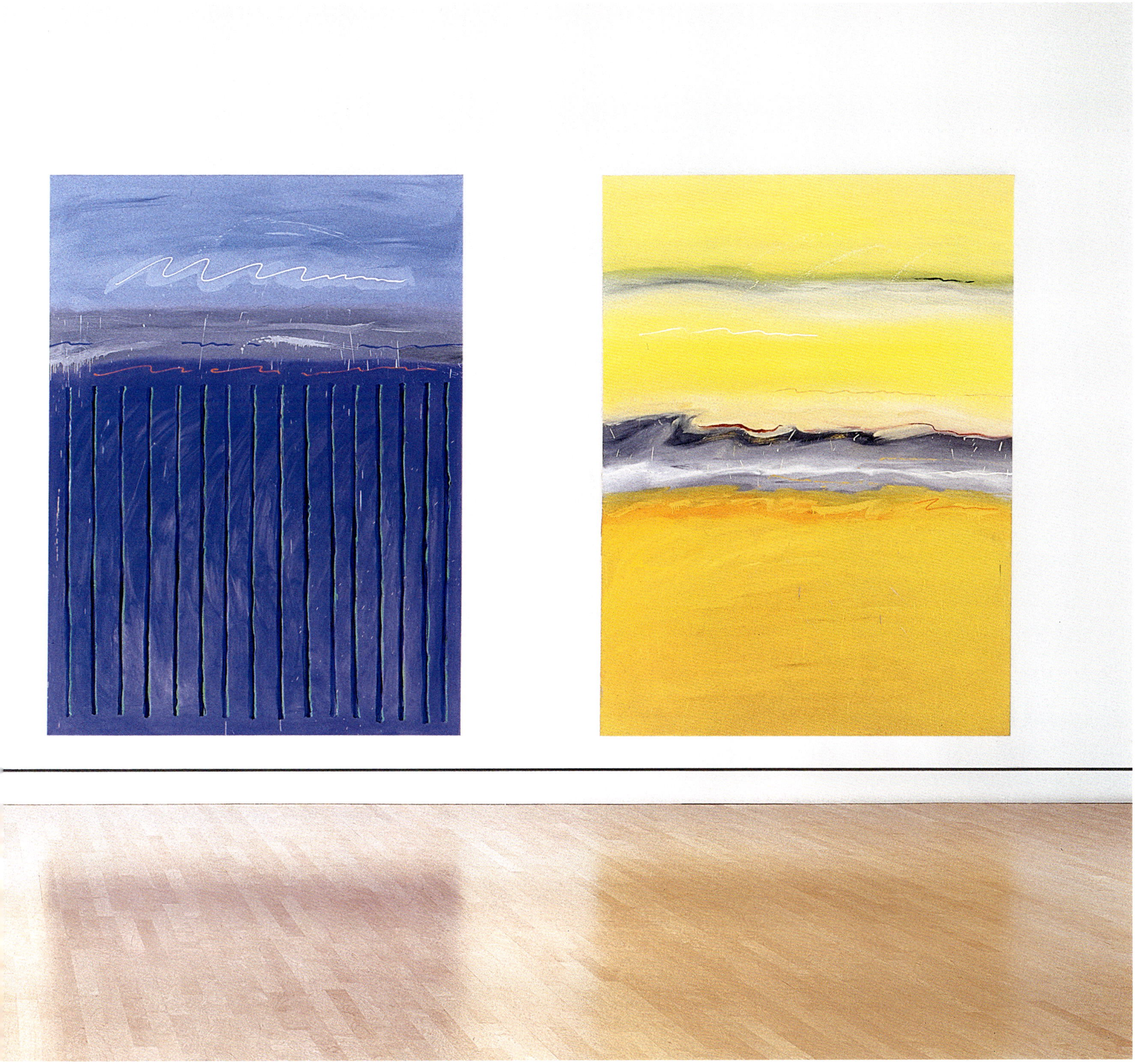

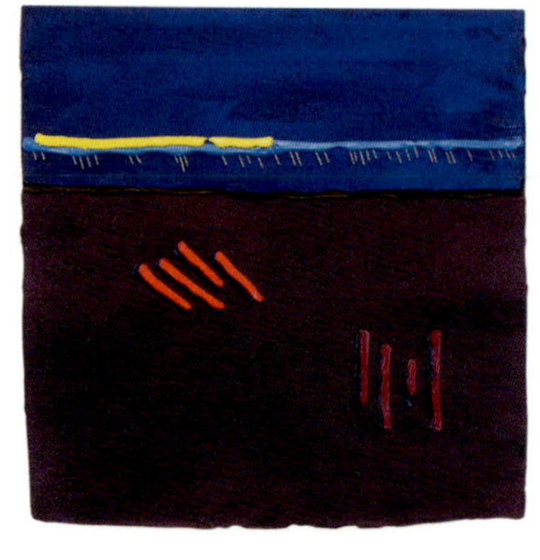
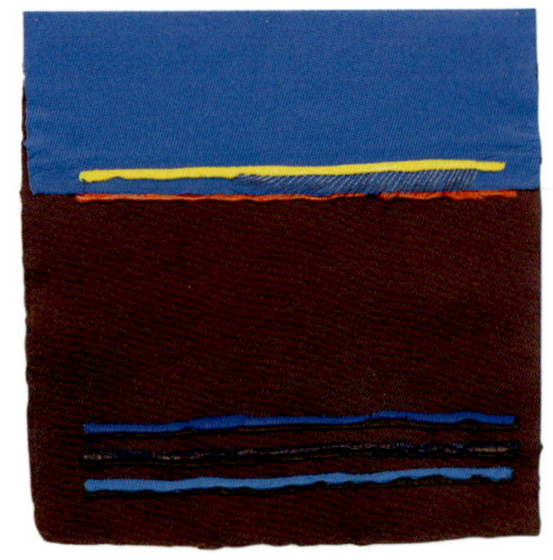
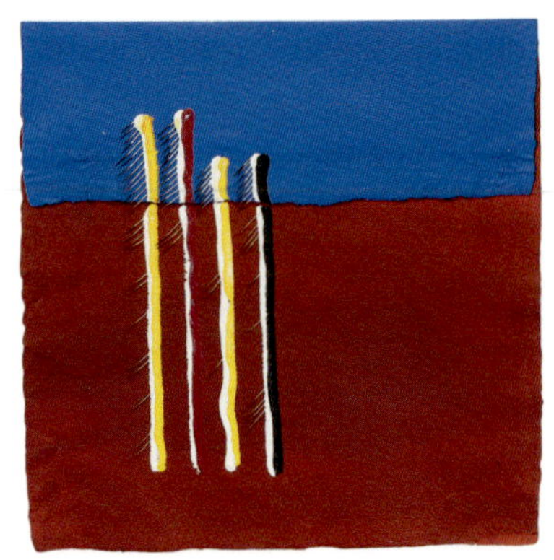
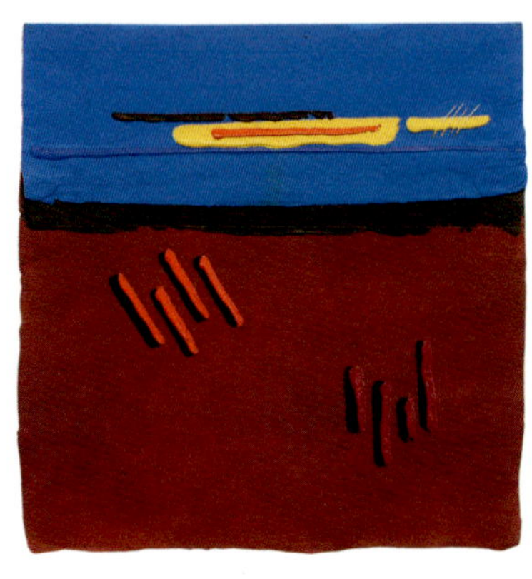
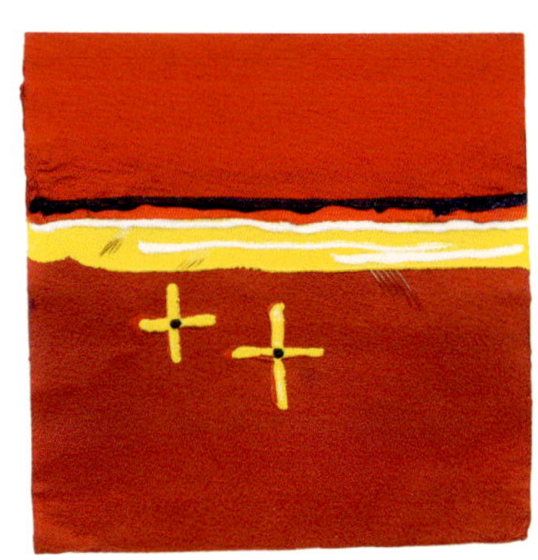
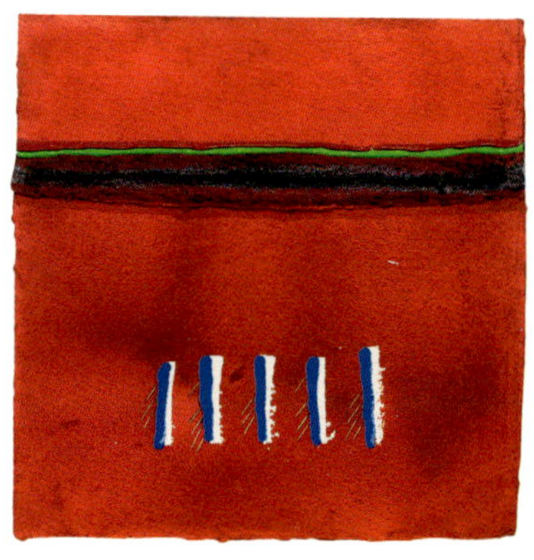
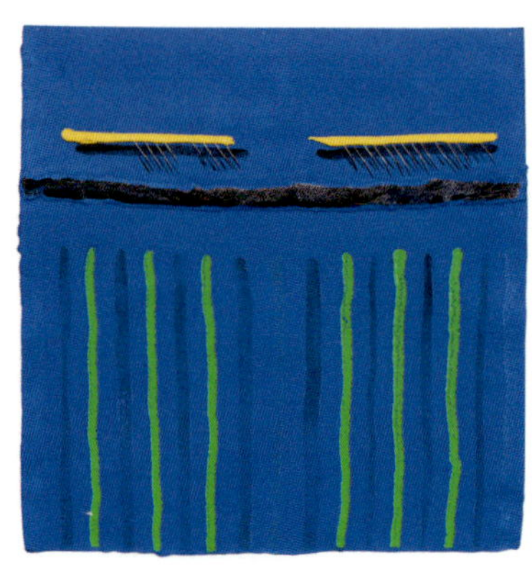
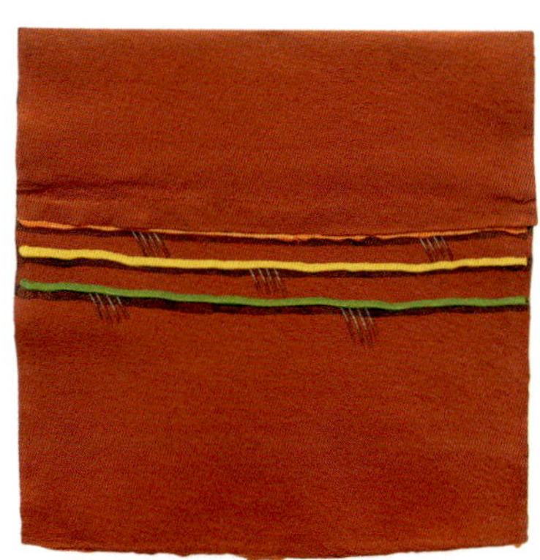
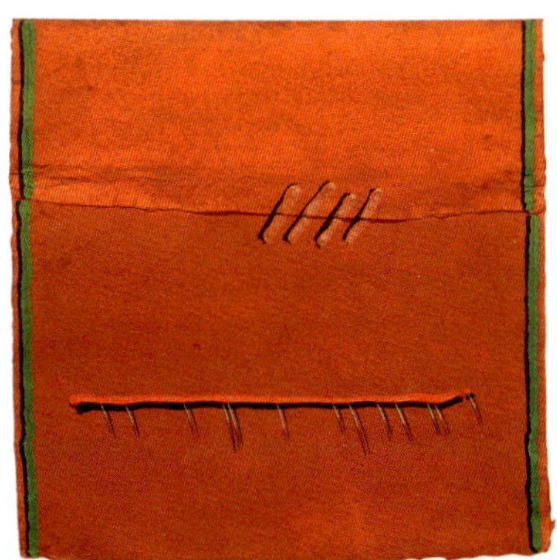

Parfleches for the Last Supper, 1983

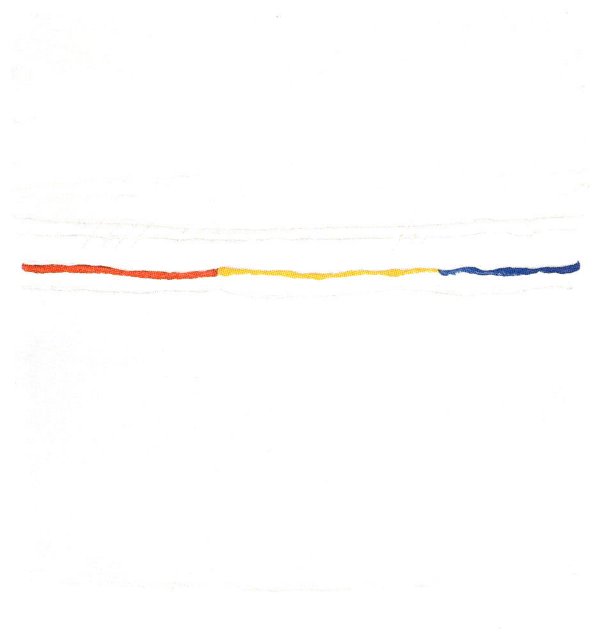
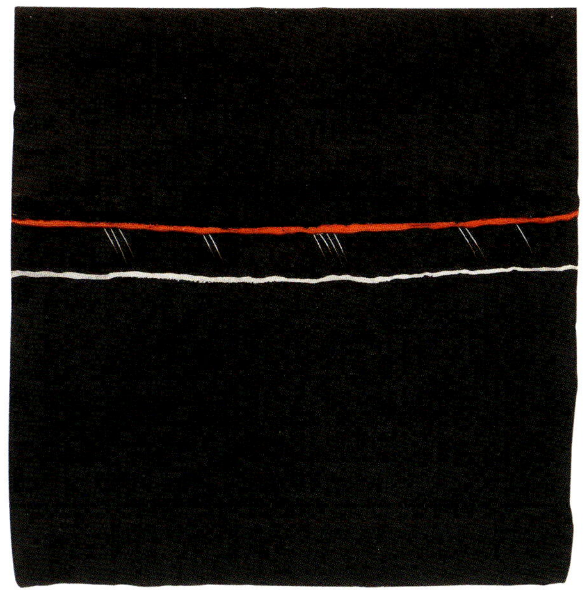
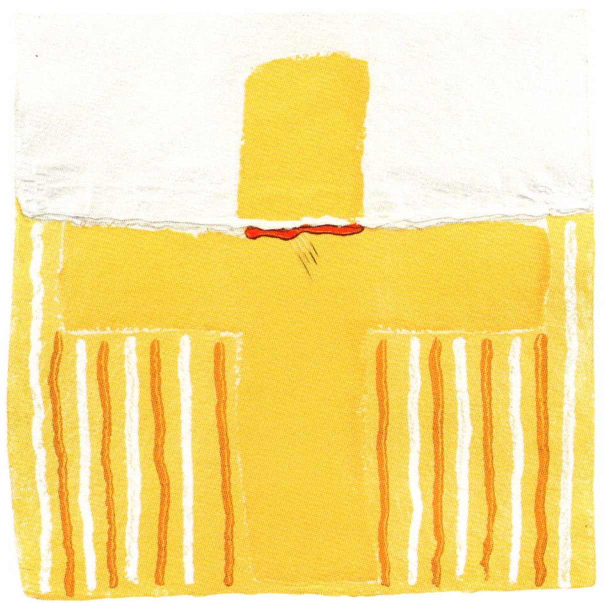
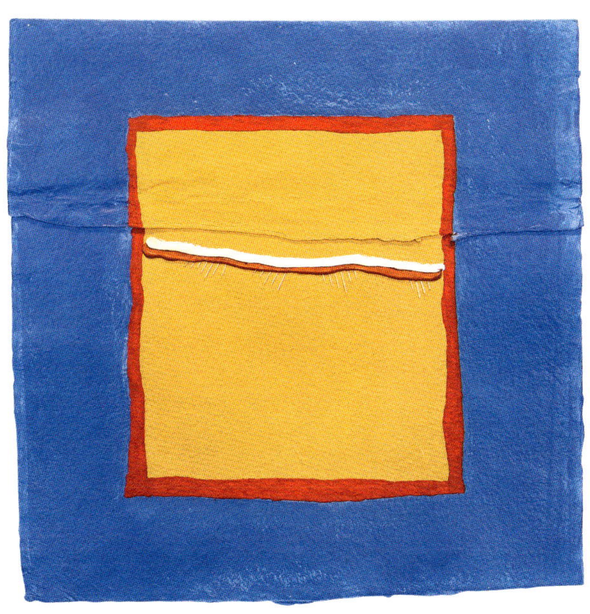

Robert Houle *Parfleches for the Last Supper*, 1983

Inscriptions on versos
(pp. 78–79, from left to right, top to bottom)

Parfleche #1: Matthew
"In the world you will have trouble, / but be brave: / I have conquered the world." (John 17:33)

Parfleche #2: James the Less
"In a short time you will no longer see me, / and then a short time later you will see me again." (John 16:16)

Parfleche #3: Jude
"If anyone loves me he will keep my word, / and my Father will love him, / and we shall come to him / and make our home with him." (John 14:23)

Parfleche #4: Simon
"I have told you all this / so that your faith may not be shaken." (John 16:1)

Parfleche #5: Philip
"To have seen me is to have seen the Father, / so how can you say, let us see the Father?" (John 14:2)

Parfleche #6: Andrew
"A man can have no greater love / than to lay down his life for his friends." (John 15:13)

Parfleche #7: Bartholomew
"If the world hates you, / remember that it hated me before you." (John 15:18)

Parfleche #8: Thomas
"I am the Way, the Truth and the Life. / No one can come to the Father except through me." (John 14:6)

Parfleche #9: James
"I tell you most solemnly, / no servant is greater than his master, / no messenger is greater than the man who sent him." (John 13:16)

Parfleche #10: John
"I give you a new commandment: / Love one another; / just as I have loved you / you also must love one another." (John 14:34)

Parfleche #11: Judas
"And yet, here with me on the table is the / hand of the man who betrays me." (Luke 22:21)

Parfleche #12: Jesus
"Then he took some bread and when he had given / thanks, broke it and gave it to them, saying, / 'This is my body which will be given for you; do this / as a memorial of me." (Luke 22:19)

Parfleche #13: Peter
"I tell you, Peter, by the time the cock crows / today, you will have denied three times that you know / me." (Luke 22:34)

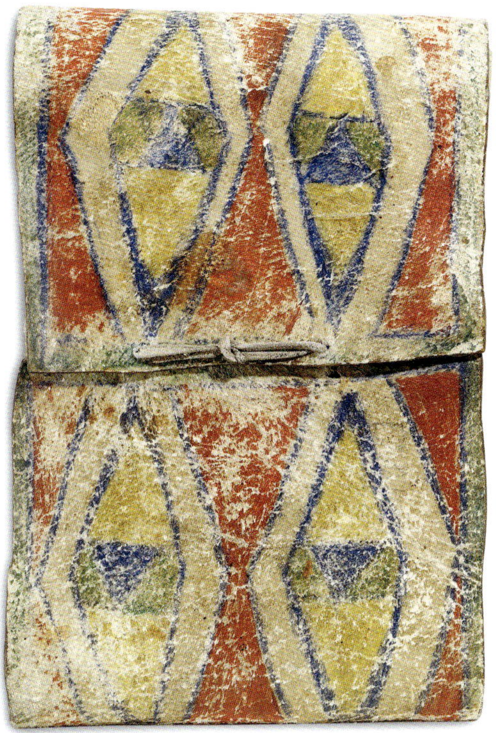

Apsáalooke (Crow) Artist once known, *a miniature parfleche,* 1890–1910

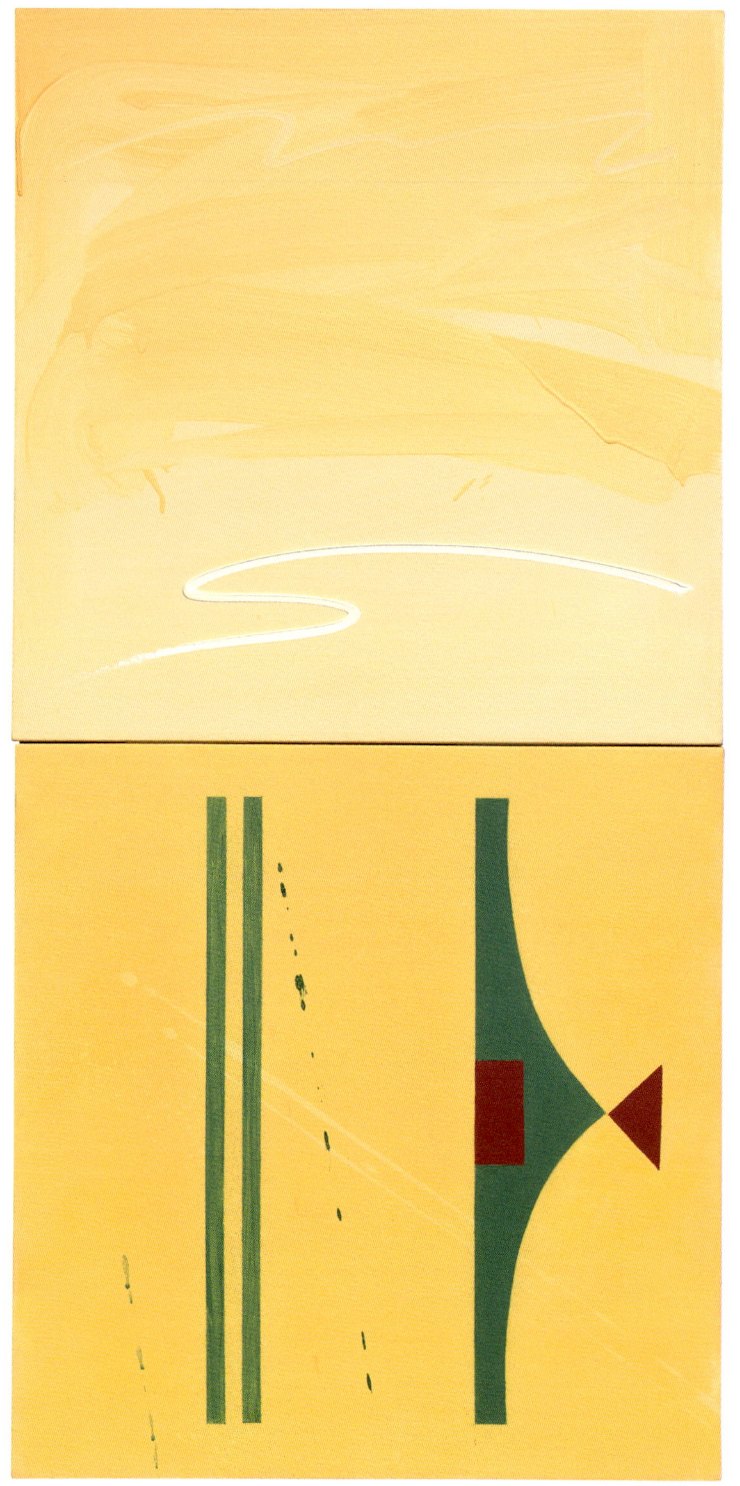

Parfleche for Alex Janvier, 1999

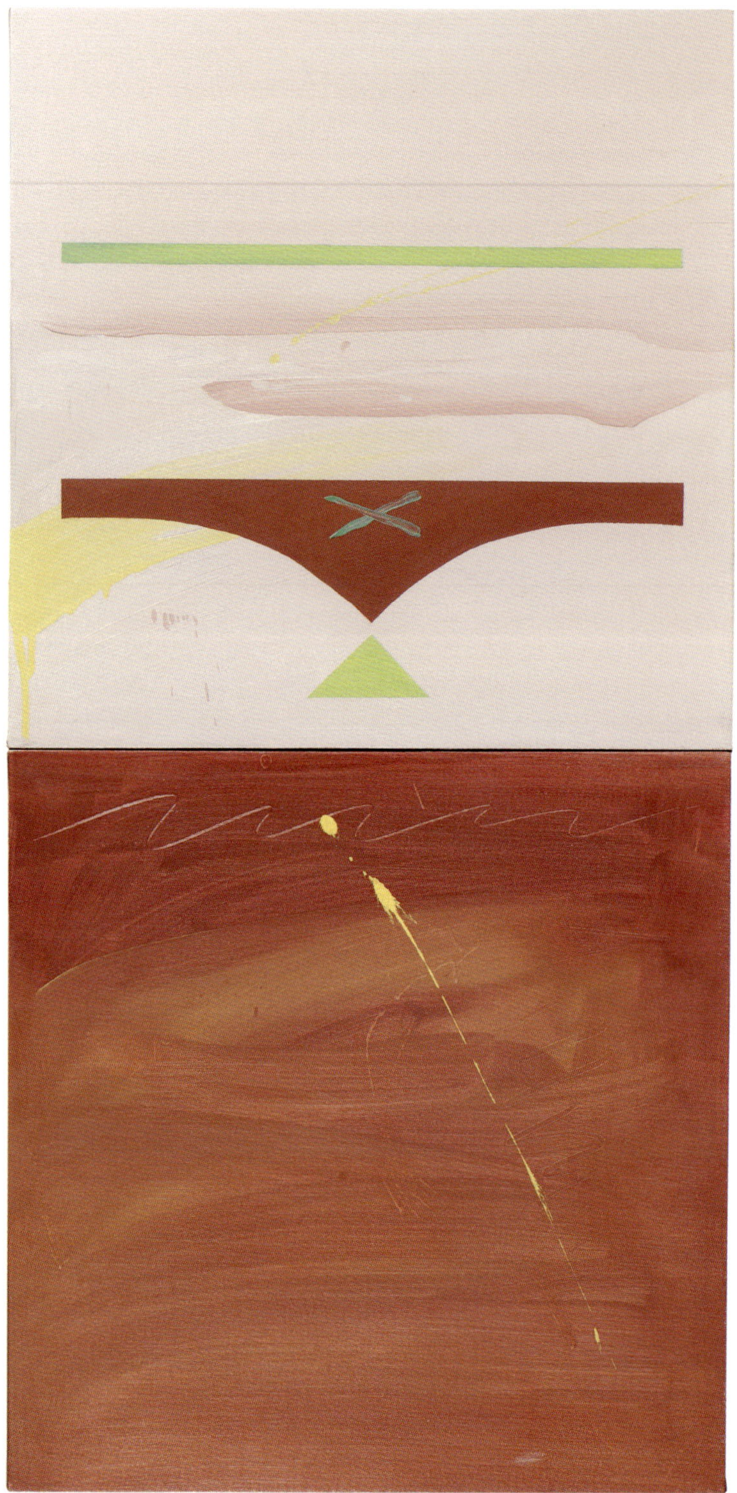

Parfleche for Edna Manitowabi, 1999

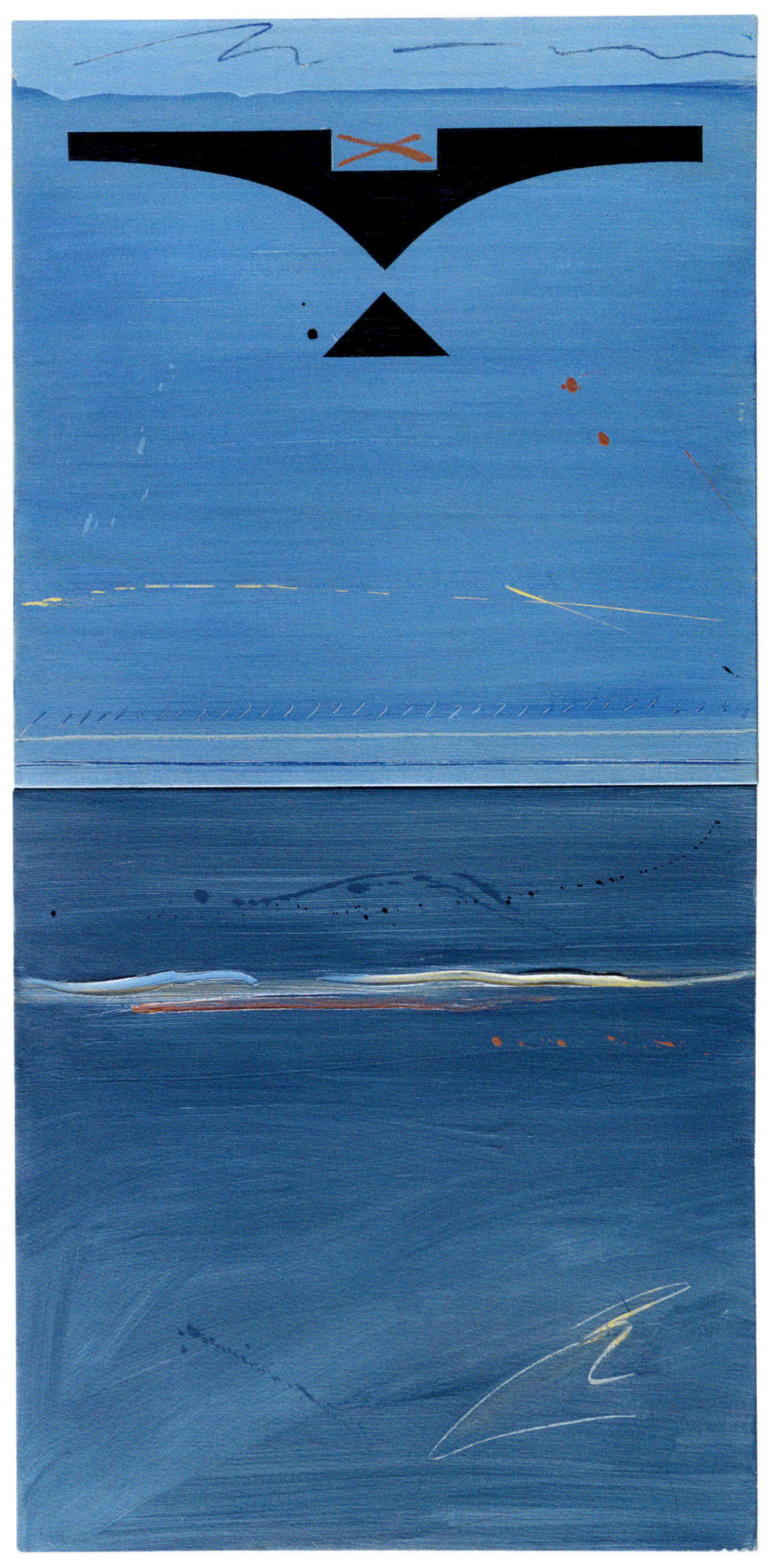

Parfleche for Norval Morrisseau, 1999

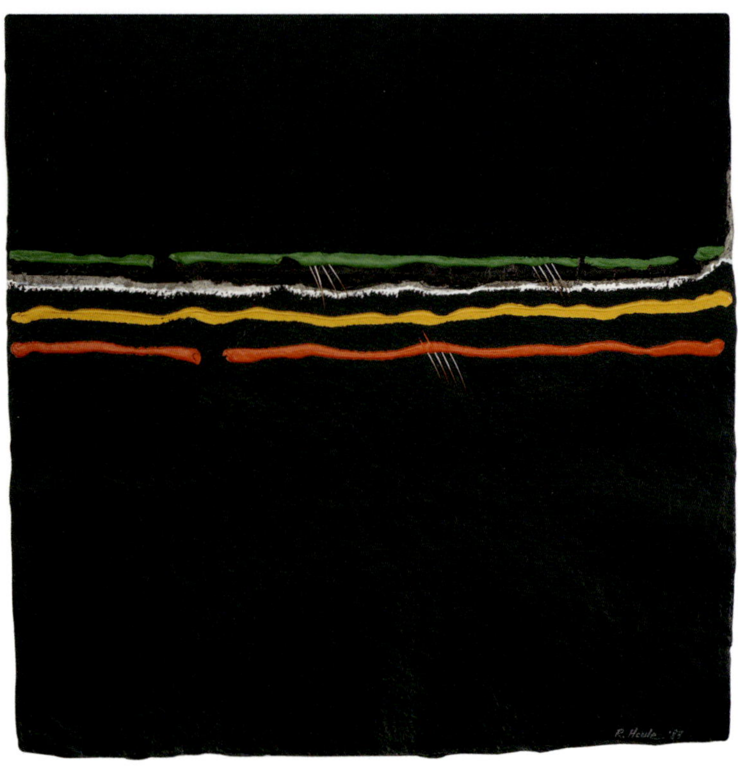

Parfleche #20/Wovoka, 1983

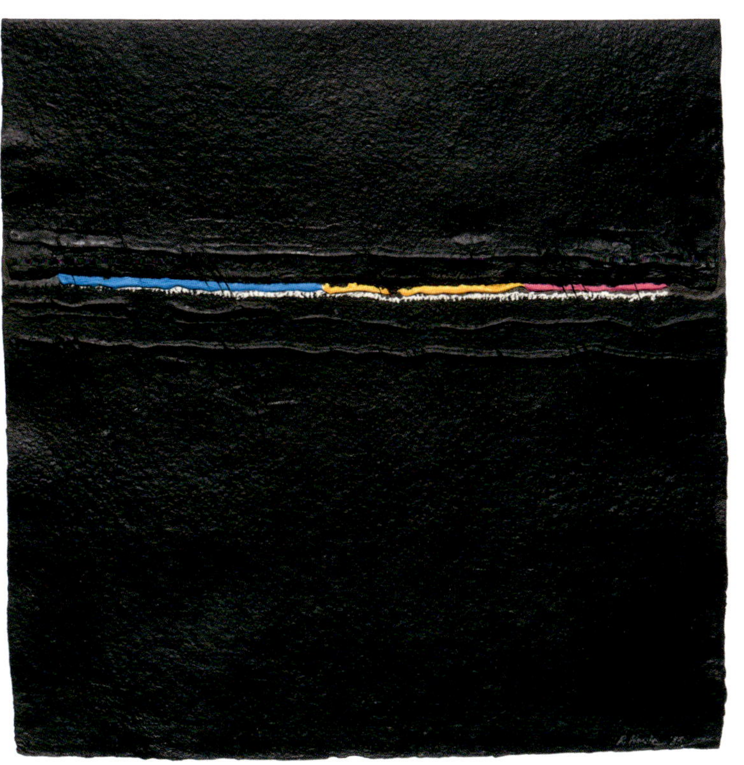

Parfleche #19 Chief Poundmaker, 1983

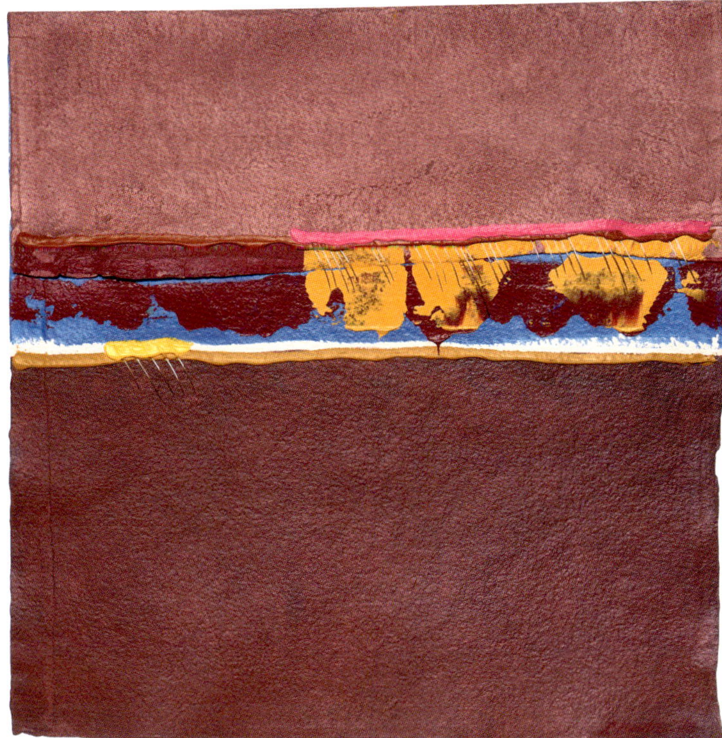

Parfleche #14 Sitting Bull Sioux, 1983

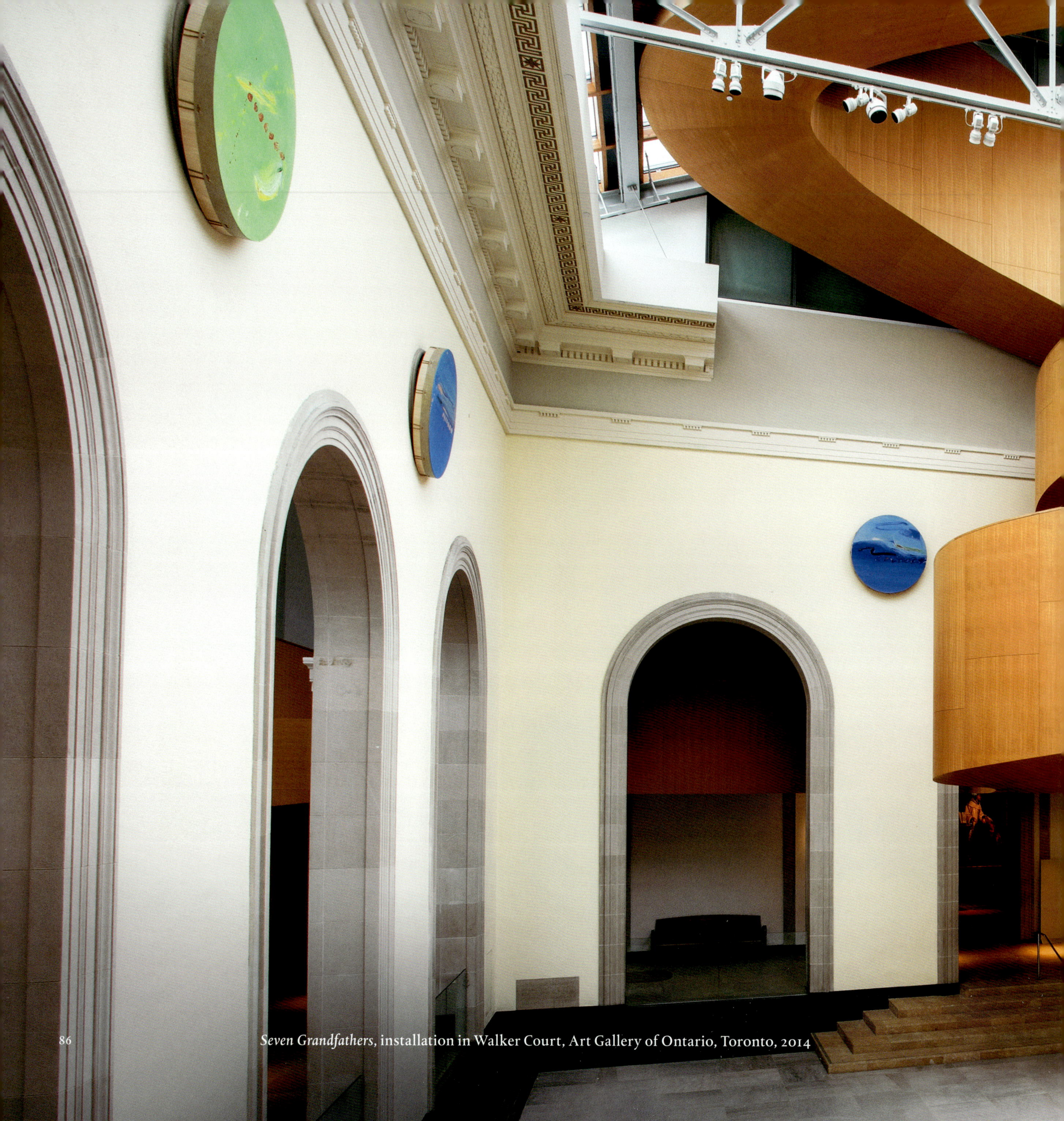

Seven Grandfathers, installation in Walker Court, Art Gallery of Ontario, Toronto, 2014

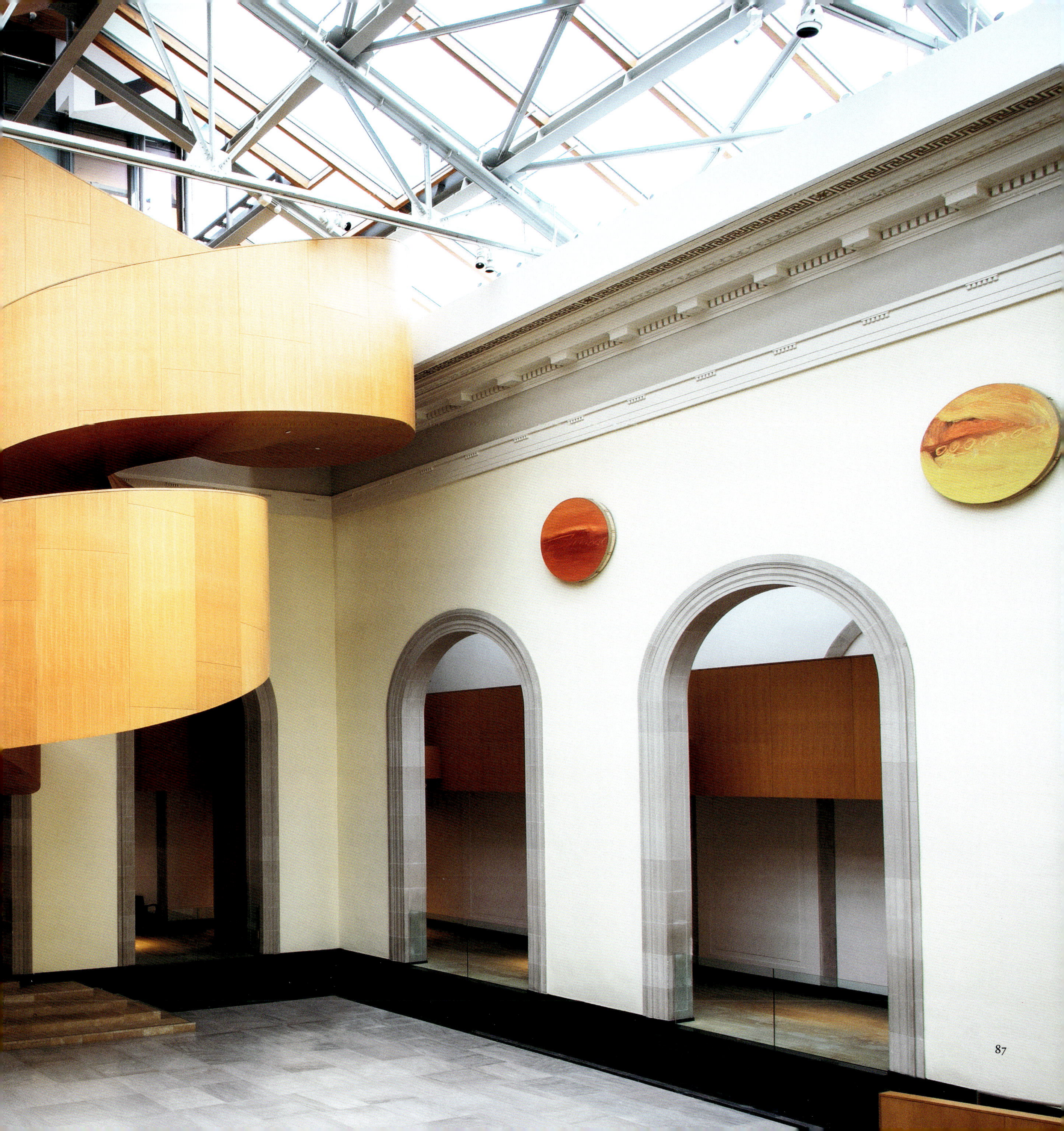

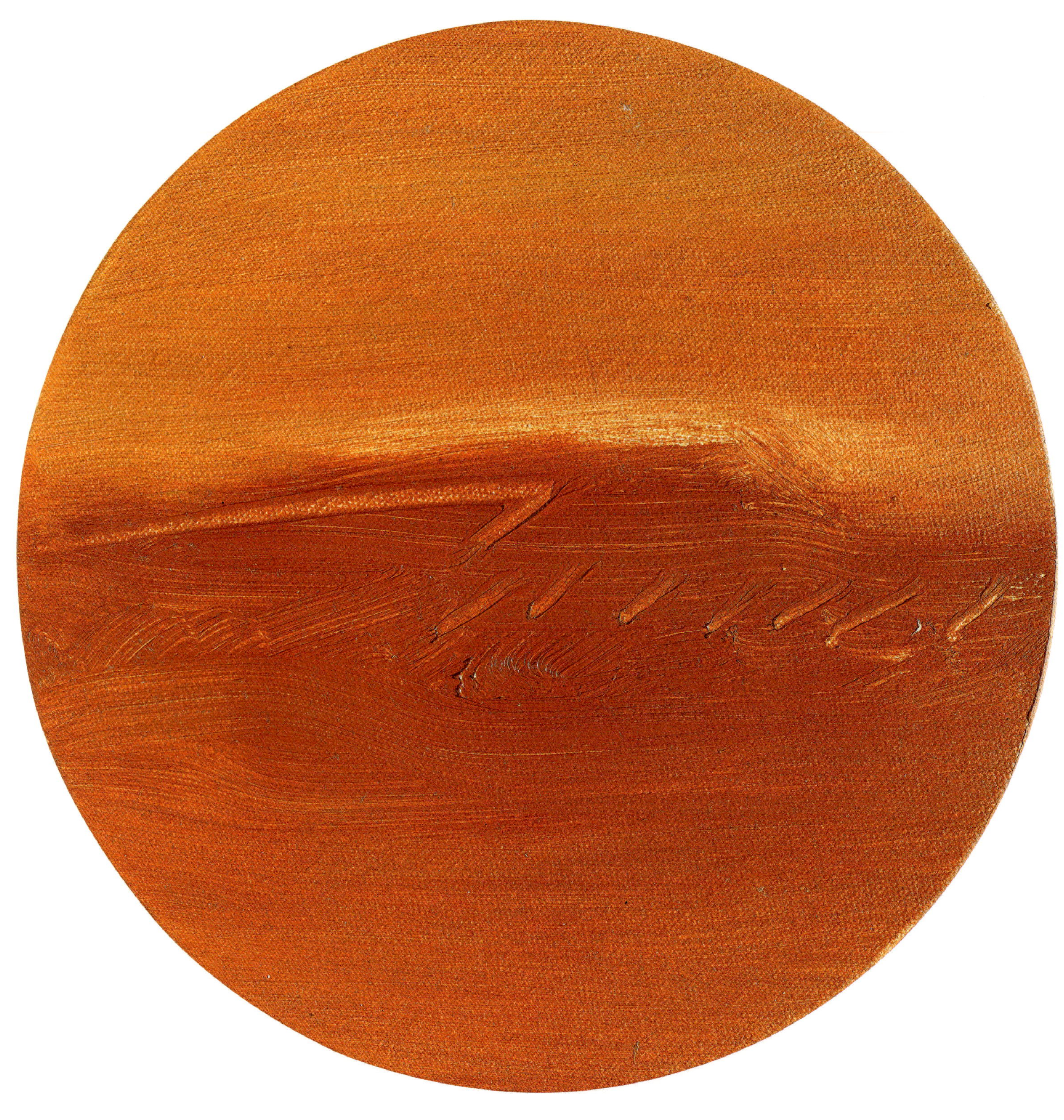

Seven Grandfathers, 2013
me ge zée (eagle), sah gee wá win (love)

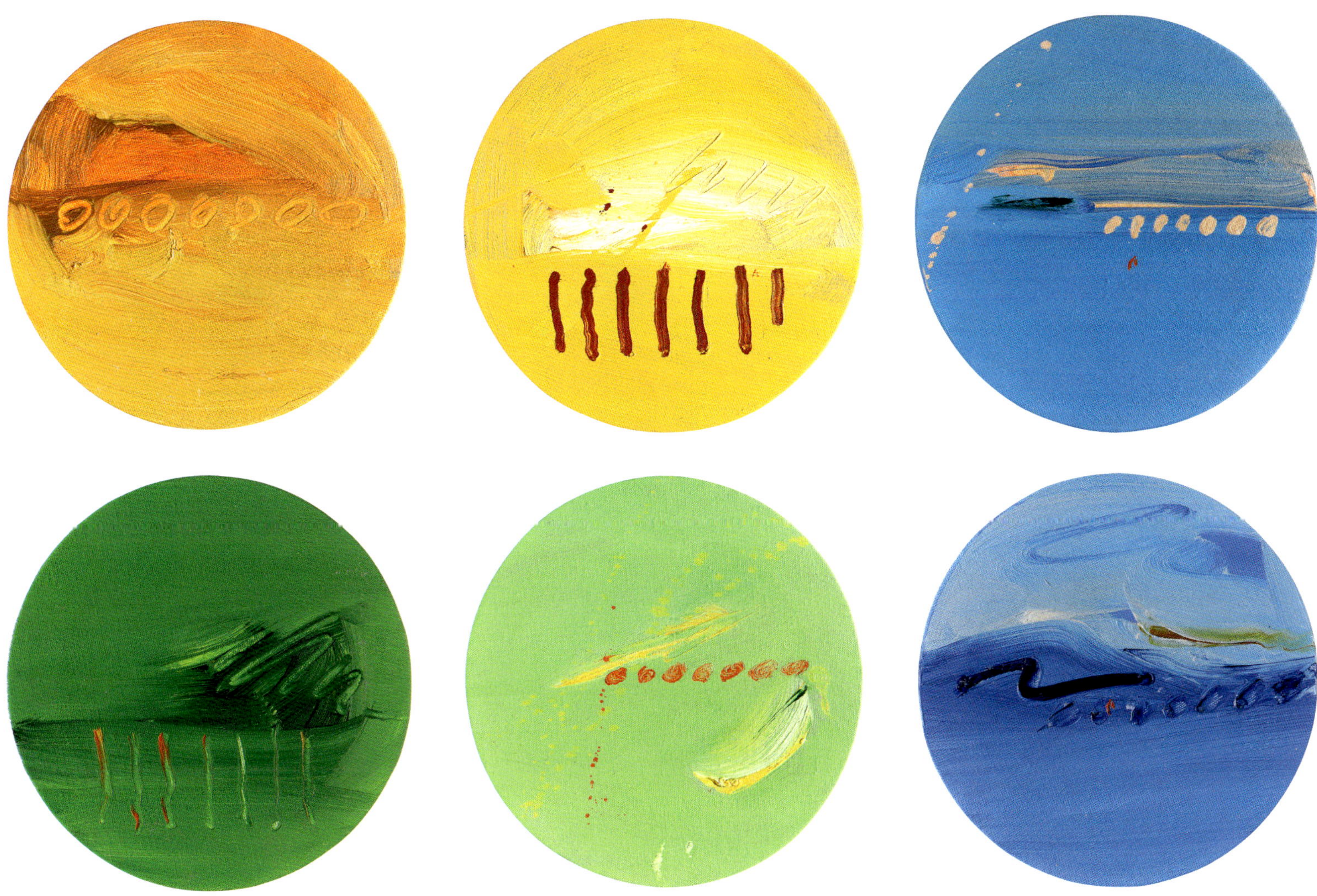

"As an Anishinaabe artist, I wanted my Saulteaux maternal language, culture and history to play an important role in defining my response to Walker Court and its institutional history. Spiritually, concepts of respect and sharing form the foundation of an Anishinaabe way of life, built around seven sacred teachings: gifts from the grandfathers. It was my desire to create a new mediated space here that would give visitors an active sense of an expanded living presence. The seven ceremonial drums specifically made for this space symbolize visions of nature and the perception and traces of memory. There are seven drums for dream songs about the presence of animals and other totemic creatures of the ancestors. Each grandfather is characterized by an animal and a teaching. *Quuh yu koo sá win (honesty)* embodies all of the other gifts because to be honest is to know the truth, to have courage, and to show respect and love. Through honesty, one attains and appreciates wisdom and humility."

— Robert Houle

Seven Grandfathers, 2013
From left to right, top to bottom:
uh mik (beaver), neb wah káh win (wisdom)
músh kooda pezhéke (buffalo), me nah da ne mo win (respect)
muh quáh (bear), sóon ge daá win (courage)
mahéen gun (wolf), tah bus sá nin de zoo win (humility)
shin gah dá me quaun (turtle), dah wa win (truth)
ma sah beh (transforming figure of the woodlands), quuh yu koo sá win (honesty)

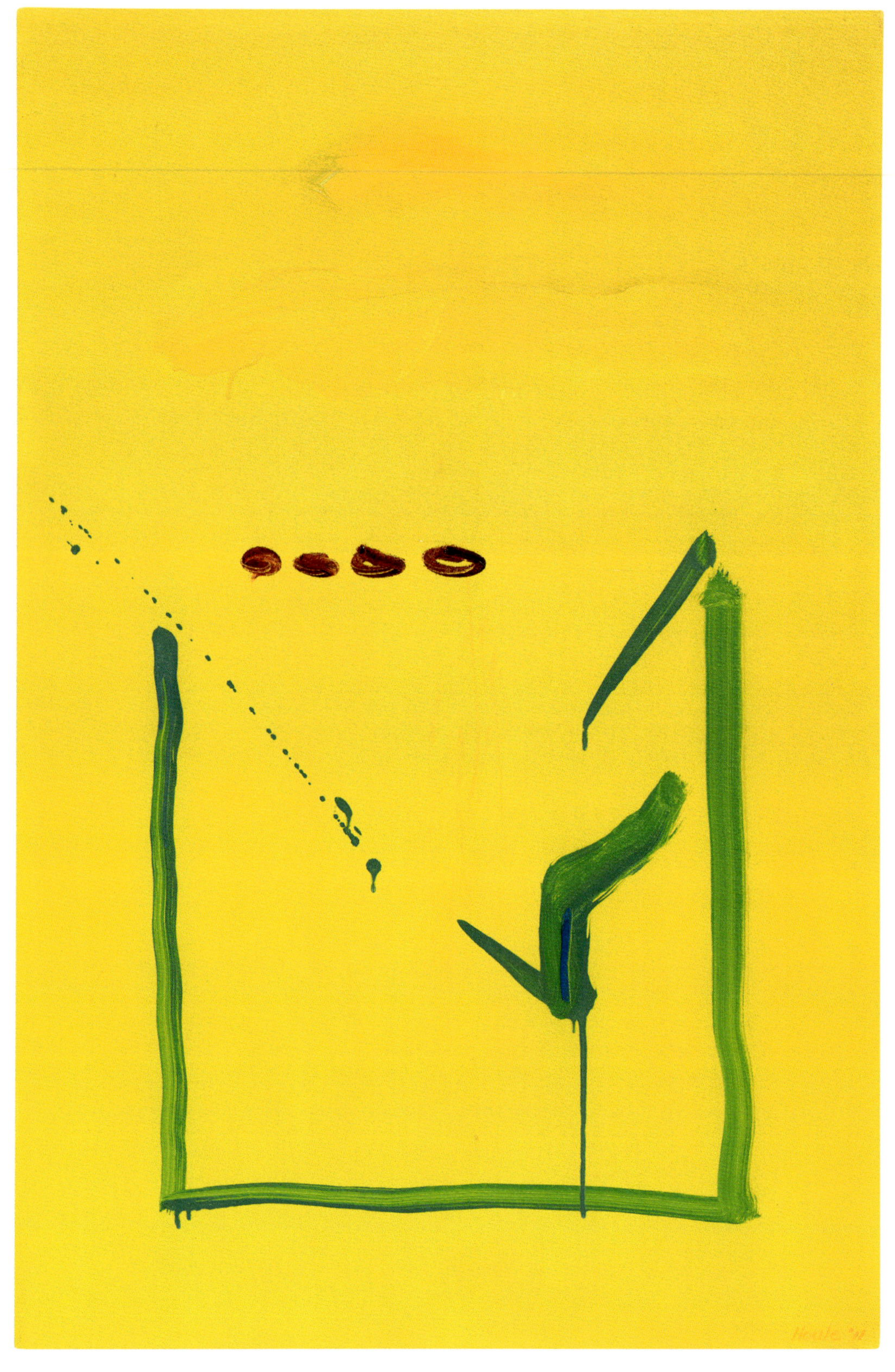

Light Box, 2011

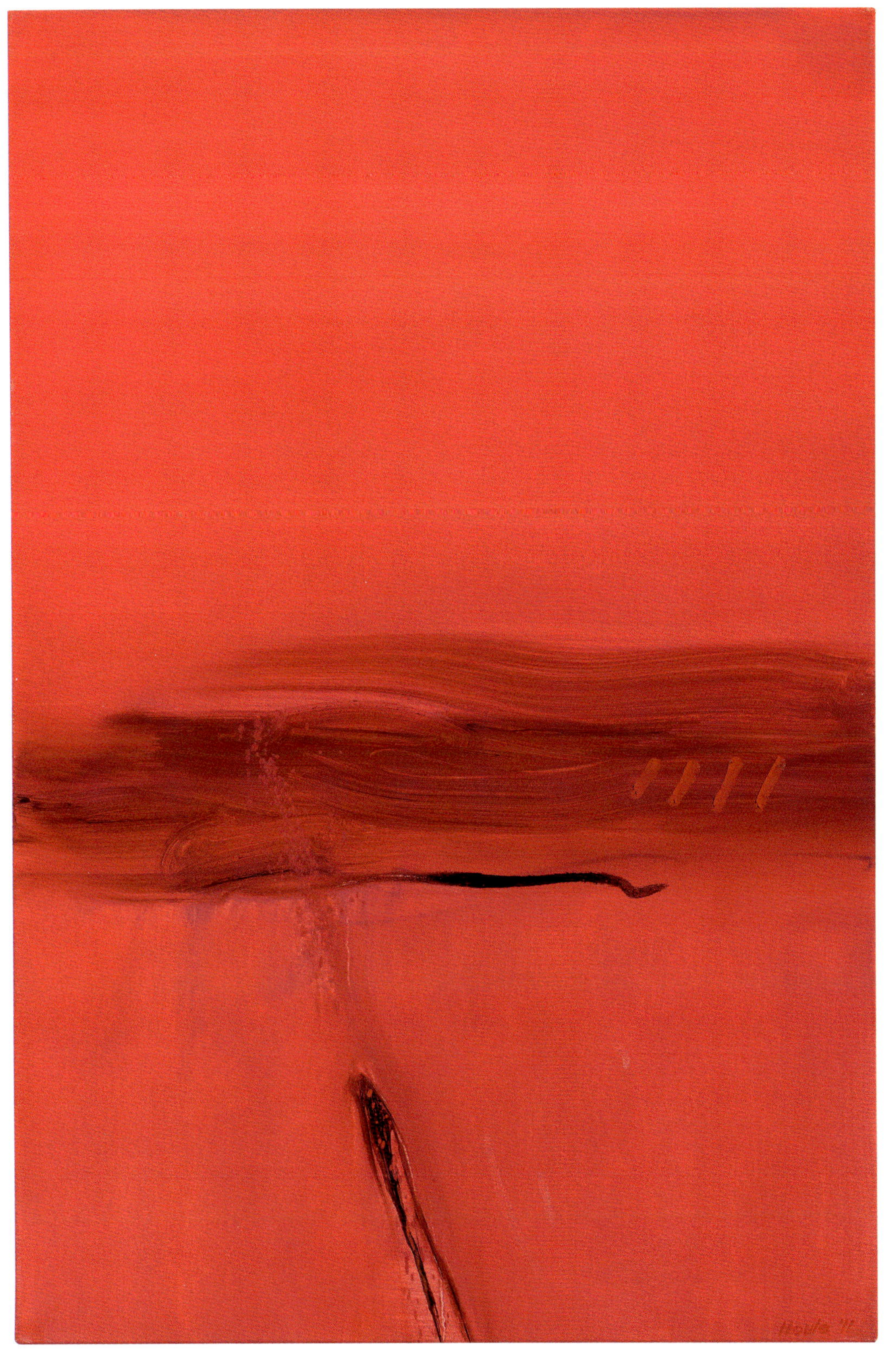

Parfleche, 2011

BEYOND HISTORY PAINTING

Robert Houle's *Kanata*: Beyond History Painting

Wanda Nanibush

The Saulteaux Anishinaabe abstract painter and installation artist, curator, and critic Robert Houle has had a profound impact on Canadian art institutions and their relationship to Indigenous art. In his best known works, Houle visually upstages Western history painting to reframe North American history from an Indigenous perspective. He mixes colour-field abstraction with mixed-media appropriations, aiming to target the grand histories of the victors by showing the constructed nature of "his-story," while also infusing his work with non-linear understandings of time and narrative from Saulteaux culture. In the following text, I examine this trajectory of Houle's work, focusing on the example of his multi-canvas painting *Kanata* (1992; page 96).

One of Houle's mid-career works, *Kanata* was created at a time when First Nations sovereignty and understandings of history were reaching the popular consciousness. The Oka Crisis or Kanehsatake Resistance of 1990 took place the year before the painting was created; the year it was finished, the celebrations marking five hundred years since Columbus's "arrival" shifted into a discourse on five hundred years of colonization. In 1991, Houle found himself standing in front of Benjamin West's *The Death of General Wolfe* (1770; fig. 1). The oil painting was being exhibited with West's collection of Native American clothing, weapons, and other so-called "artifacts" at the National Gallery of Canada. It was there that Houle began to devise a First Nations perspective on the beloved nationalist history of West's work. This rumination would become *Kanata*.

As a whole, Kanata looks like a flag constructed from three large canvases (actually four canvases). The two middle canvases are a reproduction of Benjamin West's

The Death of General Wolfe done in a bistre wash, with the colour removed from the non-Indigenous aspects of the scene. Using red and blue conté crayon, Houle subtly filled in the First Nations (Delaware) man who occupies a prominent place as a witness to the death scene. He also adds two Indigenous figures fleeing the scene in a canoe as an inside joke most viewers miss. The history painting is placed between two monochromatic flat canvases; the one on the right is in the bright red of the British flag and the one on the left is in the blue of France's flag. In his appropriation of West's work, Houle folds the time of 1771 onto 1992, resulting in a chronotopic painting. As the theorist Mikhail Bakhtin explains, in the artistic chronotope, "[t]ime ... takes on flesh, becomes artistically visible; likewise, space becomes charged and responsive to the movements of time, plot and history."[1] In foregrounding the centrality of the figure of the Delaware man in West's painting, Houle wanted to draw attention to the unending misrepresentation of Indigenous Peoples as merely passive observers, pointing instead to our direct stake in the history of Canada and the United States. He wants to "say to the viewer, 'Look, as Native people we are just voyeurs in the history of this country.' The Indian is in parentheses, the Indian is surrounded by this gigantic red and this gigantic blue and is sandwiched in that environment, is surrounded."[2]

Benjamin West's *The Death of General Wolfe*[3] was exhibited in 1771 at the Pall Mall Galleries in London, England. A mere eleven years after the British Army officer's 1759 death on the Plains of Abraham near Quebec City, West chose the event as his subject. The battle itself is thought to have been a turning point in the Seven Years' War between Britain and France, which was ultimately won by Britain in 1763. In Canadian mythology, the Battle of the Plains of Abraham marks the defeat of the French and the birth of Canada as an English-speaking British colony. Presented as a grand history painting—one that captures a crucial moment in a narrative—*The Death of General Wolfe* became very popular and was widely reproduced on everyday objects like cups.

West's painting was completed at a time when Britain was exhibiting a renewed fascination with North America and its Indigenous populace. In his essay "British Curiosity and Savage Debauchery," Timothy J. Shannon writes:

> During the 1760s Britons read a burgeoning popular literature on the empire that included pamphlets, plays and ballads about America. Veterans of the war returned home with Indian artifacts as souvenirs and exhibited such objects in cabinets of curiousities, coffeehouses, and fairs. Depictions of Native Americans in British visual culture—prints, paintings, magazines, maps, and cartoons—became commonplace and for the first time, strove for ethnographic accuracy.... Some Britons even paid to view Indians in person in theatres, taverns, and pleasure gardens.[4]

Britons were increasingly viewing so-called "Indians" as the spoils of the country's imperialist conquest of North America. West, who is embedded in this history, follows the conventions of his time by painting the "Indian's" dress, body tattoos, and tomahawk from objects he had collected on his travels. Supposed ethnographic accuracy did not imply sympathy or equality with Native Americans; instead, it was an expression of control over these subjects through the expansion of empire and its objects. "The Seven Years War brought a continental dominion under British rule and shifted notions of empire away from seventeenth-century

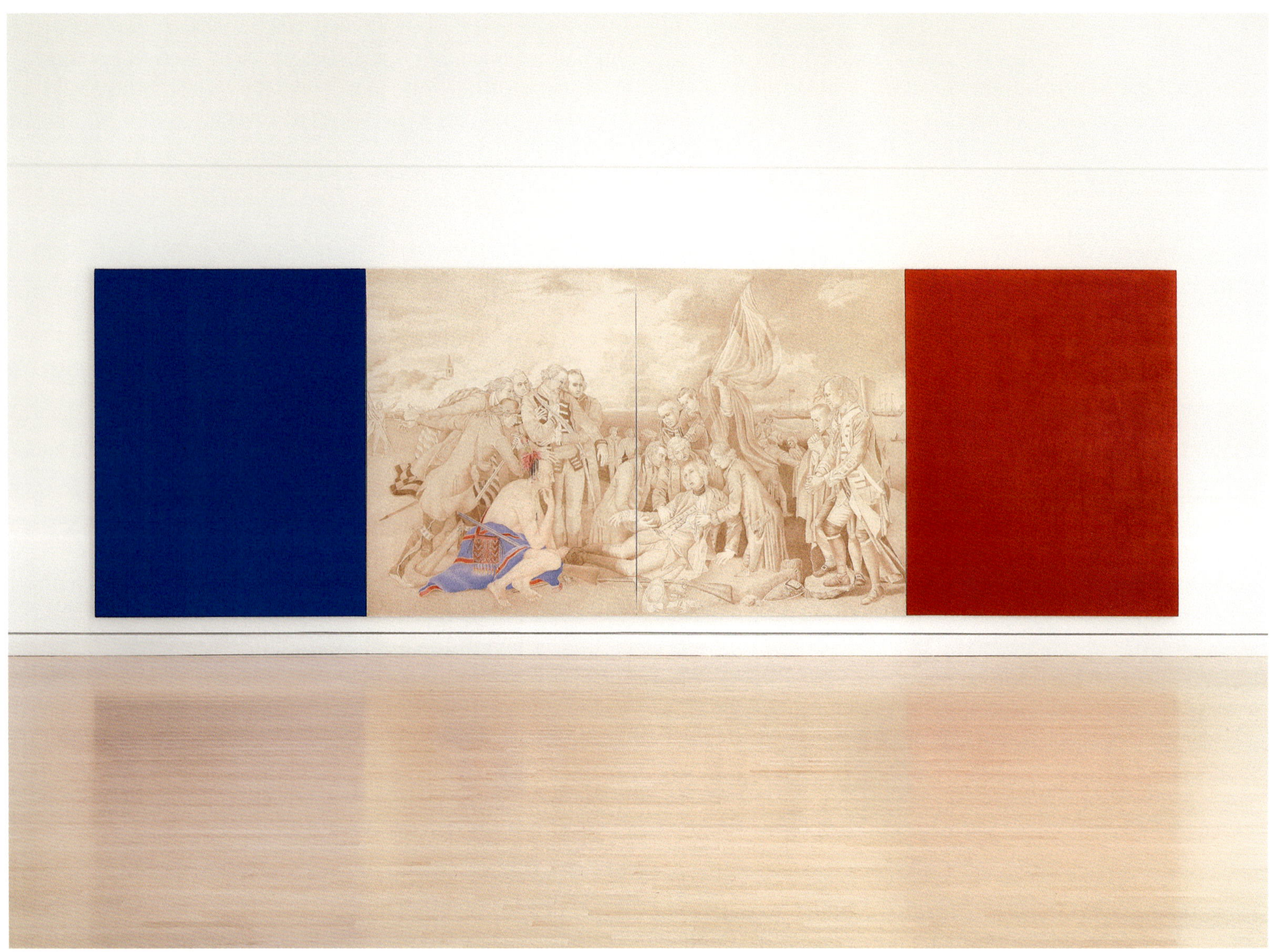

Kanata, 1992

mercantilist roots to a new emphasis on dominion over foreign lands and their native peoples."[5] In the Canadian context, West's *Death of General Wolfe* also serves as part of the nationalist project, underscoring the country's dominion over its French and First Nations "subjects."

Houle wrote about West's painting in his curatorial essay for the landmark 1992 exhibition *Land, Spirit, Power* at the National Gallery of Canada, one of the first large-scale exhibitions of contemporary Indigenous arts in a fine arts institution. Houle co-curated this exhibition the same year he finished *Kanata*. In the essay he places West's work at the beginning of the romantic movement, which, he argues, continued to disinherit Indigenous Peoples from both identity and land through visual representations of the "Indian warrior." Houle writes that "the warrior was also clearly the most logical and poignant personification of Great Britain's conquest, because the warrior symbolically affirmed the identity and place of the English on the continent."[6] Vivien Green Fryd makes a similar case in her essay "Rereading the Indian" in Benjamin West's *Death of General Wolfe*.[7] Like Houle, she argues that *The Death of General Wolfe* represents a popular rendering of what will become in the nineteenth century an enduring trope of Indianness: the Noble Savage. The "Indian" stood and stands for all that the romantics desired: a symbol of untamed nature and noble antiquity, this figure elicited awe and terror and evoked emotionalism and intuitiveness; he was exotic, unfamiliar, and anti-modern. Houle writes that "[s]adly, racism, as imagination, has a grammar and a syntax, a pervasive and impermeable narrative power; the enduring image of the "noble savage" is an empowerment that has led to disinheritance from identity."[8]

The "Indian" in West's painting is an allegory. The figure's pose is one of contemplation akin to Dürer's *Melencholia I* (1514). The melancholic woman and the Indian exist in a state of timelessness. Dürer's subject's activity of thinking is abundant but not generative, as is the case with the Indian. The woman in *Melencholia I* is surrounded by the trappings of material wealth and productivity but seems to be uninterested in those things—or at least, resigned to a melancholic state in the face of such trappings. This fits with the construction of the Indian in opposition to modernity and empire. The Indian is destined to pass away before the great states and their men. As Jennifer Raddin notes, the melancholic was "one who felt more deeply, saw more clearly, and came closer to the sublime than ordinary mortals."[9] Drawing on examples as diverse as Anne-Louis Girodet de Roucy-Trioson's *Atala at the Tomb* (1808), Thomas Crawford's Indian: *Dying Chief Contemplating the Progress of Civilization* (1856), George Catlin's illustrations (1857), F.O.C. Darley and Stephen J. Ferris's *Centennial Stock Certificate* (1874–1875), and Joseph Wright of Derby's *The Indian Widow*, as well as literary sources (like the work of James Fenimore

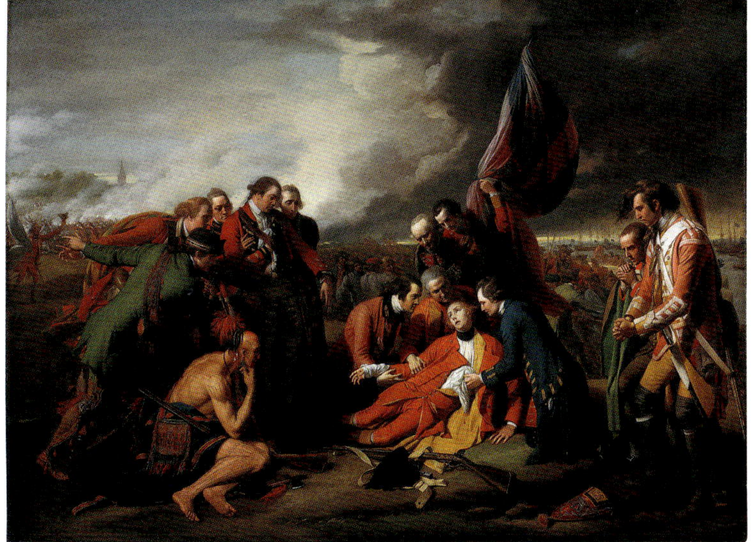

OPPOSITE PAGE:
Robert Houle, *Kanata*, 1992. Acrylic and conté crayon on canvas, 228.7 × 732 cm overall; panels: 228.7 × 183 cm each. National Gallery of Canada, Ottawa, purchased 1994. Acc. # 37479.1-4. Photo: NGC.

FIG. 1 (ABOVE)
Benjamin West, *The Death of General Wolfe*, 1770. Oil on canvas, 152.6 × 214.5 cm. National Gallery of Canada, Ottawa, gift of the 2nd Duke of Westminster to the Canadian War Memorials, 1918; Transfer from the Canadian War Memorials, 1921. Acc. # 8007. Photo: NGC.

Cooper, one of the most popular disseminators of romantic images of "Indians"[10]), Fryd argues that the pose of the "Indian" as a reiteration of the melancholic figure (fig. 2) "became codified as the Vanishing American lamenting the demise of his race."[11]

For Houle, the Delaware is not contemplating the demise of his own people, but rather, of two armies fighting over territory that wasn't theirs. Houle also identifies with this figure—in his survival as a subject and in his political/economic and social bind, caught between two colonial powers. "Our life here goes back as far as creation according to cultural memory. This spiritual legacy is what motivates me to signify the anguish I have towards our place between two European nations who have formed a nation state."[12]

The title of *Kanata* takes us beyond the two colonial powers by drawing attention to the Indigenous roots of names. Canada originates in the Mohawk[13] language as "kanata," meaning village. In 1535, Cartier wrote down "Canada," and this mistaken spelling was enshrined in the constitution of 1867. Houle has consistently drawn attention to what he terms "the aesthetics of disappearance," whereby we are disinherited from our names through their bastardization and appropriation. By using "Kanata," Houle reminds us that Canada's legitimacy as a nation is arrived at through the displacement of its original inhabitants and the dispossession of their land and languages. The word also speaks an Indigenous difference from the Canadian polity that cannot be contained within it. Lastly, *Kanata* shifts focus from the individualistic titling of West's work—from the name of a specific male hero (General Wolfe) to a concept (the village to which the Delaware might belong). In some ways, Houle is bringing the Delaware man home by highlighting him and reframing his meaning.

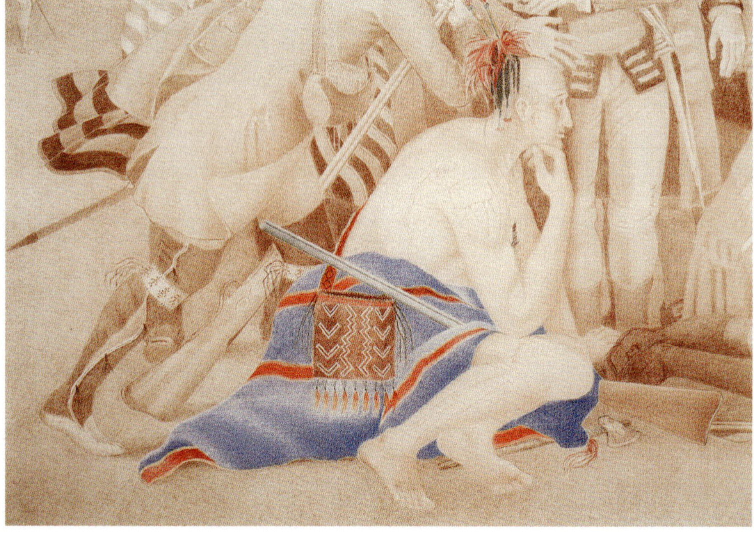

FIG. 2
Robert Houle, *Kanata*, 1992 (detail). Acrylic and conté crayon on canvas, 228.7 × 732 cm overall; panels: 228.7 × 183 cm each. National Gallery of Canada, Ottawa, purchased 1994. Acc. # 37479.1-4. Photo: NGC.

Transposing an historical event to a painting represents a move from reportage to theatre, in which history is not simply the delivery of facts but instead their truth displayed as a moral message. West reverses the classical model whereby "a classical setting is used to comment on a contemporary social or political issue" and instead uses "a recent event to preach a sermon on universal values."[14] The narrative of the eternal hero in this painted theatrical *mise en scène* then becomes a mode of ensuring man's centrality as witness to and actor in historical progress. Wolfe, a contemporary mortal represented as a heroic icon, allows the spectator to envisage the possibility of becoming a hero if they practice the values of "courage, loyalty, patriotism, and sacrifice."[15] Houle's work, on the other hand, evokes ethical questions rather than a moral message. For instance: How does history painting collude with colonialism?

Kanata constitutes an astute intervention into Eurocentric art history by challenging the representation and authority of history painting and its separation from formalism and abstraction. As an abstract painter, Houle goes beyond history painting in the grand style, although he is deliberately not working in the vein of pure modernist abstraction. For Houle, abstraction is an organic, additive spiritual process rather than a cold, reductive masculinist product. It is also a space to address the modern minefields of colonial identity issues.[16] In West's time, history became the main mode of legitimate knowledge; historians sought universal truths. And yet, the more people collected, filmed, photographed, wrote, and disseminated information, the more one realized that one's view was always incomplete, capturing only one perspective.[17] These impulses fed each other: the more collective insecurity arose about what a person could know, the more that society would seek knowledge—and the more knowledge was attained, the more it became evident that it was impossible to unify all that knowing. By the 1990s, the notion of a single grand unified version of history had long been supplanted. In Houle's time, historical narrative is no longer simply viewed as the truth gleaned from stable facts—nor is painting considered the source of universal human truths. Naming an event, as Houle understands, is also an act of rhetoric and meaning-making, one that decides the facts in advance. As Hans Kellner explicates:

> Creating the event means creating the reader who will recognize the event as an event when it is presented, and when it is presented, and who can then follow its course according to the prevailing conventions of readability. No writer can be sure of his audience, however. Genre, *topoi*, emplotment are traditional formal devices of rhetoric that are supposed to secure the adherence of a reader to a vision of the subject.[18]

History has been written by those in power; Houle uses art as a way to make *his* version of history visible. The more so-called "grand narratives" are challenged by the histories of so-called minorities, the more the conception of history as a search for truth and unity unravels. History as a discursive field has always already been about narrative; the "facts" of history are just the elements highlighted to render a particular narrative valid. What's at stake is not two different versions of history, but history-making itself. What's at stake is the place of the image in the consolidation of power through representation that still denies humanity to others.[19]

Houle's *Kanata* implicitly critiques Eurocentric versions of history that are a legacy of West's time. By repeating West's gesture with a difference (colour and abstraction), Houle shows how the original was always already a narrative in service of the interests of power and money. Translating *The Death of General Wolfe* into an Indigenous space frees its meaning to be utilized in the service of what it was against: Indigenous sovereignty. In Houle's *Kanata*, there is no lamentation, no sympathetic mourners—they have been drained of colour and emphasis so that the spectator is no longer interpellated into a drama of nationalism. All that is left is the contemplative Delaware. The figure also represents British allies, without whom the war could not have been won. Houle opens the abstract neutral space for the acknowledgement of the presence of Indigenous peoples at contact and beyond. The honour, bravery, and sacrifice that West valorized in *The Death of General Wolfe* become values of patience and negotiation for the First Nations figure in *Kanata*. From the perspective of 1992, Houle centres the continued fight for First Nations self-rule after five hundred years of contact and conquest.

I would be remiss not to end with where Houle is now in a newer work, the triptych *O-ween du muh waun (We Were Told)* (2017; page 101), which is a guide for a new century as *Kanata* was before it. Houle bypasses any circuit through European art history that may have been present in his earlier work by painting *Kanata*'s First Nations figure in vibrant oil-based colour. The absences (no scene of war, no important personages, no nation-based colour fields) reflect that this work is confident in First Nations understandings, ways of being, and histories. This confidence is also reflected in the foregrounded phrase "we were told," an acknowledgement that we were told by our ancestors about the arrival of Europeans. We were also told what we needed to save and carry forward for a peaceful future. The land here, painted in fecund greens, yellows, and browns, could be an image from before European arrival, with the First Nations figure looking out to the Atlantic, contemplating contact not as a victim but as a human with the wisdom passed down from the ancients. This scene could also be a future dreamscape where the values that came on those ships, the ones that are destroying this very land, are in the past. Houle expresses the hopes and freedoms of the new generation as they carry their drums, songs, stories, values, and creative expression with them at all times in all situations. He knows all too well how hard his ancestors and his own generation fought for this moment.

Opposite page
Robert Houle, *O-ween du muh waun (We Were Told)*, 2017. Oil on canvas, triptych, 213.4 × 365.8 cm. Confederation Centre Art Gallery, commissioned with the A.G. and Eliza Jane Ramsden Endowment Fund, 2017. CAG 2017.1.

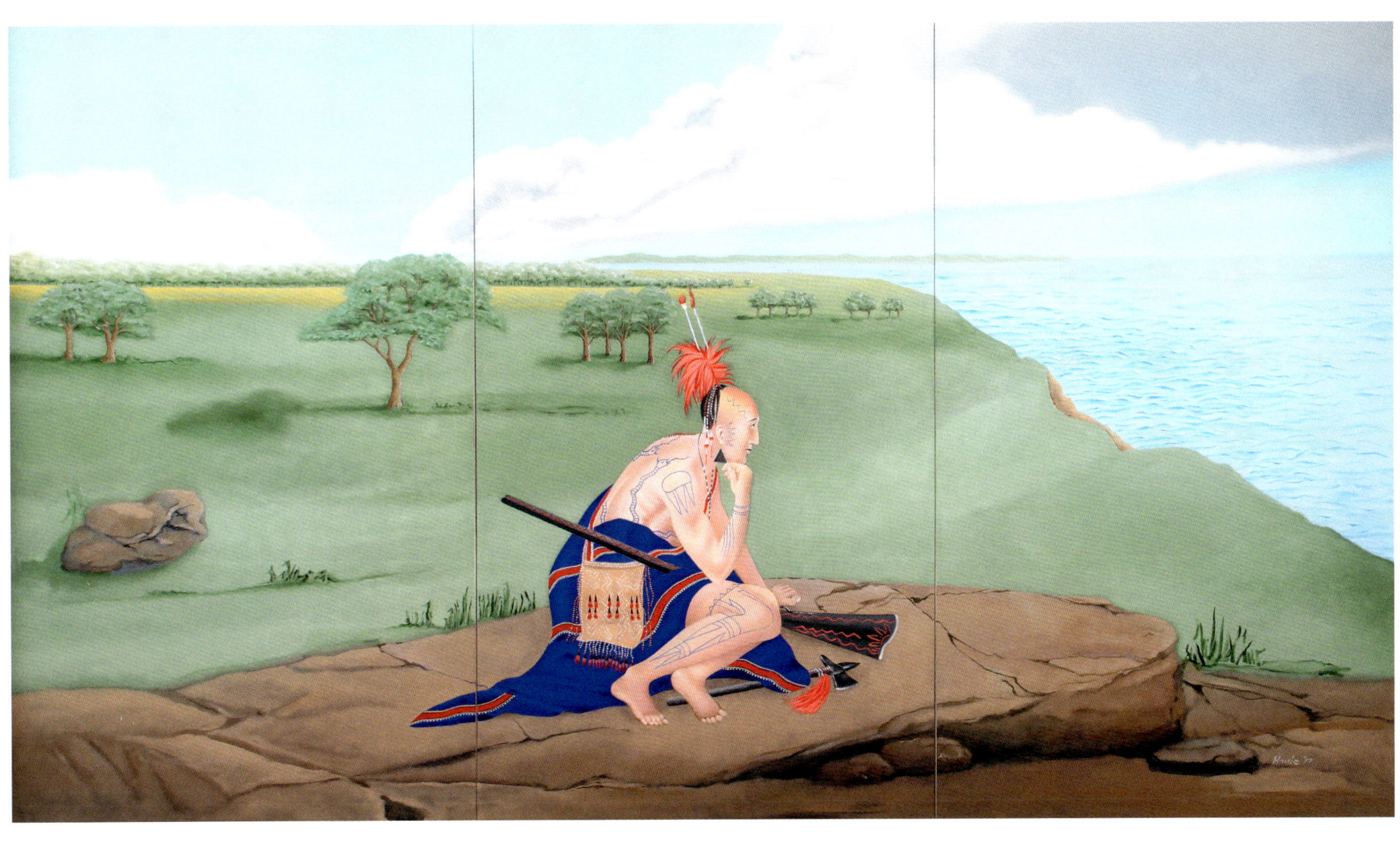

O-ween du muh *waun (We Were Told)*, 2017

1 Mikhail Bakhtin, "Forms of Time and of the Chronotope in the Novel," *The Dialogic Imagination: Four Essays*, ed. Michael Holquist (Austin: University of Texas Press, 1981), 84.

2 Robert Houle quoted in Michael Bell, *Kanata: Robert Houle's Histories* (Ottawa: Carleton University Art Gallery, 1993), 19.

3 West painted four large versions. In 1921, the original *Death of General Wolfe* was transferred to the National Gallery of Canada from the Canadian government, which had received the painting as a gift from the second Duke of Westminster, England, in 1918. The Royal Ontario Museum of Canada has the third version (dimensions 167 × 244.9 cm), which was created for the Robert Moncton Family. During the Quebec campaign in 1759, Monckton was second in command to General Wolfe. *Kanata* was purchased by the National Gallery in 1994 and joined the collection alongside West's work as an intervention. After the Art Gallery of Ontario retrospective closes, the two paintings will once again be exhibited together at the National Gallery.

4 Timothy J. Shannon. "British Curiosity and Savage Debauchery," *Native Acts: Indian Performance*, 1603-1832, ed. David Bellin and Laura L. Mielke (Lincoln and London: University of Nebraska Press, 2011), 223.

5 Shannon, "British Curiosity and Savage Debauchery," 239.

6 See Robert Houle, "The Spiritual Legacy of the Ancient Ones," *Land, Spirit, Power* exh. cat. (Ottawa: National Gallery of Canada, 1992), http://www.ccca.ca/c/writing/h/houle/hou009t.html; last accessed April 12, 2012.

7 Vivien Green Fryd, "Rereading the Indian in Benjamin West's *Death of General Wolfe*," *American Art* (Spring 1995): 73–85.

8 See Houle, "The Spiritual Legacy of the Ancient Ones," 1992.

9 Jennifer Raddin, ed. *The Nature of Melancholy: From Aristotle to Kristeva* (London: Oxford University Press, 2000), 15.

10 Raddin, *The Nature of Melancholy*, 15.

11 Fryd, "Rereading the Indian in Benjamin West's Death of General Wolfe," 81.

12 Robert Houle, *Kanata in Notion of Conflict: A Selection of Contemporary Canadian Art* (Amsterdam: Stedelijk Museum, 1995), 24.

13 New archeological evidence suggests that Cartier met St. Lawrence Iroquoian individuals who used the word "Canada," meaning village. The Canadian government has not yet revised its history of this term, which means the new information has yet to have an impact on the popular understanding of the history of the word "Canada" and thus is not relevant for my purposes. See: http://www.noslangues-ourlanguages.gc.ca/bien-well/fra-eng/vocabulaire-vocabulary/kanata-canada-eng.html; last accessed September 2, 2012.

14 Ann Uhry Abrams, "The Valiant Hero: Benjamin West and Grand Style History Painting," in *New Directions in American Art* (Washington: Smithsonian Press, 1985), 180.

15 Abrams, "The Valiant Hero," 180.

16 Robert Houle, "Artist Statement," in *Troubling Abstraction: Robert Houle* (Hamilton: McMaster Museum of Art; Oshawa: Robert McLaughlin Gallery, 2007), 15–18.

17 A case in point is the panorama, which became a site of popular history dissemination. It's impossible to view the whole thing at one time, even though the format is immersive.

18 Hans Kellner, "'Never Again' is Now," *The Postmodern History Reader*, ed. Keith Jenkins (London and New York: Routledge, 1997), 406–407. See also Roland Barthes, "The Discourse of History," in the same volume, 120–123.

19 See Judith Butler, *Precarious Life: The Powers of Mourning and Violence* (Brooklyn and London: Verso, 2006).

Selected Bibliography

Abrams, Ann Uhry. *The Valiant Hero: Benjamin West and Grand Style History Painting*. New Directions in American Art. Washington, DC: Smithsonian Press, 1985.

Bakhtin, M.M. "Forms of Time and of the Chrono-tope in the Novel," in *The Dialogic Imagination: Four Essays*. Edited by Michael Holquist. Austin: University of Texas Press, 1981, 84–258.

Bann, Stephen. *Romanticism and the Rise of History*. New York: Twayne Publishers, 1995.

Bell, Michael. *Kanata: Robert Houle's Histories*. Ottawa: Carleton University Art Gallery, 1993.

Berkhofer, Robert F., Jr. *The White Man's Indian: Images of the American Indian from Columbus to the Present*. New York: Vintage Books-Random House, 1978.

Deloria, Philip J. *Playing Indian*. New Haven and London: Yale University Press, 1998.

Fabian, Johannes. *Time and the Other: How Anthropology Makes Its Object*. New York: Columbia University Press, 1983.

Fordham, Douglas. *British Art and the Seven Years' War: Allegiance and Autonomy*. University Park: University of Pennsylvania Press, 2010.

Fryd, Vivien Green. "Rereading the Indian in Benjamin West's Death of General Wolfe." *American Art* (Spring 1995): 79.

Houle, Robert. "Artist Statement." *Troubling Abstraction: Robert Houle*. Hamilton and Oshawa: McMaster Museum of Modern Art and Robert McLaughlin Gallery, 2007, 15-18.

Houle, Robert, "Kanata," *Notion of Conflict: A Selection of Contemporary Canadian Art*. Amsterdam: Stedelijk Museum, 1995, 24.

Houle, Robert, and Shirley Madill. *Robert Houle: Sovereignty over Subjectivity*. Winnipeg: Winnipeg Art Gallery, 1999.

Houle, Robert, Nelcya Delanoë, Barry Ace, and David W. McIntosh. *Paris/Ojibwa*. Peterborough, Peterborough, ON: Art Gallery, 2011.

Jenkins, Keith, ed. *The Postmodern History Reader*. London and New York: Routledge, 1997.

Mitchell, Charles. "Benjamin West's "Death of General Wolfe" and the Popular History Piece." *Journal of the Warburg and Courtauld Institutes*, 7 (1944), 20–33.

Raddin, Jennifer, ed. *The Nature of Melancholy: From Aristotle to Kristeva*. London: Oxford University Press, 2000.

Shannon, Timothy J. "British Curiosity and Savage Debauchery." In *Native Acts: Indian Performance, 1603–1832*. Edited by David Bellin and Laura L. Mielke. Lincoln and London: University of Nebraska Press, 2011.

Wind, Edgar. "The Revolution of History Painting." *Journal of the Warburg Institute*, 2:2 (October, 1938), 116–127.

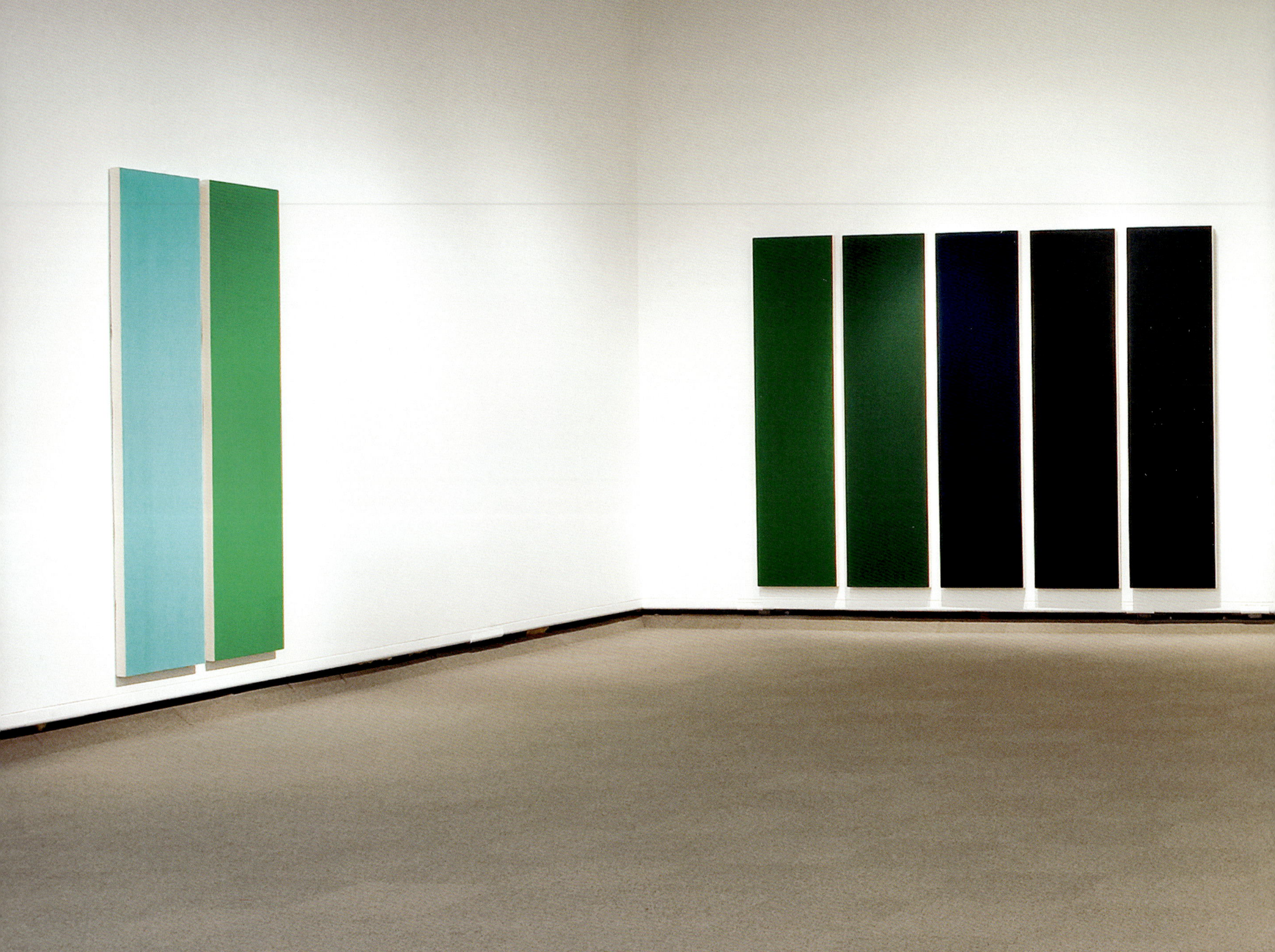

Robert Houle, *Palisade I*, 1999. Installation view of *To Be Reckoned With* at the MacKenzie Art Gallery in 2010. Oil on canvas, watercolour on paper, and lithographic print, installation dimensions variable (canvas panels are 244 × 61.2 cm each). Collection of the MacKenzie Art Gallery, purchased with the financial support of the Canada Council for the Arts Acquisition Assistance Program, 2000-001.
Installation view at the MacKenzie Art Gallery.
Photo: Don Hall, courtesy of the MacKenzie Art Gallery.

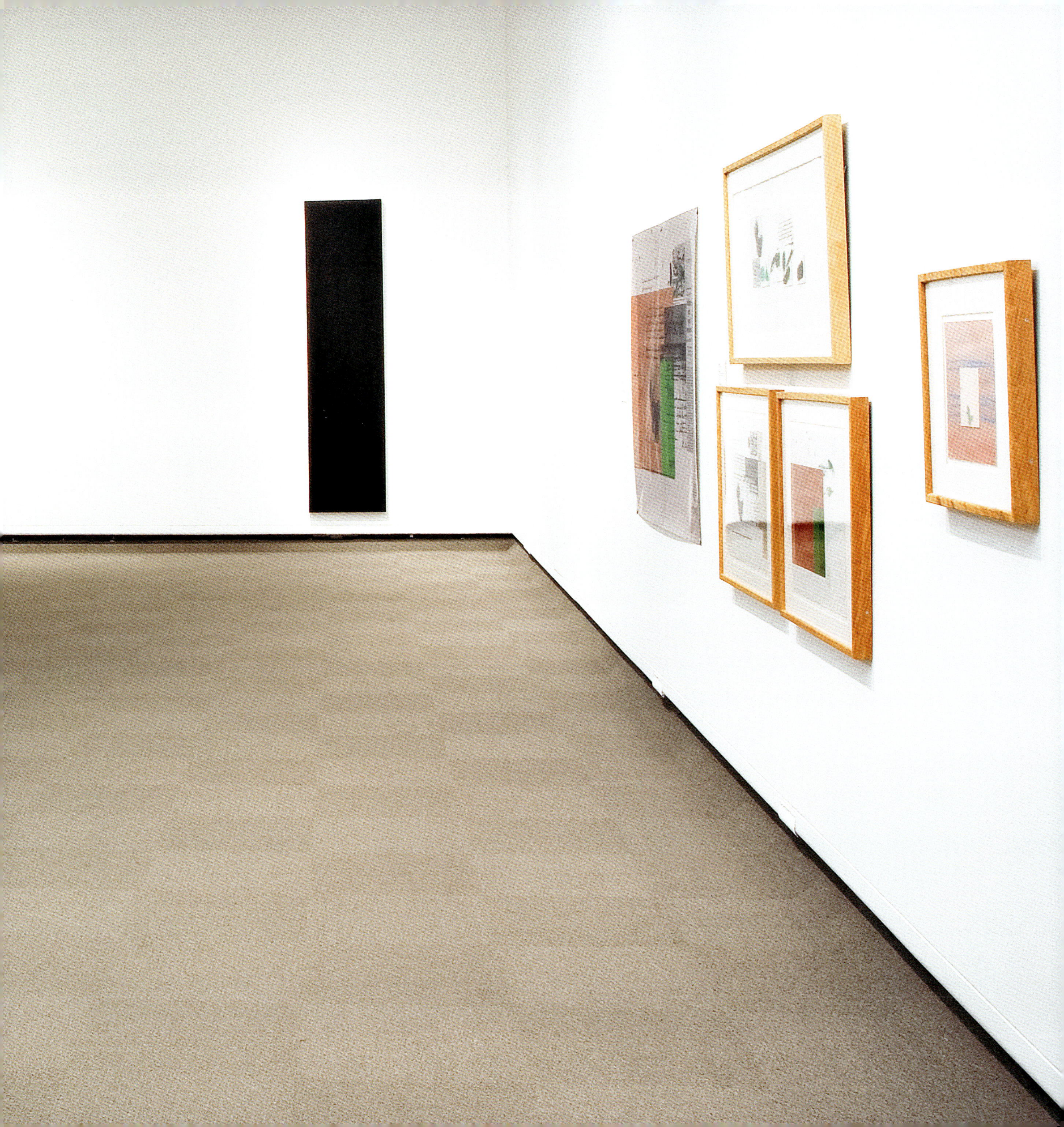

Robert Houle's *Palisade*

Michael Bell

Robert Houle's visual arts practice has successfully joined modernist formalism with activist initiatives to review the "history" of the interactions of the North American Indian and the colonizers—military and settlers. *Palisade*[1] takes its place in a group of works—for example, *Hochelaga* (1992),[2] *Kanata* (1993),[3] *Zero Hour* (1989),[4] *Pontiac Conspiracy* (1996),[5] and *Premises for Self Rule: The Royal Proclamation* (1994)[6] —that examine the intersection of Amerindian history and contemporary issues. These intersections inform the relationship between North America's First People and those Europeans who have encountered them since 1492, in the course of the establishment of a Neo-European society in North America.

I. *Palisade*

palisade: noun, verb, a fence of pales or stakes set firmly in the ground, as for enclosure or defense.[7]

The installation *Palisade* comprises eight vertical canvases, each eight feet high and two feet wide,[8] a group of studies for the project, and a digitally collaged graphic, produced originally to be used in the production of outdoor billboards in the first occurrence of the installation in Saskatoon (pages 104–105).

The eight green canvases are each painted a solid, distinct hue, moving sequentially in value from the first panel, from the lightest to the last one, which is the darkest. The sequence of colours is: Cobalt Green, Winsor Emerald #708, Chrome Green Deep Hue, Terre Verte, Winsor Green #720, Prussian Green, Sap Green, Olive Green. Pontiac's intended signal to his warriors to attack the occupants of Fort Detroit was to turn the wampum belt to show its green side. Each of the eight panels stands for one of the eight forts captured by the tribes in Pontiac's Confederacy in 1763. The panels are installed in three groups: one group of two, one group of five, and a single panel. Each group occupies, in a "virtual" manner, the same conceptual space on the wall: precisely seventeen feet, nine inches (sixteen feet for the panels and three inches between each panel). Where you see two panels, you must imagine all eight; where you see five panels, you must imagine all eight; and, where you see one panel, you must imagine all eight. The result is to construct around the gallery walls the conceptual effect of a palisade.

The digital graphic collages many of the elements developed in the studies (fig. 1). In addition, Houle introduces disturbing documentation. The first is a *National Post* column (after the *New York Times*)[10] discussing the fate of the last five stocks of variola virus—commonly known as smallpox. The other documentation—reproductions of the postscripts of letters exchanged between Lord Jeffrey Amherst, commander-in-chief of British Forces in North America during Seven Years' War (1756–63) and the Swiss mercenary, Colonel Henry Bouquet, stationed at Fort Pitt—advocates the "inoculation" of the Indians gathered loosely under the leadership of Pontiac, with gifts of blankets infected with the smallpox virus.[11]

...

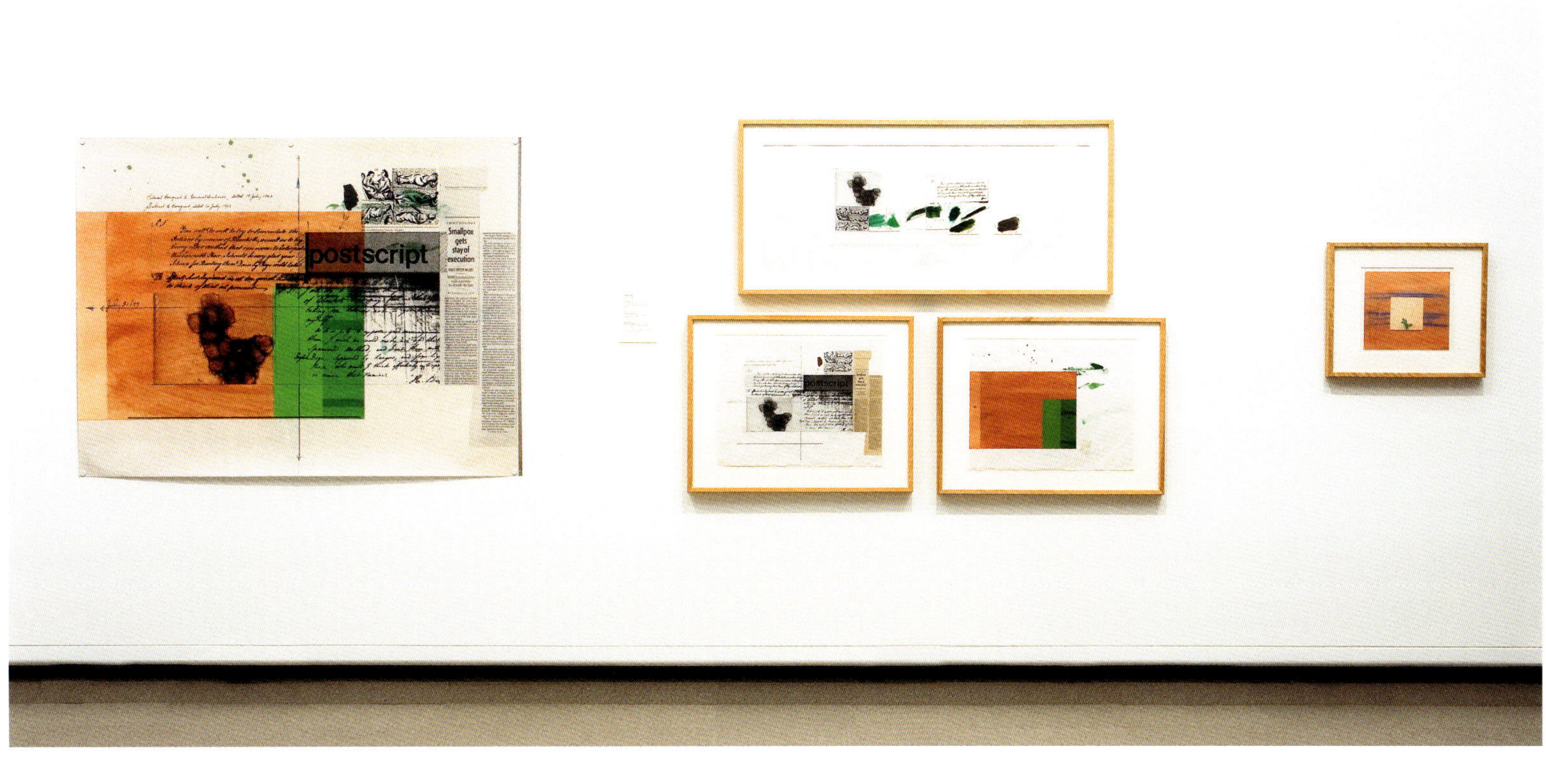

FIG. 1
Robert Houle, *Palisade I*, 1999 (detail). Watercolour on paper, lithographic print, installation dimensions variable. Collection of the MacKenzie Art Gallery, purchased with the financial support of the Canada Council for the Arts Acquisition Assistance Program. 2000-001-001 through 005.
Photo: Don Hall, courtesy of the MacKenzie Art Gallery.

IV. Amherst and the infected blanket[12]

infect: verb, to affect or contaminate (a person, organ, wound, etc.) with disease-producing germs.

In the Americas, the Seven Years' War was a dispute between the English and the French. France—with its colony New France along the St. Lawrence and a series of posts south and west of the Great Lakes and into the Mississippi River valley—reaching as far as the Gulf of Mexico, seemed to be closing off the potential for expansion by England's Thirteen Colonies, ranged along the eastern seaboard.

By 1760, the English forces and their Indian allies had vanquished the French forces and their Indian allies, and sought to establish their military presence wherever the French had set down posts.[13] Commander-in-chief of the British Forces in North America, Lord Jeffrey Amherst, systematically took charge. He sent small detachments to forts scattered around the Great Lakes, restricted trade to these forts, thus controlling the flow of liquor and ostensibly stopping the worst trading practices, and halted the practice of giving "presents" to Indigenous groups.[14] The Indian allies of the French felt some degree of disappointment, especially as they realized that settlers would continue to move into and occupy their territory.

Rumours abound, and hatchets and Seneca war belts circulated among the disaffected groups, culminating in what conventional Neo-European "history" considers the Pontiac Rebellion or Conspiracy, and what contemporary First Nations call Pontiac's Confederacy. In front of the Ottawas and a Huron band, Pontiac proclaimed:

> It is important for us, my brothers, that we exterminate from our lands this nation which seeks only to destroy us. You see as well as I that we can no longer supply our own needs, as we have done from our brothers, the French. The English sell us goods twice as dear as the French do, and their goods do not last.
>
> Scarcely have we bought a blanket or something else to cover ourselves with before we must think of getting another; and when we wish to set out for our winter camps they do not want to give us any credit as our brothers the French do ... we must all swear their destruction and wait no longer. Nothing prevents us; they are few in numbers, and we can accomplish it.
>
> All the nations who are our brothers attack them—why should we not strike too? Are we not men like them? Have I not shown you the wampum belts which I received from our Great Father, the Frenchman? He tells us to strike them ... I have sent wampum belts and messengers to our brothers, the Chippewas of Saginaw, and to our brothers, the Ottawas of Michilimackinac, and to those of the Thames River to join us. They will not be slow in coming, but while we wait let us strike anyway. There is no more time to lose.[15]

Loosely confederated under the leadership of Pontiac, who in turn was influenced by the Delaware Prophet, Neolin,[16] the tribes captured eight palisaded forts and killed or took captive the British soldiers: Fort Venango (13 June, 1763); Fort LeBoeuf (18 June, 1763); Fort Sandusky (16 May, 1763); Fort Miami (27 May, 1763); Fort Ouiatenon (31 May, 1763); Fort Joseph (25 May, 1763); Fort Michilimackinac (2 June, 1763); and Fort Edward Augusta (15 June, 1763).[17] The Amerindians also laid siege to Fort Pitt (where Amherst corresponded also with Captain Simeon Ecuyer) and Detroit. The latter siege lasted from May 9 to October 31, 1763, under the direction of Pontiac, whose original plan to attack from inside the fort during talks with the commander had been revealed to the British, who could then be prepared.

After bringing his forces inside the fort ostensibly to talk peace with Major Gladwin, Pontiac held up "a belt of wampum, white on one side and reputedly green on the other," and displaying the white side, Pontiac spoke at length. But "according to two contemporaries, the turning of this belt from the white to the green was the signal for the massacre ... Pontiac gave no sign,"[18] faced as he was with an English garrison prepared to defend itself.

Needless to say, Amherst, stationed in New York, was not pleased with the murder and mayhem in the territory that he had believed to be under the control of his sparsely manned forts; in the captured forts, the British presence ranged from twelve to twenty-eight enlisted men and officers, and they were all killed or taken captive.

V. Postscripts

postscript: noun, a paragraph or phrase etc. added to a letter that has already been signed by the writer.

It is in this context that Amherst corresponded with his commanders in the field, specifically with Colonel Henry Bouquet and Captain Ecuyer. In postscripts to the correspondence Amherst exchanged comments about the potential use of smallpox-infected blankets to spread the disease among the Indian groups causing so much

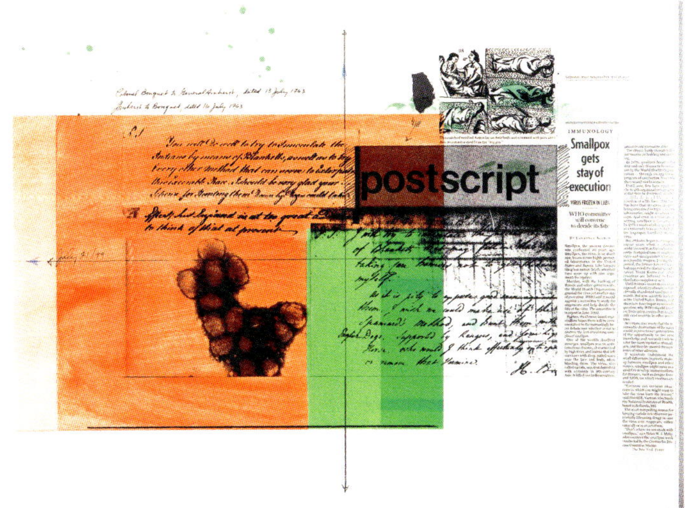

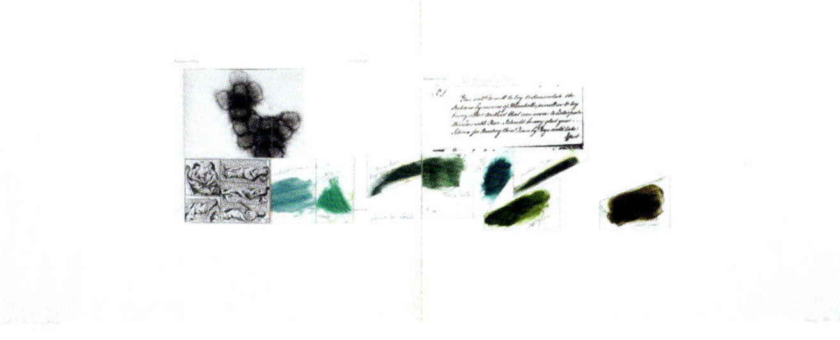

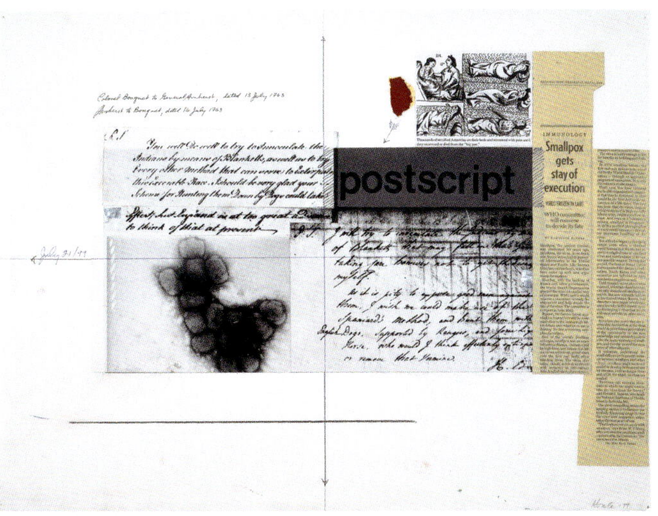

FIG. 2 (TOP)
Robert Houle, *Postscript*, 1999. Lithographic print on paper, 121.9 × 163.2 cm. 2000-001-001.

FIG. 3 (MIDDLE)
Robert Houle, *Postscript*, 1999. Acrylic, graphite, ballpoint ink, computer printout from WWW site, photocopy, and mat board on paper, 45.7 × 121.9 cm. 2000-001-005.

FIG. 4 (BOTTOM)
Robert Houle, *Postscript (study)*, 1999. Acrylic, ink, Xerox image, newsprint, vinyl lettering, and ball point pen ink on paper, 45.5 × 60.7 cm. 2000-001-002.

Figures 2–4: Collection of the MacKenzie Art Gallery, purchased with the financial support of the Canada Council for the Arts Acquisition Assistance Program.
Photos: Don Hall, courtesy of the MacKenzie Art Gallery.

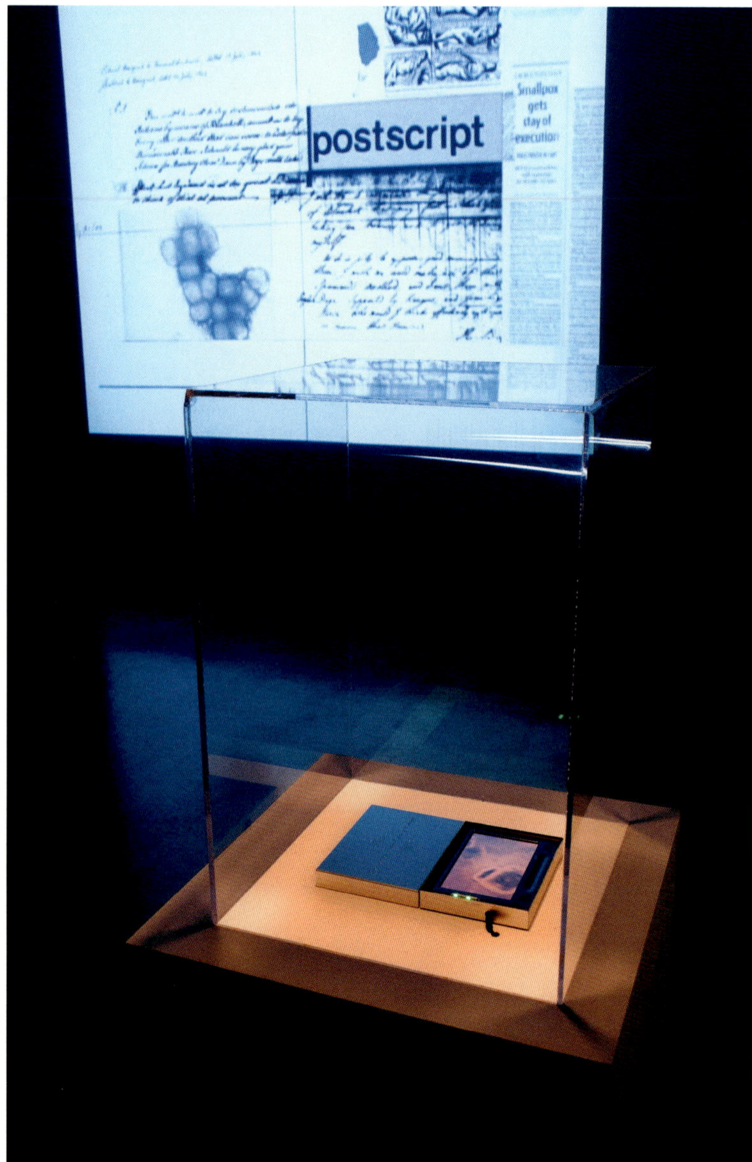

FIG. 5
Robert Houle, *Do Not Open Until You Get Home*, 2007. Installation: video, player, video projection, and vinyl lettering, dimensions variable. Courtesy of the artist.

disturbance.[19] It is this series of letters, particularly the postscripts, that inspired the *Palisade* project (figs. 2–5) just at the time when the World Health Organization (WHO) was entering into the discussion regarding the destruction of the last live stocks of smallpox virus held in Atlanta (the Centers for Disease Control) and in Koltsovo, Novosibirsk Region (Russian State Research Centre of Virology and Biotechnology). WHO had, in the mid-century, successfully mounted a massive vaccination program in many of the world's most poverty-stricken and populous countries to eradicate smallpox. It is ironic that the same organization was trying to determine whether these remaining sources of live virus should be destroyed or preserved. The only justification that seems possible to be mounted to follow the latter course of action is to be able to deter bio-terrorist attacks. Houle's linkage of this contemporary dilemma with the historic actions of the British military in the eighteenth century serves to highlight the revulsion and fear we experience at the prospect of the deliberate release of any deadly virus as an act of war:

> The deliberate reintroduction of smallpox into the population would be an international crime of unprecedented proportions. A spreading, highly lethal epidemic in an essentially unprotected population, with limited supplies of vaccine, no therapeutic drugs, and with shortages of hospital beds suitable for patient isolation is an ominous spectre.[20]

Houle's interpretation of the historical event documented in the Amherst correspondence is necessarily shaped by his own heritage as a First Nations person, a different "history," but one which carries an enormous moral and ethical potential. As almost all historians agree, the intentions of

Amherst and his field commanders were unambiguous: The records for about this time contain more than one specific incident showing the introduction of smallpox among the Indians by a voluntary act of the whites. Such acts were possibly not all malicious ... but another incident occurred in the same year (1763) *from which the conclusion of malice aforethought and deadly intent seems unescapable*. During an Indian uprising when attempts were being made to destroy the British garrison and the posts west of the Allegheny Mountains, Sir Jeffrey Amherst, commander-in-chief of the British forces, harassed by the knowledge of his limited resources and by the extent and seriousness of the revolt, wrote in a postscript of a letter to Bouquet the suggestion that smallpox be sent among the disaffected tribes. Bouquet replied, also in a postscript, "I will try to inoculate the ... with some blankets that may fall into their hands, and take care not to get the disease myself." This could easily have been done since smallpox had broken out in Fort Pitt, where Bouquet was stationed. To Bouquet's postscript Amherst replied, "You will do well to try to inoculate the Indians by means of blankets as well as to try every other method that can serve to extirpate this exorable race." On June 24, Captain Ecuyer, of the Royal Americans, noted in his journal: "Out of our regard for them [i.e., two Indian chiefs] we gave them two blankets and a handkerchief out of the smallpox hospital. I hope it will have the desired effect." A few months later the smallpox raged among the tribes of the Ohio...[21]

Nevertheless, it is all too evident from the account from which the above was taken, that for two centuries, smallpox epidemics had cycled throughout the Americas repeatedly without intentional infection by foes, but still with tragic consequences.

VI. Smallpox present

World Health Assembly: noun, representatives of the entire membership of the World Health Organization, who govern this specialized United Nations agency.

The WWW site for the Center for Civilian Biodefense Studies provides access to a memorandum of the meeting of the WHO Variola Research Committee, a committee mandated by the 52nd World Health Assembly through the Director-General to "establish what research, if any, must be carried out to reach global consensus on the timing for the destruction of existing variola virus stocks." The Assembly also "reaffirmed the decision of previous Assemblies that the remaining stocks of variola virus should be destroyed and authorized retention of the virus "up to not later than 2002 and subject to annual review." The research program proposed by the committee dealt with obtaining DNA sequence information, the development of novel diagnostic techniques, the need for antiviral drugs, the need for monoclonal antibodies, the need for novel smallpox vaccines, the need for a non-human primate or other animal model for smallpox infection, and the need for basic research. The committee arrived at consensus on all these points subject to time limitations (complete before 2002): a laudable goal.[22]

On the other hand, there are those who advocate maintaining stocks of the live virus as part of an ethos of deterrence, in the Cold War mode. Articles abound, in 1999 some two hundred or more, addressing the notion of smallpox as a biological weapon, either by nation states or by bio-terrorists. Those who engage in this line of argument seem to have learned little from the past, and certainly do not subscribe to the views of D.A. Henderson, who countered their main reasons effectively in January 1999.[23] U.S. President Bill Clinton, however, decided to retain the U.S.-held stocks of smallpox virus.

VII. Houle's History

"history": noun, the branch of knowledge dealing with past events.

Houle's construction of *history* is ironic. The juxtaposition of the Amherst correspondence with the newspaper accounts recounting some of the discussions surrounding the destruction of the last living stocks of smallpox virus highlights the powerful ethical and moral potential in Houle's reading of the past (figs. 6 and 7). Houle always reads the past in ways that serve the present and open paths to a better future. The irony?[24] European powers were instrumental in the spread of the smallpox virus to the Americas, and the British military, at least in the persons of Amherst and his field commanders Bouquet and Ecuyer, intended to infect the Indians involved in Pontiac's Confederacy.[25] Two centuries later, through the programs of the WHO, these same European powers, with the assistance of the Neo-European powers, carried out a global campaign of vaccination to rid the world of smallpox. The campaign was successful.

Houle's two events, separated by two centuries, relate a *history* in an unconventional way, not in a linear narrative, but in ironic juxtaposition. In *Why Ethics?*, Robert Gibbs' exegesis on Benjamin's critique of "history" is pertinent here:

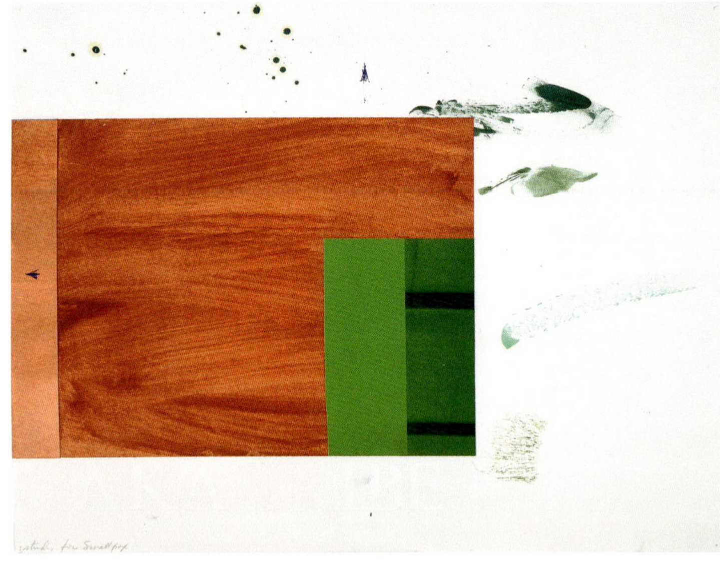

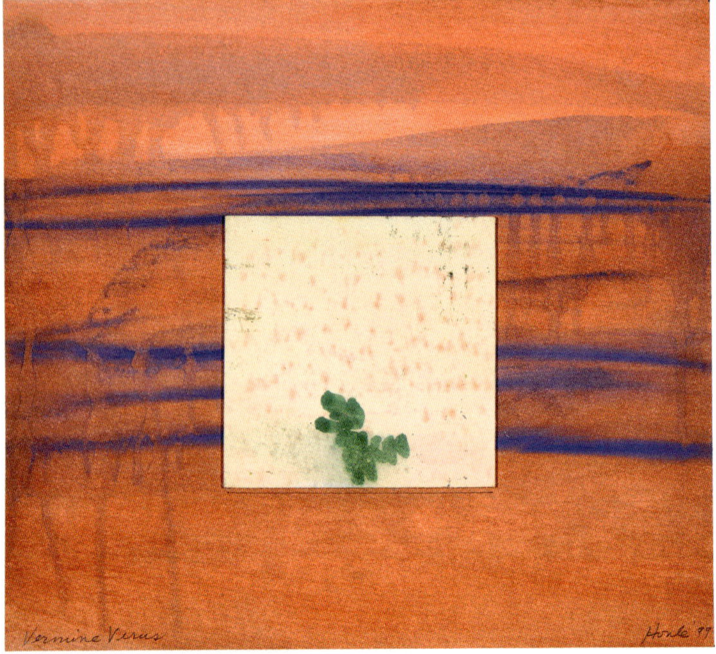

FIG. 6 (TOP)
Robert Houle, Study for *Smallpox*, 1999. Acrylic, collage, vinyl lettering, and graphite on paper, 45.7 × 61 cm. 2000-001-003.

FIG. 7 (BOTTOM)
Robert Houle, *Vermine Virus*, 1999. Watercolour and graphite on paper, 27.8 × 31 cm. 2000-001-004.

Both works: Collection of the MacKenzie Art Gallery, purchased with the financial support of the Canada Council for the Arts Acquisition Assistance Program.
Photos: Don Hall, courtesy of the MacKenzie Art Gallery.

> The risk of studying "history" is that one will not challenge the present, but will interpret it as justified (The world's history as the world's judgment). That challenge to the winners, moreover, is distributable over not only the past, but also the transmission of the past, the winner's stories through time. The task of juxtaposing dialectical images is not merely asymmetric with respect to time, but also bears a unique responsibility for the past ... for the past as unjust.[26]

This is the kind of *history* advocated by some critics of conventional "history"[27] following suggestive insights of authors such as Baudrillard, who advocated alternatives to the familiar conventional linear forms. The notion of a "poetic alternative to the disenchanted confusion, the chaotic profusion of present events"[28] has some definite resonance with Houle's eight green monochrome panels placed deliberately to insist upon their completion as poetic postmodern "imaginaries."

Houle's *history* holds much in common with the *petit-narratives* advocated by Lyotard as an antidote to the erasure of particulars in the metanarratives of universal "history." The proliferation of local narratives offers the possibility of survival for difference and radical alterity. Conventional "history," exclusively past-looking, is no longer suitable in our postmodern times. Robert Jenkins extends his polemical argument to the notion of ethics: "its demise coincides with the rise of 'knowledge' of the undecidability of the (moral) decision."[29]

Excerpt from the exhibition catalogue for Robert Houle's Palisade *(2001). Carleton University Art Gallery.*

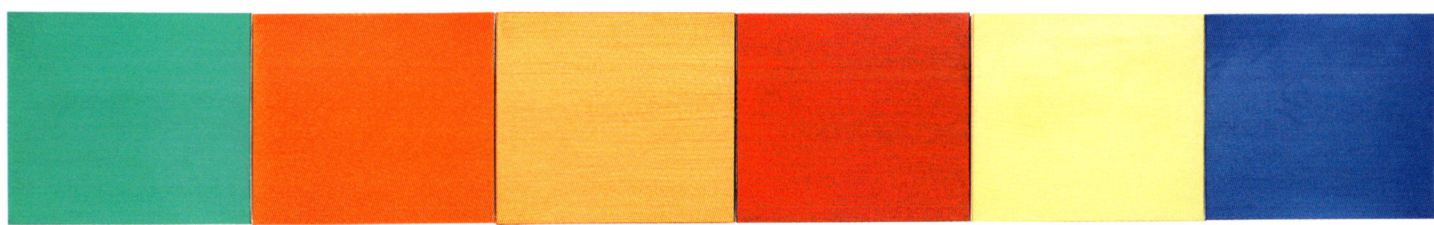

FIG. 8
Robert Houle, *Untitled (Palisade colour bar)*, 2006. Oil on wood, 25 × 183.5 × 4 cm.
Collection of Grant Wedge & Bob Crouch.
Photo: Art Gallery of Ontario

1. First installed in Saskatoon under the auspices of TRIBE, and subsequently purchased by the Mackenzie Art Gallery, Regina. Carleton University Art Gallery undertook to exhibit the installation in the interim.
2. See Curtis J. Collins, *Hochelaga: A Multi-Media Installation by Robert Houle* (Montreal: Articule, 1992).
3. Michael Bell, *Kanata: Robert Houle's Histories* (Ottawa: Carleton University Art Gallery, 1993). The mixed-media work central to this installation, the multi-panelled painting/drawing containing a grisaille replica of Benjamin West's *The Death of General Wolfe*, is in the collection of the National Gallery of Canada, where the most important version of the West painting is located.
4. Originally installed in the Vancouver Art Gallery exhibition, *Beyond History* (1989), this multimedia installation was reinstalled, for a second time, in the Agnes Etherington Art Centre, Queen's University, Kingston, in 1992. It was reinstalled again (October 21, 2000 – March 18, 2001), subsequent to its purchase by the Kingston gallery in 1998 with a grant from the Canada Council for the Arts Acquisition Assistance program.
5. Garnet Press Gallery, Toronto, 1996.
6. Included in the exhibition *Sovereignty Our Subjectivity* (Winnipeg Art Gallery, 1999) and now in the collection of the Museum of Contemporary Art Toronto.
7. The dictionary definitions throughout are derived from *The Random House Dictionary of English Usage* (unabridged edition), 1974—with one exception: the World Health Assembly.
8. The artist conceived the work in imperial measure. With a modest reduction in size, the panels echo the proportions of the body. The repetitive application of colour, contributing to intense depth, also gives each canvas a strong presence of the body.
9. See note 17.
10. *National Post*, 29 May 1999 (reprint of a column from *The New York Times*).
11. The relevant sections are excerpted in *Jeffrey Amherst and Smallpox Blankets*: http://nativeweb.org/pages/legal/amherst/lord_jeff.html (2000.10.11). Houle obtained his images of the manuscripts from this site.
12. The *infected blanket* is echoed in Eric Robinson and Henry Bird Quinney, *The Infested Blanket* (Winnipeg: Queenston House Publishing, 1985), xx–xxi: "When Canada brought its Constitution 'home' from London in 1982, it knowingly backed out of the Treaty agreements which were solemnly signed between the First Nations and the British Crown... The first colonialists were sometimes not aware that the blankets they distributed to the Indians were festering with disease, and so too now, many Canadians think that they are doing Indians a big favour by weaving Indians into the fabric of Canada's Constitution and Confederation. Yet to do so and the way it is set-out and determined by non-Indians, is to kill off the Sovereignty of Indian Nationhood.... Unfortunately, too many Indian people and leaders are craving so desperately for political recognition of any type from Canada, that they are willing to accept the deluding warmth of the Constitutional blanket. Just as Indians before did not know that the blankets needed for warmth were disease-ridden, so, also today many do not realize the killing power of the Constitution. Yet the result is the same as before—genocide."
13. "After the surrender of Canada in 1760, fighting ceased in North America, although the war continued elsewhere in the world and French forces in the west remained ready to resume hostilities if given the opportunity. In military calculations the western garrisons of the French represented a threat to security that Amherst with habitual thoroughness determined to eliminate by systematically replacing French troops with British." Francis Jennings, *Empire of Fortune*, 439.
14. Sir William Johnson was the consummate negotiator with the Indigenous peoples [amended from "Indians" to reflect the Art Gallery of Ontario's house style as of 2018], although Amherst would ignore his recommendations. The denial of presents—especial ammunition so that they could hunt to feed themselves—condemned them to starvation. See Olive P. Dickason, *Canada's First Nations: A History of Founding Peoples from Earliest Times* (Toronto: McClelland and Stewart, 1992), 181.
15. Howard H. Peckham, *Pontiac and the Indian Uprising*, 119–120. See also Olive P. Dickason, Canada's *First Nations*, 179 ff.
16. See Anthony F.C. Wallace, *The Death and Rebirth of the Seneca* (New York: Alfred A. Knopf, 1970), 117.
17. The clearest and most succinct presentation of this Indian Defensive War (1763–1764) occurs in R. Cole Harris, ed., and Geoffrey J. Matthews, cartographer, *Historical Atlas of Canada*, Vol. 1, *From the Beginning to 1800* (Toronto: University of Toronto Press, 1987), plate 44 (W.J. Eccles, M.N. McConnell, and Susan L. Laskin).
18. Howard H. Peckham, *Pontiac and the Indian Uprising*, 131–132.
19. The director of the Center for Civilian Biodefense Studies, D.A. Henderson, wrote in January 1999: "Smallpox was probably first used as a biological weapon during the French and Indian Wars (1754–1767) by British forces in North America ... the potential threat of smallpox as a bioweapon greatly diminished after Jenner's discovery of vaccination in 1796 ... in fact, the possible use of smallpox as a biological weapon received almost no attention until the last few years." *Risk of a Deliberate Release of Smallpox Virus; Its Impact on Virus Destruction*: http://www.hopkinsbiodefense.org/pages/news/meeting.html (2000.10.11). Henderson led the WHO program to eradicate the smallpox virus.

[20] D.A. Henderson, *Risk of a Deliberate Release on Smallpox Virus*, n.p.

[21] E. Wagner Stearn and Allen E. Stearn, *The Effect of Smallpox on the Destiny of the American Indian*, 45 (my emphasis). There is still discussion about this event and the British intention. See the newsgroup archive posted as http://www2.hnet.msu.edu/~west/threads/disc-smallpox.html

[22] D.A. Henderson, Unofficial memo for the record, Meeting of the WHO Variola Research Committee, December 6–9, 1999: http://hopkinsbiodefense.org/pages/news/meeting.html (2000.10.11).

[23] D.A. Henderson, *Risk of a Deliberate Release on Smallpox Virus*, n.p.

[24] For an engaging and wide-ranging discussion of irony in contemporary culture, see Linda Hutcheon, *Irony's Edge: The Theory and Politics of Irony* (London: Routledge, 1994). Chapters 1, 4, and 7 are particularly relevant.

[25] Wars were notorious for spreading disease, since there was often rapid movement of potentially infected individuals over large distances.

[26] Robert Gibbs, *Why Ethics?*, 365.

[27] See Keith Jenkins, *Why History? Ethics and Postmodernity* (London: Routledge, 2000).

[28] Jean Baudrillard quoted in Jenkins, *Why History?*, 69.

[29] Keith Jenkins, *Why History?*, 89.

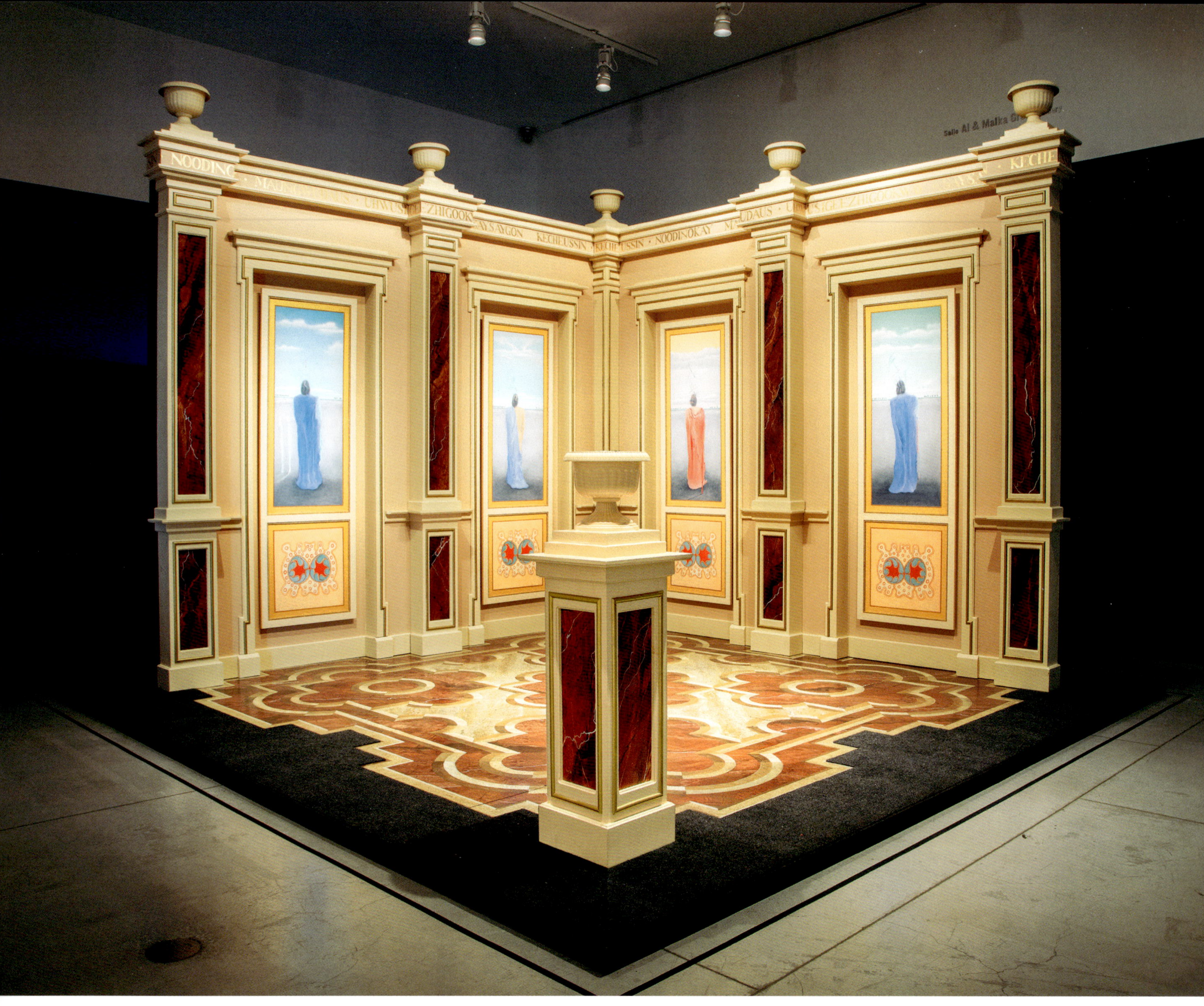

Installation view of *Paris/Ojibwa*, 2010, at the Art Gallery of Ontario

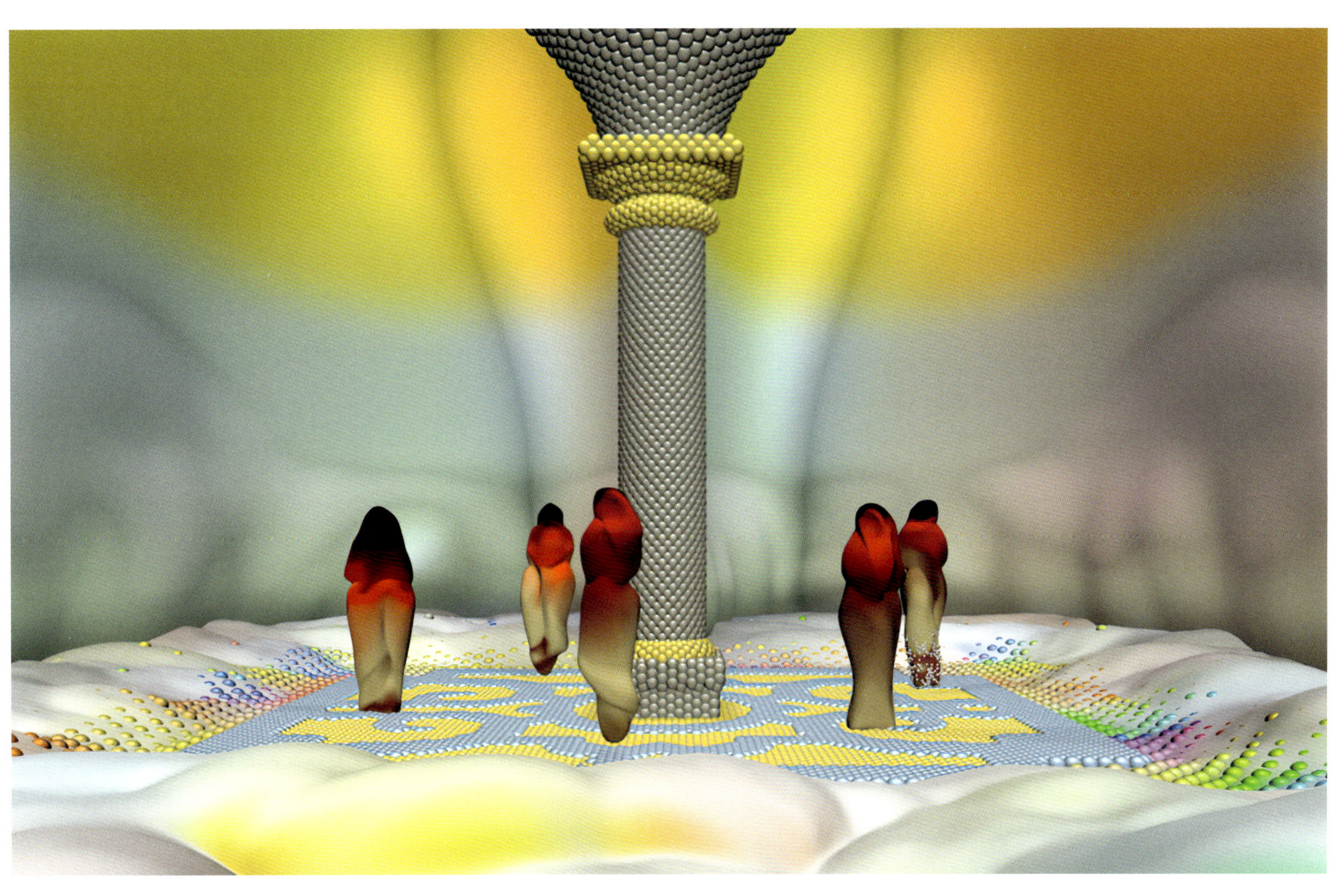

Paris/Ojibwa, 2010 (video still detail of *uhnemekéka*)

Ojibwa *Tableaux Vivants*: George Catlin, Robert Houle, and Transcultural Materialism

Jessica L. Horton

In 1846, thirteen Ojibwa men, women, and children performed *tableaux vivants* or "living pictures" for audiences in Paris. In 2010, Saulteaux artist, curator, and critic Robert Houle (b. 1947) created *Paris/Ojibwa* (fig. 1), an archive, salon, and stage set in which paintings of the past Ojibwa appear poised to perform again.[1] Crossing the historical distance between 1846 and 2010, as well as the ontological distinction typically drawn between live bodies and static pictures, Houle's installation prompts timely questions about the "new materialisms" that have lately preoccupied scholars across disciplines.[2]

...

Paris/Ojibwa

Paris/Ojibwa evolved from Houle's encounter with a sketch by French painter Eugène Delacroix (1798–1863) during a residency at Cité des Arts in Paris in 2006. *Cinq etudie d'Indiens* depicts members of a party of travelling Ojibwa performers led by the Methodist-educated Maungwudaus in Paris in 1846, all wearing robes and head ornaments and in various states of repose (fig. 2) Houle recalls the first time he saw it:

> Seeing the sketch at the Louvre's Pavillon de Flore, le department des arts graphique was like traveling back in time to when [Delacroix] first drew it, looking fresh, every line an immediacy of romantic passion. Foreign and coming from a former colony, I sat at a large table in a salon with a gilded ornate ceiling, putti holding garlands at the cornices, and drew directly from the study. The moment was intimidating and inspirational, surrounded by empire and glory, art as a frontier without cultural borders (fig. 3).[3]

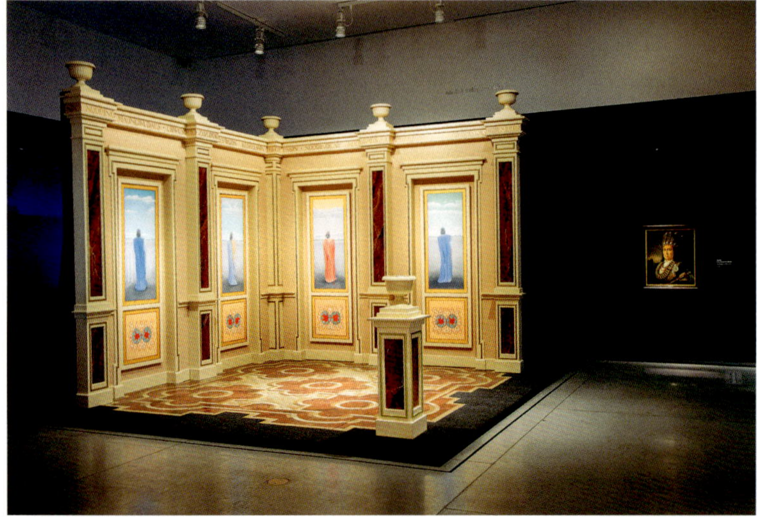

FIG. 1
Robert Houle, *Paris/Ojibwa*, 2010. Installation view as part of *Toronto: Tributes + Tributaries, 1971–1989*, at the Art Gallery of Ontario, September 29, 2016 – May 22, 2017. Photo: Art Gallery of Ontario.

The resulting sketches provided source material for four painted panels, which the artist embedded in the bas-relief walls of *Paris/Ojibwa*.[4] Together with the raised faux marble floor and abbreviated freestanding colonnade, the panels bring to mind the grand salons of "Paris, capital of the nineteenth century," where Ojibwa and French elites entertained one another in 1846 (fig. 1).[5] At the Canadian Cultural Center in Paris where *Paris/Ojibwa* was first exhibited in 2010, visitors could walk around the facade to witness exposed wooden beams suggestive of a stage set. They could also browse nearby displays of preliminary sketches, reproductions of artworks, and historical documents that informed Houle's process. *Paris/Ojibwa* is simultaneously a salon, theatre, and archive. The painted Ojibwa people the otherwise empty stage, encouraging us to imagine that pictures might perform.

Paris/Ojibwa reformulates the history and function of *tableaux vivants*, a pastime in which human actors assume static positions to mimic scenes culled from painting and literature. Popular in public theatres and private parlours on both sides of the Atlantic in the eighteenth and nineteenth centuries, *tableaux vivants* appealed to American artist and entrepreneur George Catlin, who was in the business of picturing Natives. When he toured his famed Indian Gallery across Europe from 1839 to 1846, he hired groups of British actors, followed by three travelling parties of Iowa and Ojibwa performers, to stage variations on his painted portraits and scenes of Native Americans. Today, the Indian Gallery is widely recognized as an archetype of salvage ethnography, representing Catlin's attempt to preserve cultures that he believed were disappearing due to the advent of modernity.[6] We are left to recollect the travelling Ojibwa in two dimensions, primarily through Catlin's many words and pictures.

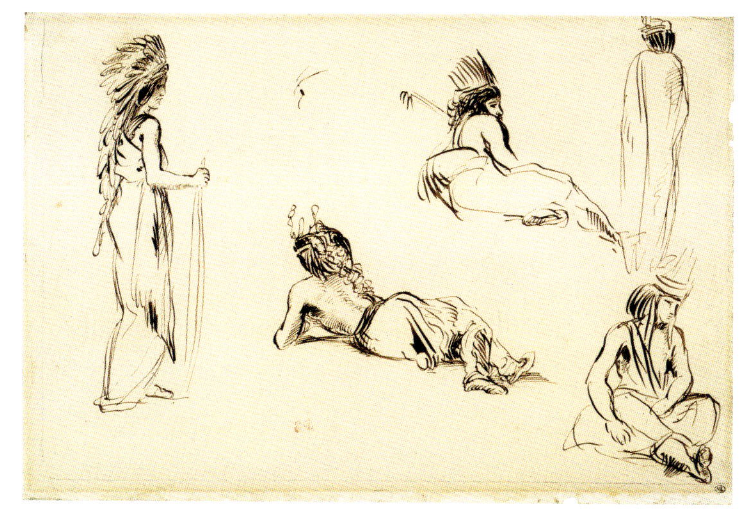

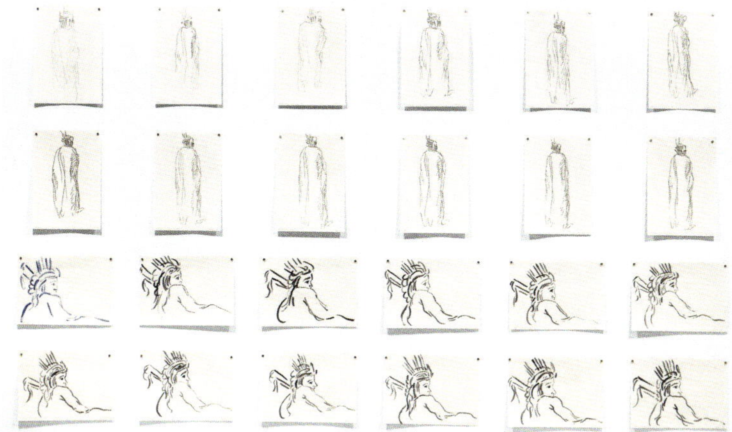

FIG. 2 (TOP)
Eugène Delacroix, *Five Studies of Ojibwa Indians [Cinq études d'indiens Ojibwas]*, 1845. Pen and brown ink on vellum, 25.6 × 38.7 cm. Musée du Louvre, Paris. RF 9311 recto. Photo: Thierry Le Mage; © RMN-Grand Palais / Art Resource, NY.

FIG. 3 (BOTTOM))
Robert Houle, *Paris/Ojibwa Studies*, 2006. Graphite on paper and watercolour on paper, each 27.9 × 21.6 cm. Courtesy of the artist.
Photo: Michael Cullen, TPG Digital Art Services.

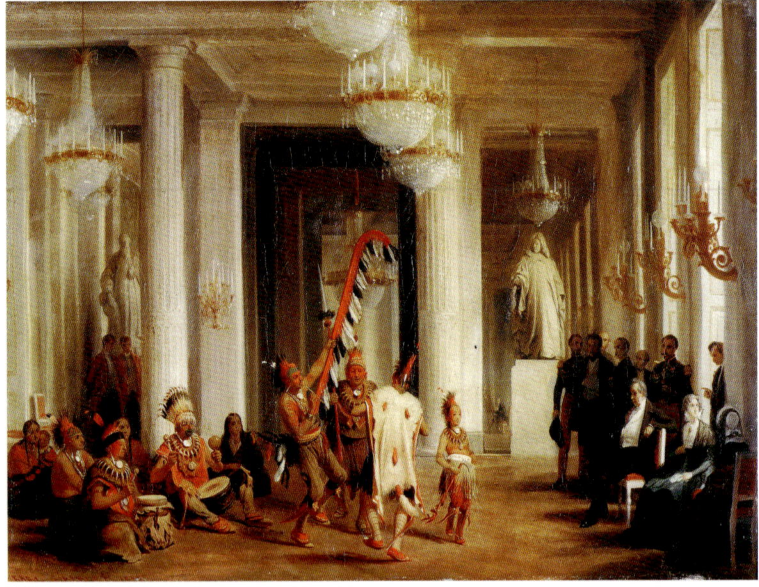

Paris/Ojibwa looks to *tableaux vivants* to enliven a different story. As Indigenous men, women, and children performed alongside the Indian Gallery, they were painted and sketched by Catlin, Delacroix, and other European artists, participating in an unsettling chain of bodies-turned-pictures-turned-bodies-turned pictures. As I will explore, *tableaux vivants* gave shape to … hybrid forms that mediate between modern, European categories of human and nonhuman, nature and culture. Furthermore, *Paris/Ojibwa* helps us to see that Indigenous performances of *tableaux vivants* incorporated an Ojibwa understanding of the potential liveliness of images and objects. Embodying complex notions of personhood, *tableaux vivants* reversed the ambitions of nineteenth-century ethnography: instead of turning living Natives into static images, they made way for the reanimation of pictures. By inviting contemporary visitors to realize this potential, Houle makes visible "the possibilities hidden on the canvases, invisible in public records, and therefore hidden from history."[7] …

FIG. 4
Karl Girardet, *Danse d'Indiens Iowas aux Tuileries*, 1845. Oil on canvas, 39 × 53.5 cm. Chateaux de Versailles et de Trianon, France. MV 6138.

Infecting Abstraction

Paris/Ojibwa reinterprets the archive of Ojibwa *tableaux vivants* in Europe. But understanding Houle's methods first requires a detour through another, specifically art historical narrative: modernism as a sequence of developments in abstraction. I begin by defining abstraction in conventional terms as the emptying out—to varying degrees—of the referent. The painted panels of the installation pointedly omit references to the fulsome details of Catlin's portraits as well as European artists' contemporaneous paintings of Natives, such as Delacroix's iconic *The Natchez* (1835), dramatizing the fate of the Natchez during the eighteenth-century French and Indian War, and French court painter Karl Girardet's image of the Iowa performing for King Louis Philippe in 1845 (fig. 4).[8] Such saturated paintings of dark-skinned peoples functioned, in Linda Nochlin's words, as "a stage for the playing out, from a suitable distance, of forbidden passions—the artist's own fantasies."[9] Instead, Houle chose to foreground Delacroix's spare and comparatively undervalued drawing of the performers, a work whose high degree of abstraction heralded modernism for some, even as it participated in a French academic tradition of freehand drawing from models (see fig. 2).[10]

Paris/Ojibwa deepens Houle's prior engagement with abstraction's multicultural heritage. Scholars have by now thoroughly critiqued the colonial dynamics of art history for valorizing the formal innovations of primarily white modernists in Europe and the U.S., many of whom drew inspiration from the arts of "primitive" peoples but relegated their makers to the parallel, self-contained discourse of ethnography.[11] Beginning in the 1980s, Houle dedicated much of his oeuvre to redressing this exclusionary narrative by merging celebrated characteristics of paintings by Kazimir Malevich, Piet Mondrian, Barnett Newman, and others with Indigenous iconographies, materials, and histories. Art historian Mark Cheetham analyzes Houle's grids and colour-field paintings using a metaphor of contamination, arguing that they "infect" the classic Greenbergian account of modern painting as an evolution toward "optical purity." Reversing the process whereby the canvas is emptied of outside referents, Houle deploys abstraction to *fill in* what is missing from a dominant art historical genealogy, namely the agency of Indigenous subjects and objects.[12]

...

If quills were agents of infection in Houle's early work, paint in turn promised rehabilitation. The artist saw in painting the potential to restore life to Indigenous materials left for dead inside of ethnographic museums. His intimate experiences with a range of Canadian institutions undoubtedly shaped this dual approach. Houle grew up with the trauma of an abusive residential school system designed to assimilate Indigenous children through Christian edification, still active until 1996.[13] At the same time, he spent weekends on the Sandy Bay First Nation Reserve in Manitoba, where he received an education in Saulteaux spirituality and oral culture.[14] In 1977 he was appointed the first Curator of Contemporary Indian Art at the National Museum of Man (now the Canadian Museum of History), only to resign three years later. He protested the institution's treatment of historical and contemporary Native art as "extensions of the ethnological collections, without any appreciation of their esthetic values." He recalled spending his last day sketching in the galleries:

> [S]urrounded by all those objects, presented in a context that isolated them from life and reality, all I could think of was that I wanted to liberate them. How do I do that? I am leaving. What can I do to breath life into them, to show that they still matter? In desperation I sketched these lifeless objects, and decided that this would be my project for the next little while. Up until last year [1987] I concentrated on making parfleches and warrior staffs, trying to rehabilitate those objects I left behind.[15]

Houle further elaborated his vision that contemporary art might redress Indigenous objects "despoiled through curatorial greed" when he co-curated the influential exhibition, *Land, Spirit, Power: First Nations Art at the National Gallery of Canada*, in 1992, the year of the Columbus Quincentennary. In the accompanying catalogue he wrote that living artists, heirs to "the spiritual legacy of the ancient ones," could "make use of the powers evoked by this historic backdrop in their own artworks."[16]

...

Paris/Ojibwa brings these ideas to fruition and takes a step beyond them. Houle's prior work privileged the contemporary artist as the agent responsible for "rehabilitating" the past from a present vantage point. He implicitly accepted the power of Western institutions and discourses to render historical materials "lifeless," awaiting rescue. Houle's postmodern mission left the parallel pasts of modernism and ethnography intact without touching. Translating between "the spiritual legacy of the ancient ones" and Delacroix's drawing, *Paris/Ojibwa* locates Indigenous meanings near the beginning, rather than the end of the modernist queue, reminding us that art history and ethnography have long been mutually "infected." By drawing out possibilities

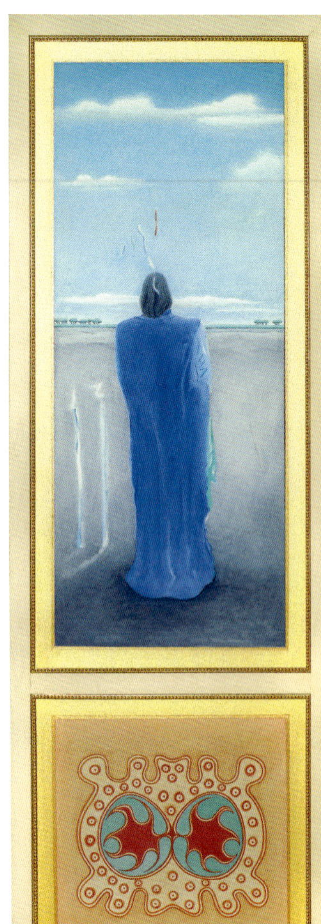
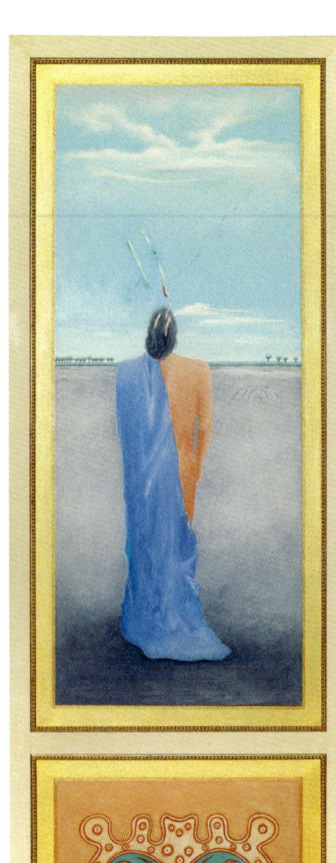
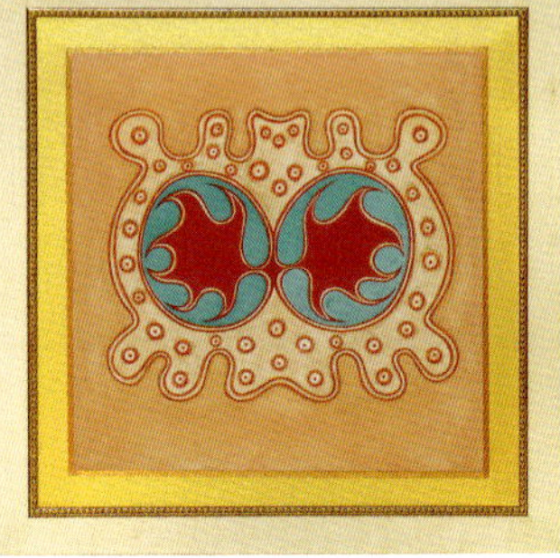
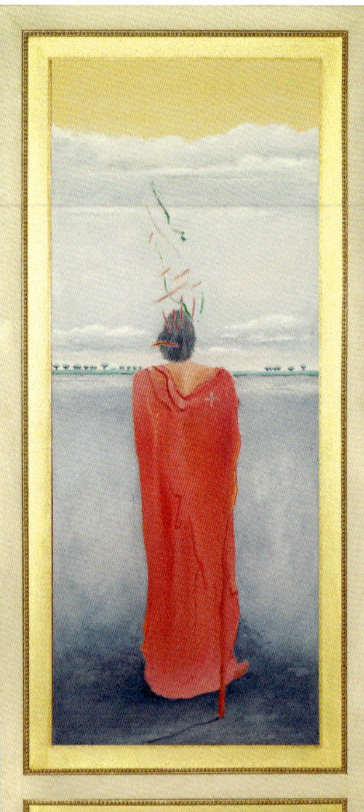
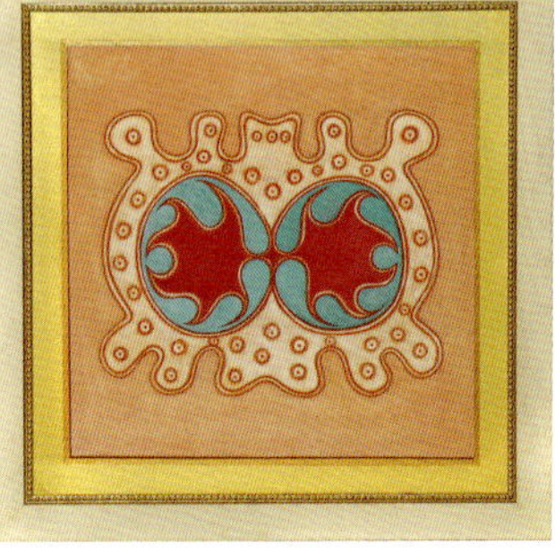
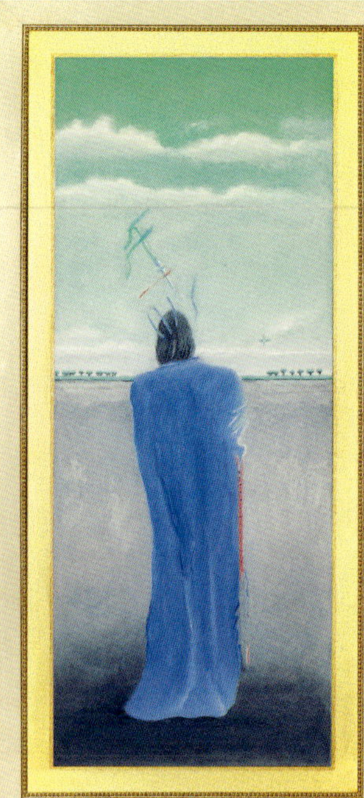
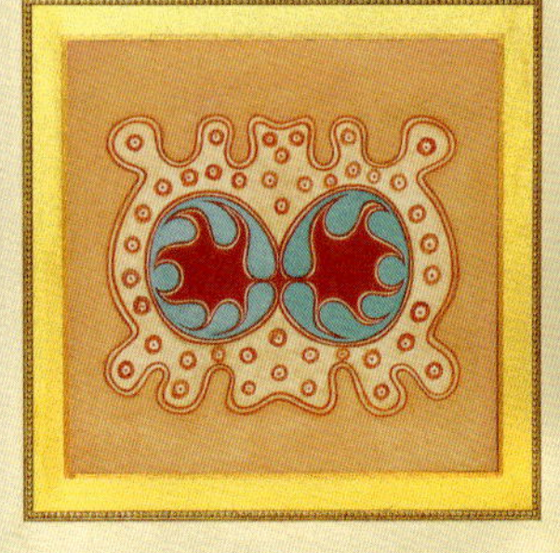

that were present in archives all along, the contemporary artist becomes the recipient, as well as the purveyor, of historical lessons. As Houle translated sketches of Delacroix's drawing into oil paint, headdresses worn by the Ojibwa disintegrated into a confetti of bright wavy lines (see fig. 5). It is as if the ghostly extraneous squiggles found elsewhere on Delacroix's page, likely contours begun and abandoned, migrated and concentrated above the heads of the Ojibwa. As I will elaborate, abstraction fills in what Catlin and Delacroix could not see: the presence of an Ojibwa spirit world manifested in images and objects. The lines suggest powers of vision beyond the average human eye, underscoring the spiritual capabilities that Houle ascribed to the figures by titling them Shaman, Healer, Dancer, and *Warrior* (generic English translations of complex Ojibwa concepts of *medáwenene, nóojemowenene, nahmidwenene,* and *megahzoownene*).[17] Rather than *look at* the figures (as Catlin's Indian Gallery and French Romantic canvases compel us to do), we are invited to *see like* them.

Other-than-Human Persons

The halos surrounding the figures' heads bring to mind the "wavy or castellated … power lines" that art historian Ruth Phillips identifies surrounding representations of spiritual helpers, or *manitos*, on Ojibwa twined bags from the eighteenth century.[18] Similar abstract renditions of powerful cosmological beings appear on a wide range of Ojibwa objects before and after contact with Europeans, including painted robes, quillwork pouches, *parfleche*, birchbark scrolls used by shamans of the still-active Midewiwin Society, and musical instruments used to communicate with spirits (fig. 6). Phillips explains that "representations were not merely mementos of [an individual's] vision, they were imbued with a part of the power he had received."[19] Images are an extension of the *manitos*, upon whose goodwill the Ojibwa depend for mental and physical thriving. *Manitos* can also be present in nondescript environmental features such as certain stones and plants. This begins to explain why objects understood to be wholly static in a European worldview are classified as animate in the Ojibwa language. Anthropologist Irving A. Hallowell summarizes this difference in a respected essay first published in 1960: "The concept of 'person' is not, in fact, synonymous with human being but transcends it … '[S]ocial relations' between human beings and other-than-human 'persons' are of cardinal significance."[20] One characteristic that all persons

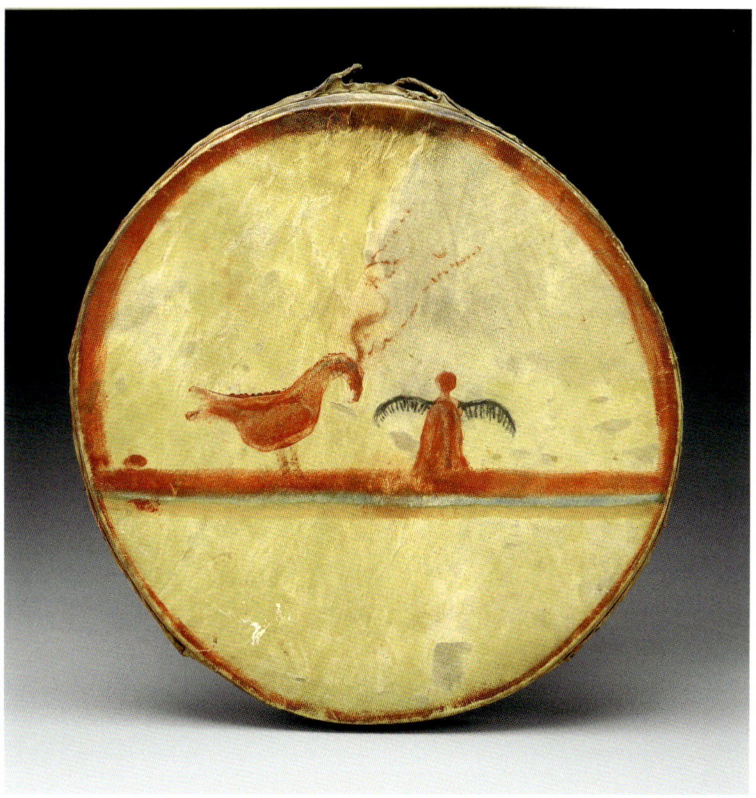

FIG. 5 (OPPOSITE)
Robert Houle, "Shaman," "Warrior," "Dancer," and "Healer" details from *Paris/Ojibwa*, 2010. Framed oil on canvas, each 71.5 × 214 cm. Art Gallery of Ontario, gift of Robert Houle, with funds by exchange from a gift in memory of J.G. Althouse from Isobel Althouse Wilkinson and John Provost Wilkinson, 2020. 2020/3.
Photo: Michael Cullen, TPG Digital Art Services.

FIG. 6 (ABOVE)
Chippewa Culture (possibly), Drum, c. 1840. Wood, deerhide, iron nails, and pigment, 53.3 × 52.7 × 7.6 cm. Detroit Institute of Arts, gift of Deborah S. and Richard A. Pohrt, Jr., 1991.1022.

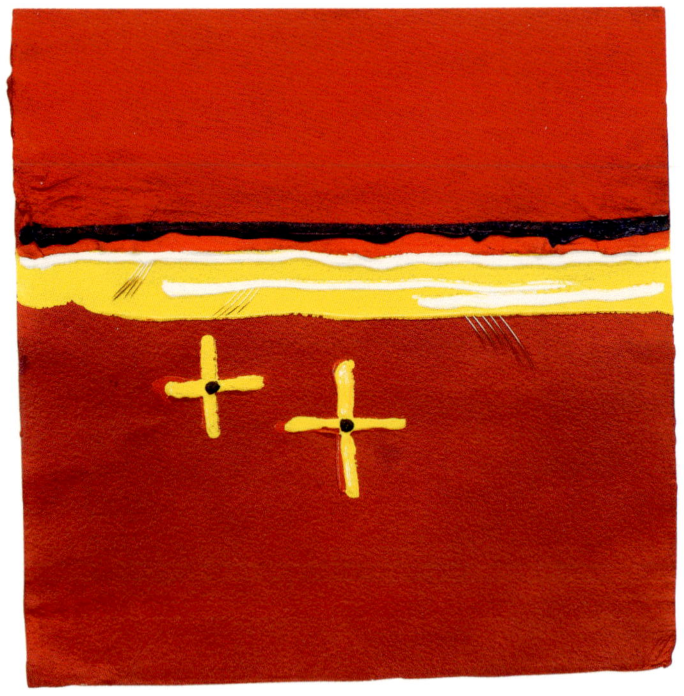

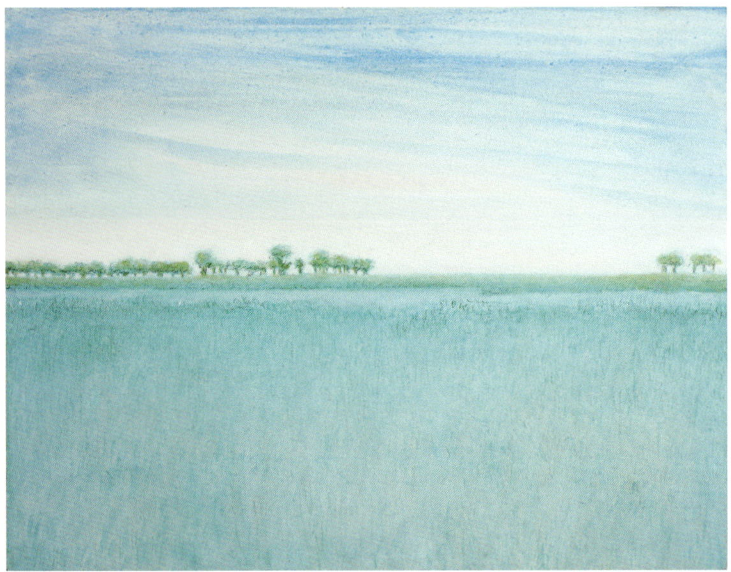

share is a vital part, a soul, which is detachable from the body and may reappear in a new form in another time and place.[21] Representations are privileged sites within the larger class of materials imbued with soul, allowing humans to directly influence the *manitos* through formal means. Ojibwa "living pictures" inscribed on clothing, pouches, and drums invite spiritual guardianship for precarious life journeys.[22]

...

By the mid-nineteenth century, the missionization of the Ojibwa led many—Maungwudaus, for one—to revise Ojibwa spiritual practices to accommodate Christian ideas and stories, while stopping short of full religious assimilation.[23] The testimonies that Hallowell gathered from Saulteaux individuals in the 1930s described a physical world alive with other-than-human transactions, undivided by missionary accounts of a distant heaven.[24] *Paris/Ojibwa* likewise attests that Ojibwa philosophies have persisted, absorbing new meanings through colonization, to offer valid perspectives on a modernity shared with Europeans.[25]

As I have already hinted, the installation shares this "spiritual legacy of the ancient ones" with visitors in the form of a visual lesson. The abstract lines that congregate over the figures heads simultaneously deflect ethnographic curiosity and redirect our gaze over their shoulders, toward a shimmering horizon. The mottled colour-field skies echo the backdrops of Catlin's portraits, only beneath Houle's hand they grow and command attention. While the blue skies of *Warrior* and *Shaman* appear naturalistic, the green and orange expanses opening beyond the clouds in *Healer* and *Dancer* hint at the celestial origin narratives of the Ojibwa.[26] A narrow treed horizon line, repeated in all four panels, separates vivid skies from the liminal fields of grey in which the figures stand. The horizon has a physical referent: it is a view of the prairie

FIG. 7 (TOP)
Robert Houle, *Parfleche #5, Philip*, 1983, from *Parfleches for the Last Supper*. Acrylic and porcupine quills on paper, 56 × 56 cm. Collection of the Winnipeg Art Gallery, gift of Mr. Carl T. Grant, Artvest Inc., G-86-464.
Photo: Serge Gumenyuk courtesy of the Winnipeg Art Gallery.

FIG. 8 (BOTTOM)
Robert Houle, *Sandy Bay*, 2007. Oil on Masonite, 22.9 × 29.8 cm. Courtesy of the artist.
Photo: Michael Cullen, TPG Digital Art Services.

from the First Nations cemetery near Lake Manitoba, where Houle's grandfather harvested marsh grasses for his cattle and horses. The equal-arm cross visible in *Parfleches for the Last Supper #5: Philip* reappears above the horizon lines in the *Warrior* and *Healer* paintings, again calling to mind the Christian crosses that mark the Indigenous graves (see fig. 5 and fig. 7). The artist has photographed and painted the horizon many times; one small canvas appears among the exhibited research materials of *Paris/Ojibwa* (fig. 8). When recycled in the panels, the view becomes a physically impossible one. Houle paints Ojibwa who didn't make it home alive, but rather faced their lands from a cemetery across the ocean. To glimpse the same green horizon snapped by Houle's twentieth-century camera, they—and those of us peering over their shoulder—must look beyond the limits of the body, across temporal and spatial boundaries, over the very threshold of death.

Ojibwa life after death corresponds to an actual geography: the spirits of the dead, or *djibaiyak*, travel a long road to the south to the land of *djíbaiaking*, where they carry on lives parallel to those of their living relatives, though with more plentiful resources and without threat of death. Knowledge of this locale, at least as described by twentieth-century Ojibwa, is experiential rather than dogmatic; the living catch glimpses when, in rare circumstances, individuals transcend mundane flesh during severe illness, dreams, or ceremonies to travel south for a visit with the dead, returning to tell of their experience.[27] *Medáwenene, nóojemowenene, nahmidwenene,* and *megahzoownene* are especially powerful communicators across the permeable and occasionally reversible boundary between living and dead. Humans may also contact ancestors by leaving offerings of food, tea, and tobacco at their graves. When travellers encounter these sites, they are invited to enjoy the offerings as they would during a hospitable visit with the living, thus carrying on a relationship with the deceased. In turn the *djibaiyak* may occasionally return in physical form to their burial sites, retaining a friendly interest in their living kin.[28] This material tradition is invoked in *Paris/Ojibwa* by a tobacco offering, visible in the urn atop the shortened column that marks the fourth corner of the stage (fig. 1).[29]

In addition to food, drink, and smoke, music travels easily from north to south. The *djibaiyak* are happy when they hear human drumming and in turn they sing, dance, and drum at night (see fig. 6). The deceased may be sent to the grave with a drum as company in the afterlife; the Ojibwa sometimes call the drum "grandfather," a flexible term used for ancestors, in recognition of the liminal qualities of travelling sound. Recorded drums permeate the stage of *Paris/Ojibwa*. They are entwined with the voices of a Blackfeet band, Kicking Woman Singers, performing a traditional Grand Entry song, and carry forward the rhythmic sound of water striking stone that begins the looping soundtrack. The audio of *Paris/Ojibwa* extends the centuries-old role of the drum, a social link between humans and other-than-human persons, across the ocean.

Smallpox and Steamboats

The affirmative sound and images of *Paris/Ojibwa* are shadowed by an entity aligned with death in both European and Native imaginations: the smallpox virus. The appearance of the disease is critical to Houle's treatment of Indigenous performers in Europe, given that it has powerfully shaped their legacy as victims of colonial objectification. Below *Shaman, Warrior, Dancer,* and *Healer* are square paintings of fleshy pink containing identical turquoise ovals with scalloped edges and vivid, spiny splashes of red at centre (fig. 5). Together with the painted Ojibwa, they form a vertical diptych; neither can be read without the other in mind. The graceful, stylized forms call to mind images of the peanut-shaped microorganism tinted and viewed through the lens of a microscope. Houle's motif merges this ominous reference with yet another that connotes Indigenous flourishing: an abstract design repeated across the surface of a buffalo robe he encountered in the collections at the Musée du quai Branly in Paris, reproduced in the archival section of the installation (fig. 9). Although little is known about the buffalo robe's ovoid motif, Houle refers to it as a "mnemonic style of painting" traditional to his culture.... Painted hides like this were traded or gifted between nations, communicating the political sovereignty, cultural survival, and adaptability of Native groups.... Can the ancestral power adhering in aged robes be reconciled with smallpox, a disease long associated with colonial exploitation and the decimation of Indigenous communities?

Smallpox devastated Indigenous populations across the Americas from the earliest moments of European contact.... Although exact numbers are difficult to ascertain, the Ojibwa were hit especially hard in the eighteenth century; an estimated fifty to seventy-five percent of those living west and north of Grand Portage (including Manitoba) died in the great epidemic of 1780–1783. Another wave struck the Ojibwa and their neighbours in Manitoba, Saskatchewan, and Alberta in 1837, although vaccination campaigns significantly reduced the death toll. Ojibwa historical accounts regularly blamed the French and British colonialists for deliberately spreading smallpox to the Indians, as the mixed-heritage author William Warren notes in his *History of the Ojibway Nation*, first published in 1885.[33] ...

But the archive of the Ojibwa in Europe suggests an alternative to the neat bifurcation of life and death in familiar smallpox narratives.[34] In the materials exhibited alongside the stage of *Paris/Ojibwa*, Houle included a travelogue that Maungwudaus authored and published in 1848. The educated leader showed great promise as a missionary among his people following his conversion to Christianity in 1825, deemed "a good divine, a tolerable poet, and an excellent translator," by one Anglo reverend.[35] But he abruptly left the church following a disagreement with his half-brother, respected missionary Peter Jones, in 1840. To Jones's consternation, Maungwudaus inserted Ojibwa spiritual concepts into his translations of Christian hymns, a wilful "cross-pollinization of cultures" that he continued by organizing a dance troupe to travel in Europe four years later.[36] Upon his return, Maungwudaus put his pen to work, offering a counter-narrative to Catlin's mournful travelogue of the same year. In a terse thirteen pages, he litanies the travels, illnesses, and deaths of his Ojibwa family and friends in Europe. Yet he lavishes surprising detail on an account of peering, for the first time, into a microscope at a piece of cheese. He sees "hundreds of living creatures swimming in it: some like beasts, some like snakes, some like fish; some had wheels on each side of their bodies, and with these they were moving about like steamboats, hooking, chasing, fighting, killing and eating one another."[37] The microscope reveals an unexpected, lively world beyond the everyday appearance of objects. Here a tool of science, capable of

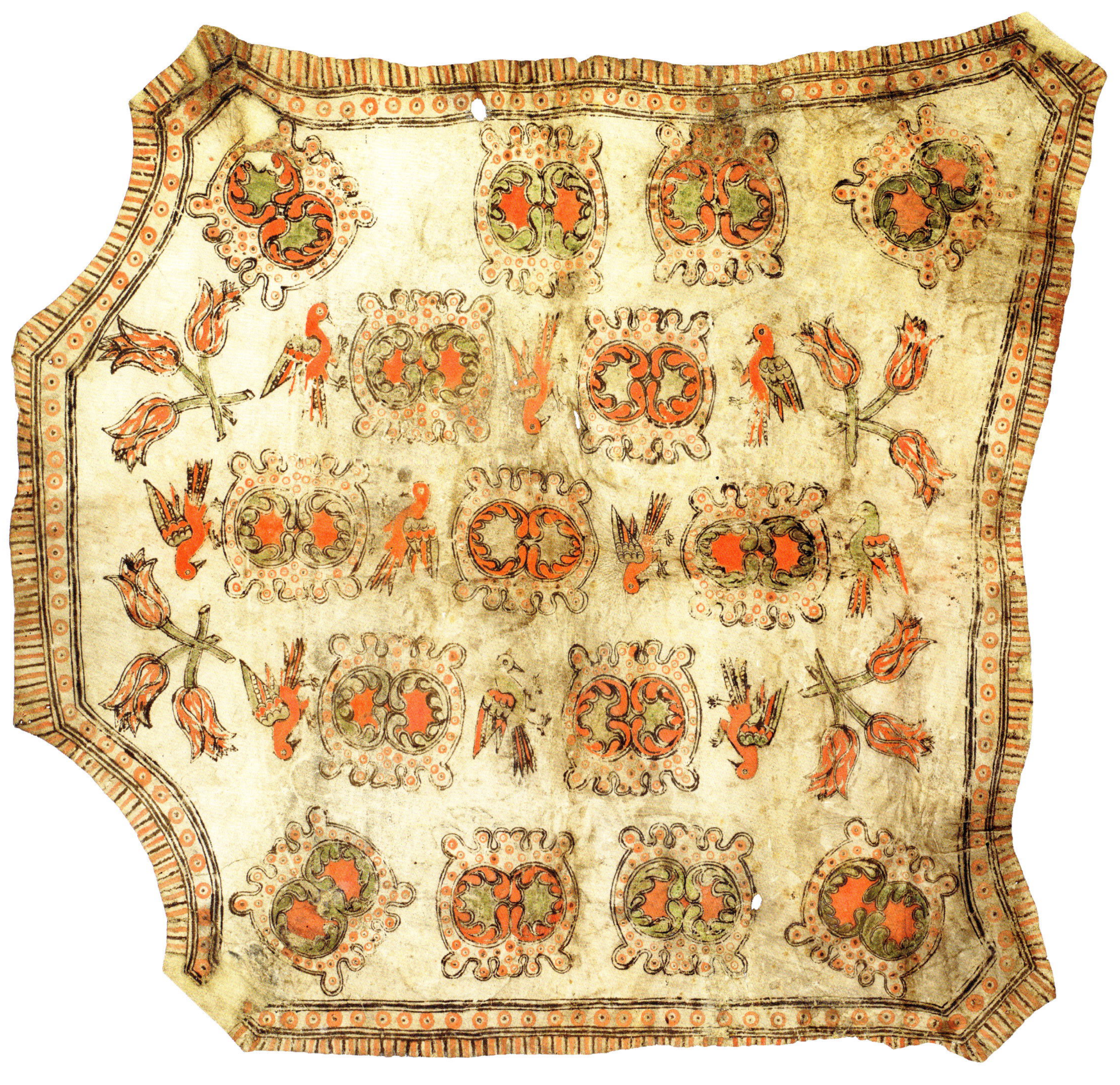

FIG. 9
Robe with birds and cartouches, eighteenth-century painted hide, 107 × 100 × 2 cm. Musée du quai Branly, Paris. Inv. 71.1878.32.161 Photo: Claude Germain © Musée du quai Branly – Jacques Chirac, Dist. RMN-Grand Palais / Art Resource, NY.

powerfully augmenting human vision, doubles back on itself, undermining the objectivity of the thing studied. Mediated by the microscope, cheese, that most mundane of French consumables, turns out to be a quasi-object.[38] Maungwudaus aptly links swimming microscopic organisms with the colonial vehicles that moved cheeses and diseases around the Americas and across the Atlantic.[39] He focuses on the unfixed nature of things, their transport across permeable boundaries between cultures and places as well as life and death.

In *Paris/Ojibwa*, Houle similarly channels viral imagery through a lively, travelling Ojibwa form, the buffalo robe. Smallpox joins the cast of living pictures, embedded in the stage alongside the upright figures of *Shaman*, *Warrior*, *Dancer*, and *Healer*, who see across the ocean and beyond the threshold of death. Ojibwa motifs appearing on painted drums, buffalo robes, and contemporary paintings attest that ancient ones may persist and reappear. As Hallowell explained, Saulteaux temporal orientation treats past and present as "part of a whole because they are bound together by the persistence and contemporary reality of mythological characters not even now grown old."[40] Likewise, Houle wrote, "The lack of a linear chronology in myth, storytelling, and dreams [recorded in art], the interchangeable grammar and the interchangeability of perception is what makes wonderful, rhythmical patterns of thought in the oral traditions of the ancient ones."[41] Humans may recall the upheavals of colonialism, acknowledge the horrors of disease, and mourn the death of loved ones. But they can also bring ancestors near again by performing songs and stories, touching a robe, or painting a line.

Transcultural Materialism

In *Paris/Ojibwa*,… Houle's earlier goal to "liberate" objects, "breathe life into them, to show that they still matter," is bolstered by a collaboration between contemporary and historical agents that counters the deadening effects of colonial institutions.… I close by imagining Ojibwa *tableaux vivants* as models of transcultural materialism, in which Europeans' own impurities meet those of colonized peoples and undergo translation in the same form. In his travel notes, Catlin describes the first time Ojibwa performers encountered his paintings in the Egyptian Hall in London, a scene with all the characteristics of a *tableau vivant:*

> As they entered the hall, the portraits of several hundred of the chiefs and warriors of their own tribe and of their enemies were hanging on the walls and staring at them from all directions, and wigwams, and costumes and weapons of all constructions around them: they set up the most frightful yells and made the whole neighbourhood ring with their howlings; they advanced to the portraits of their friends and offered them their hands; at their enemies, whom they occasionally recognized, they brandished their tomahawks or drew their bows as they sounded the war-whoop.[42]

Catlin hints that the response of the Ojibwas stemmed from their naive confusion between bodies and pictures; they mistook paintings for friends and enemies in the flesh. At the edges of the salon stood the mayor of London and his newspapermen, invited by Catlin to record the spectacle. The Ojibwas' behaviour flattered his abilities as an ethnographic painter and offered yet another "primitive" spectacle. Yet the scene perpetuated a chain of transactions that Catlin had already exposed by staging *tableaux vivants* with British actors, quasi-objects whose pleasures lay in their contamination of European categories of human and nonhuman, culture and nature. The Ojibwas introduced another, critical link in the chain, making it impossible to ignore Indigenous perspectives on the very pictures they came to embody. I think they knew exactly what they were looking at: powerful representations in which the souls of friends and enemies reside, other-than-human persons who demand social engagement in the form of a greeting.…

I have explored how *Paris/Ojibwa* draws this potential out of the archive, transforming the abstraction of Delacroix's lines into paintings of an Ojibwa environment enlivened by spiritual exchanges. Let us finally bring the four upright figures back into focus (see figs. 1 and 5). They stand at the border between a Manitoba landscape and a Parisian stage. Facing them from the other side of the theatre/archive/salon, we contemporary audiences are left with a choice of how to see. We can resume Catlin's ethnographic prompt to locate the Ojibwa in "their" world, assumed to be culturally, geographically, and temporally distant from ours. In this case the stage remains empty, a site for mourning Indigenous bodies razed by smallpox and the "animist" beliefs buried with them. Alternatively we might follow Houle's lesson and "offer them [our] hands." Now the stage expands in both directions, enveloping the figures and us in a chain of mediations linking pictures and bodies, Manitoba and Paris, Natives and Europeans, the nineteenth century and the present. The entire site of exhibition becomes a *tableaux vivant*, a generous space for transcultural materialism.

1 The Saulteaux are a branch of the Ojibwa First Nations who migrated into the western plains of present-day Canada from the Great Lakes region in the late eighteenth century under pressure from colonial settlement, epidemic disease, and the fur trade. The name means 'people of the falls' in French, referring to the concentration of Indigenous peoples French colonizers first encountered in the area of the trading post, Sault Ste. Marie. Many living today in northwestern Ontario and southern Manitoba prefer to call themselves Anishinabeg, meaning "first peoples." Laura Peers, *The Oj of Western Canada, 1780–1870*, St. Paul, 1994, ix–xviii. The Ojibwa who travelled under the leadership of Maungwudaus to Europe in 1845 were Mississauga from headwaters of the Grand River in south-central Ontario, not directly related to Houle.

2 See, for example, Jane Bennett, *Vibrant Matter: A Political Ecology of Things*, Durham, 2010; Bill Brown, ed., *Things*, Chicago, 2004; Diana Coole and Samantha Frost, eds., *New Materialisms: Ontology, Agency, and Politics*, Durham, 2010.

3 Robert Houle, 'A Transatlantic Return Home Through the Magic of Art' in Robert Houle et al., *Robert Houle's Paris/Ojibwa*, Peterborough, 2011, 52.

4 Houle commissioned the stage for *Paris/Ojibwa* from the Centaur Theatre scenery shop in Montreal upon his return from Paris. Although *Paris/Ojibwa* has travelled to exhibition venues in the U.S. and Canada, I focus on architectural and archival details from its debut at the Canadian Cultural Center in 2010. Beyond the scope of this essay is an animated video Houle commissioned from Parisian artist Hervé Dagois, titled *uhnemekéka* (2010), depicting a twentieth-century Ojibwa healing dance. Also not discussed are four performances by Barry Ace, a friend of Houle's and "a contemporary Southern Straight powwow dancer" who felt "an overwhelming sense of affinity with [the Ojibwa] dancers," in front of the Louvre and on the stage of *Paris/Ojibwa* at the opening in 2010. See Barry Ace, 'A Reparative Act,' 34 and Nelcya Delanoë, 'Making the Past Dance,' 24–33 in Houle et al., *Robert Houle's Paris/Ojibwa*.

5 Walter Benjamin coined this enduring phrase in a famous essay from 1935, "Paris, Capital of the Nineteenth Century," in *Reflections: Essays,* Aphorisms, *Autobiographical Writings*, ed. Peter Demetz, New York, 1986, 146–162.

6 For example, William B. Truettner calls Catlin's Indian Gallery a "beguiling veil of primitivism that he cast across the American West" in Truettner, *The Natural Man Observed: A Study of Catlin's Indian Gallery*, Fort Worth and Washington DC, 1979, 9. Contemporary Cree artist Kent Monkman has mocked and appropriated Catlin's legacy, primarily through the escapades of his alter-ego, Miss Chief Eagle Testickle, a sequined and feather-bedecked artist-anthropologist who undertakes an exhaustive taxonomy of the European male. On Monkman's subversive reformulation of Catlin's painting, *Dance to the Berdache*, see my essay "Of Mimicry and Drag: Homi Bhabha and Kent Monkman," *Theorizing Visual Studies: Writing Through the Discipline*, New York and London, 2013, 169–191. Monkman comments at length on Catlin's legacy when he appears as a character in Norman K. Denzin's experimental book, *Indians on Display: Global Commodification of Native America in Performance, Art, and Museums*, Walnut Creek, 2013, 75–113.

7 James Tweedie, "The Suspended Spectacle of History: Derek Jarman's Caravaggio," Screen, 44: 4, Winter 2003, 396.

8 *The Natchez* is the only known oil painting of Native American subjects completed by Delacroix. It imagines a scene from François-René de Chateaubriand's popular 1801 novel, Atala, in which the 'last' Natchez couple on the banks of the Mississippi watch their baby die because the mother is unable to produce milk. The painting (in the Metropolitan Museum of Art collection, 1989.328) is reproduced in Houle et al., *Robert Houle's Paris/Ojibwa*, 53. See also John F. Moffitt, "Native American 'Sauvage' as Pictured by French Romantic Artists and Writers," *Gazette des Beaux-Arts*, 134: 1568, September 1999, 120–126.

9 Linda Nochlin, "The Imaginary Orient," Art in America, May 1983, 123. Nochlin is referring specifically to Delacroix's *Death of Sardanapalus*. While Catlin was perpetuating mythologies of the American West, Delacroix, Girardet, and others helped to produce and circulate the visual culture of French empire in Africa and Southeast Asia.

10 Clement Greenberg, for one, declared, "Delacroix marked one of the great turning-points in the history of Western painting … after him … all turns and goes toward a new future." Clement Greenberg, *The Collected Essays and Criticism Vol. 1: Perceptions and Judgments*, 1939–1944, ed. John O'Brian, Chicago and London, 1986, 243 (first published in *The Nation*, 30 Dec., 1944). French historian Nelcya Delanoë recounts sharing her essay about the French response to the Ojibwa in Paris with Houle prior to the creation of Paris/Ojibwa, which inspired him to come to Paris to see Delacroix's sketches and other collections in person. See Delanoë, "Making the Past Dance," 27; Nelcya Delanoë, "Dernière recontre, ou comment Baudelaire, George Sand et Delacroix s'épirent des *Indiens du peintre Catlin*," in *Destins croisés: Cinq siècles de recontres avec les Amérindiens*, Paris, 1992, 263–281.

11 This literature is large. Useful critiques of primitivism that address the occluded agencies of *Native* Americans include Bill Anthes, *Native Moderns: American Indian Painting, 1940–1960*, Durham, NC, 2006; Ruth B. Phillips, "The Turn of the Primitive: Modernism, the Stranger and the Indigenous Artist," in *Exiles, Diasporas and Strangers*, ed. Kobena Mercer, Cambridge, MA, 2008, 46–71; Elizabeth Hutchinson, *The Indian Craze: Primitivism, Modernism, and Transculturation in American Art*, 1890–1915, Durham, NC, 2009.

12 Cheetham's understanding of infection draws upon Kazimir Malevich's supremetist theories, which also directly influenced Houle. Mark Cheetham, "The Transformative Abstraction of Robert Houle," in Houle et al., *Robert Houle's Paris/Ojibwa*, 27. See also Mark A. Cheetham, *The Rhetoric of Purity: Essentialist Theory and the Advent of Abstract Painting*, Boston, 1994.

13 Houle in conversation with the author, Toronto, Dec. 12, 2013. As I write in 2014, hearings on this subject through Canada's Truth and Reconciliation Commission are ongoing. For a series of works based on Houle's abuse at the residential school at Sandy Bay First Nation Reserve, **see** *Robert Houle: enuhmo andúhuaun (the road home)*, Winnipeg, 2012.

14 Michael Bell and Robert Houle, "Conversation," in Michael Bell, *Kanata: Robert Houle's Histories*, (Ottawa: Carleton University Art Gallery, 1993), 13; 19. Today, Houle describes himself as a "non-practising Catholic." Houle, email to the author, January 29, 2015.

15 Robert Houle in conversation with Clara Hargittay, "The Struggle Against Cultural Apartheid," *Muse*, Autumn 1988: http://ccca.concordia.ca/c/writing/h/houle/hou003t.html (12 August 2014).

16 Houle, "The Spiritual Legacy of the Ancient Ones," 53.

17 The titles are translated in David McIntosh, "Travelling Light: Paris/Ojibwa," Houle et al., *Robert Houle's Paris/Ojibwa*, 16.

18 Phillips, *Patterns of Power*, 25.

19 Phillips, *Patterns of Power*, 26. Houle similarly states, "The point of putting things together is to create a paradigm to create some type of power." Bell and Houle, "Conversation," 15.

20 A. Irving Hallowell, "Ojibwa Ontology, Behavior, and World View," in *Culture in History: Essays in Honor of Paul Radin*, ed. Stanley Diamond, New York, 1960, 20–22.

21 Hallowell, "Ojibwa Ontology, Behavior, and World View," 33–34.

22 Phillips, *Patterns of Power*, 26.

23 Donald B. Smith, *Mississauga Portraits: Ojibwe Voice from Nineteenth-Century Canada*, Toronto, 2013.

24 For example, Hallowell notes the influence of Christianity in Ojibwa understandings of success in the afterlife as a reflection of proper behaviour during one's lifetime, but notes that his informants remained skeptical about a concept of hell. Hallowell, *Contributions to Ojibwe Studies*, 414.

[25] Houle, "Spiritual Legacy of the Ancient Ones."

[26] Ojibwa stories relate that the first people came down from the star world through a hole in the sky. See accounts by contemporary shamans recorded in Thor Conway, "The Conjurer's Lodge: Celestial Narratives from Algonkian Shamans," in *Earth and Sky: Visions of the Cosmos in Native American Folklore*, eds. Ray A. Williamson and Claire R. Farrer, Albuquerque, 1992, 236–259.

[27] Hallowell, *Contributions to Ojibwe Studies*, 406.

[28] Hallowell, *Contributions to Ojibwe Studies*, 415–417.

[29] Houle discusses the sacred importance of tobacco and its role in his work in Bell and Houle, "Conversation," 15–16.

[30] Thomas Vennum, *The Ojibwa Dance Drum: Its History and Construction*, Washington, DC, 1982, 33. See also Beth Southcott, *The Sound of the Drum: The Sacred Art of the Anishnabec*, Erin, 1984.

[31] Houle states, 'The ancestors and the manitous will hear the entry song." Houle, 'A Transatlantic Return Home Through the Magic of Art' in Houle, et al., *Robert Houle's Paris/Ojibwa*, 44.

[32] Peers, *The Ojibwa of Western Canada*, 18–19; 141–142. See also Elizabeth Fenn, *Pox Americana: The Great Smallpox Epidemic of* 1775–82, New York, 2001.

[33] Warren, the son of an Ojibwa woman and a French fur trader, did not believe these accounts and gave an alternative version of the notorious smallpox outbreak of 1780–1783. *William W. Warren and Theresa Schenck, History of the Ojibway people*, St. Paul, 1999 [1888], 228–233. On the historical evidence for germ warfare, see Fenn, "Biological Warfare in Eighteenth-Century North America: Beyond Jeffery Amherst", *Journal of American History*, 86:4, March 2000, 1552–1580. A key article that set off these debates is Bernhard Knollenberg, "General Amherst and Germ Warfare," *The Mississippi Valley Historical Review*, 41:3, 1954, 489–494. Adrienne Mayor explores the discursive resonance of these and other circulating accounts of smallpox infested blankets in "The Nessus Shirt in the New World: Smallpox Blankets in History and Legend," *Journal of American Folklore*, 108:427, 1995, 54–77.

[34] Kate Flint argues that the Iowa and Ojibwa used their travels as an opportunity "that the British should recognize how the host country was implicated in the causes of the Indian poverty that underlay their reasons for crossing the Atlantic to raise money, including the introduction of smallpox, venereal disease, and the sale of 'fire-water.'" Flint, *The Transatlantic Indian*, 79. Native responses are also discussed in Christopher Mulvey, "Among the Sag-a-noshes: Ojibwa and Iowa Indians with George Catlin in Europe, 1843–1848," in *Indians and Europe: An Interdisciplinary Collection of Essays*, ed. Christian F. Feest, Lincoln, 1999, 253–276.

[35] Benjamin Slight, *Indian Researches; or, Facts concerning the North American Indians; Including Notices of Their Present State of Improvement, in Their Social, Civil and Religious Condition, with Hints for Their Future Advancement*, Montreal, 1844, 43.

[36] Houle in conversation with the author, Toronto, December 12, 2013; Smith, *Sacred Feathers*, 187–188. For a detailed account of the life of Maungwudaus, see Smith, *Mississauga Portrait*, 126–163.

[37] Maungwudaus, *An Account of the Chippewa Indians*, 11.

[38] Some of Latour's most convincing illustrations of quasi-objects appear in his studies of nineteenth-century laboratories and the development of microbiology. For example, in an analysis of French scientist Louis Pasteur's famous 1857 essay on lactic acid yeast, Latour writes, "The reader [of Pasteur's text] lives in a world where a ferment is as lively as a specific life form." Bruno Latour, "Pasteur on Lactic Acid Yeast: A Partial Semiotic Analysis," *Configurations*, 1:1, Baltimore, 1993, 133.

[39] The first transatlantic steamship service began in 1838. *Steamships: Wester's Timeline History*, 1762–2007, San Diego, 2007, n.p. It is not clear what type of service Maungwudaus and the other Ojibwa used to travel to London in 1843, although we know that they returned aboard the Yorktown, a conventional sailing ship, in 1848. Maungwudaus, *An Account of the Chippewa Indians*, 9.

[40] Hallowell, *Contributions to Ojibwe Studies*, 135.

[41] Robert Houle, "The Spiritual Legacy of the Ancient Ones," 44.

[42] Catlin, *Catlin's* Notes, 107.

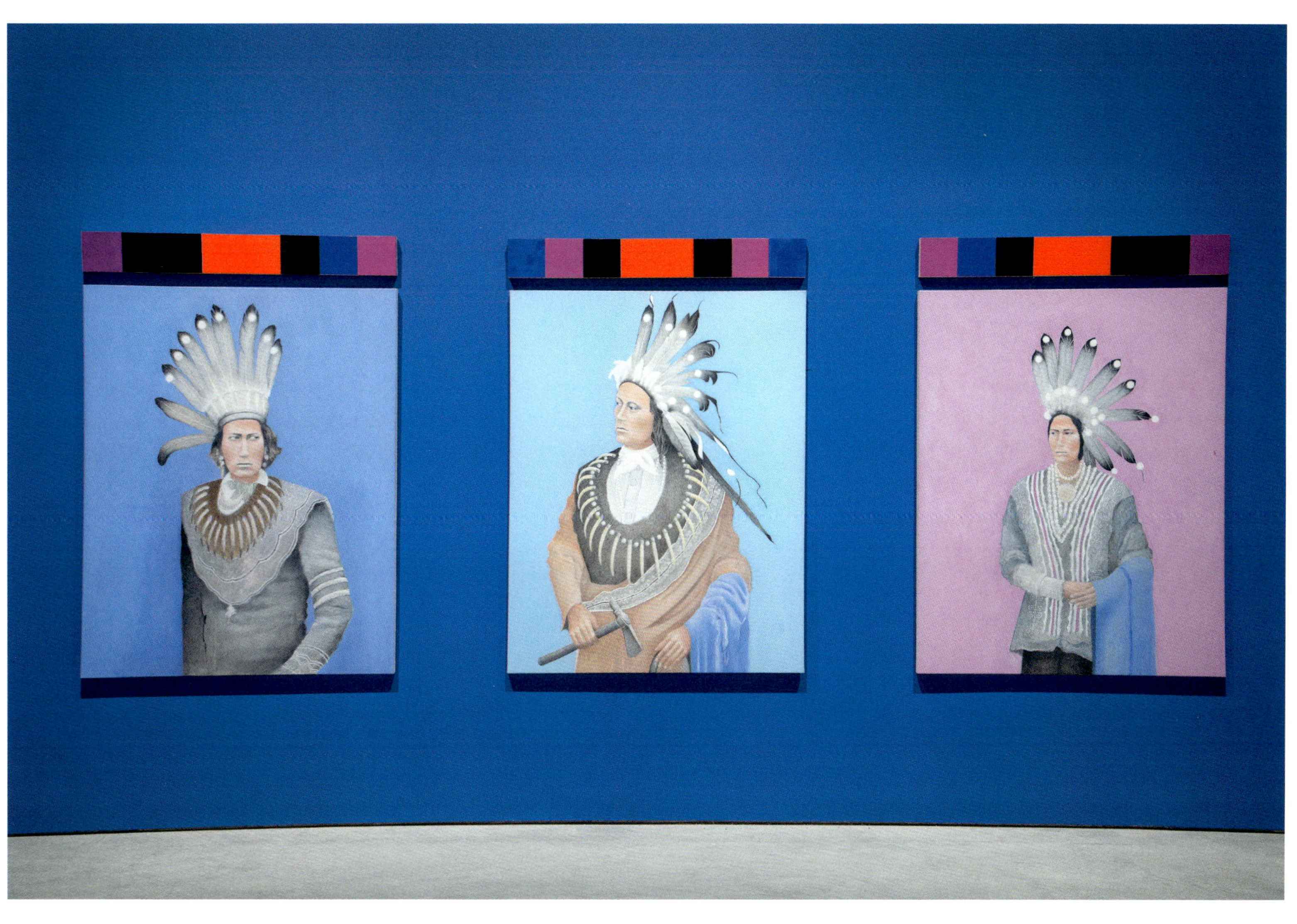

Mississauga Portraits (Waubuddick, Maungwudaus, Hannah), 2012

THE AESTHETICS OF DISAPPEARANCE

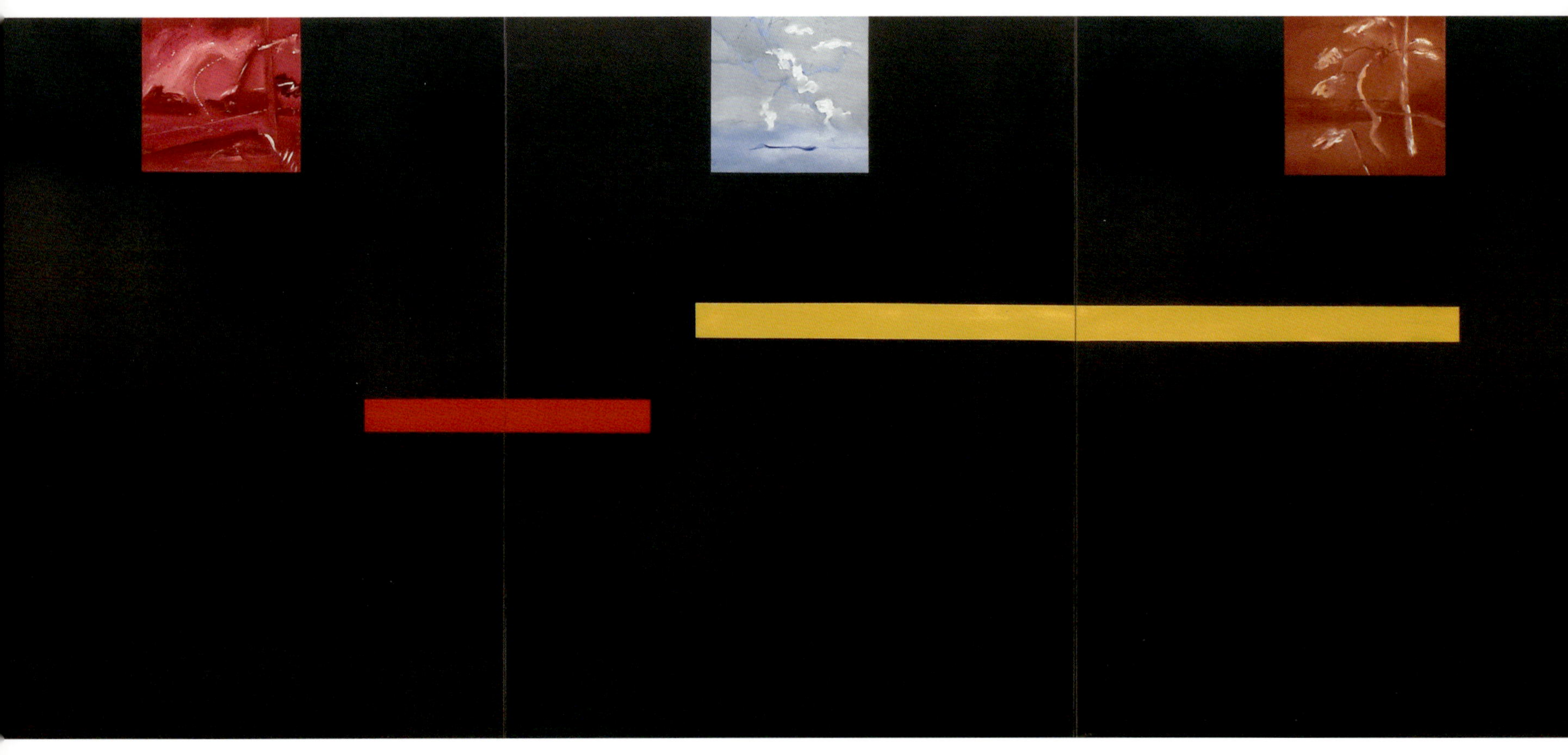

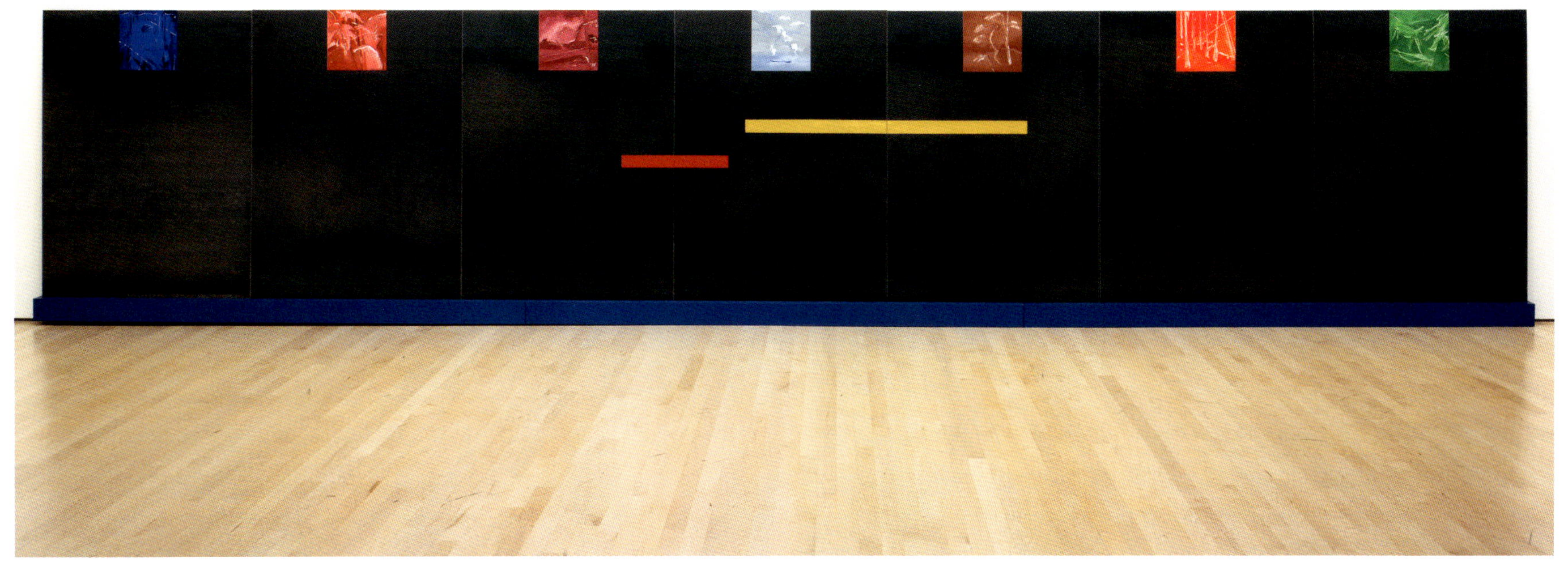

Seven in Steel, 1989

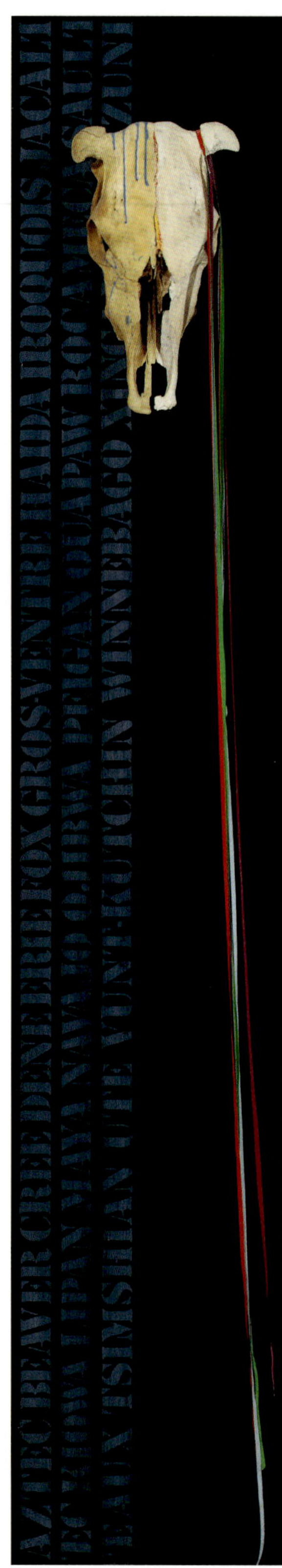

New Sentinel, 1987

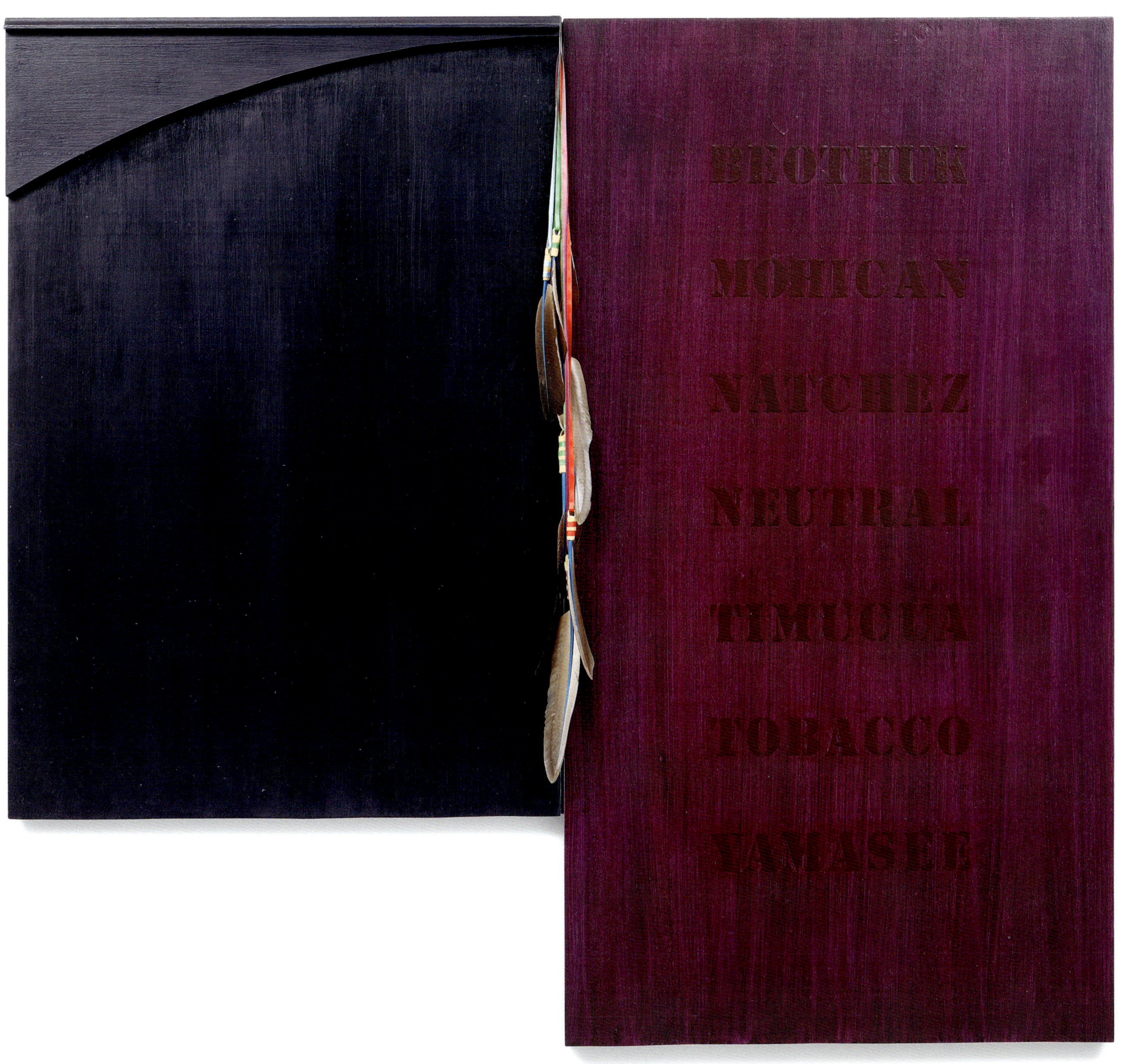

In Memoriam, 1987

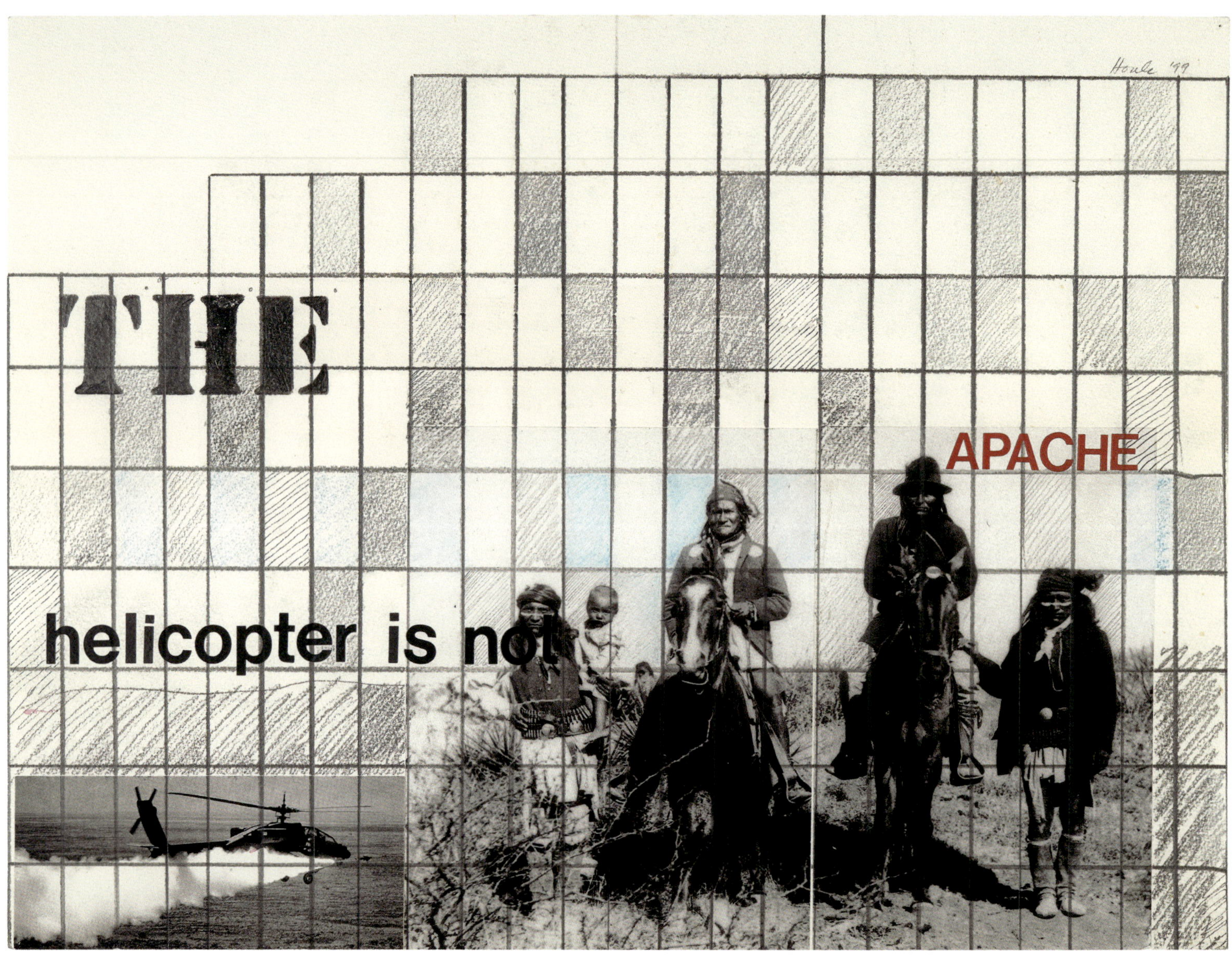

Study for *These Apaches Are Not Helicopters*, 1999

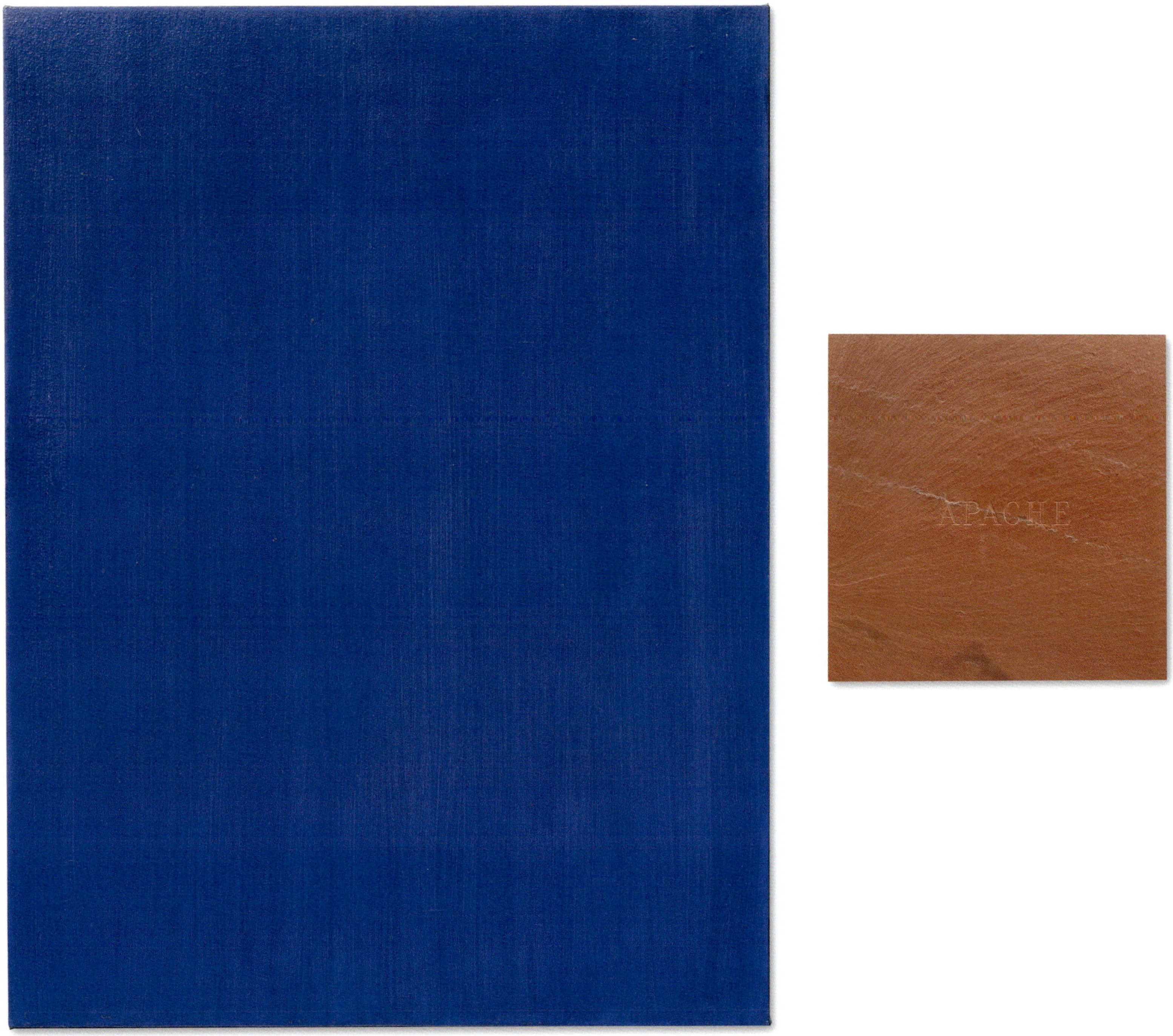

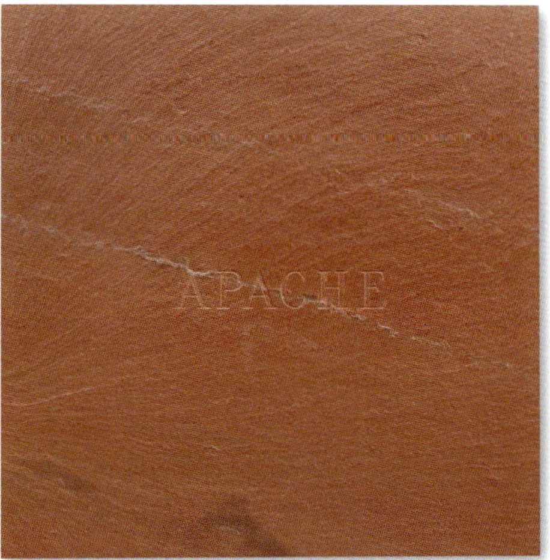

Blue Apache, 2003

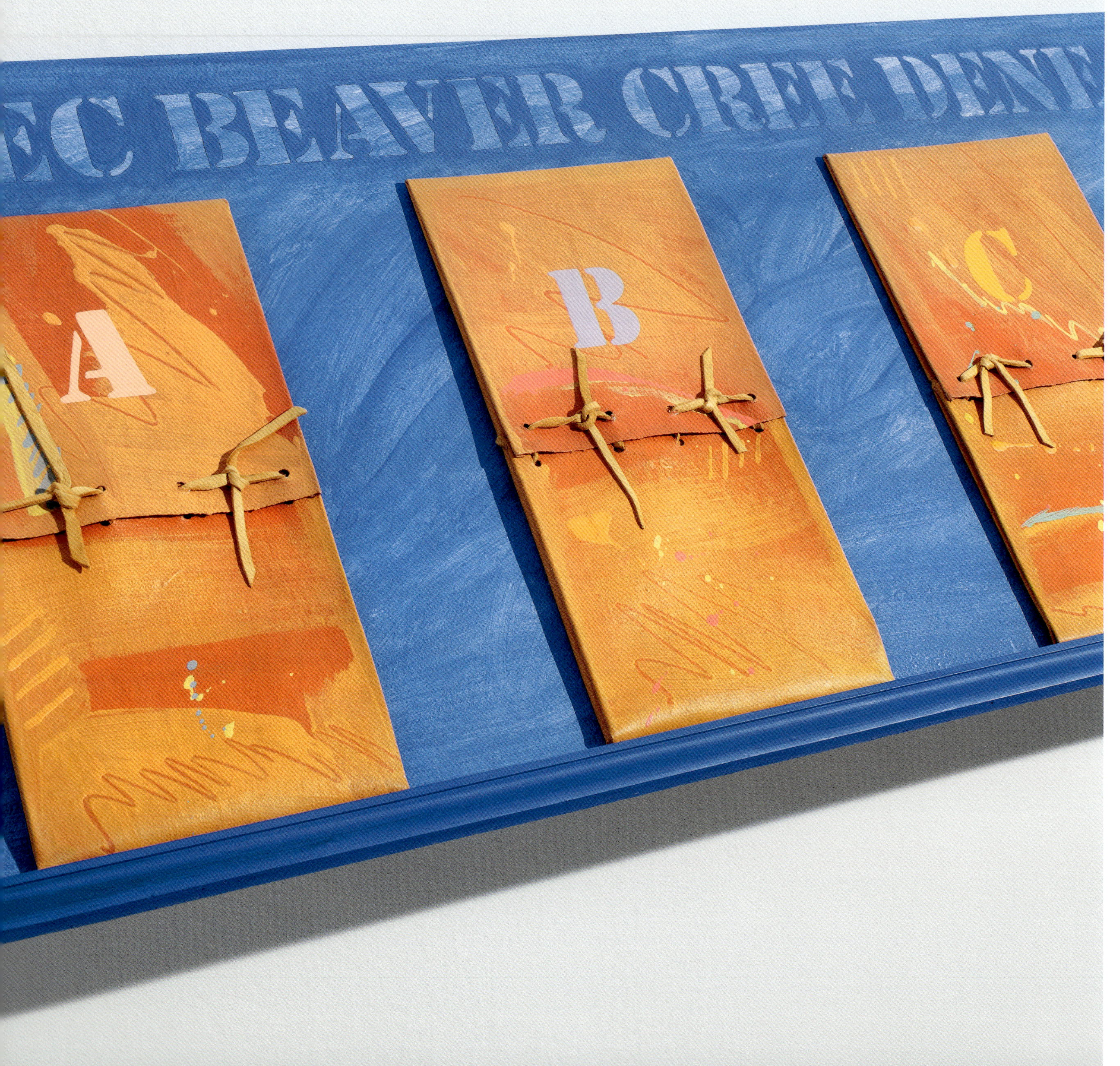
EC BEAVER CREE DENE
A
B
C

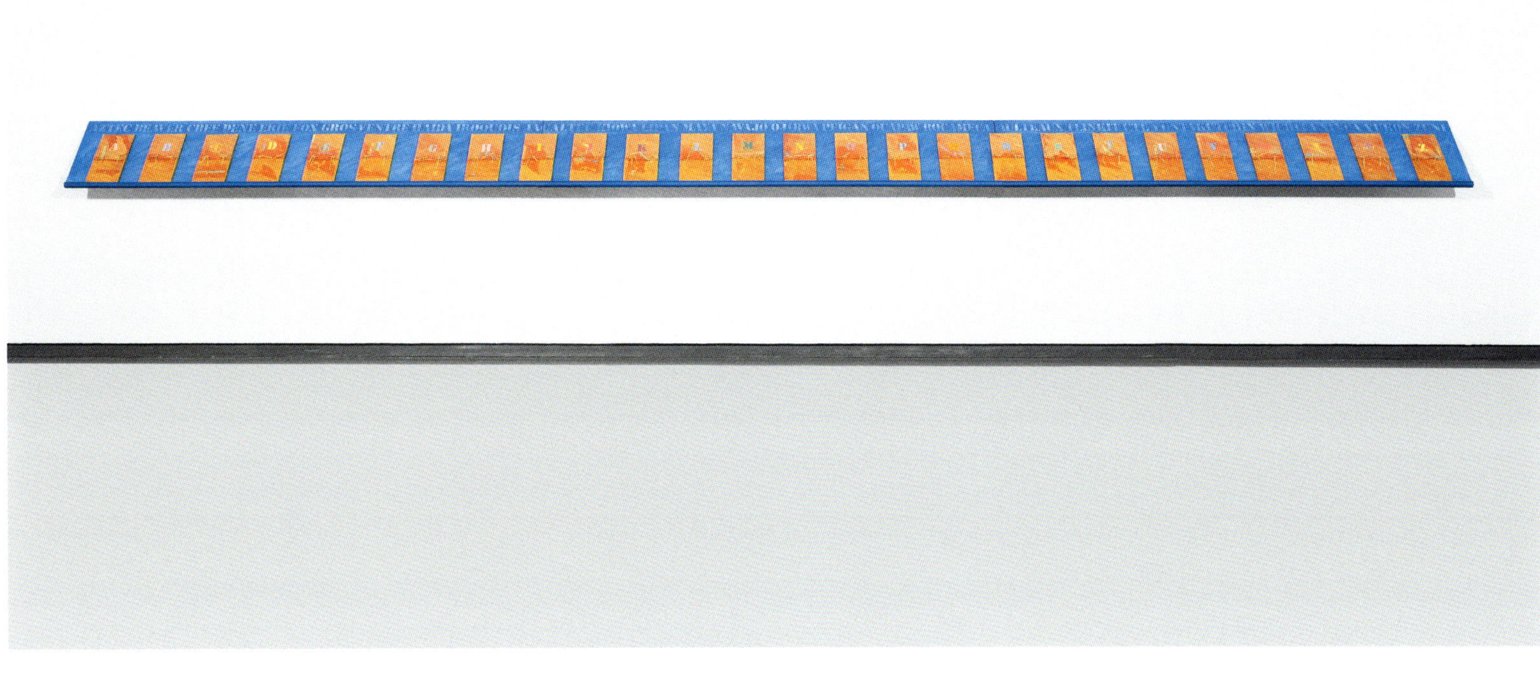

Everything you ever wanted to know about Indians from A to Z, 1985

PONTIAC

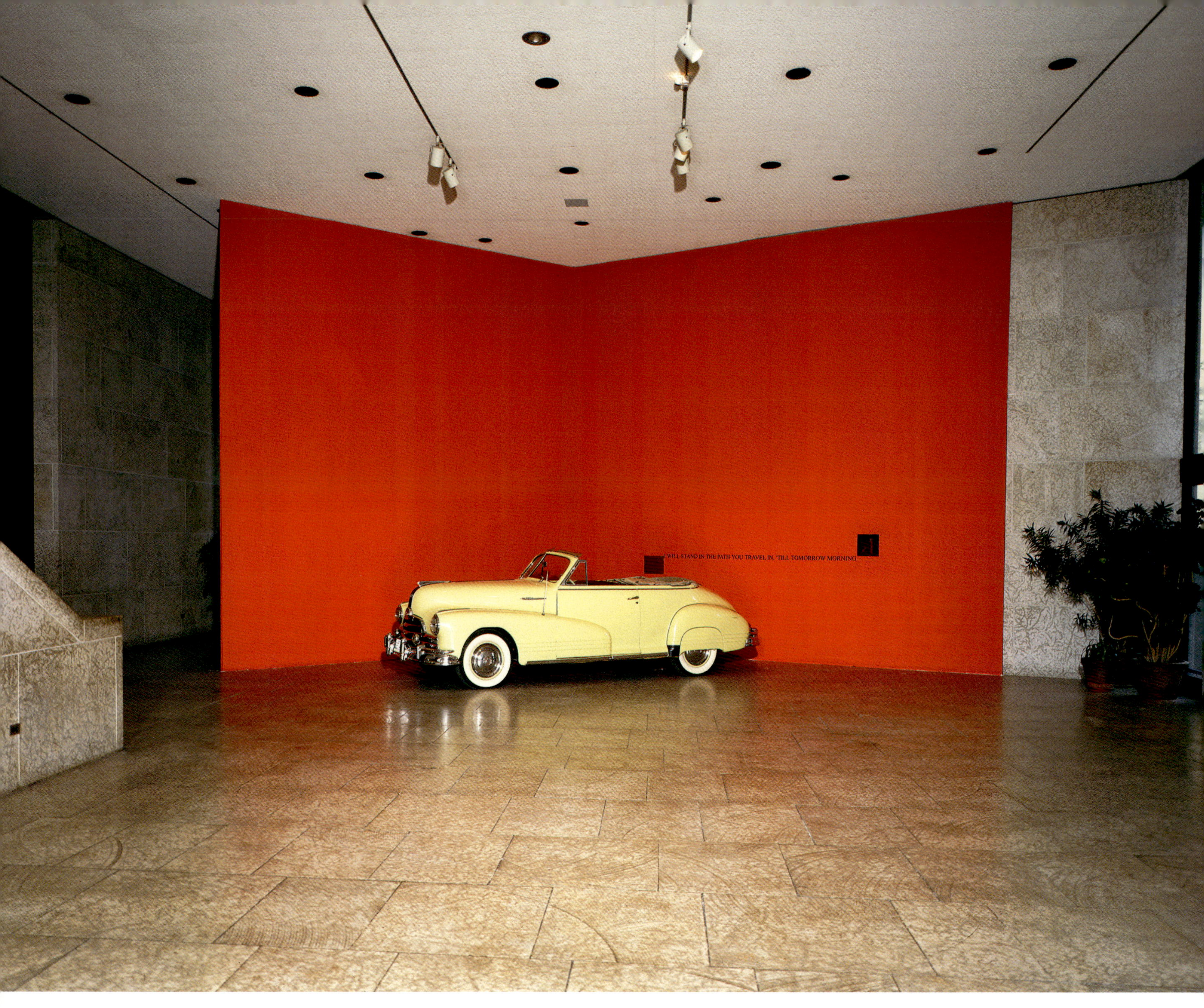

I Stand, 1997

Installation view of *Robert Houle: Sovereignty Over Subjectivity* at the Winnipeg Art Gallery, March 7 – September 5, 1999.

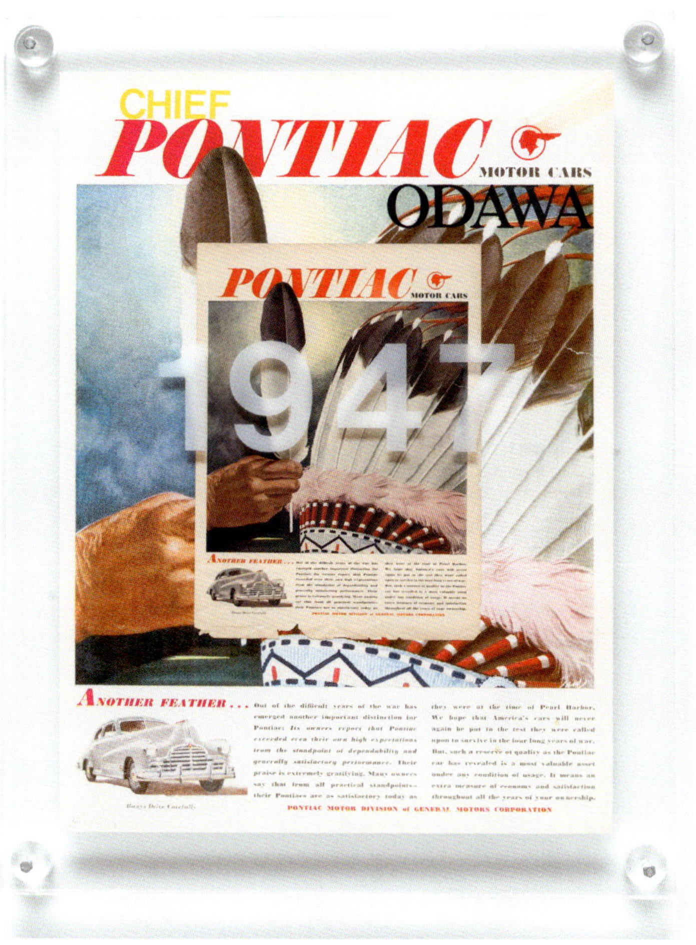

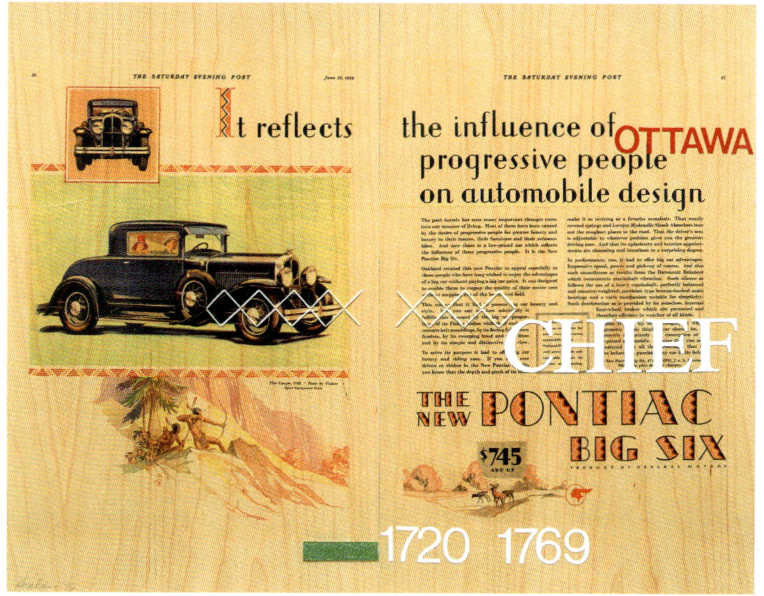

1947, 1996

Chief, the New Pontiac Big Six, around 1997

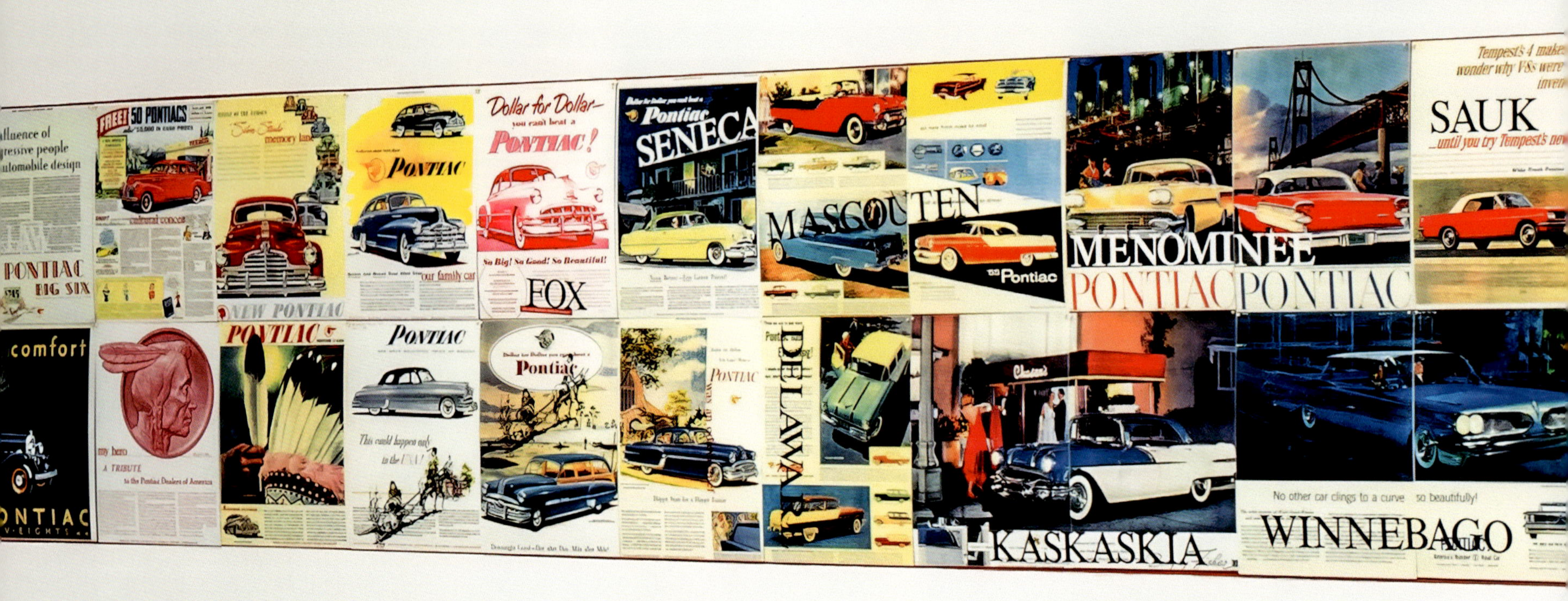
FREE! 50 PONTIACS
PONTIAC
NEW PONTIAC
Dollar for Dollar—
you can't beat a
PONTIAC!
So Big! So Good! So Beautiful!
FOX
SENECA
MASCOUTEN
'55 Pontiac
MENOMINEE
PONTIAC
PONTIAC
SAUK
comfort
my hero
A TRIBUTE
to the Pontiac Dealers of America
POINTIAC
This could happen only
in the U.S.A.!
Pontiac
DELAWA
KASKASKIA
No other car clings to a curve so beautifully!
WINNEBAGO

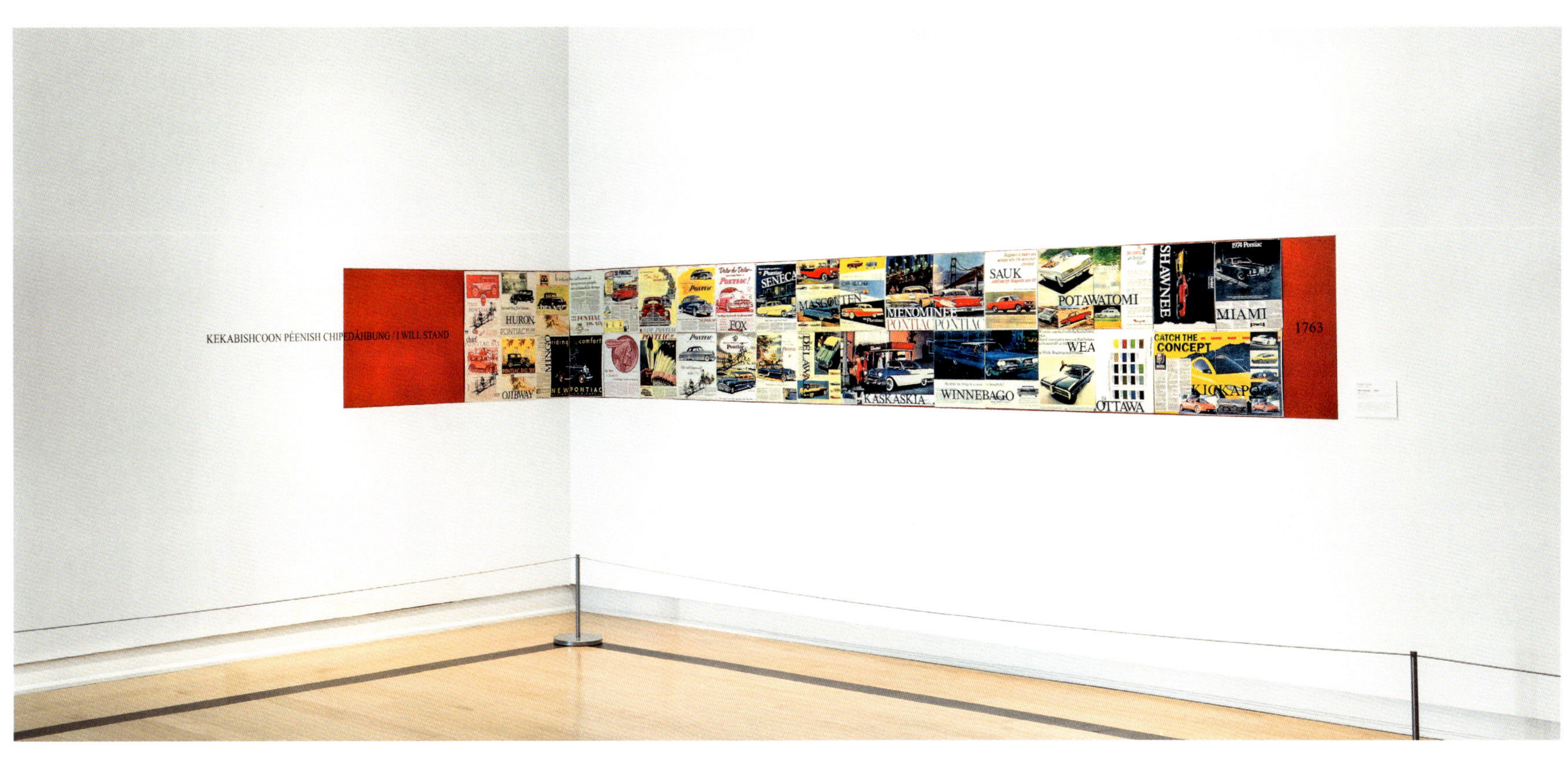

Kekabishcoon Peenish Chipedahbung (I Will Stand in Your Path Till Dawn), 1997

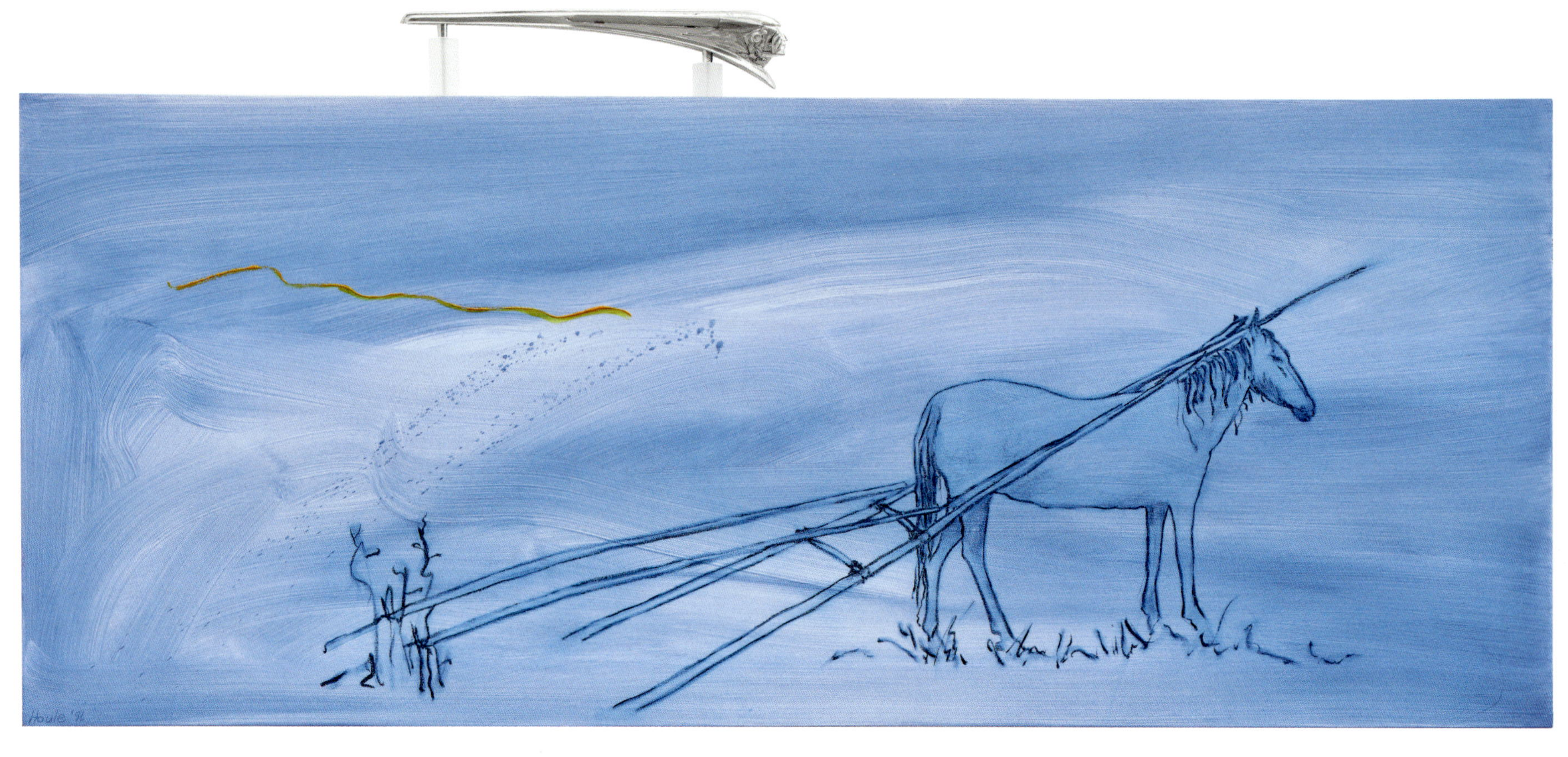

The Chief, 1996

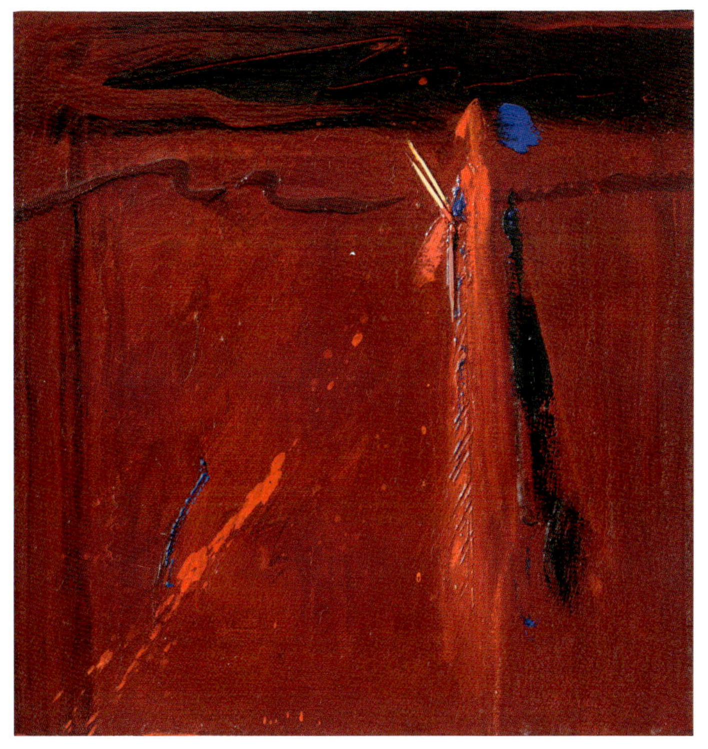

Pontiac, 1996

RESIDENTIAL SCHOOL YEARS

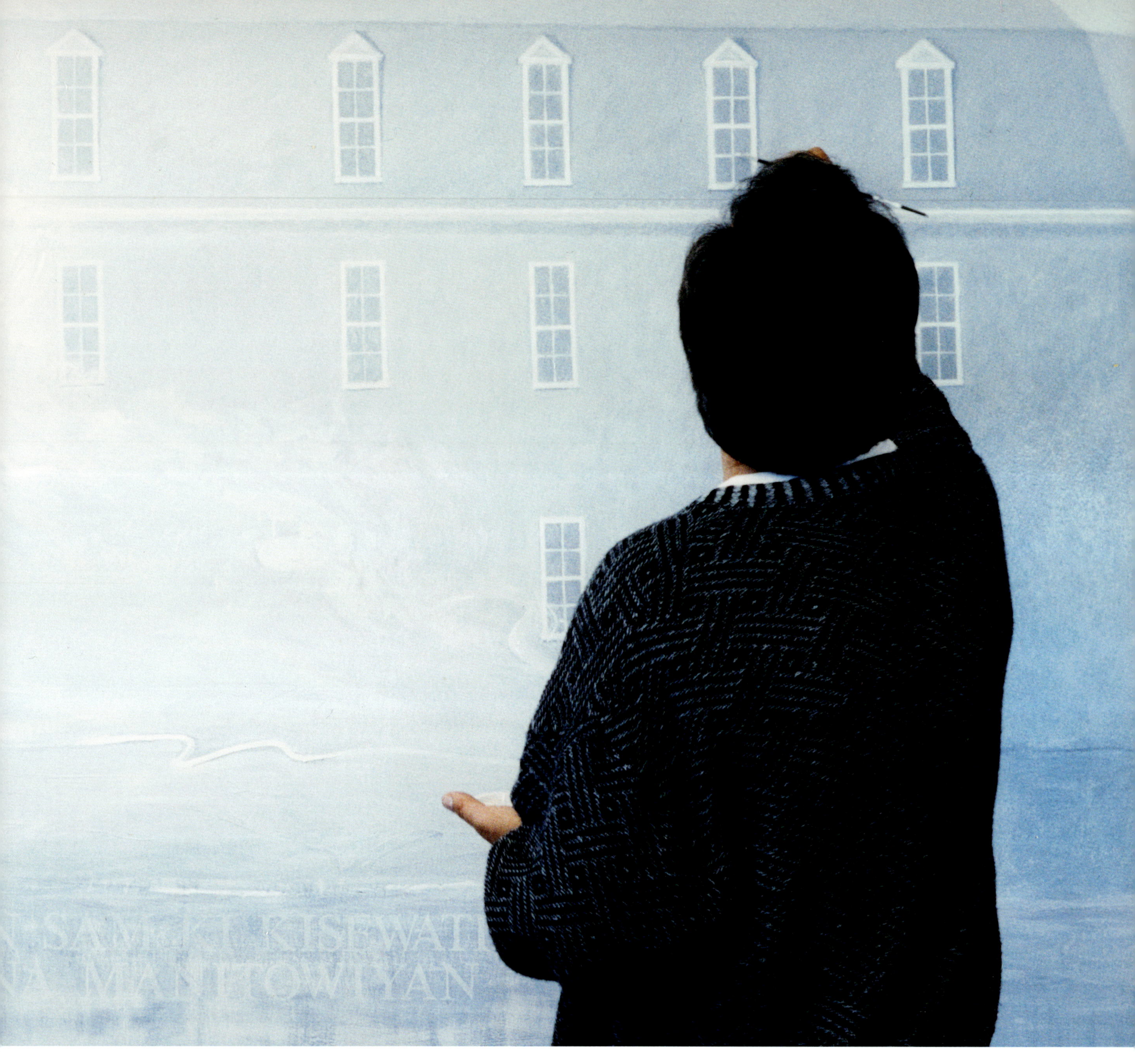

Robert Houle painting *Sandy Bay* in his Spadina Avenue studio in 1999. Photographed by David Recollet. Image courtesy of the artist.

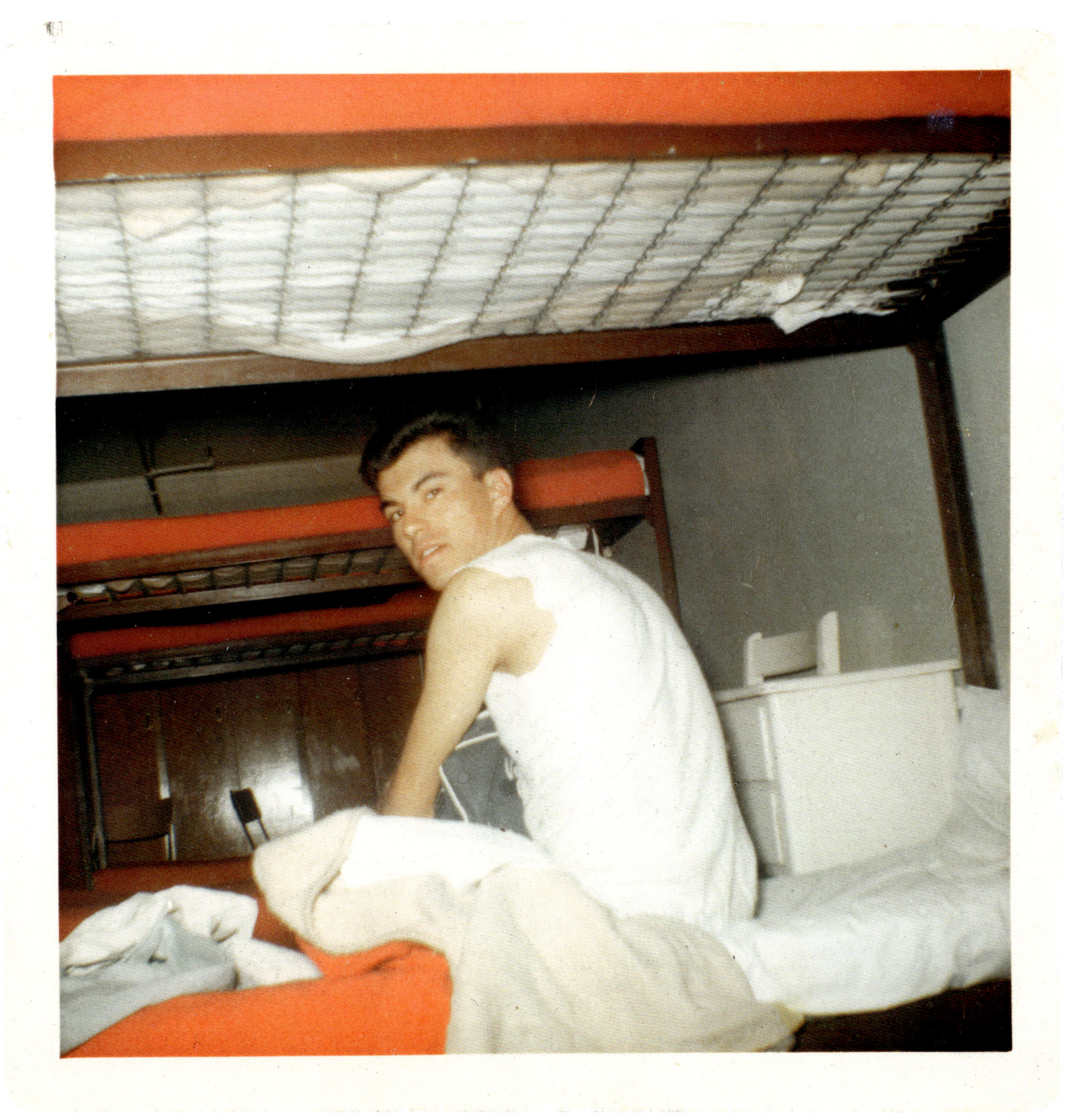

Robert Houle at the Assiniboia Residential High School dormitory in Winnipeg, preparing to go on the Confederation Train, which travelled across the country telling the story of "Canada," in 1967. Photographer unknown. Image courtesy of the artist.

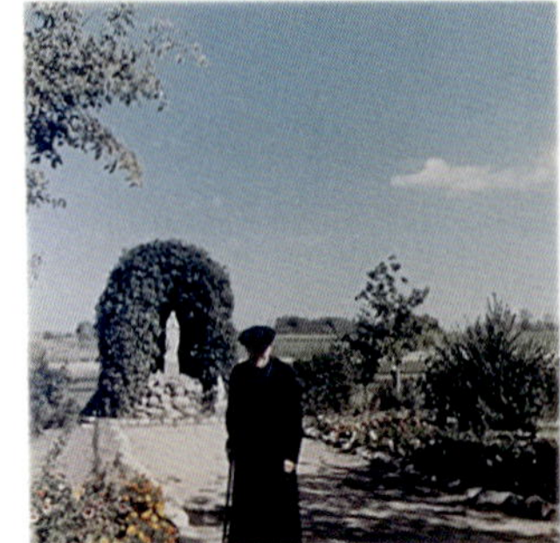

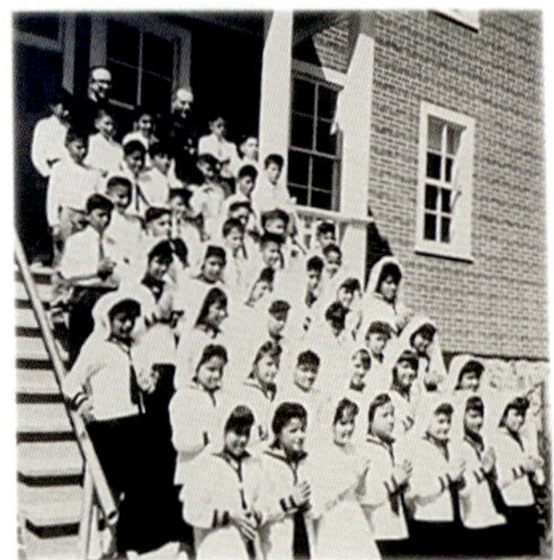

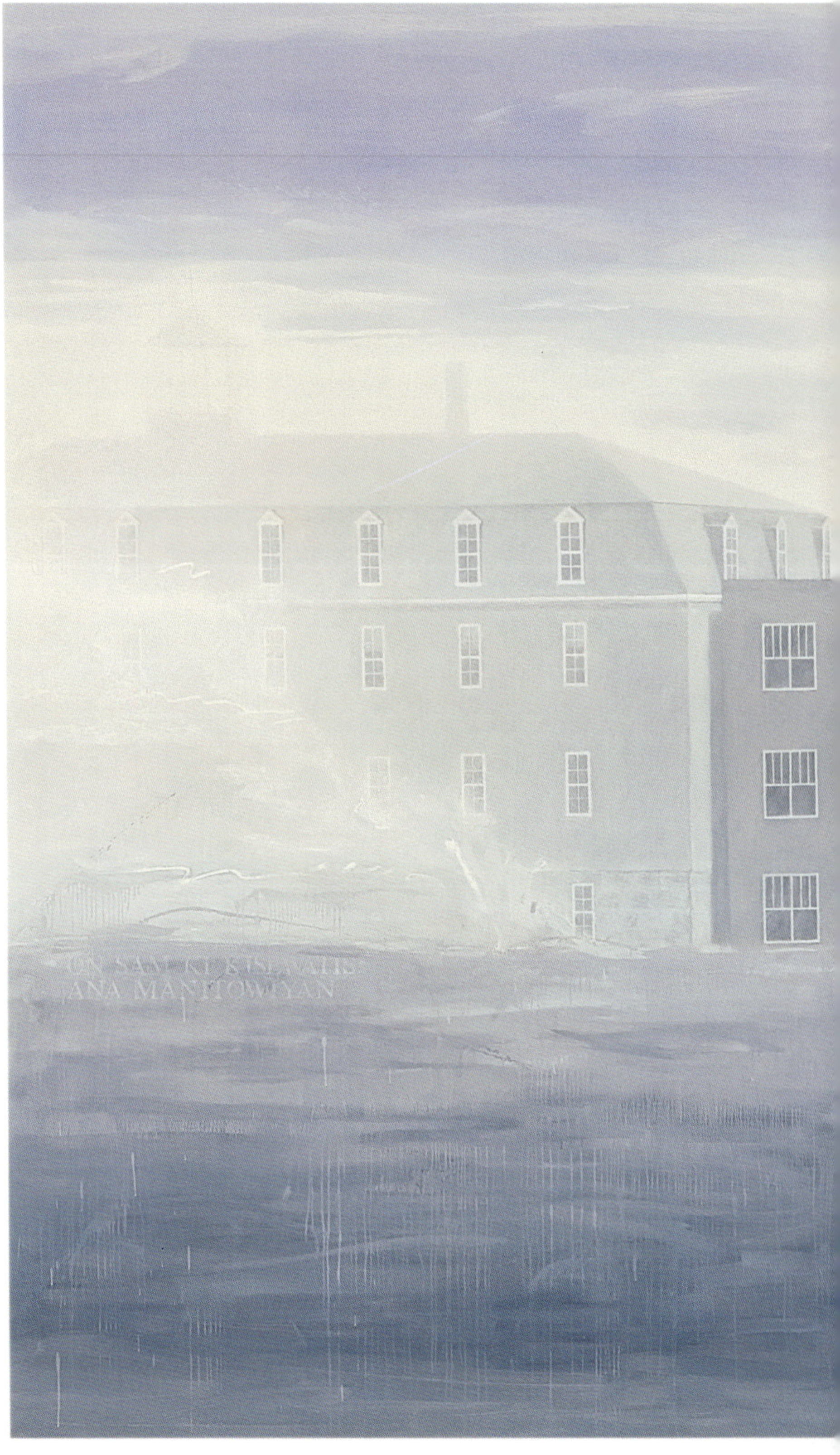

Sandy Bay, 1998–1999

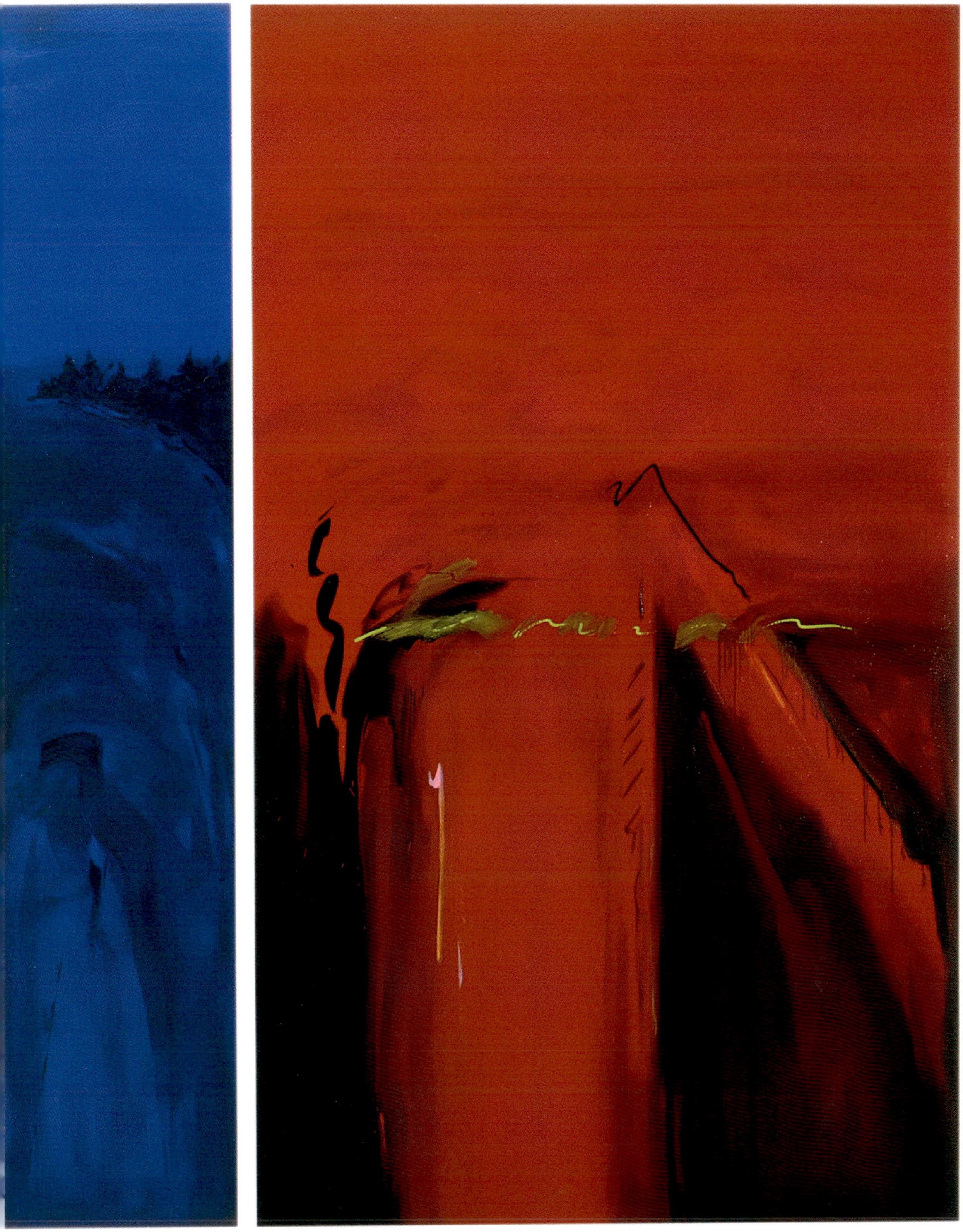

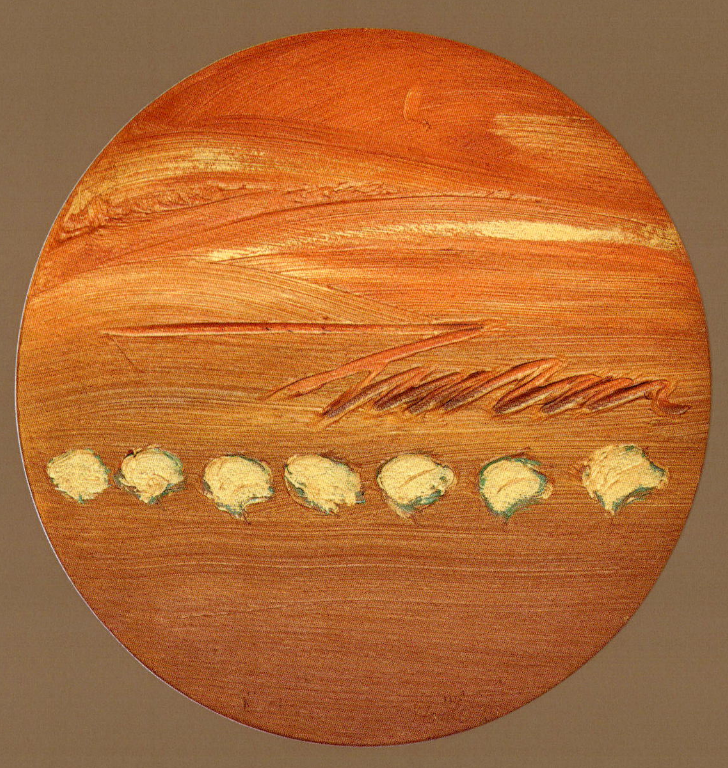

Grandmother (drum), 2015

"When the school is on the reserve the child lives with its parents who are savages; he is surrounded by savages and though he may learn to read and write, his habits and training and mode of thought are Indian. He is simply a savage who can read or write."

— Sir John A. Macdonald, 1883

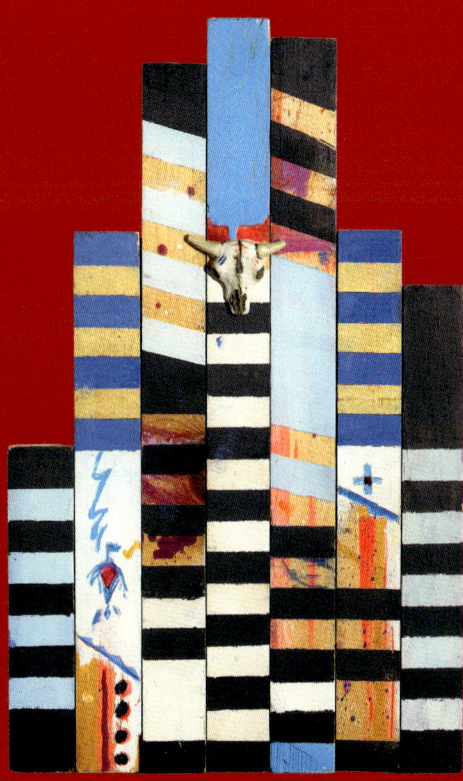

Cathedral, 2016

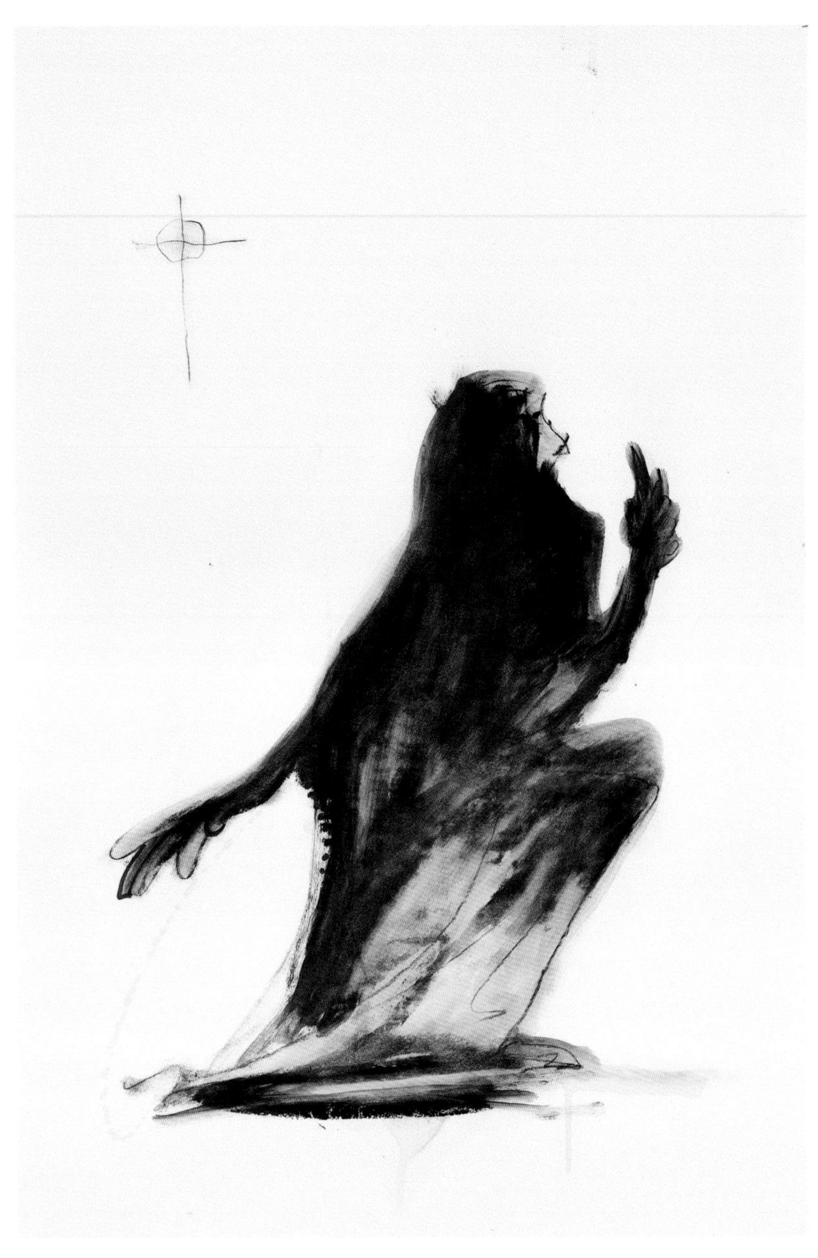

Sister Clothilde, 2009

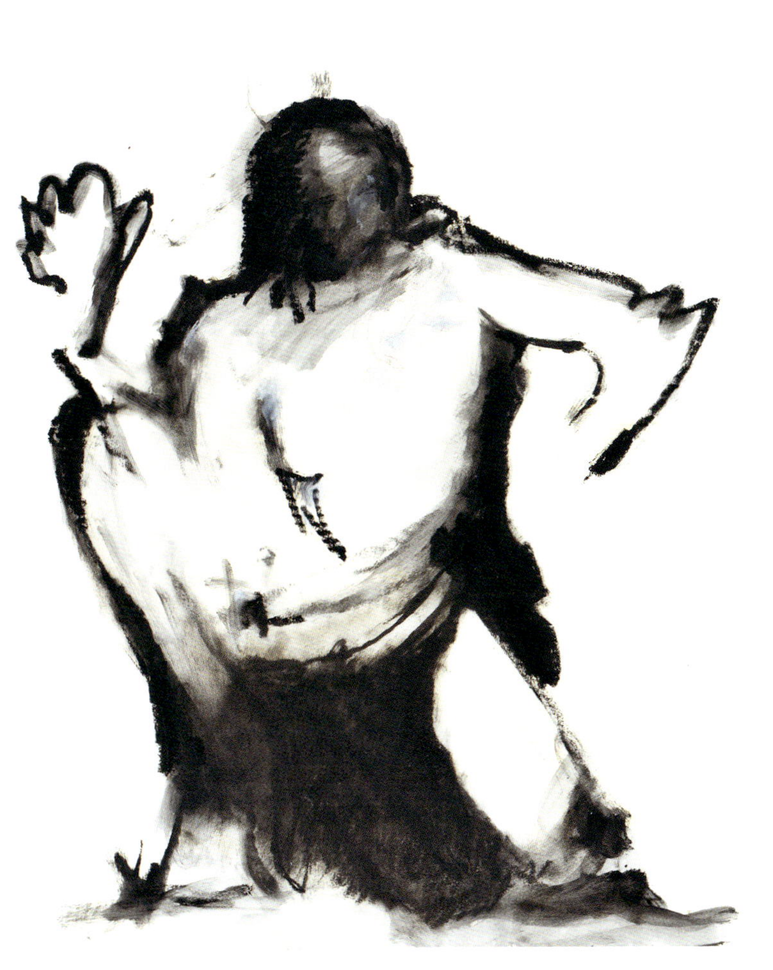

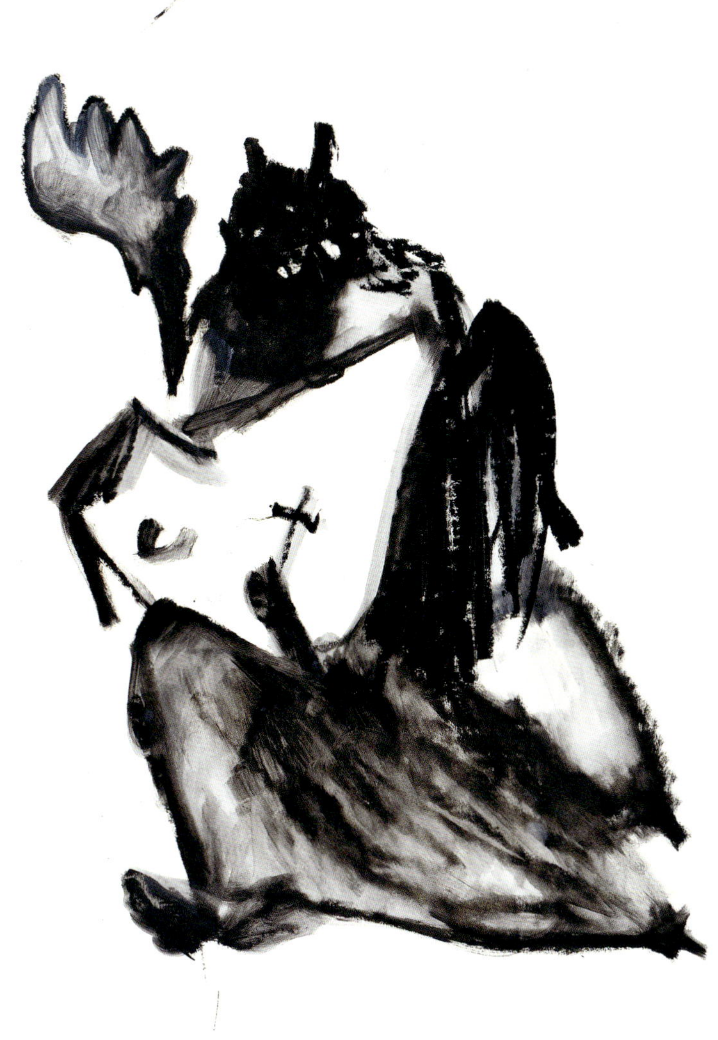

Dark Moses, 2009

Shape Shifter, 2009

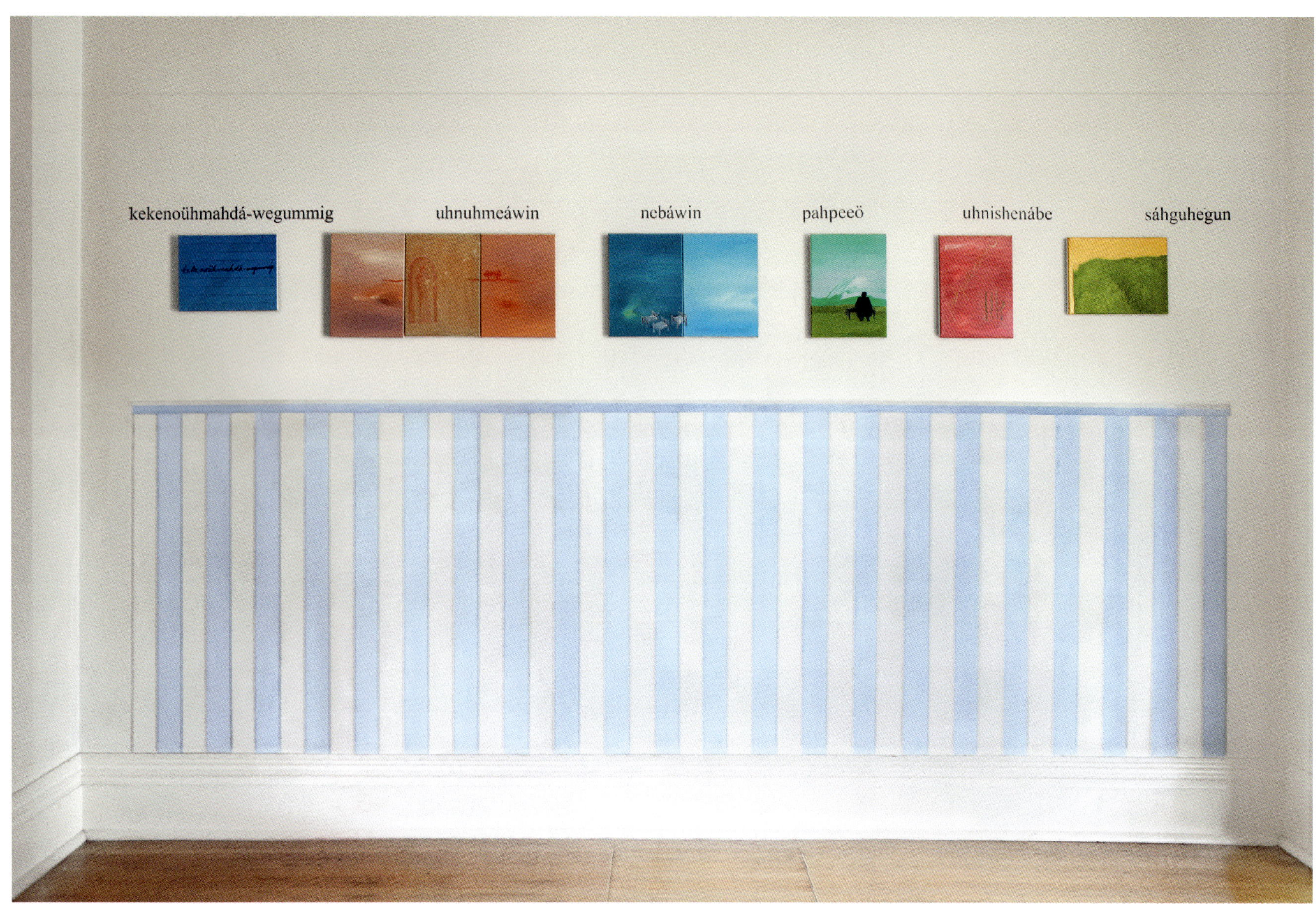

Sandy Bay Indian Residential School I (schoolhouse, praying, sleeping, waiting, people, lake), 2010–2011

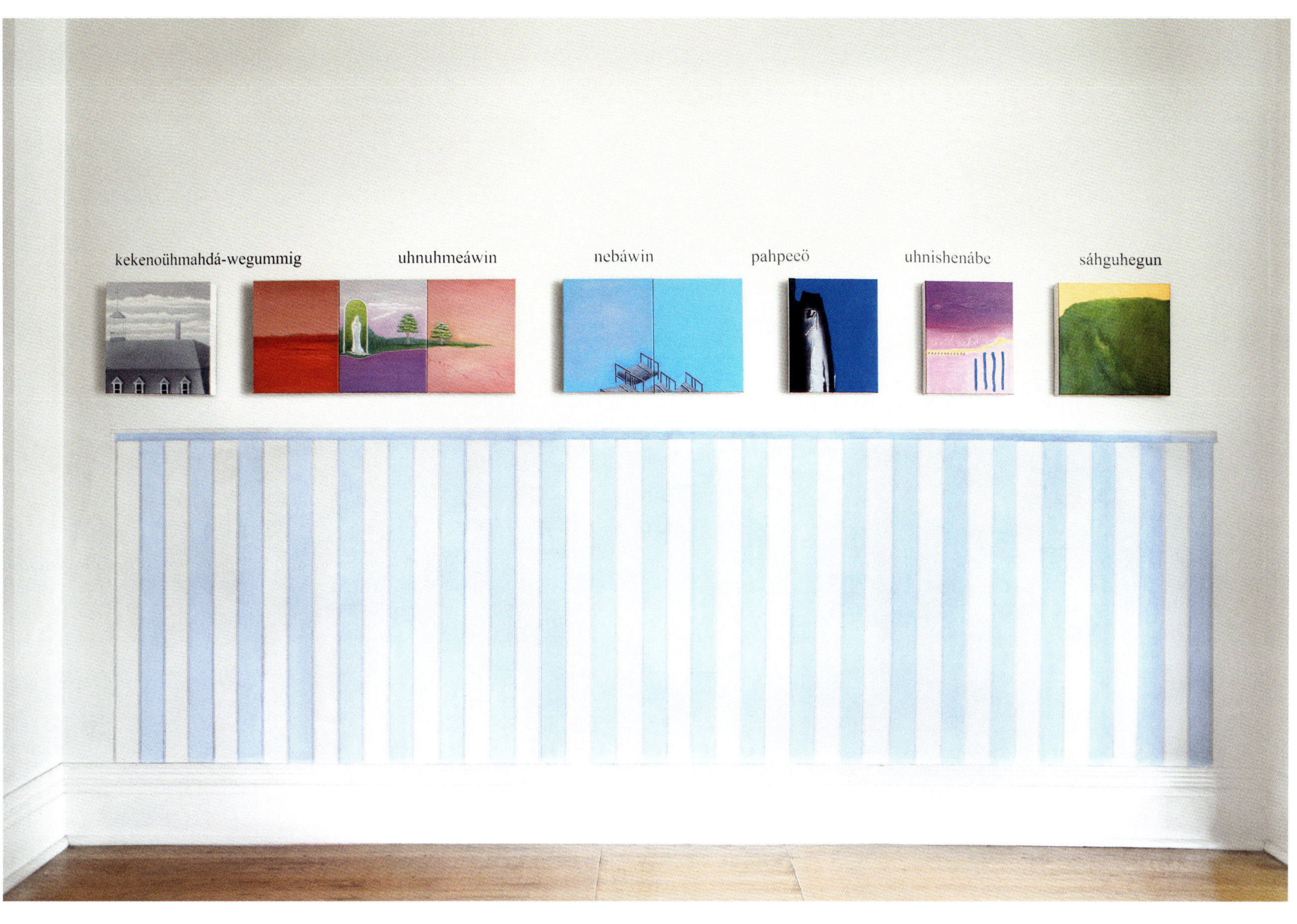

Sandy Bay Indian Residential School II (schoolhouse, praying, sleeping, waiting, people, lake), 2010–2011

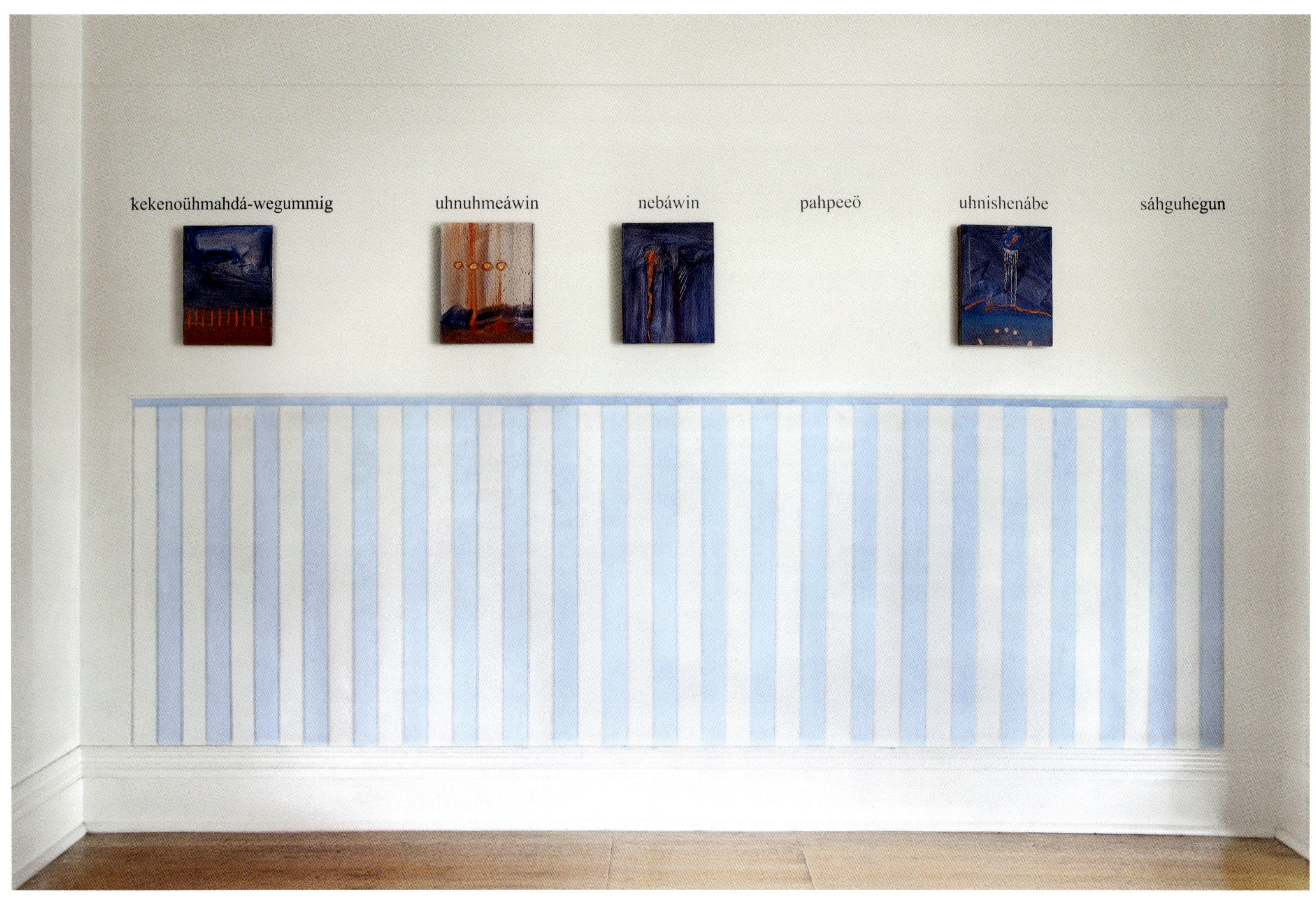

Sandy Bay Indian Residential School III (schoolhouse, praying, sleeping, people), 2012

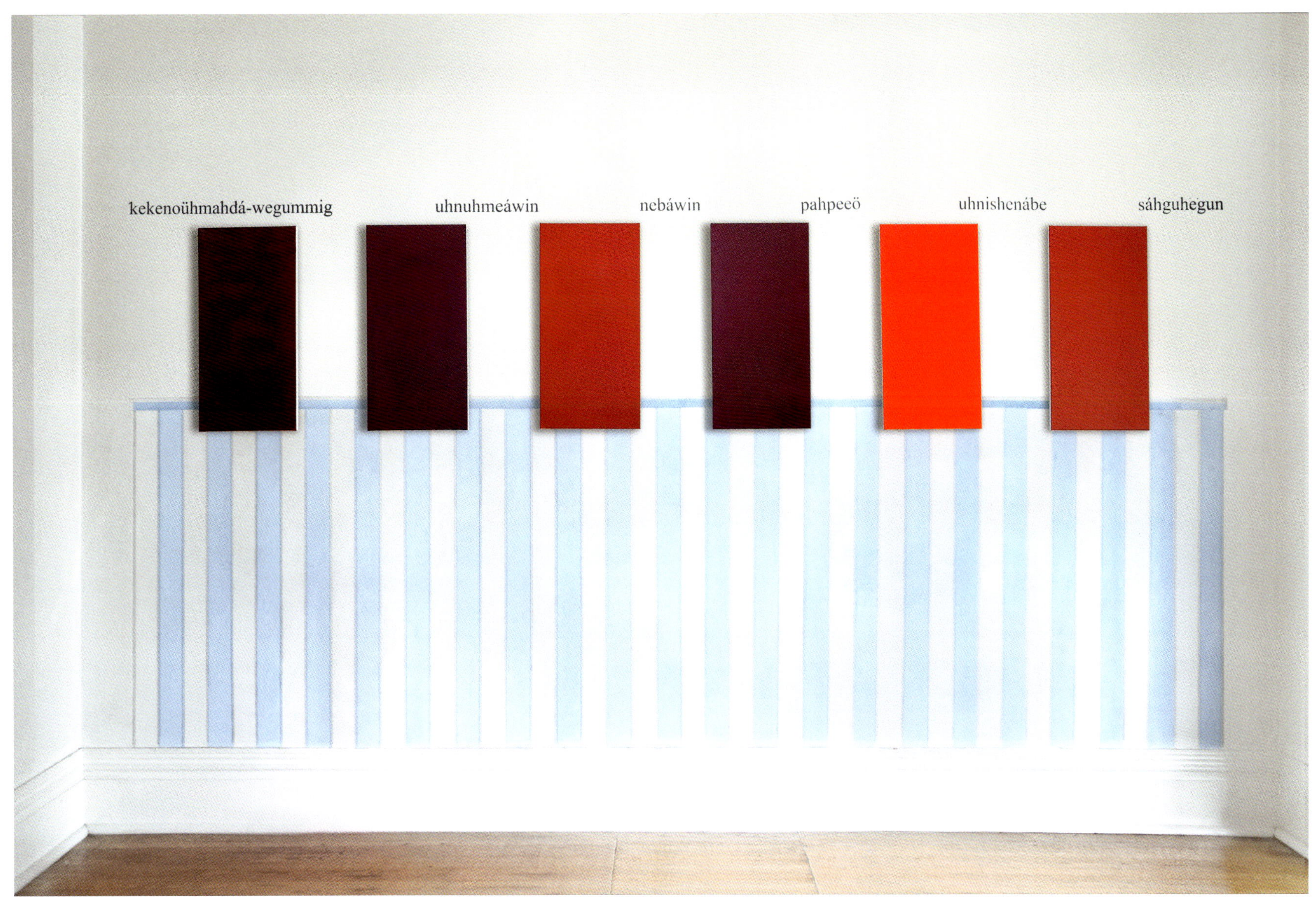

Sandy Bay Indian Residential School IV (alizarin crimson, cobalt violet, winsor red deep, magenta, cadmium red light, cadmium red deep), 2012

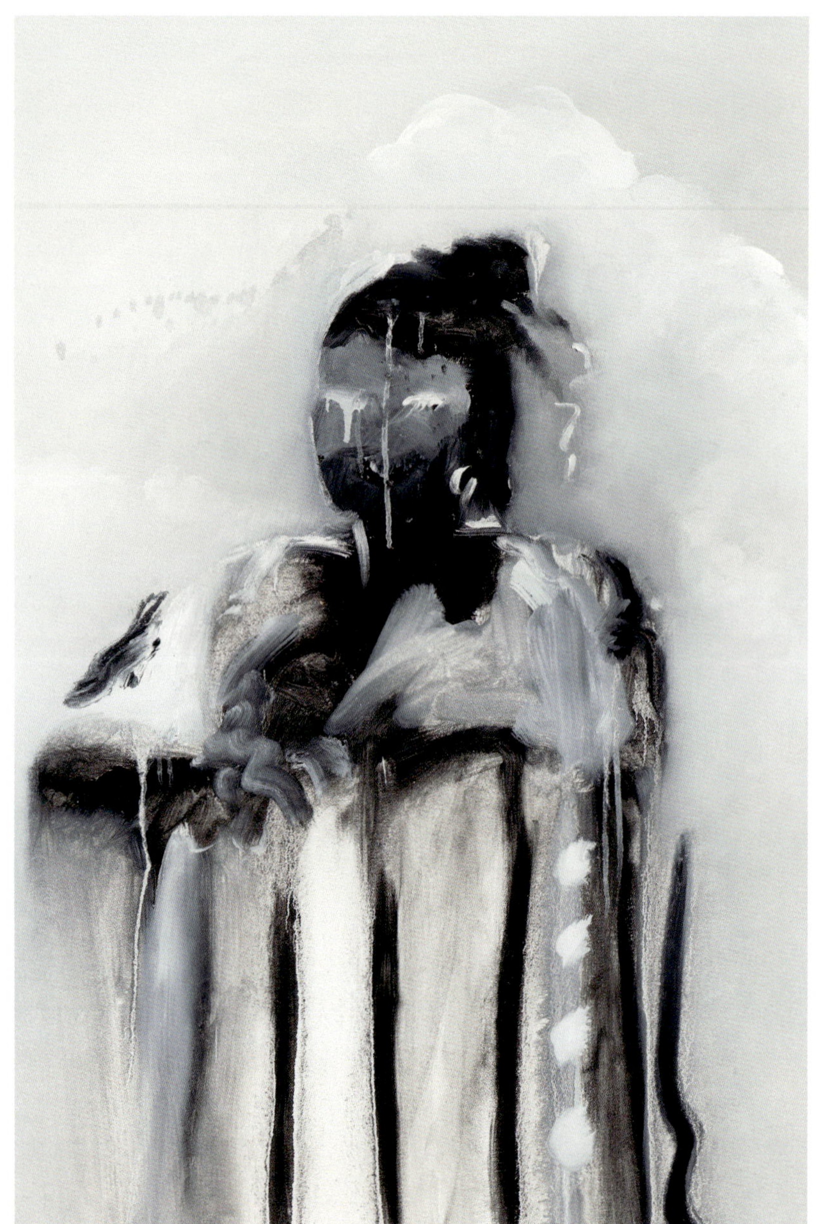

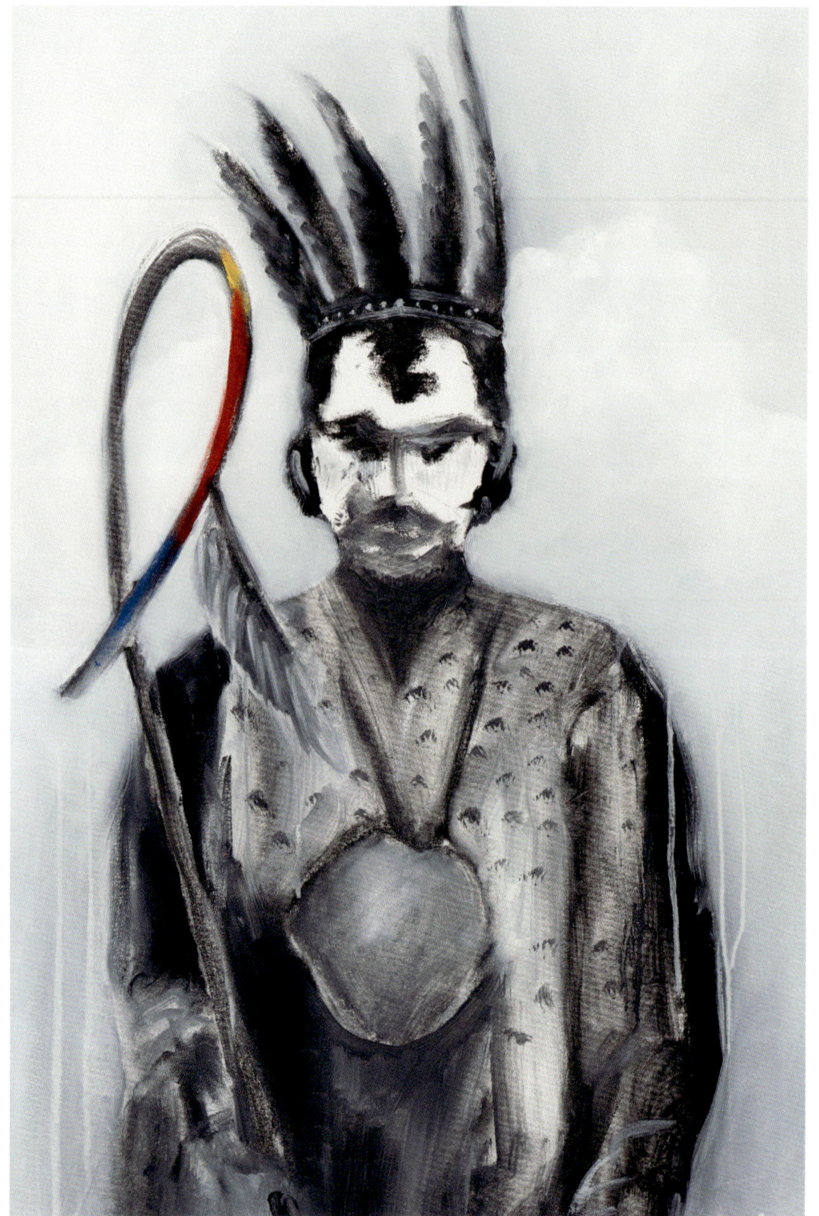

Shaman Takes Away the Pain, 2015

Shaman Dream in Colour, 2015

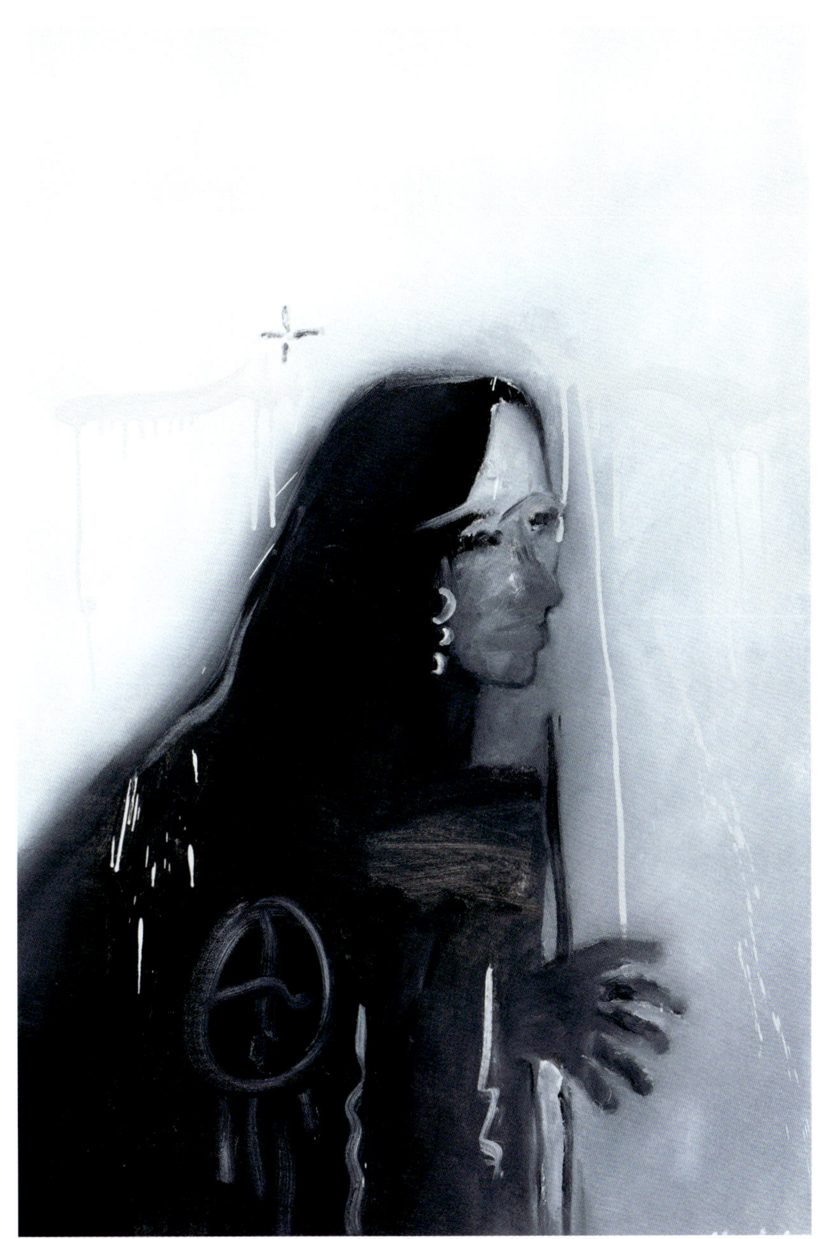

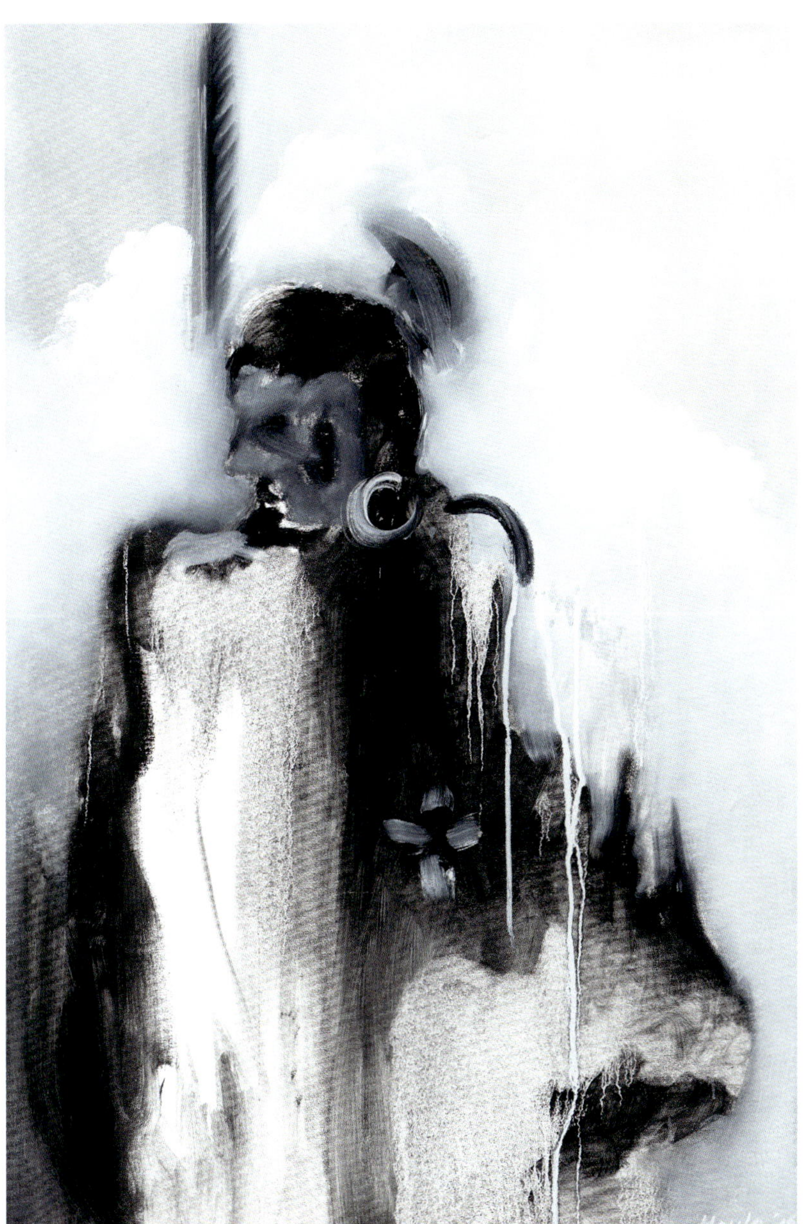

Shaman Heals by Touching, 2015

Shaman Never Die, 2015

SOVEREIGNTY

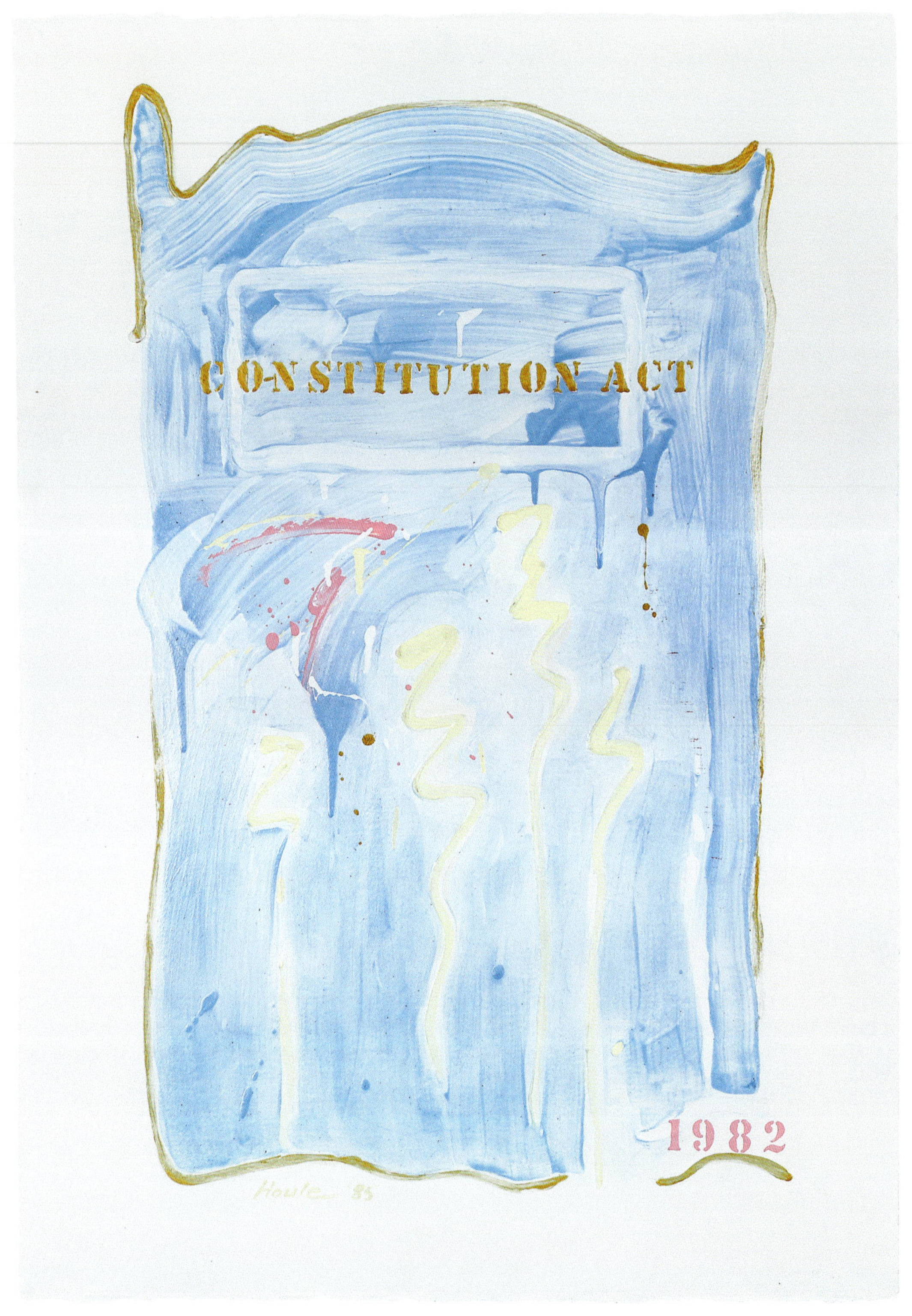

Constitution Act 1982, 1985

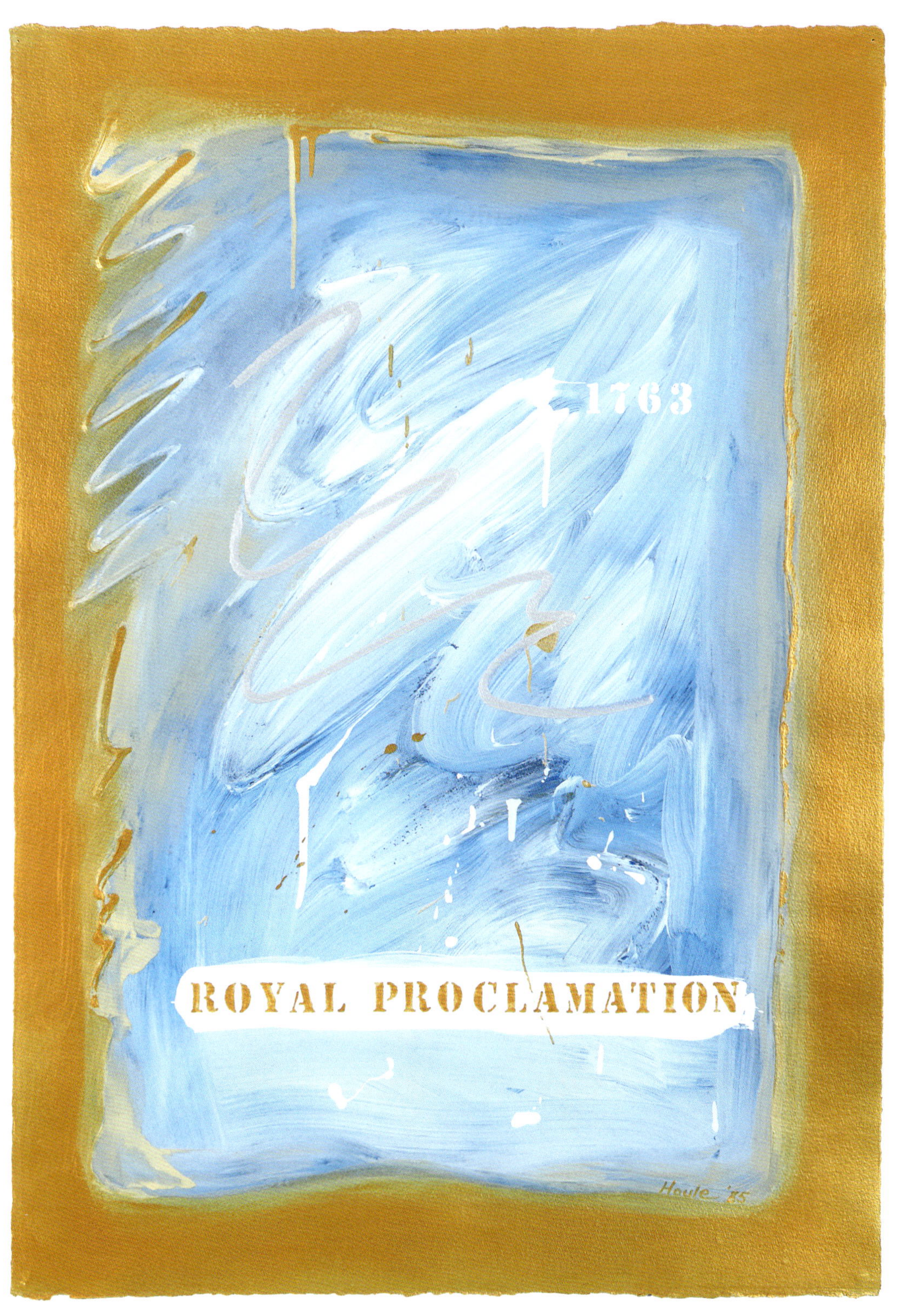

Royal Proclamation 1763, 1985

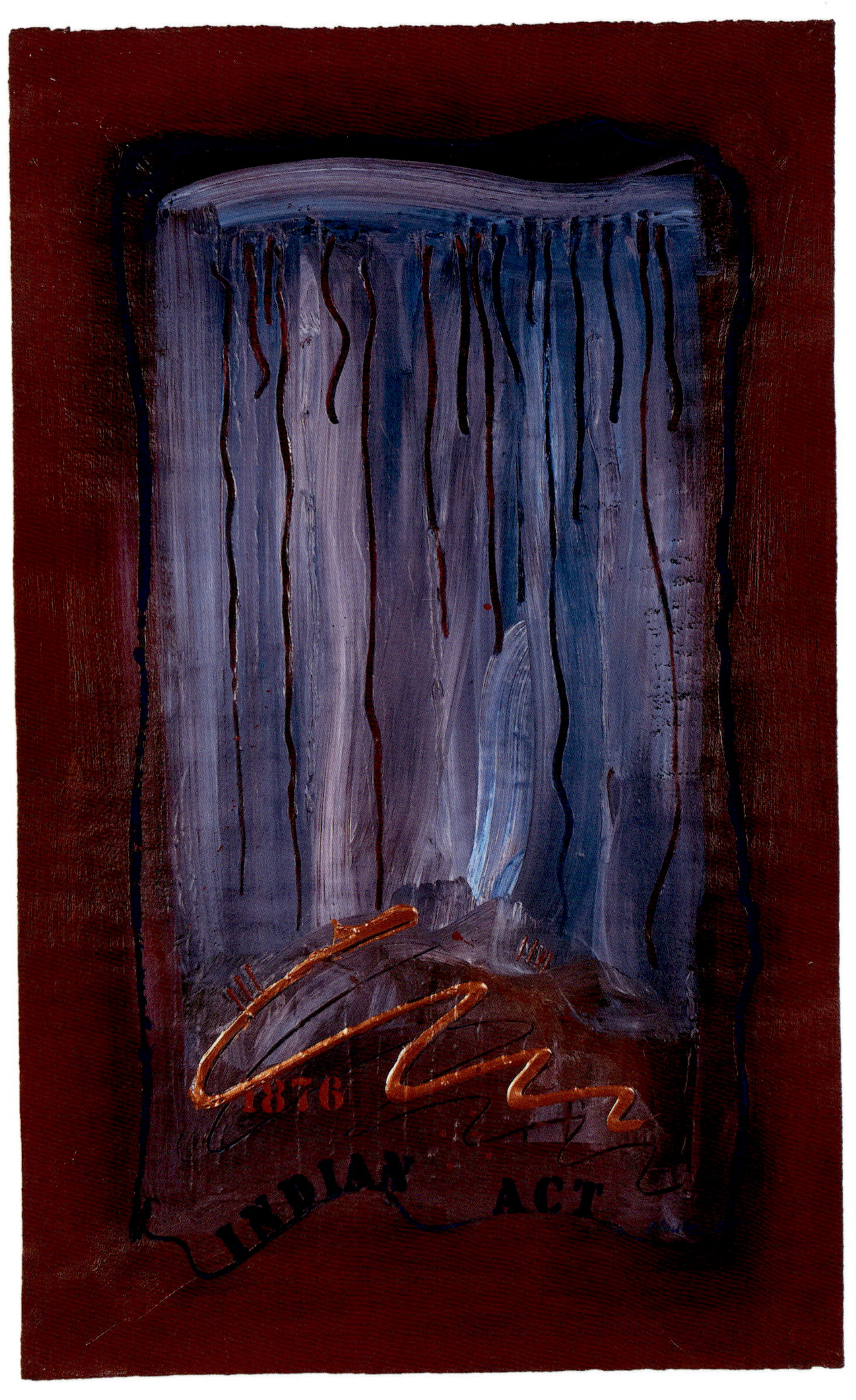

Indian Act 1876, 1985

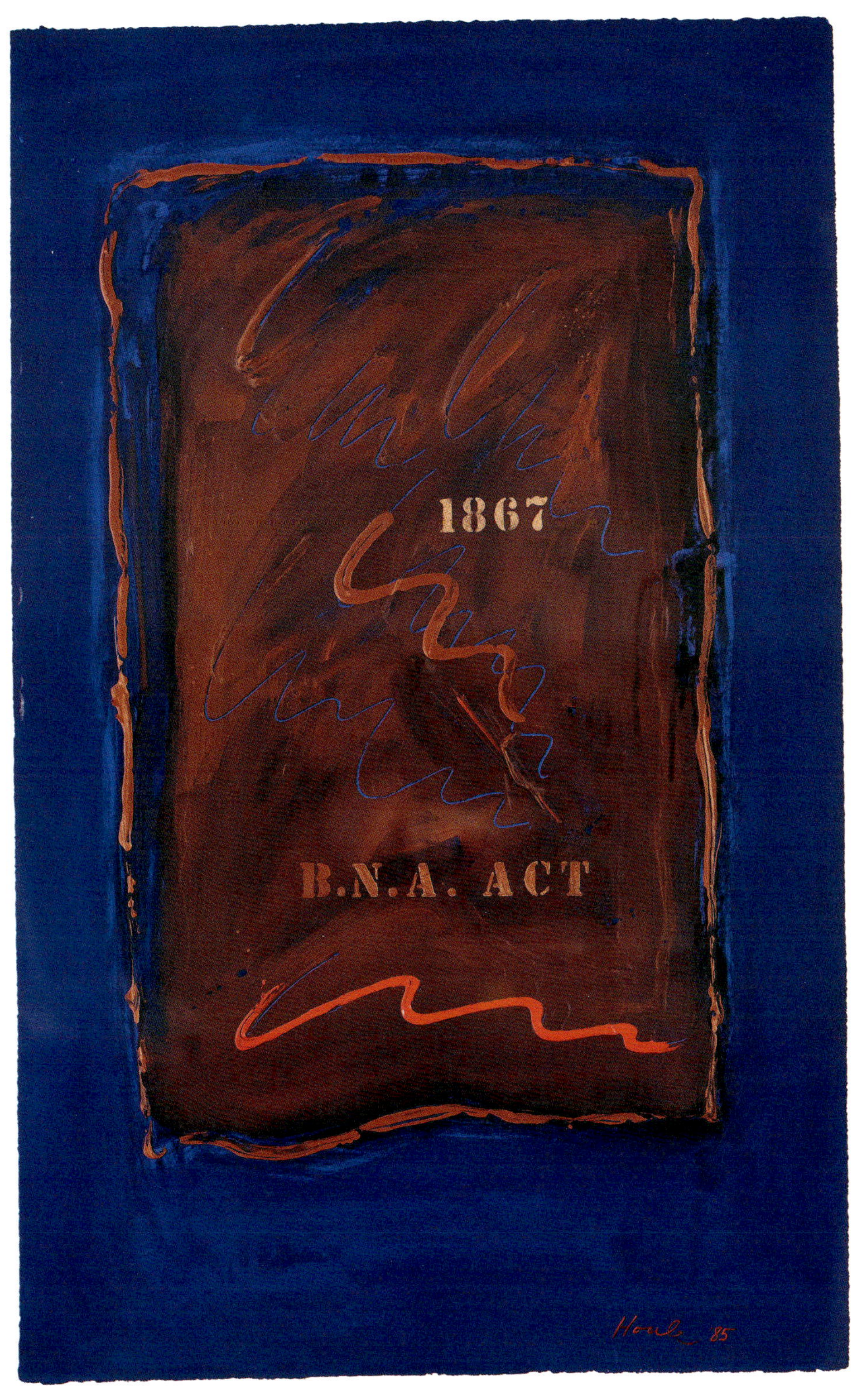

B.N.A. Act 1867, 1985

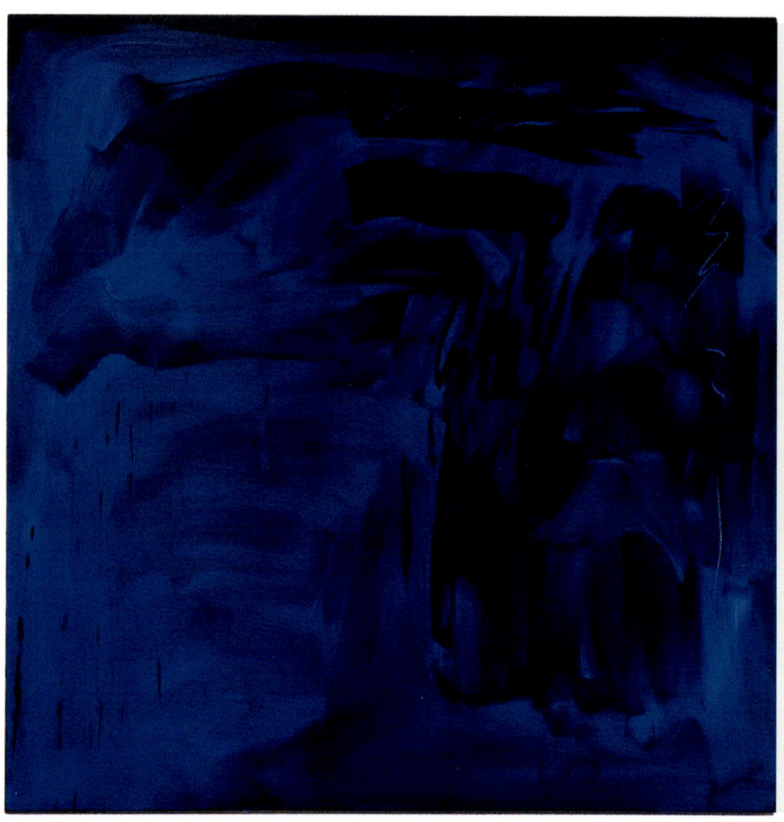

THE ROYAL PROCLAMATION October 7, 1763 BY THE KING, A PROCLAMATION GEORGE R. Whereas We have taken into Our Royal Consideration the extensive and valuable Acquisitions in America, secured to our Crown by the late Definitive Treaty of Peace, concluded at Paris, the 10th Day of February last; ....And whereas it is just and to our Interest, and the Secur at the several Nations or Tribe We are connected, and who live hould not be molested or distu of such Parts of Our Domi not having been ceded to or purchased by Us, are reserved to them, or any of them, as their Hunting Grounds. - We do therefore, with the Advice of our Privy Council, declare it to be our Royal Will and Pleasure, that no Governor or Commander in Chief in any of our Colonies of Quebec, East Florida, or West Florida, do presume, upon any Pretence whatever, to grant Warrants of Survey,....or upon any Lands whatever, which, not having been ceded to or purchased by Us as aforesaid, are reserved to the said Indians, or any of them. And We do further declare it to be Our Royal Will and Pleasure, for the present as aforesaid, to reserve under our Sovereignty, Protection, and Dominion,

Premises for Self Rule: The Royal Proclamation, 1763, 1994

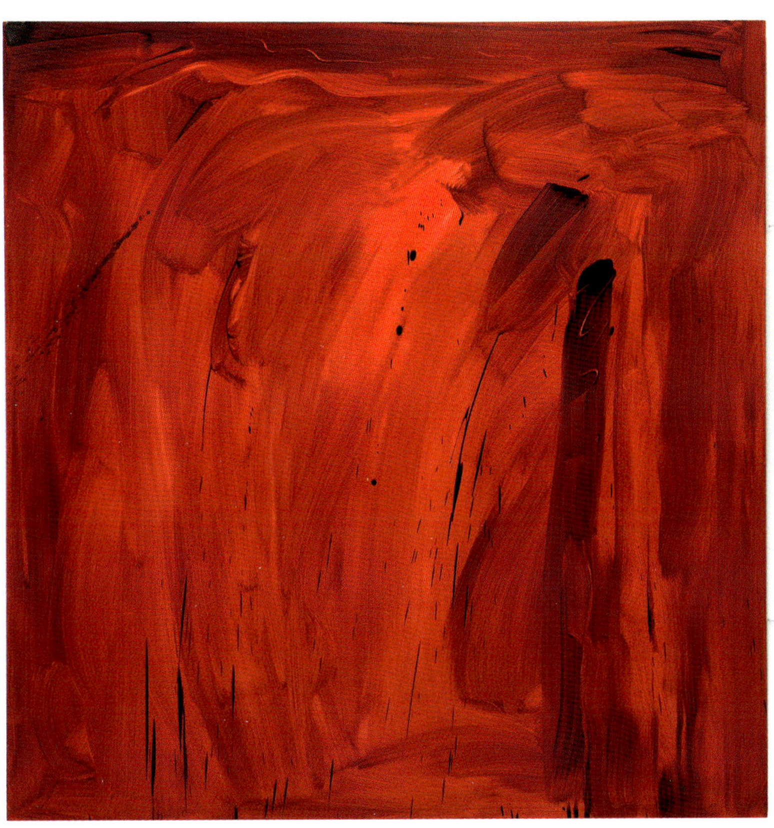

An Act for the Union of Canada, Nova Scotia, and New Brunswick, and the Government thereof; and for Purposes connected therewith. [29*th March* 1867.]....WHEREAS the Provinces of Canada, Nova Scotia, and New Brunswick have expressed their Desire to be federally united into One Dominion under the Crown of the United Kingdom of Great 1 a Constitution similar in Princ Kingdom:....1. This Act may be ci America Act, 1867. 2. The Provi: to Her Majesty the Queen exten ccessors of Her Majesty, Kings 1 Kingdom of Great Britain and Ireland....*Powers of the Parliament...**91.*** It shall be lawful for the Queen, by and with the Advice and Consent of the Senate and House of Commons, to make Laws for the Peace, Order, and good Government of Canada, in relation to all Matters not coming within the Classes of Subjects by this Act assigned exclusively to the Legislatures of the Provinces; and for greater Certainty, but not so as to restrict the Generality of the Foregoing Terms of This Section, it is hereby declared that (notwithstanding anything in this Act) the exclusive Legislative Authority of the Parliament of Canada extends to....24. Indians, and Lands reserved for the Indians.... And

Premises for Self Rule: The British North America Act, 1867, 1994

An Act to amend and consolidate the laws respecting Indians....[*Assented to 12th April, 1876*]....WHEREAS it is expedient to amend and consolidate the laws respecting Indians: Therefore Her Majesty, by and with the advice and consent of the Senate and House of Commons of Canada, enacts as follows:-**1**. This Act shall be known and may
Act, 1876;" and shall apply
to al
the North West Territories,
incluc
Keewatin....**3**. The following
terms
shall be held to have the
mean
d to them, unless such
mean
subject or inconsistent with
the context:-1. The term "band" means any tribe, band or body of Indians who own or are interested in a reserve or in Indian lands in common, of which the legal title is vested in the Crown, or who share alike in the distribution of any annuities or interest moneys for which the Government of Canada is responsible; the term "the band" means the band to which the context relates; and the term "band" when action is being taken by the band as such, means the band in council....**6**. The term "reserve" means any tract or tracts of land set apart by treaty or otherwise for the use or benefit of or granted to a particular band of Indians, of which the legal title is in ..

Premises for Self Rule: Indian Act, 1876, 1994

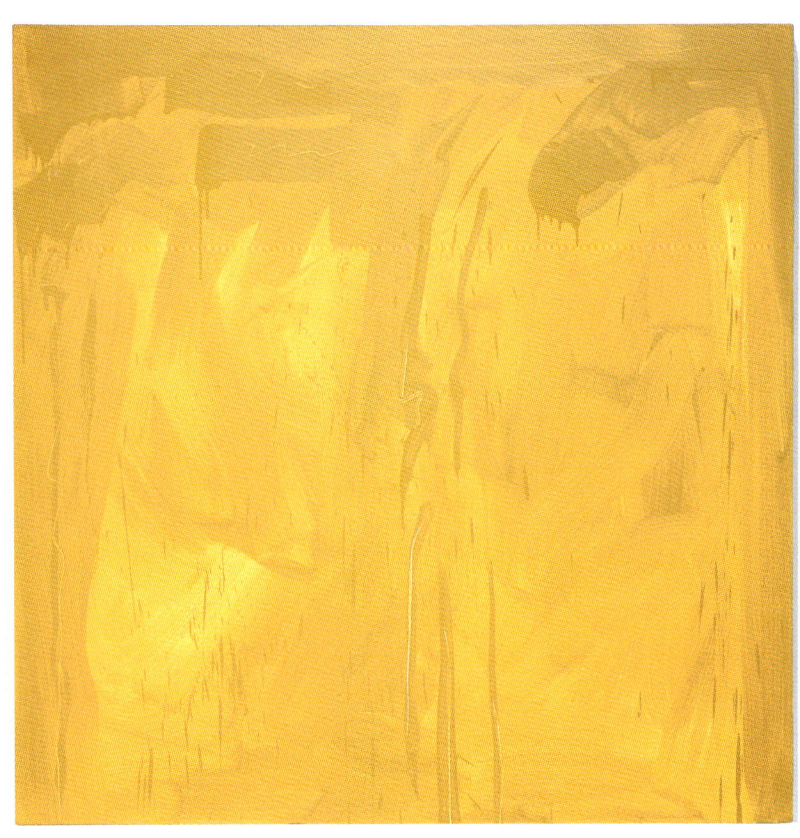

An Act to give effect to a request by the Senate and House of Commons of Canada.... WHEREAS CANADA has requested and consented to the enactment of an Act of the Parliament of the United Kingdom to give effect to the provisions hereinafter set forth and the Senate and the House of Commons of Canada in Parliament assembled have s Her Majesty requesting that H sly be pleased to cause a Bill t rliament of the United Kingd he *Constitution Act, 1982* set out t is hereby enacted for and shall h anada and shall come into force as provided in that Act....2. No Act of the Parliament of the United Kingdom passed after the *Constitution Act, 1982* comes into force shall extend to Canada as part of its law.... This Act may be cited as the *Canada Act 1982*.... PART I. CANADIAN CHARTER OF RIGHTS AND FREEDOMS....25. The guarantee in this Charter of certain rights and freedoms shall not be construed so as to abrogate or derogate from any aboriginal, treaty or other rights or freedoms that pertain to the aboriginal peoples of Canada including (a) any rights or freedoms that have been recognized by the Royal Proclamation of October 7, 1763; and (b) any rights or freedoms that may be acquired

Premises for Self Rule: Constitution Act, 1982, 1994

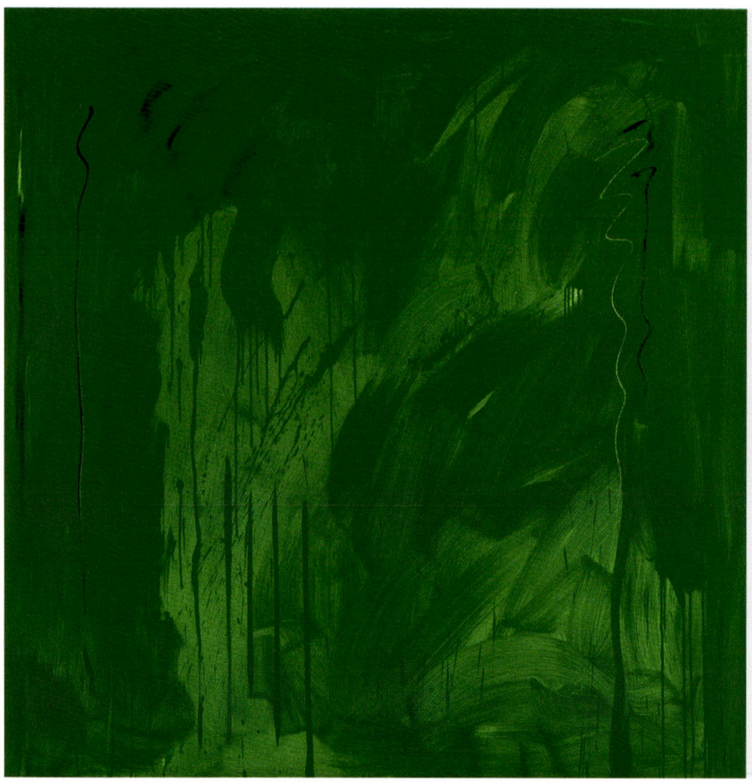

Premises for Self Rule: Treaty No. 1, 1994

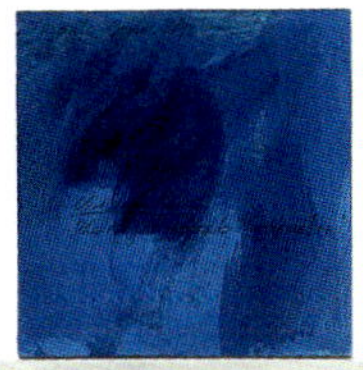
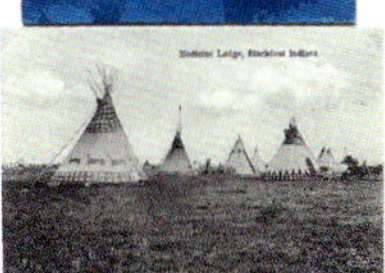

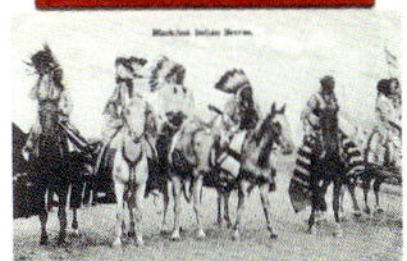

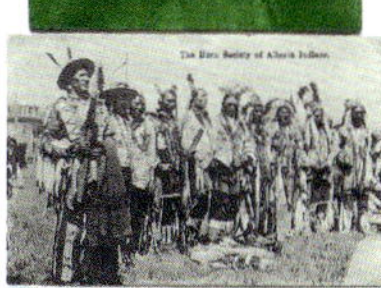

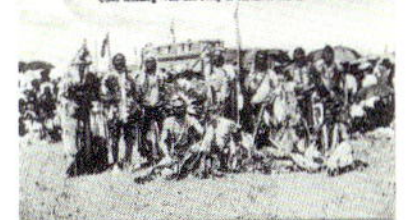
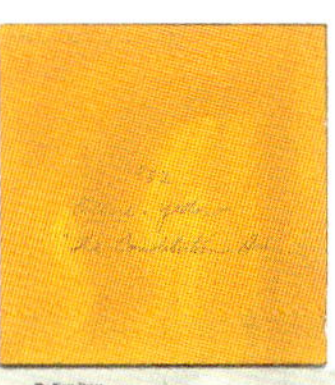

Study for *Premises for Self Rule*, 1994

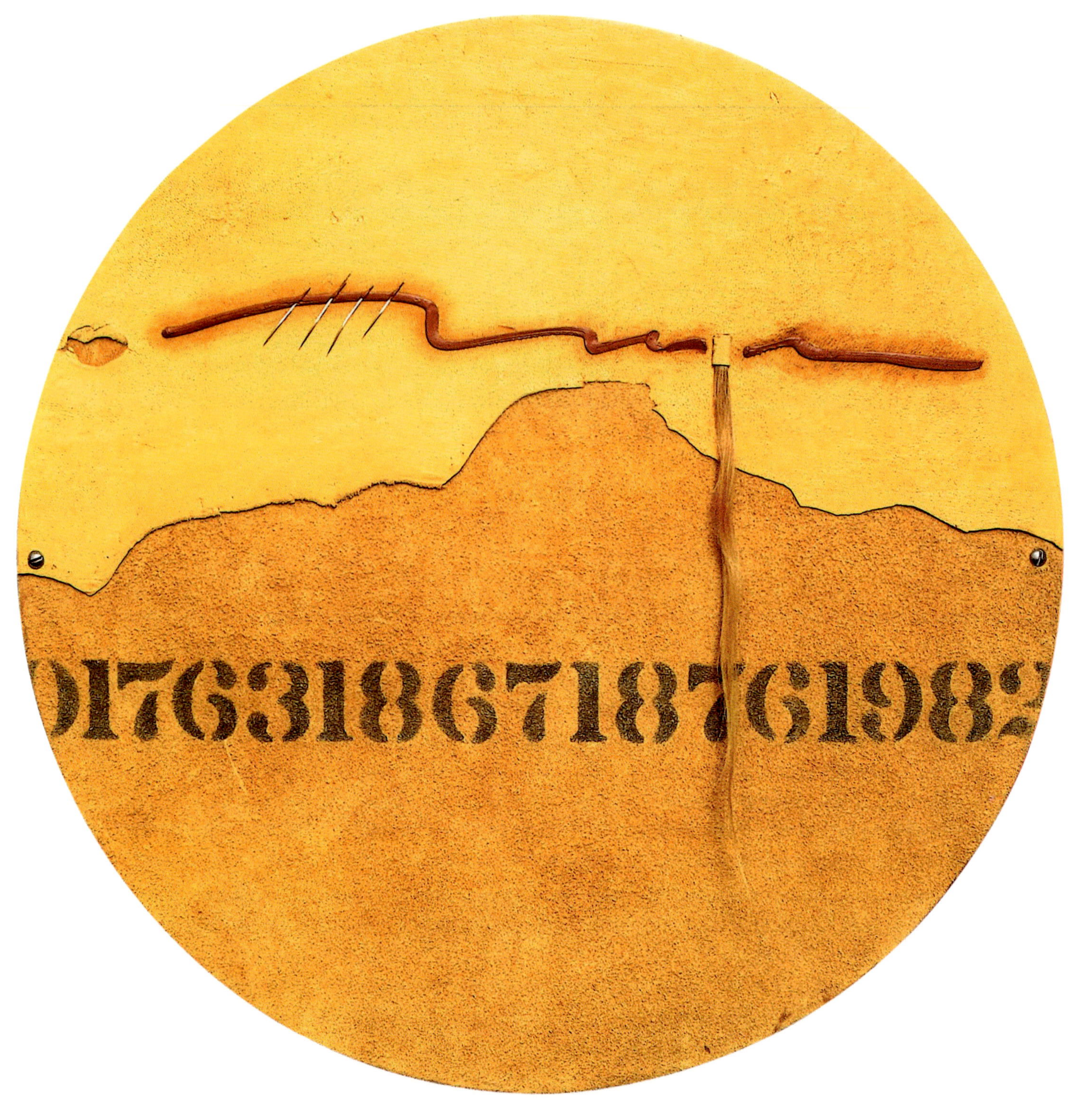

Shield for Aboriginal Title, 1990

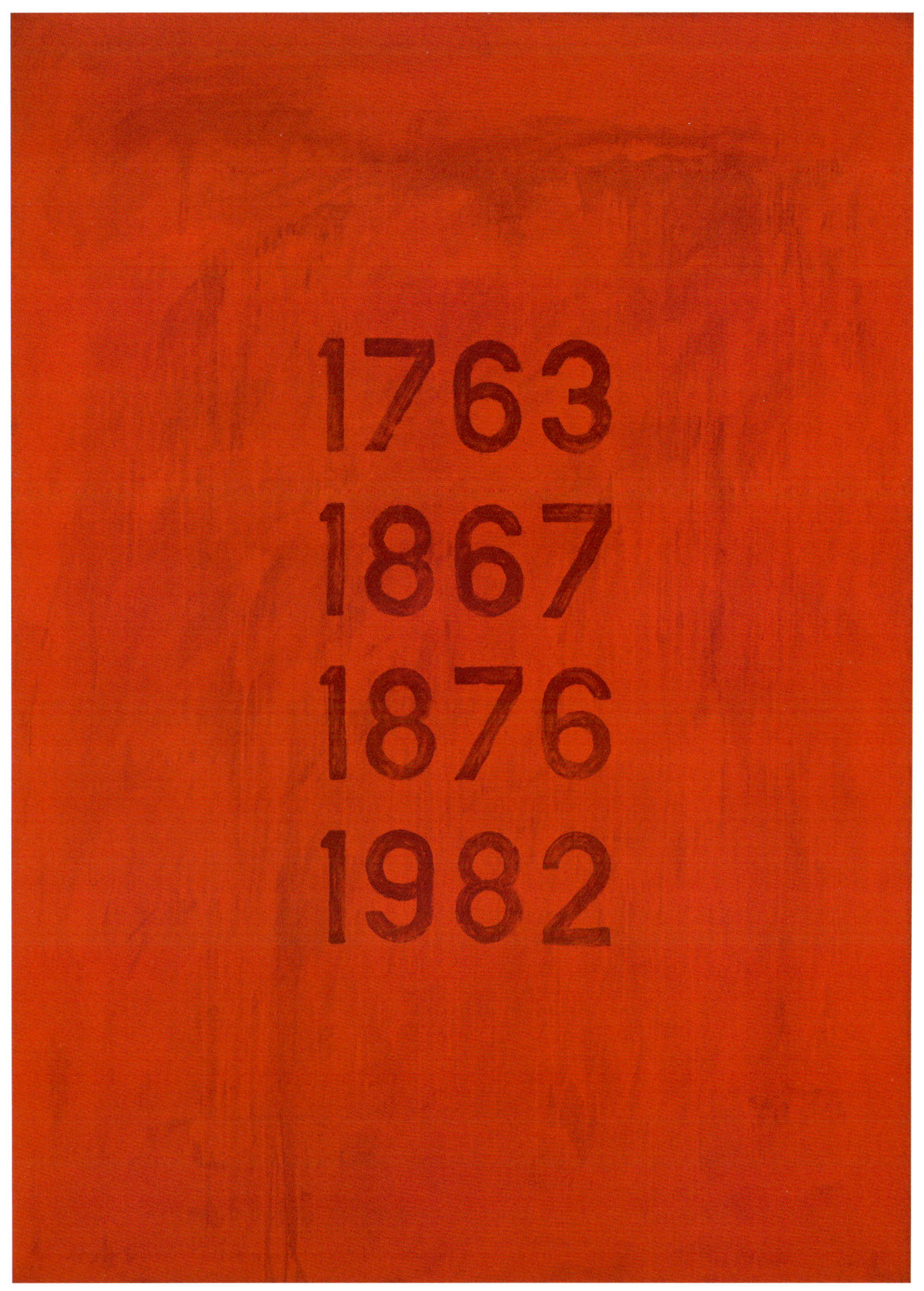

Aboriginal Title, 1989–1990

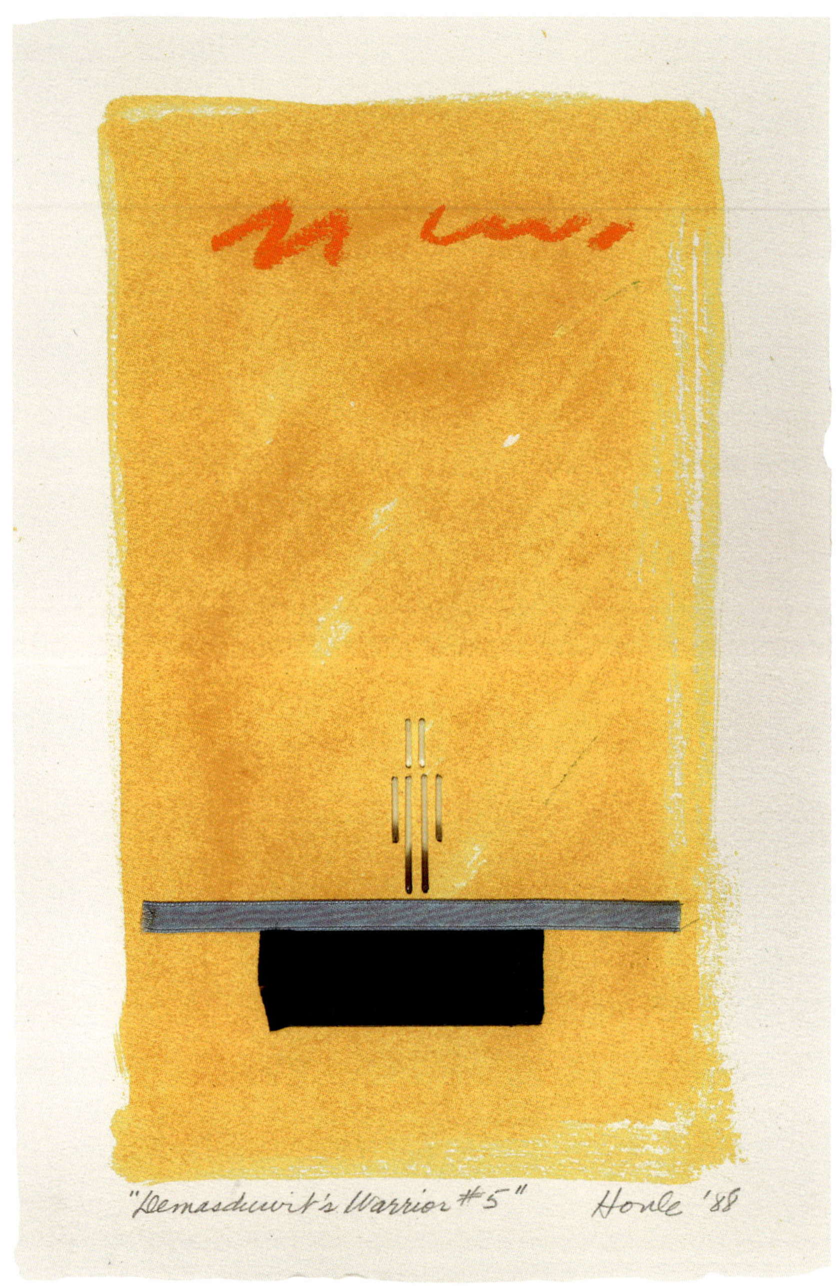

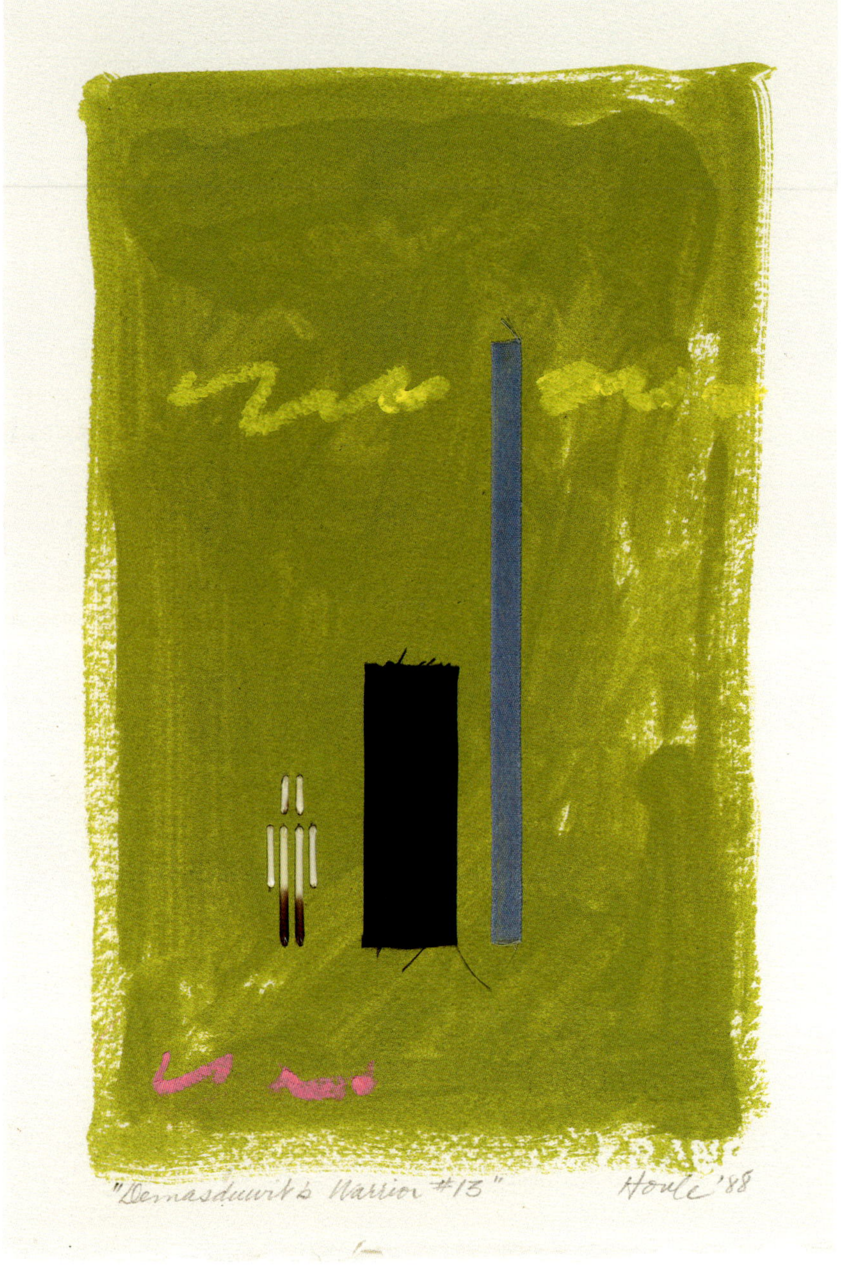

Demasduwit's Warrior #5, 1988

Demasduwit's Warrior #13, 1988

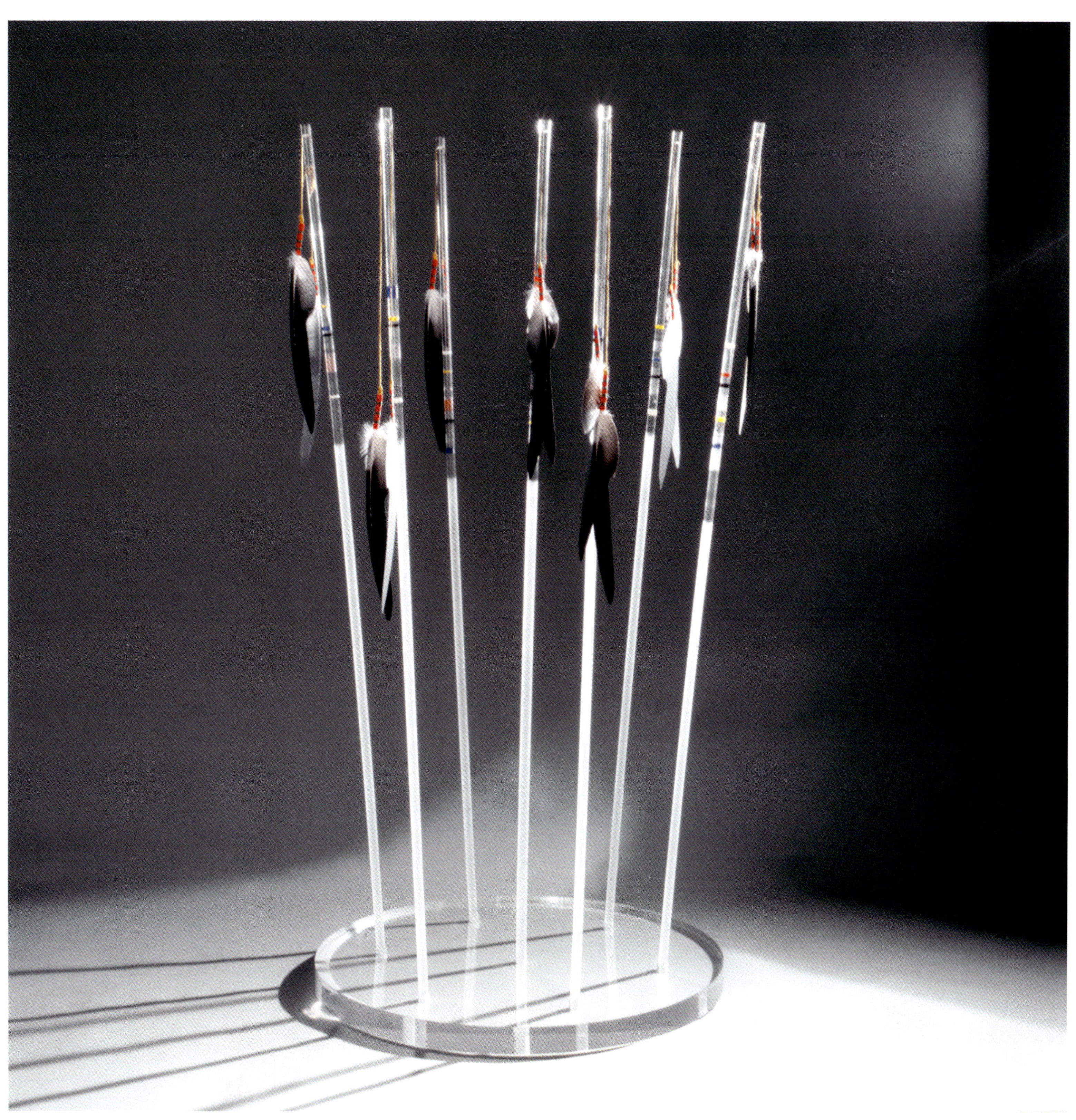

Warrior Lances for Temagami, 1989

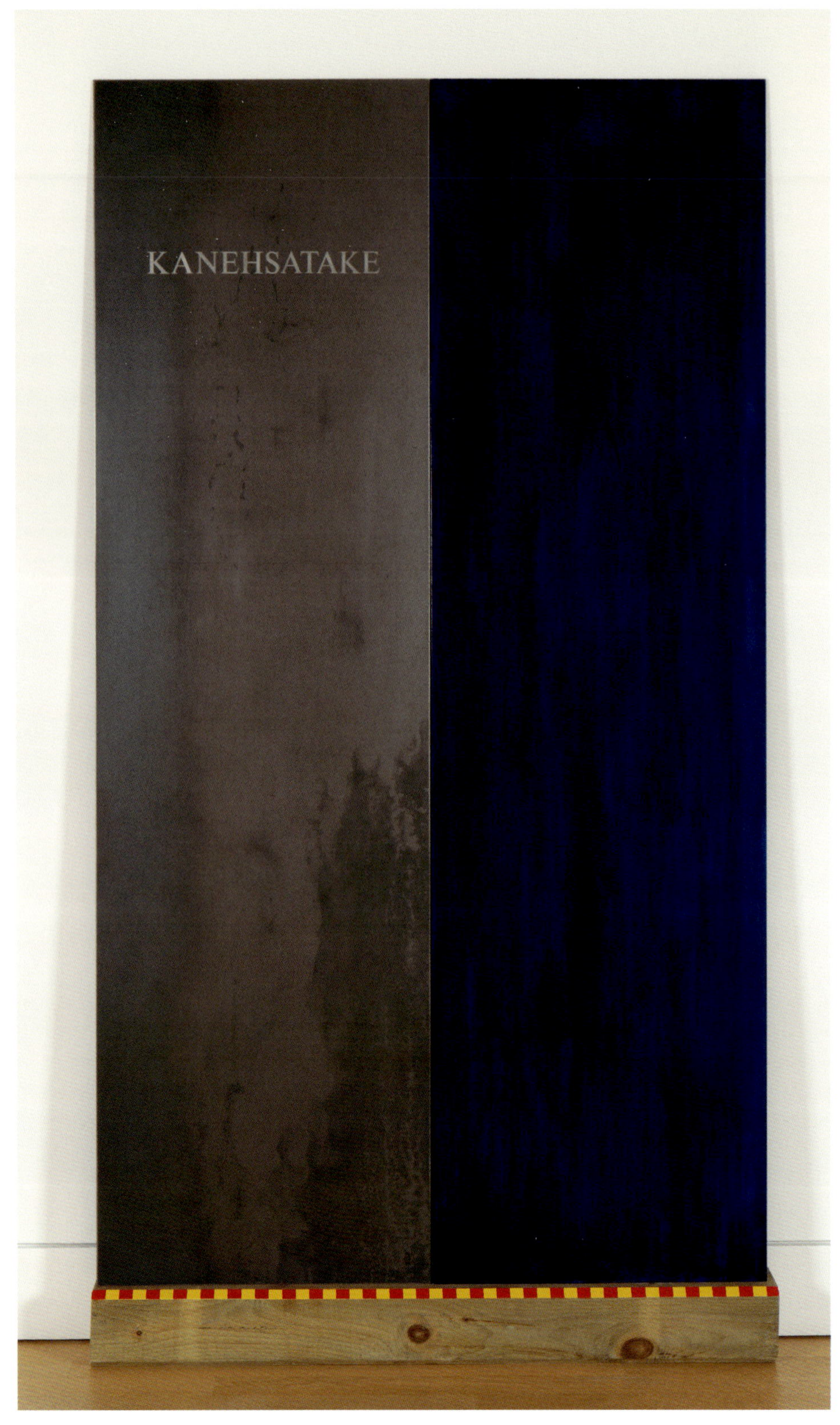

Kanehsatake, 1990–1993

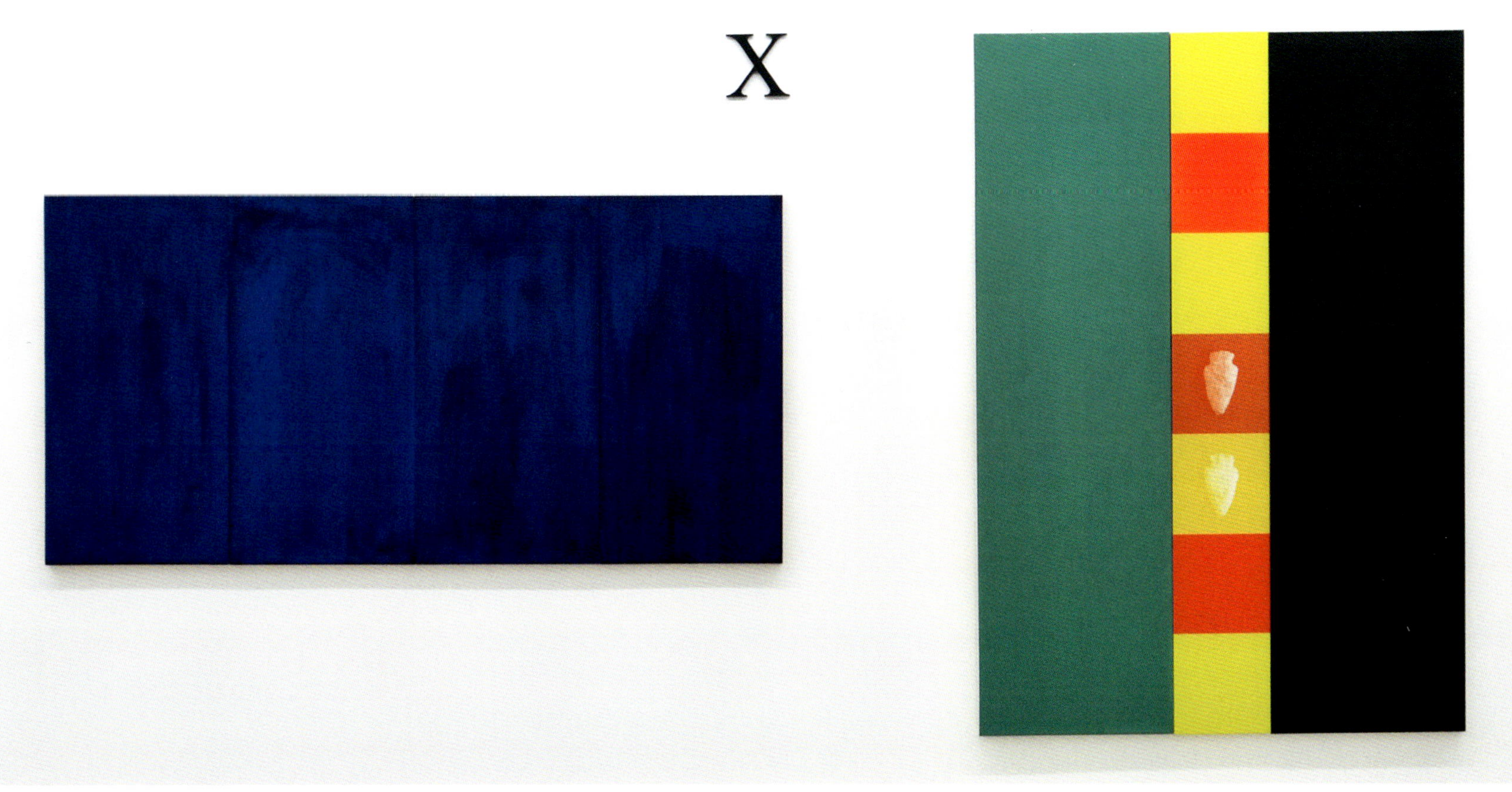

Kanehsatake X, 2000

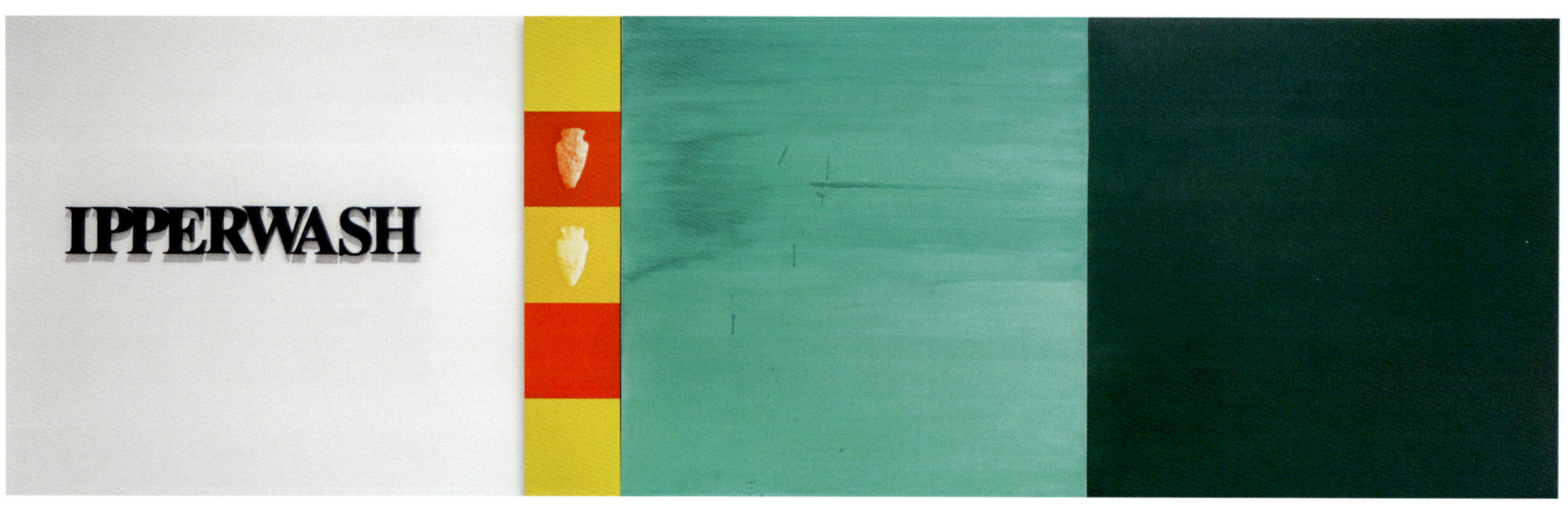

Ipperwash, 2000–2001

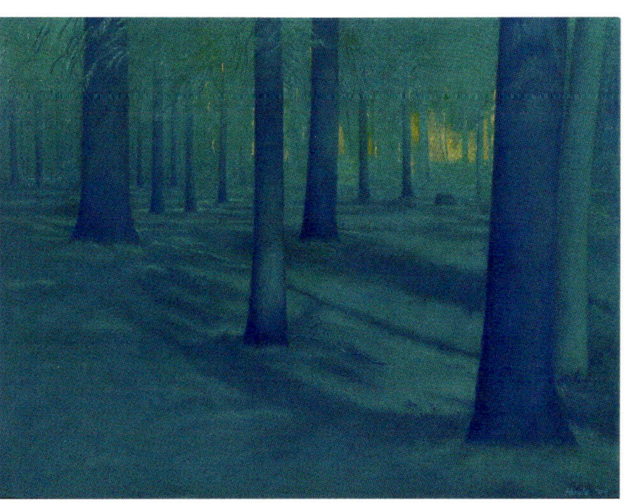

The Pines, 2002–2004

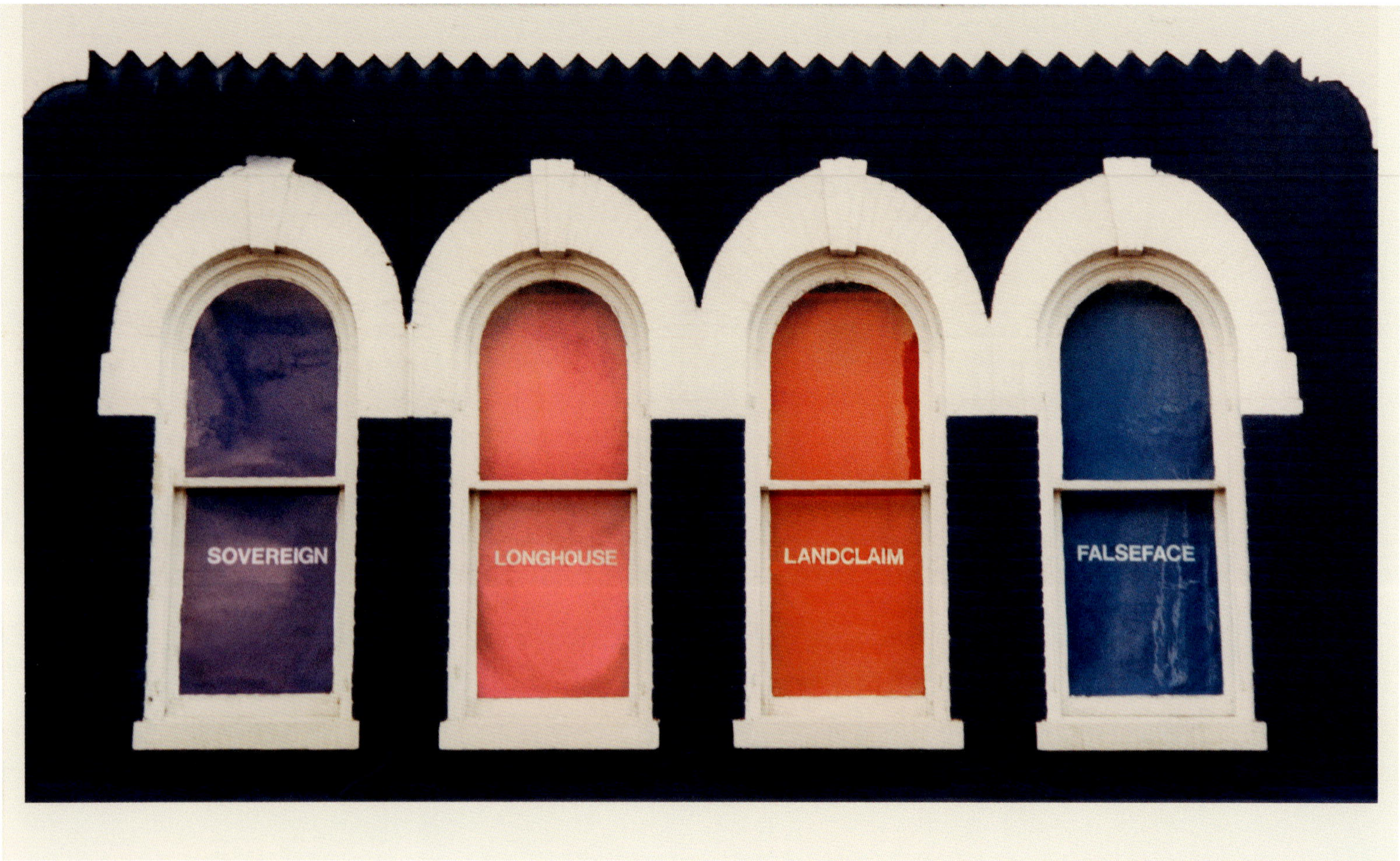

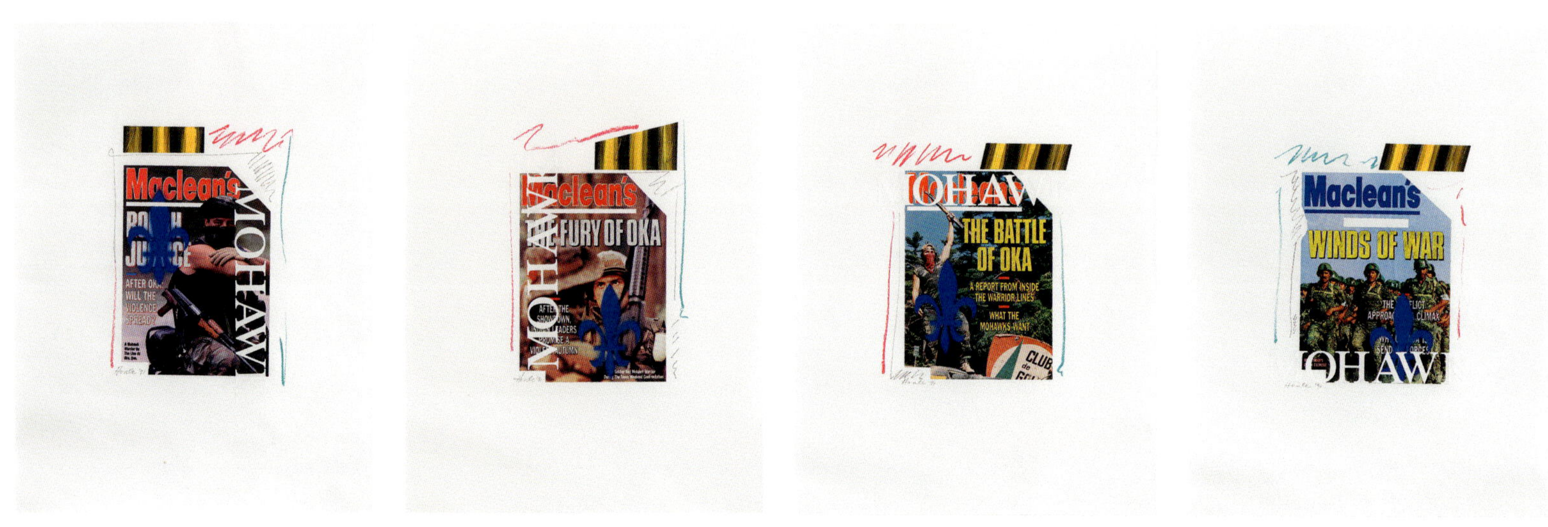

Mohawk Summer, 1990

Mohawk Summer Collages, 1991

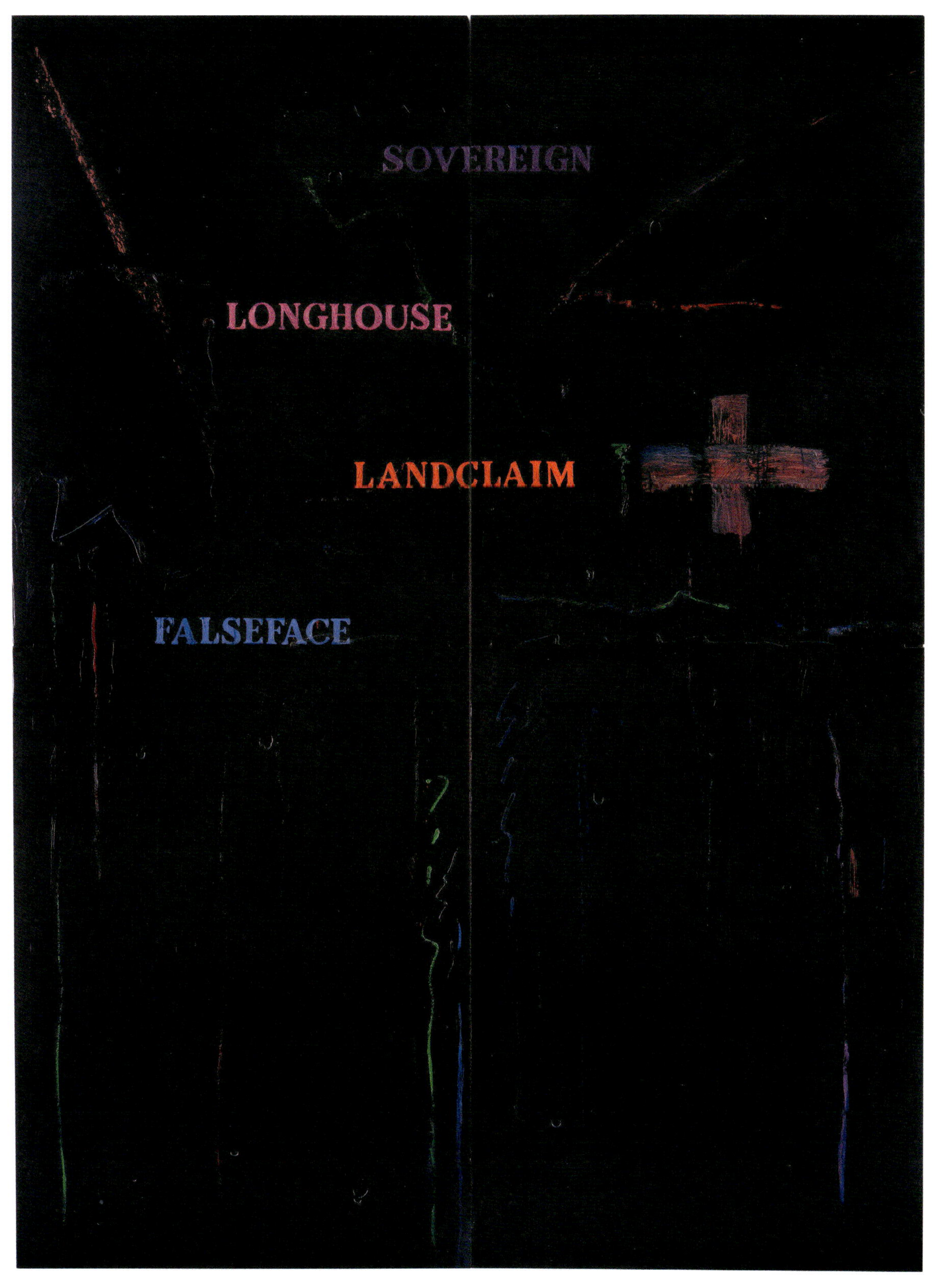

Oka, 1991

ZERO HOUR

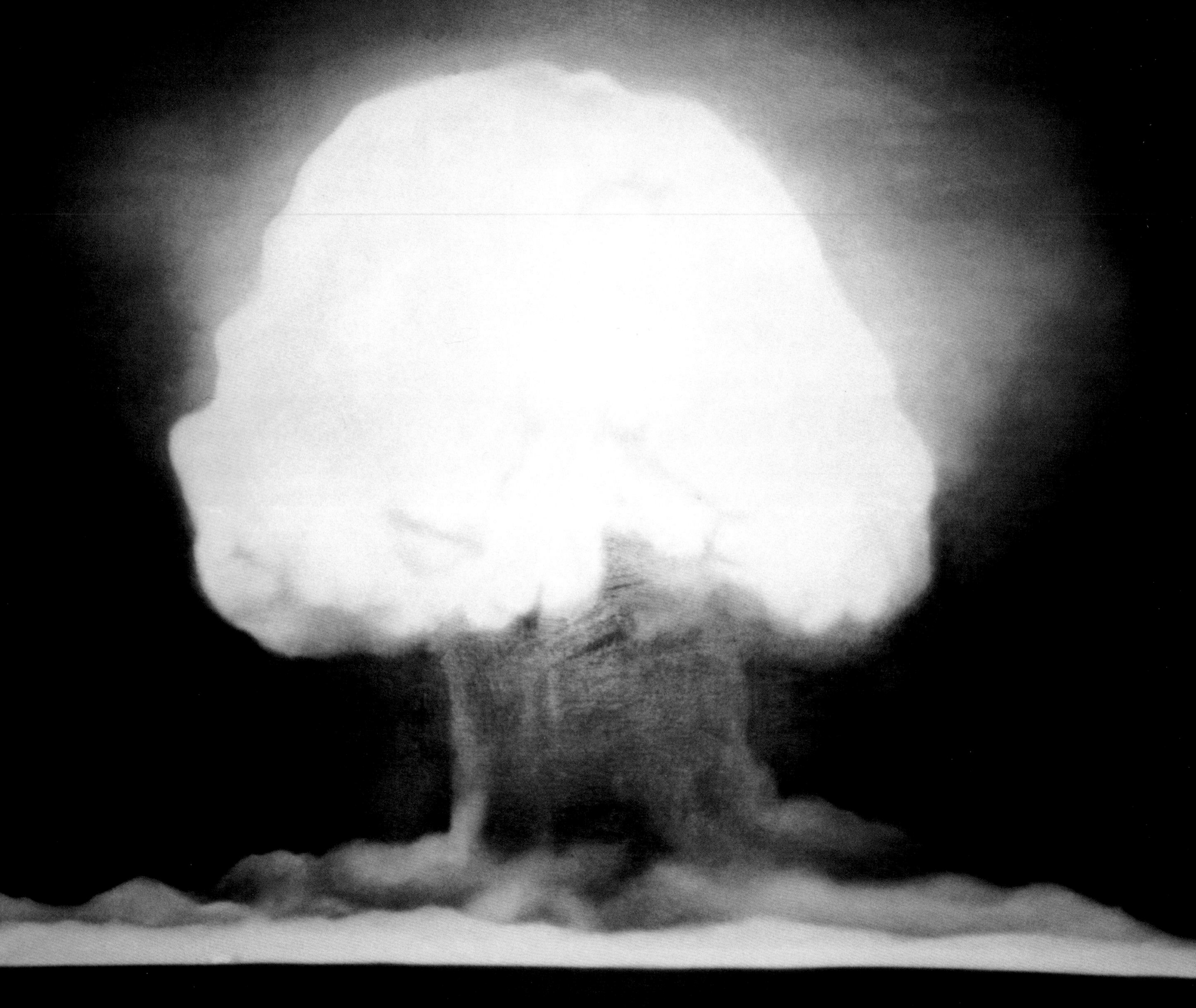

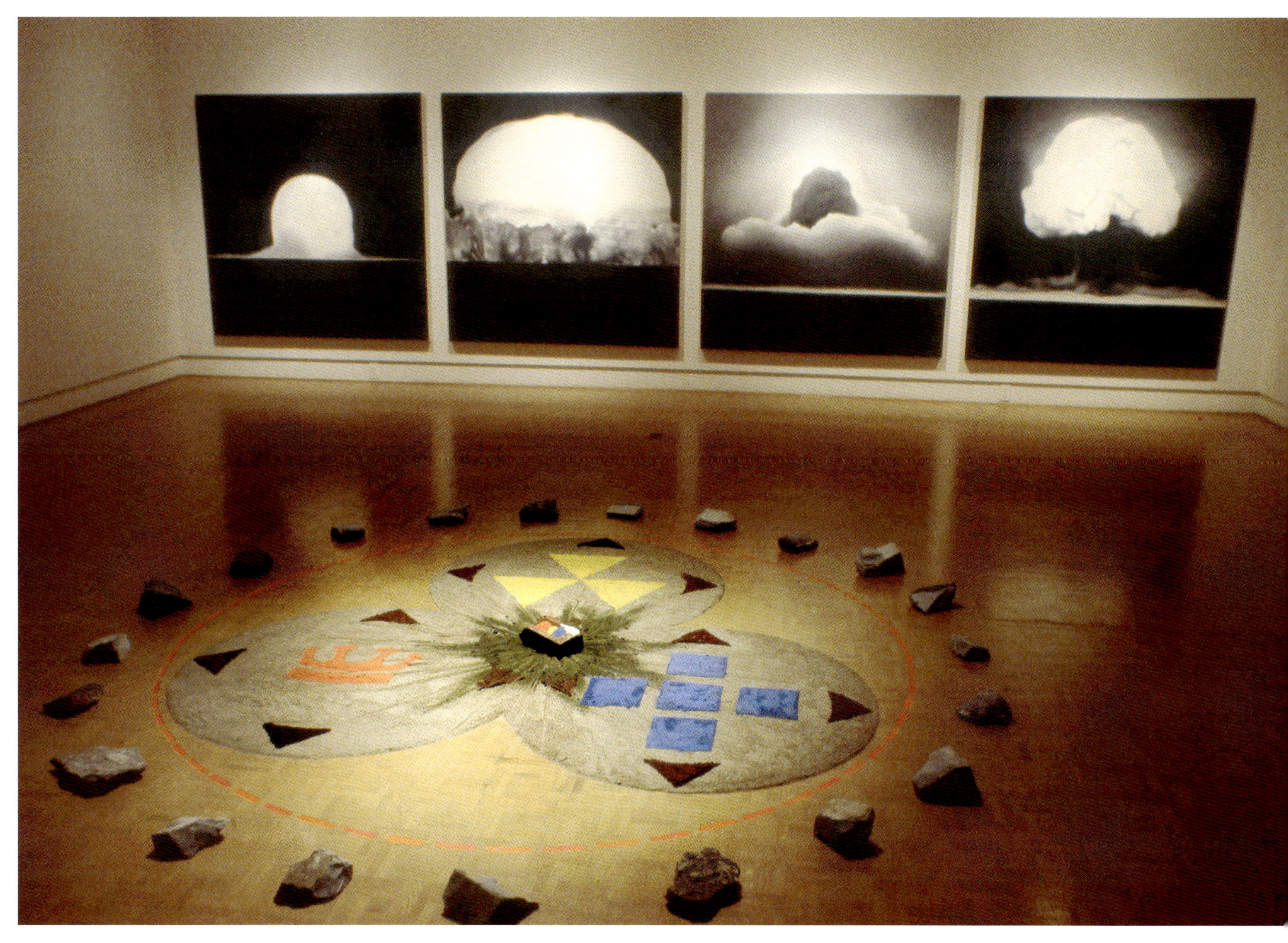

OPPOSITE PAGE:
Zero Hour, 1988 (detail)

ABOVE:
Installation view of *Robert Houle: Zero Hour* at Agnes Etherington Art Centre, Queen's University, May 3 – June 28, 1992

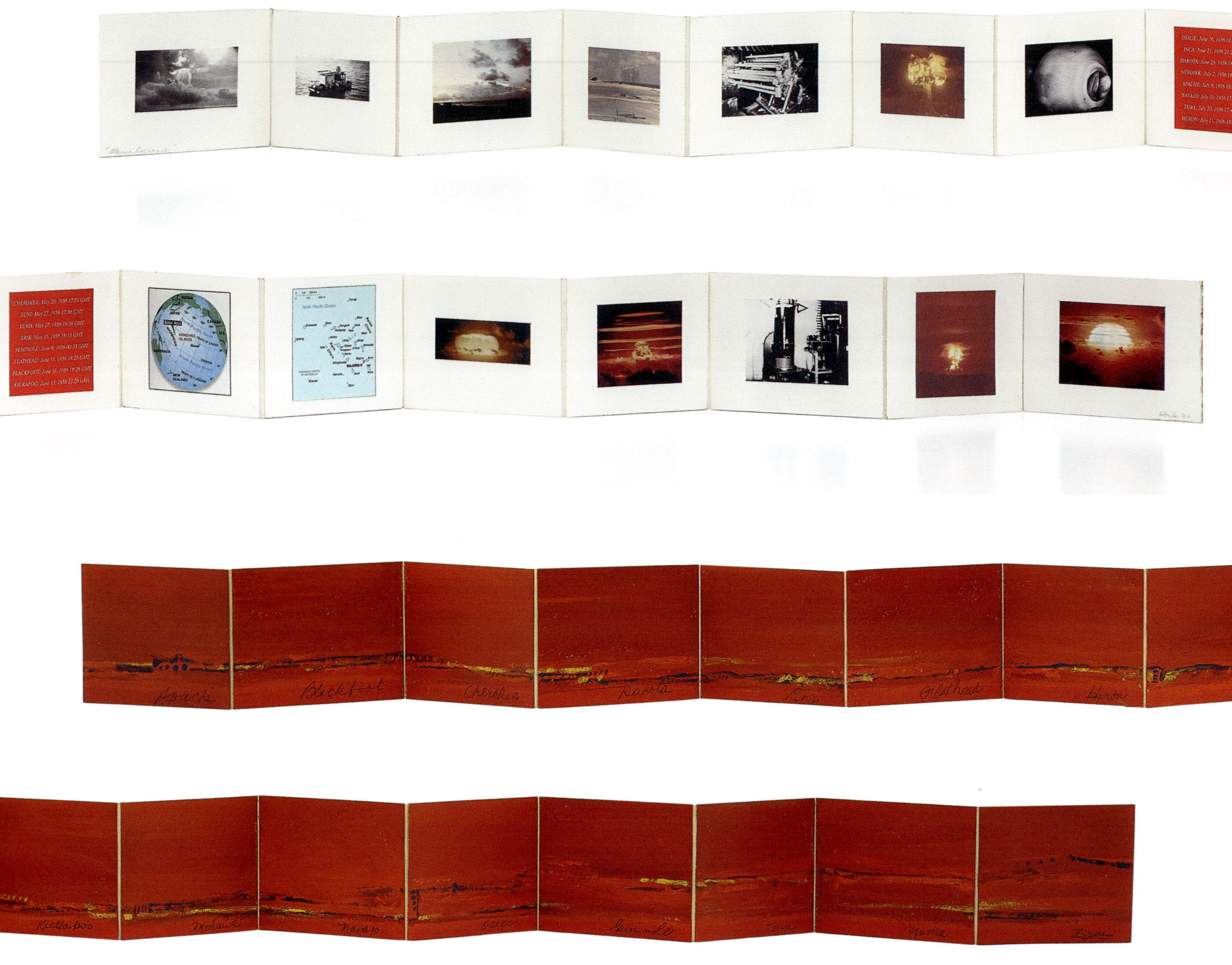

Atomic Lacrosse, 2005

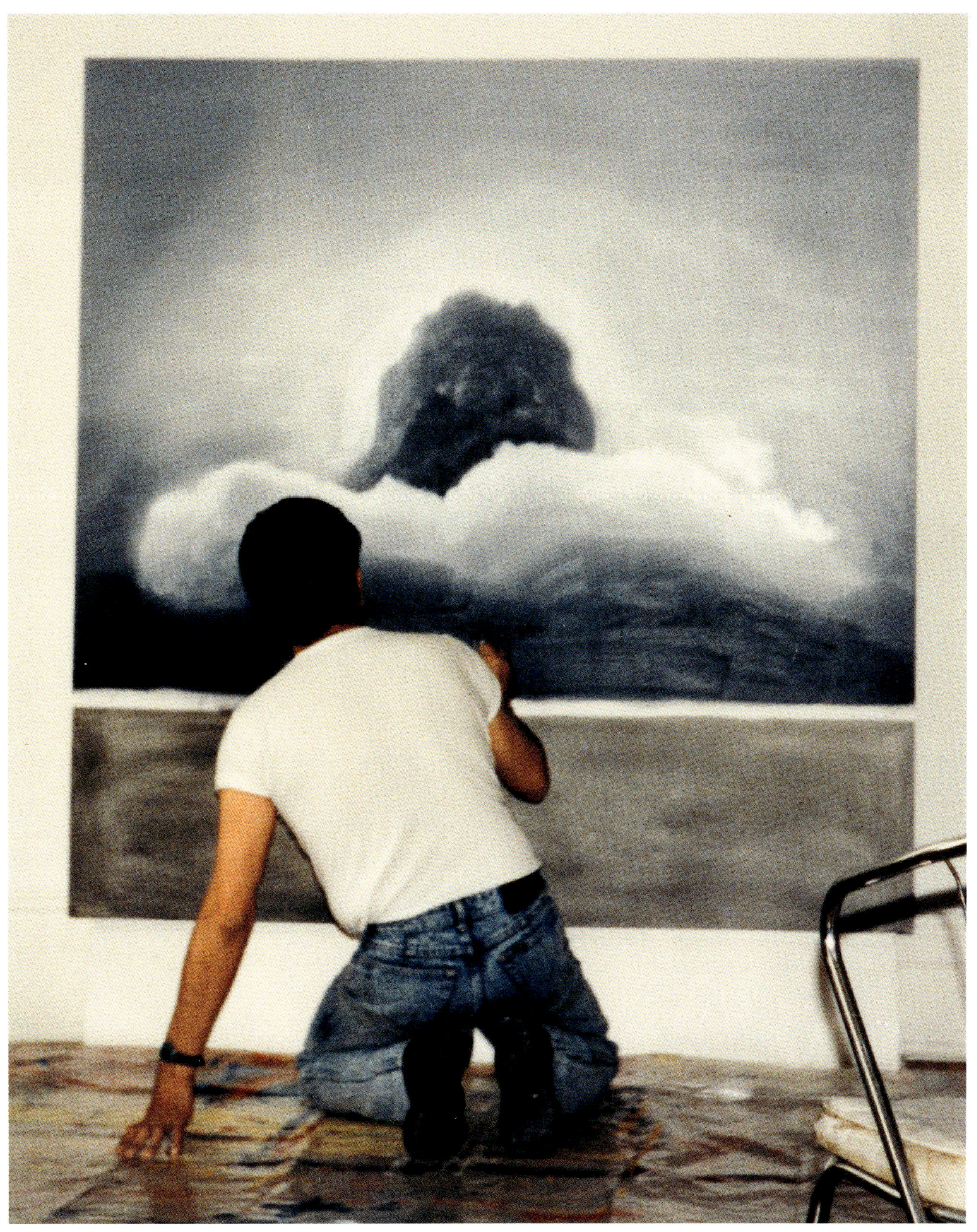

Robert Houle painting *Zero Hour* in his Queen West studio in 1988. Photographed by André Leduc. Image courtesy of the artist.

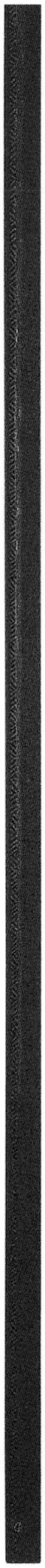

Falklands, 1982

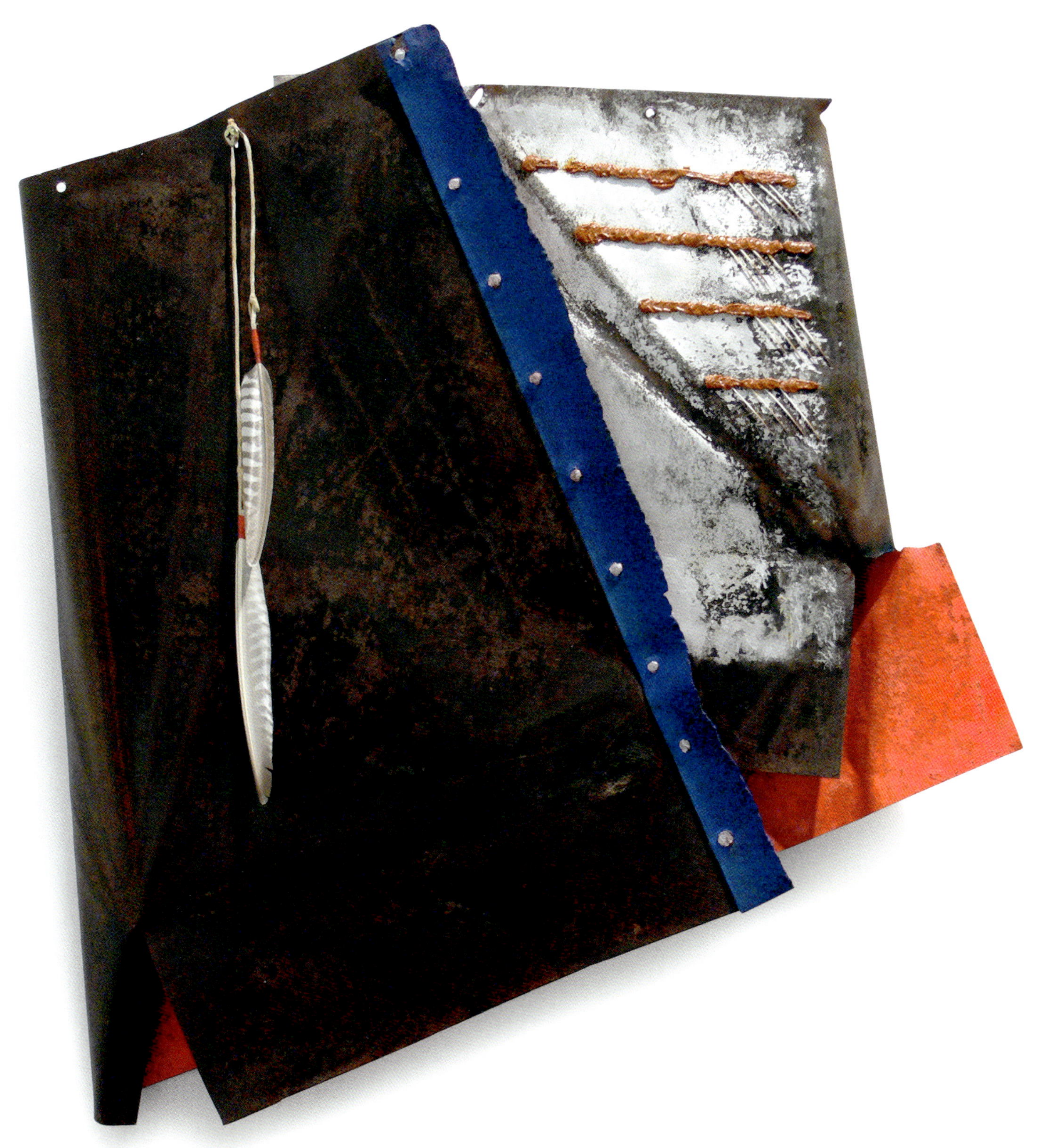

Innu Parfleche, 1990

GESTURES OF INTIMACY

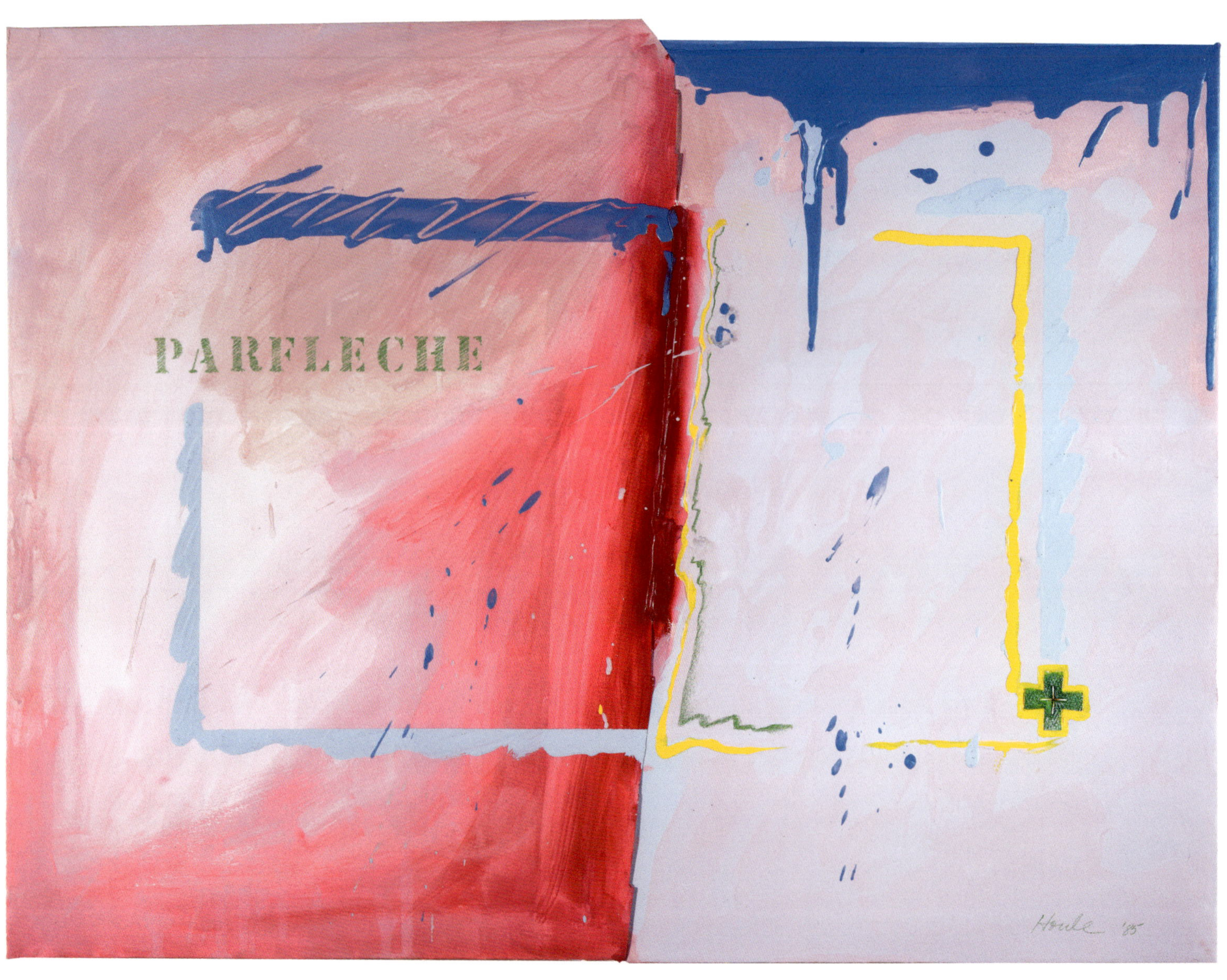

Parfleche for Rock Hudson, 1985

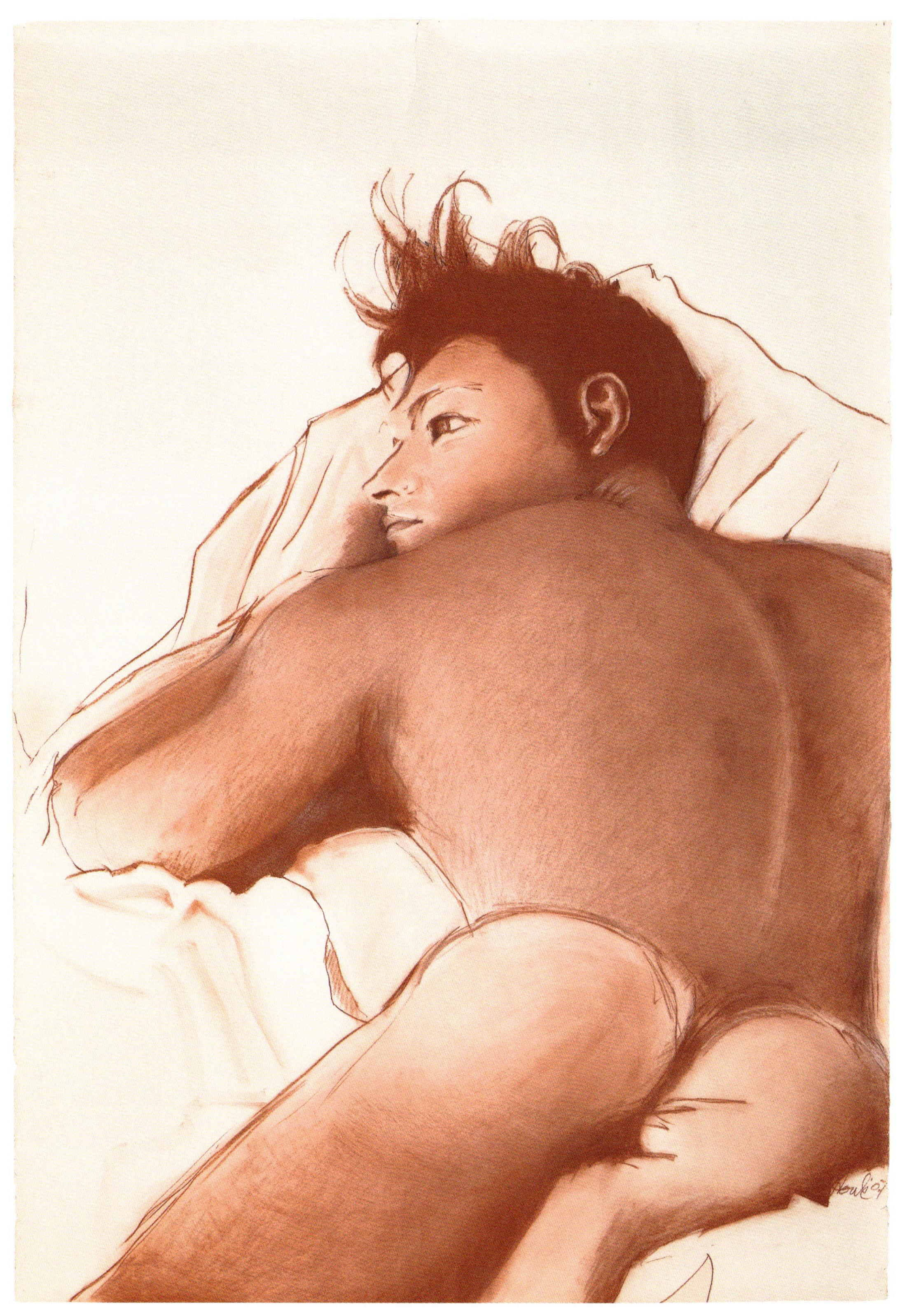

Untitled (Male Nude), 2007

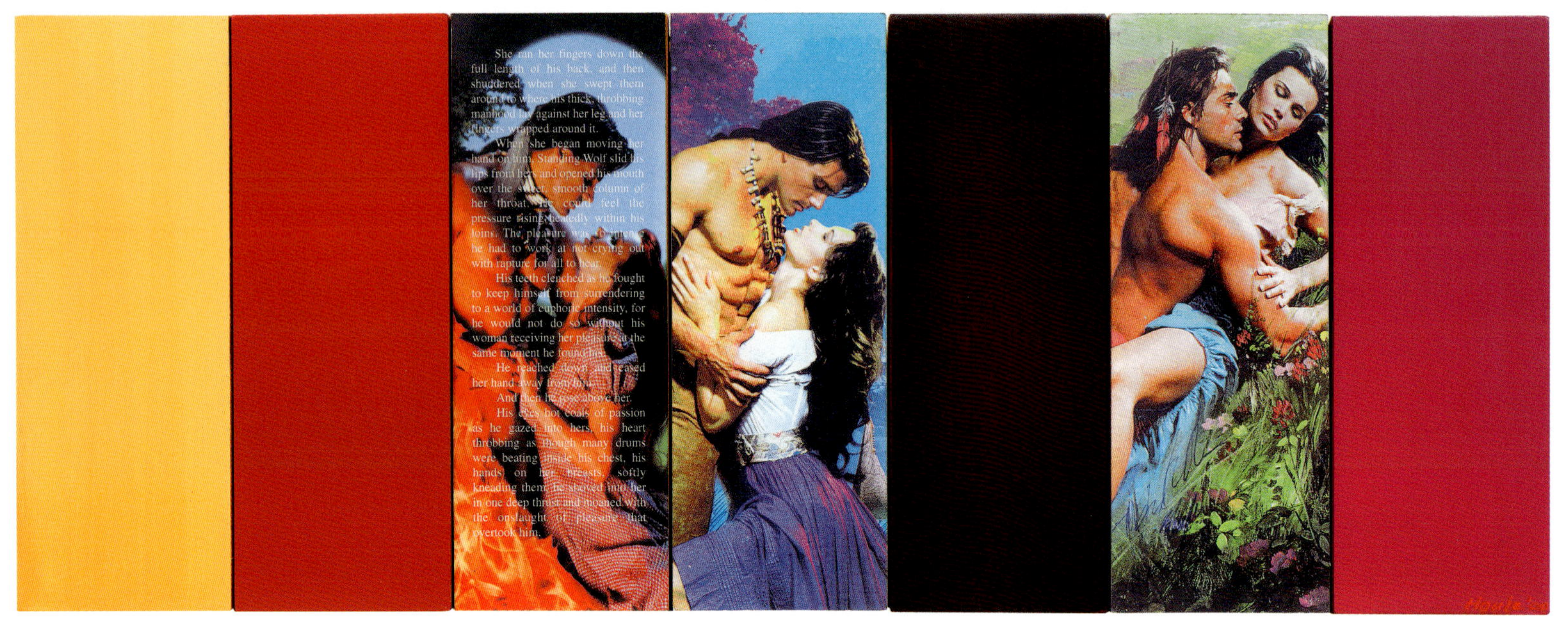

Savage Love, c. 2003

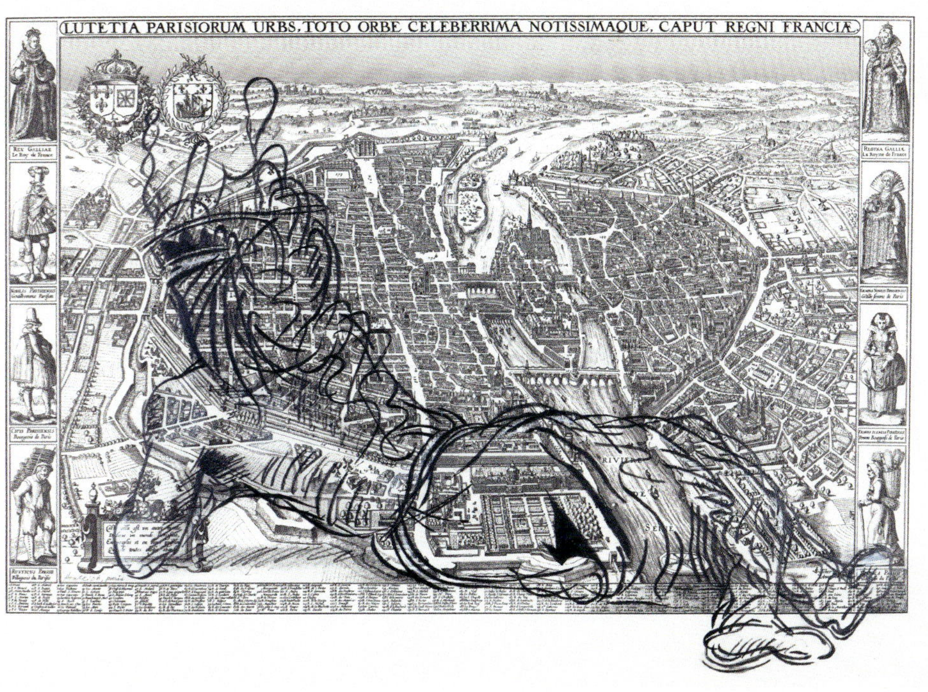

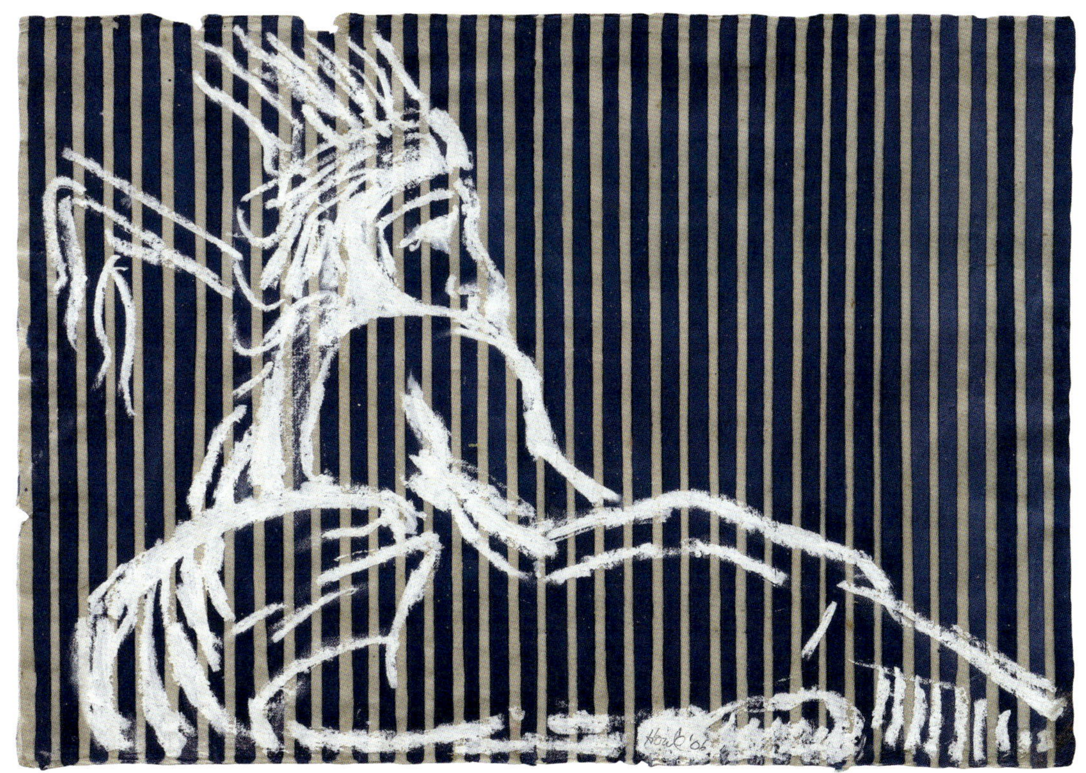

Warrior Resting on Map of Lutetia, 2010

Warrior à la Buren, 2010

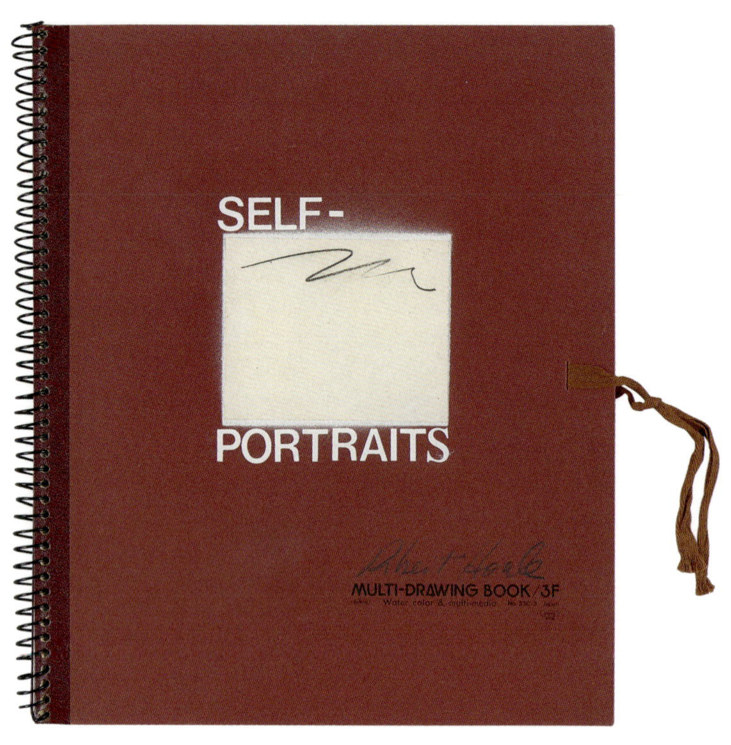
SELF-
PORTRAITS
MULTI-DRAWING BOOK/3F

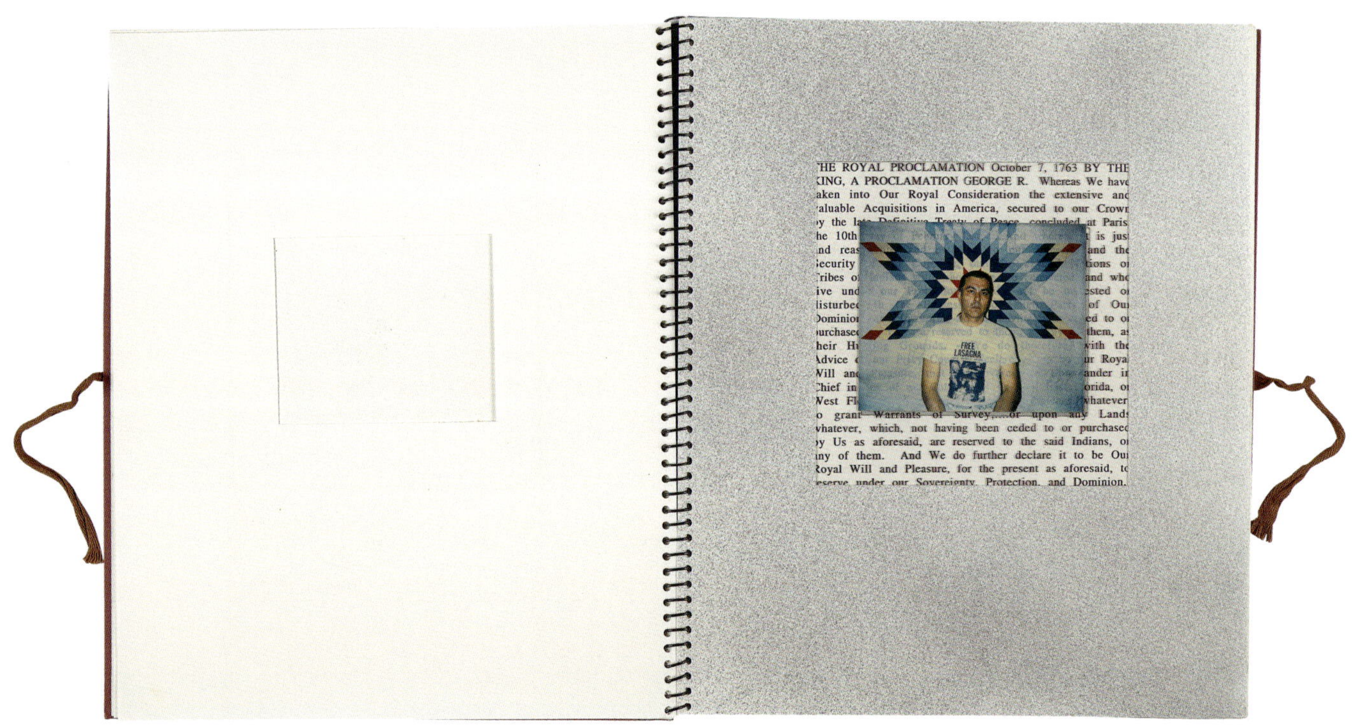
THE ROYAL PROCLAMATION October 7, 1763 BY THE
KING, A PROCLAMATION GEORGE R. Whereas We have
aken into Our Royal Consideration the extensive and
valuable Acquisitions in America, secured to our Crown
whatever, which, not having been ceded to or purchased
by Us as aforesaid, are reserved to the said Indians, or
any of them. And We do further declare it to be Our
Royal Will and Pleasure, for the present as aforesaid, to
FREE
LASAGNA

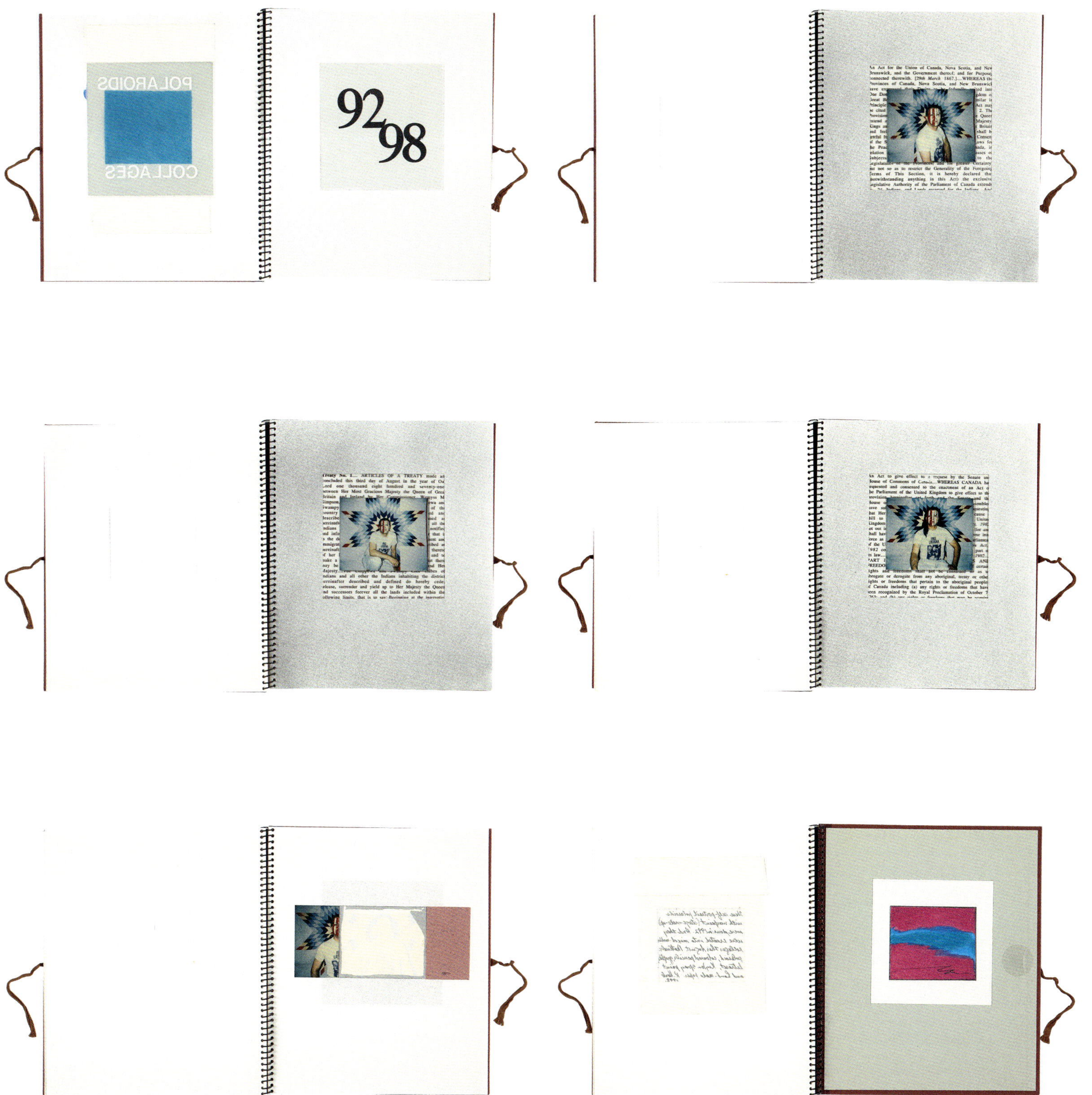

Self Portraits, 1990–1995

Analogues of Indigenous Materiality

David Penney

In 1983, Robert Houle produced a set of four large-scale, precisely rendered drawings in conté crayon inspired by the Canadian Constitution Act, which had been signed in an internationally televised event on April 17, 1982, by Prime Minister Pierre Trudeau, Queen Elizabeth II, and others. The Act severed Canada's final ties of sovereignty to Britain by granting the country the authority to amend its own constitution. Reflecting on this event, Houle said recently that the event of the signing saddened him at the time, surprisingly so: the Indigenous nations of what had become the nation state of Canada had forged relations spanning many generations of alliance and episodic enmity with the Crown, and that was coming to an end.[1] Uncertainty about Indigenous status in the constitution had prompted intense lobbying and negotiations by Indigenous organizations and activist demonstrations during the years preceding the signing. The effort led to Section 35 of the Act, affirming existing treaties and opening the potential for further negotiations over unceded lands that continue to this day. In 1983, Houle's 1983 drawings were the first of several artistic responses to the Act and its implications for Aboriginal sovereignty and self-determination under the new constitution.[2]

Houle titled the suite of drawings *Constitutional Wampum* (figs. 1–4). The images, arranged across the lower halves of oversized paper (120 × 80 cm), represent wampum belts in appearance and scale: sash-like "belts" woven with white and purple shell beads. Wampum belts functioned as the principal instruments of diplomacy among northeastern Indigenous nations, most often associated with the Haudenosaunee Confederacy, but also among other confederacies in the American Northeast and Great Lakes

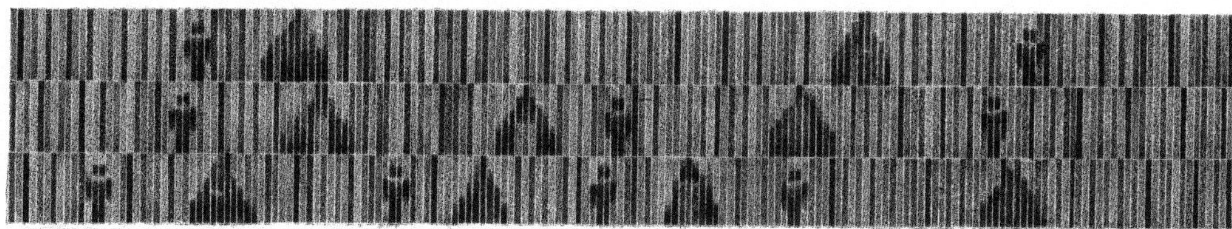

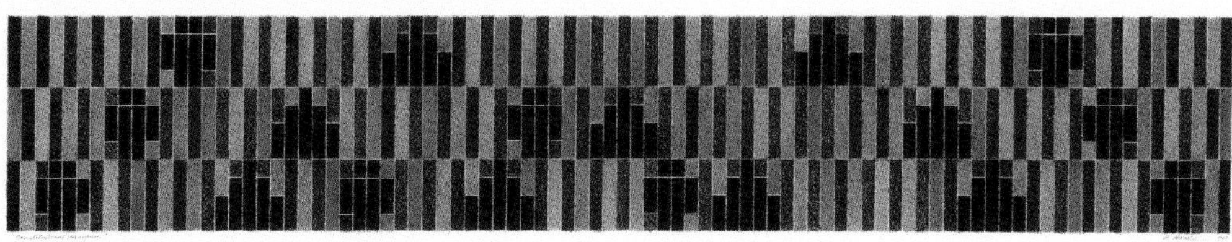

FIG. 1
Robert Houle, *Constitutional Wampum*, 1983. Conté crayon on paper, 79.5 × 120 cm. Courtesy of the National Museum of the American Indian, Smithsonian Institution, purchase, 2009. 26/7195. Photo: Ernest Amoroso. (Detail on page 215.)

FIG. 2
Robert Houle, *Constitutional Wampum*, 1983. Conté crayon on paper, 79.5 × 120 cm. Courtesy of the National Museum of the American Indian, Smithsonian Institution, purchase, 2009. 26/7196. Photo: Ernest Amoroso.

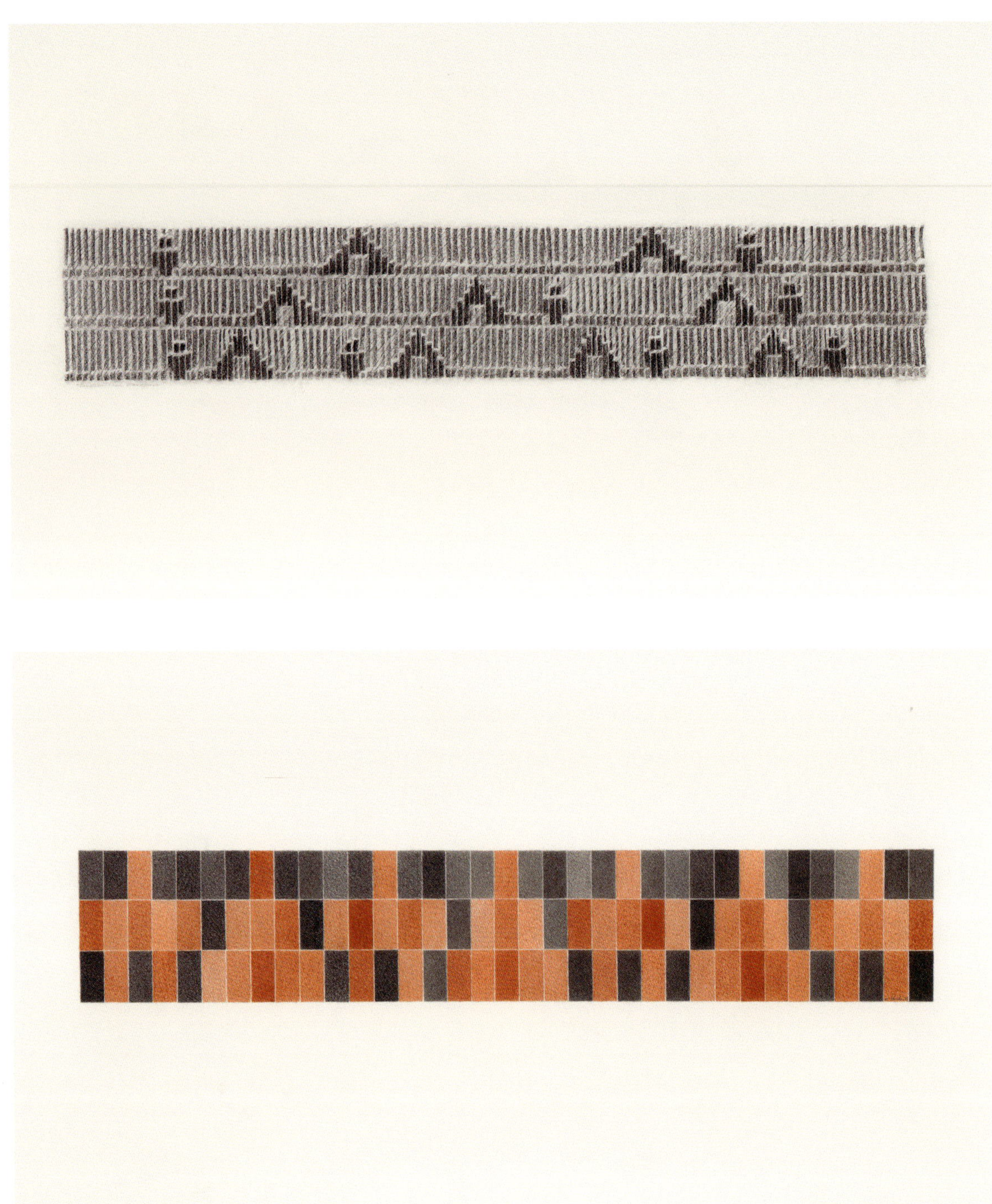

FIG. 3
Robert Houle, *Constitutional Wampum*, 1983. Conté crayon on paper, 79.5 × 120 cm. Courtesy of the National Museum of the American Indian, Smithsonian Institution, purchase, 2009. 26/7197. Photo: Ernest Amoroso.

FIG. 4
Robert Houle, *Constitutional Wampum*, 1983. Conté crayon on paper, 79.5 × 120 cm. Courtesy of the National Museum of the American Indian, Smithsonian Institution, purchase, 2009. 26/7198. Photo: Ernest Amoroso.

regions. Their exchange documented agreements, alliances, and promises, with no less authority than the signatures on written treaties, often more so. Houle remarked recently that the drawings are best viewed horizontally, as if holding a wampum belt on one's lap.

Houle conceived the four drawings as a set; each one features variations of technique and composition that progress toward increasing abstraction. Each variation presents an identically scaled motif, the horizontal belt, structured by three horizontal registers or lanes. The variations concern ways of rendering the wampum beads, the first by means of lighter and darker vertical markings, the others with increasingly scaled oblongs separated by thin frames in negative reserve, an exacting technique requiring precise measurement and masking. Houle created variations in tone and colour by careful layering of conté—as many as four layers for some panels. The technique resulted in dense, rich, and complex effects.

As with heritage wampum belts, Houle introduced figuration to signify meaning. The first three of the series (fig. 1-3) feature nine stick figures and nine triangular "houses." These reference the nine provincial signatories of the Act and the nine provinces they represented. The tenth Canadian province, Quebec, dissatisfied with its status after decades of separatist resistance, refused to sign. Houle had followed the debates about Quebec status on television with great interest. The fourth, most abstract drawing (fig. 4) introduces pale blues, pinks, and oranges with larger-scaled panels where four figures alternate with three "houses" arranged side-by-side across the length of the wampum belt drawing. Houle does not now recall the numerical significance of that arrangement, but suspects there was one.

Around the time he produced those drawings, Houle had been pursuing the reconciliation of what he described as "two different aesthetic systems: North American and Western European" in a catalogue essay for *New Work by a New Generation,* an exhibition he curated for the Norman MacKenzie Art Gallery[3] in 1982. He included himself as part of that generation; his arts training at McGill University had committed him to modernist studio practice. "The transformations experienced in the studio make the artist emerge as a new aesthetic personage," he wrote.[4] He had also served (and resigned) as the honorific first Indigenous curator of contemporary Indigenous art at the National Museum of Man (now the Canadian Museum of History).[5] There, he reported, he had felt dismayed over the mistreatment and misunderstanding of Indigenous heritage items. But his experiences with the collections prompted later insights. In his 1982 essay he proposed that modernist studio practice approached the "power to evoke the supernatural creatures found in the meditative formalism of Haida graphic art, to echo the incantations recorded with a secret code on a Potawatomi prescription stick, and to summon the animal spirits found in the fetish assemblages of shamanistic art." Here, Houle argued, lay the common ground between a "North American" aesthetic, with its material traditions, and a modernist "Western European" studio practice where the Indigenous modern artist might pursue the "ritualistic will to uphold their highest uses of art."[6]

Wampum belts, for Houle, embodied such "higher uses" or purpose. "They are sacred," he acknowledged recently. The formalist theme and variations that worked through his four drawings seemed to "associate contemporary imagery and form with such mystical and existential visionary iconography… to reaffirm the notion that the creative process is guided by a ritualistic will," as Houle expressed it.[7] The drawings are constructed of countless markings laboriously repeated with ritual-like focus and precision requiring exacting, repetitive gestures like stitching or weaving.

Houle's relationship with the "motif" for these drawings is complex. Wampum references, for Houle, Indigenous ideas and protocols about treaty-making as an Indigenous analogy to the Constitution Act. Yet it is not simply the instrumental qualities of wampum that interest him, but also its sacred, ritual, epistemological resonances. Wampum signifies an Indigenous worldview, Indigenous understandings, all by way of the Indigenous materiality of shell beads woven into a belt. The drawings are analogs to wampum belts as things, and this synthesis of analogous materiality—a belt woven of beads or a precisely rendered drawing—provided for Houle a basis for studio-based abstraction. The drawings prompt questions about Houle's engagements with Indigenous materiality, with heritage items, in the development of his modernist, "bicultural" artistic practice. "My abstraction arises from the traces left on an unsmoked caribou skin," he wrote twenty-five years later in 2007, "aesthetics coded in aboriginal art… about creation, celebration and passage to the other side and shar[ing] the mythological generosity of the caribou."[8] Heritage items and Houle's perceptions of their material, aesthetic, ritual, and conceptual qualities, helped shape his approach to creating art. Houle spent his last day of employment at the National Museum of Man drawing heritage items in the galleries—a headdress, a staff, a parfleche—before offering his resignation. "All I could think of is that I wanted to liberate them," he said later.[9] By drawing, did he intend to reclaim them in some sense? For what purpose?

The parfleche, as a material item and as an idea, catalyzed for Houle a prolonged and fruitful examination of these questions. A parfleche is a simple folded envelope made of rawhide, often painted with abstract geometric patterns, traditionally produced by women of several Plains tribes. But for Houle, the parfleche drew upon particular memories. Houle's home community of Sandy Bay First Nation, Manitoba, had provided limited opportunity for experiencing traditional Saulteaux culture, although he grew up speaking Anishinaabemowin and his family occasionally attended an annual summer Sun Dance. The reserve was administered under the strict supervision of the Catholic Church, including a repressive local residential school that Houle attended and where he experienced abuse. Houle recalled his mother's worry about her children's spiritual health in this environment. And so, in secret and risking censure, she periodically hired a community shaman, as Houle referred to him, to give her children traditional names. As the eldest of fifteen children, Houle says he witnessed this ceremony many times. His mother would cover the windows with paper to keep out prying eyes, but also to create a private, ritual space. The shaman brought with him a sacred bundle kept inside a parfleche container that he opened on the floor of the darkened room, taking out a rattle and other items while addressing spirit beings and asking them to name the child.

The year Houle created the wampum drawings, he also produced a number of works based on parfleches, significantly the ambitious series *Parfleches for the Last Supper*, thirteen paintings on paper with the addition of porcupine quills. The thirteen paintings are named for the twelve Apostles and Jesus (in Houle's series, Jesus is number twelve and Peter number thirteen) (figs. 5 and 6).

Houle, whose childhood had been shaped by the repressive Church, is explicit about his effort to reconcile the idea of the Eucharist and Communion—the most holy ritual of the Catholic liturgy—with Indigenous religious thought and practice. Both taking Communion and receiving a name from spirits summoned by a shaman reference for Houle heightened moments of ritual where the material leads to the divine. As with the wampum drawings, Houle emphasized the materiality of these parfleche paintings as things: heavy, hand-crafted paper folded over at the top to create the appearance of a flap, the addition of porcupine quills, like fasteners, adhered to thick strips of paint in high relief, all made more dimensional with the shadowing technique of "abstract illusionism."[10] Houle established analogies between the materiality of a parfleche with its sacred bundle inside and his modernist drawings and paintings as things. "Each artist is invariably and intimately involved in recording personal experiences determined by tribal culture," he wrote. "This leaves the artist to create works of art traditionally inspired, but expressed through modern concepts and techniques.... Being modernists, they carry the privilege of appropriating bits of their traditional and contemporary cultures to form an amalgam strictly reflective of their own identity."[11] As with the wampum drawings, the parfleche is not simply a starting point for formalist development and elaboration, but instead inspired a synthesis of Indigenous and modernist art making.

The parfleche would become an enduring theme for Houle: when he returned to consideration of *Constitution Act 1982* (fig. 8); his *Innu Parfleche* of 1990 (fig. 7); and a 1999 series of commemorative works honouring Indigenous cultural leadership, *Parfleche for Norval Morrisseau* (fig. 9), *Parfleche for Edna Manitowabi*, *Parfleche for Alex Janvier*, *Parfleche*

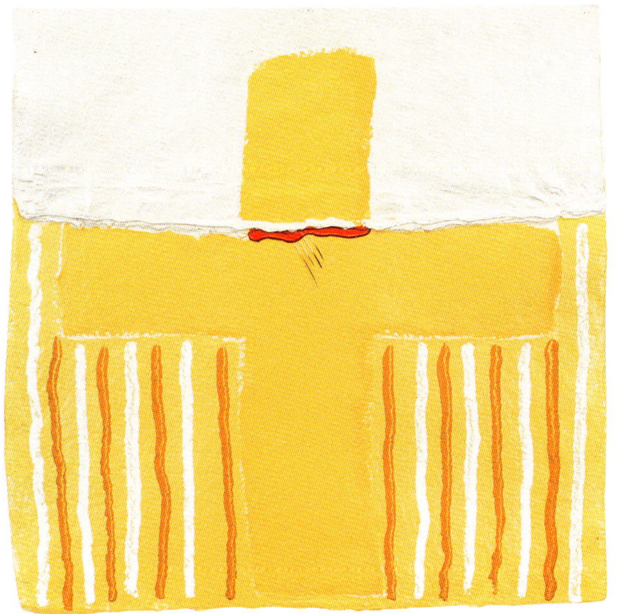

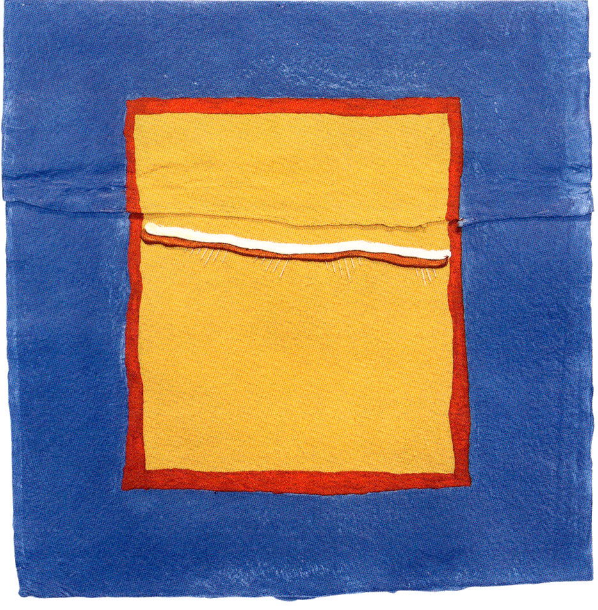

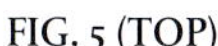

FIG. 5 (TOP)
Robert Houle, *Parfleche #12, Jesus*, 1983, from *Parfleches for the Last Supper*. Acrylic and porcupine quills on paper, 56 × 56 cm. Collection of the Winnipeg Art Gallery, gift of Mr. Carl T. Grant, Artvest Inc., G-86-471. Photo: Serge Gumenyuk courtesy of the Winnipeg Art Gallery.

FIG. 6 (BOTTOM)
Robert Houle, *Parfleche #13, Peter*, 1983, from *Parfleches for the Last Supper*. Acrylic and porcupine quills on paper, 56 × 56 cm. Collection of the Winnipeg Art Gallery, gift of Mr. Carl T. Grant, Artvest Inc., G-86-472. Photo: Serge Gumenyuk courtesy of the Winnipeg Art Gallery.

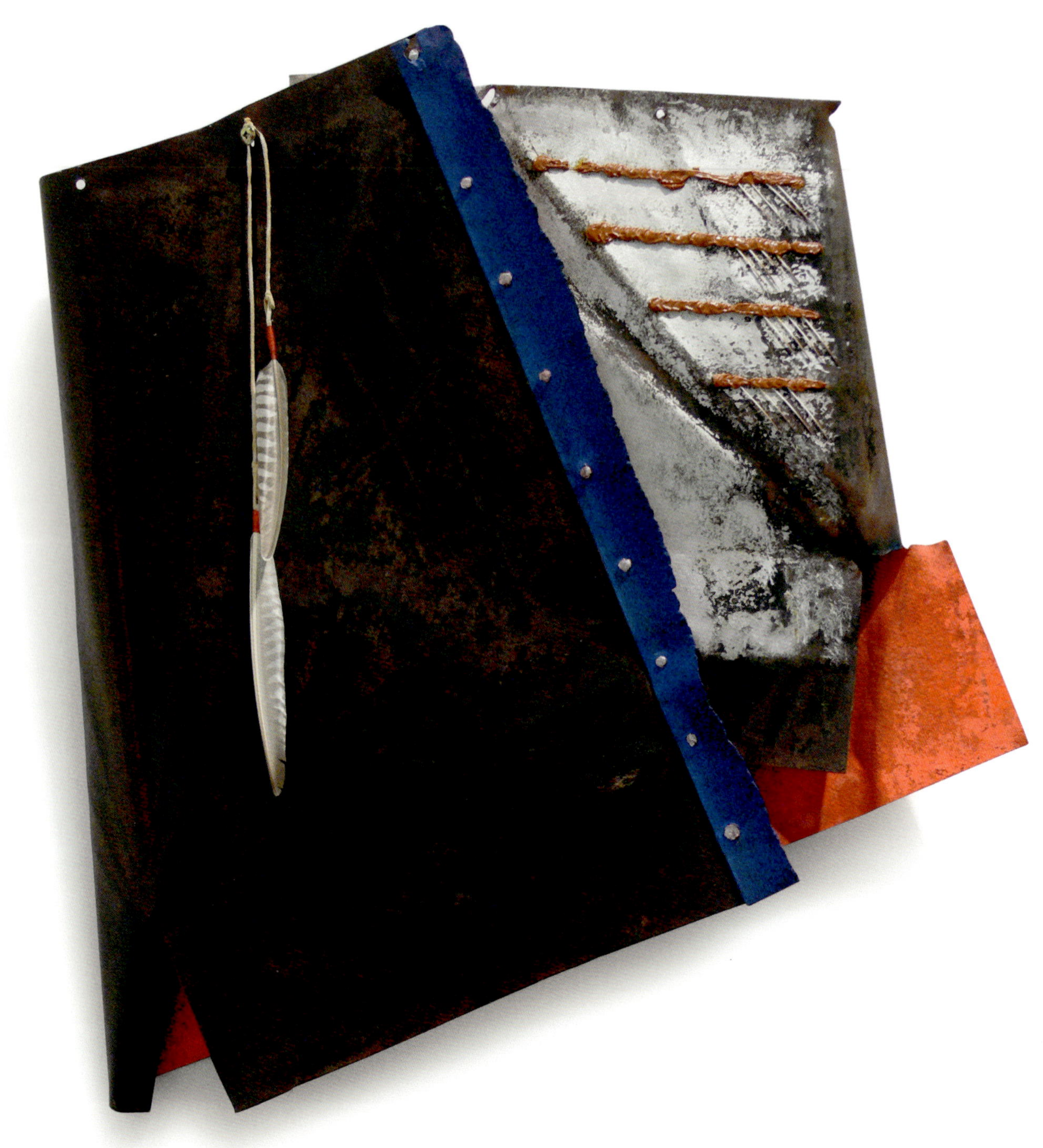

FIG. 7
Robert Houle, *Innu Parfleche*, 1990. Oil, acrylic, iron, ink, metal, owl feather, and mammal leather, 66.2 × 68 × 8 cm. Musée canadien de l'histoire / Canadian Museum of History. V-F-190. Image courtesy of McMaster Museum of Art, Hamilton.

for Bea Medicine, Parfleche for Ernie Benedict, and others.[12] It is worth emphasizing that a parfleche is a container; the sacred bundle itself is kept inside, shielded from casual view and inappropriate exposure. The geometric abstractions customarily painted on heritage parfleches may signal the presence of the bundle within but do not signify it. As Gerald McMaster remarked, "it is difficult to argue that [heritage parfleche paintings] are non-objective in that so much significance was attached to every symbol: 'the four directions,' 'sun,' 'moon,' 'stars,' 'mountains,' or 'insects.'"[13] These cosmological referents provide an appropriate housing or frame for the sacred materials inside, just Houle's personalized colour, gesture, and quotation (for the Apostles) signal yet do not signify the individuality of his commemorative subjects. As such, the parfleche provides an apt metaphor for the human individual, a soul or spirit housed in the human body of flesh and bone, whose individuality is signalled by outer physiognomy while the mystery of spirit remains hidden within. The commemorative parfleche paintings become a kind of portraiture, an Indigenous alternative to a portraiture of appearances.

The notion of wampum belts as an alternative and more Indigenous expression of the significance of the Constitution Act, and Houle's much longer-term engagement with the concept of the parfleche, became for him ways to link Indigenous epistemologies and perspectives to modernist studio practice. His early engagement with heritage items—during rituals at home, or in museum collections as a curator—inspired deep reflections about the relations between Indigenous "North American" and modernist "Western European" artistic practices, as he expressed it in 1982. These insights provided durable considerations developed in his work thereafter and the intellectual and aesthetic ideas that informed them.

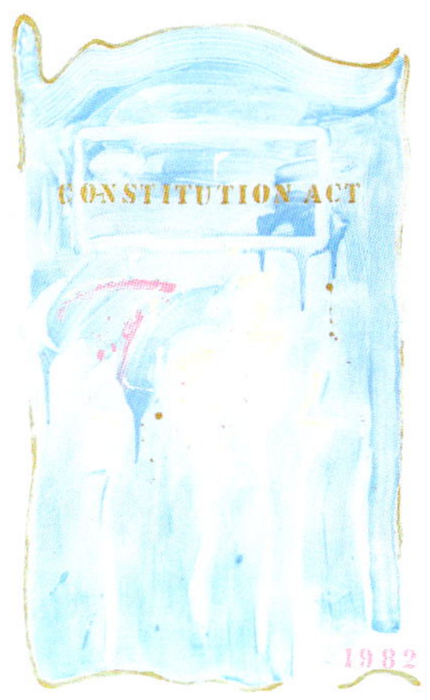

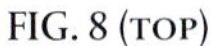

FIG. 8 (TOP)
Robert Houle, *Constitution Act 1982*, 1985. Acrylic on paper, 106 × 75 cm. Indigenous Art Collection, Crown-Indigenous Relations and Northern Affairs Canada / Collection d'art autochtones, Relations Couronne-Autochtones et Affaires du Nord Canada.
Photo: Lawrence Cook.

FIG. 9 (BOTTOM)
Robert Houle, *Parfleche for Norval Morrisseau*, 1999. Oil paint on canvas, mounted to wood, 51 × 101 × 6 cm. Courtesy of the National Museum of the American Indian, Smithsonian Institution, purchase from the artist, 2012. 26/9030.
Photo: R.A. Whiteside.

1 Unless otherwise noted, citations of Houle are from telephone interviews with the author in February and March 2021.

2 "Robert Houle: Premises for Self-Rule: Constitution Act 1982, 1994," Art Gallery of Ontario, accessed September 28, 2021, https://ago.ca/sites/default/files/ago_TeacherResource-Houle.pdf. Stacy A. Ernst, "Indigenous Sovereignty and Settler Amnesia: Robert Houle's Premises for Self Rule," *RACAR : Revue d'art canadienne / Canadian Art Review* 42:2 (January 2018): 108–120, https://doi.org/10.7202/1042950ar

3 Now the MacKenzie Art Gallery.

4 Robert Houle, "The Emergence of a New Aesthetic Tradition," *Canadian Art Database: Canadian Writers Files* by the Centre for Contemporary Canadian Art (originally published in the catalogue for *New Work by a New Generation*, Norman Mackenzie Art Gallery, University of Regina, 1982), http://ccca.concordia.ca/c/writing/h/houle/hou002t.html

5 Now the Canadian Museum of History; Houle served from 1977–1981.

6 Houle, "Emergence."

7 Houle, "Emergence."

8 Robert Houle, "Artist Statement for Troubling Abstraction," in *Robert Houle: Troubling Abstraction*, eds. W. Jackson Rushing et al. (Hamilton: McMaster Museum of Art, 2007), 15–17.

9 Clara Hargittay in conversation with Robert Houle, "The Struggle Against Cultural Apartheid," Muse 6:3 (Autumn 1988): 58–60.

10 The works have been discussed by several critic-scholars. See Clara Hargittay, "Robert Houle: Creative Spirit Journey, 1980–1990," and Shirley J. R. Madill, "Robert Houle: Dual State of Being in Robert Houle: Indians from A to Z. ed. Jennifer S.H. Brown et al. (Winnipeg: Winnipeg Art Gallery, 1990), 13–14 and 25–26; Nooshfar B. Afnan, "Concepts of Spirituality in the Works of Robert Houle and Otto Rogers with Special Considerations to Images of the Land" (Master's Thesis, Carleton University, 2000), 55–62.

11 Houle, "Emergence."

12 The commemorative parfleches of 1999 are illustrated and discussed in Bonnie Devine, "Robert Houle," in *Path Breakers: The Eiteljorg Fellowship for Native American Fine Art*, eds. Suzanne G. Fox, and Lucy R. Lippard (Indianapolis: Eiteljorg Museum of American Indians and Western Art, 2003), 49–58.

13 Gerald McMaster, "The Symbolic Field," in *Robert Houle: Troubling Abstraction*, ed.W. Jackson Rushing et al. (Hamilton: McMaster Museum of Art, 2007), 84.

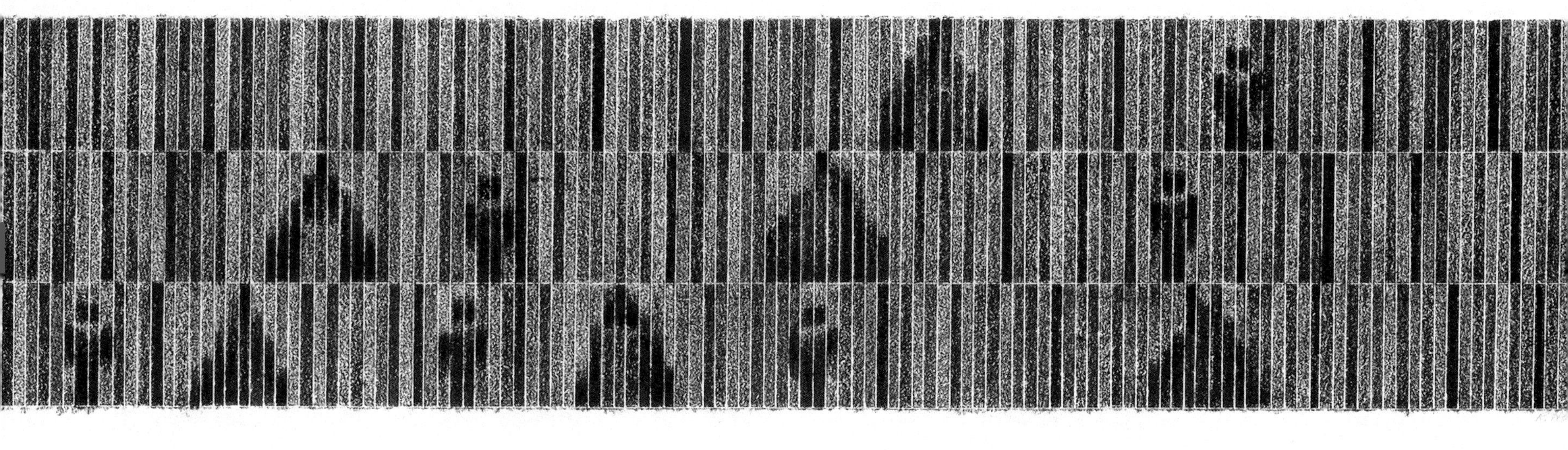

Installing *Sandy Bay* and the parfleches with Robert Houle

Stephen Borys

Most of my encounters with Robert Houle have related to the installation of his paintings at the Winnipeg Art Gallery (WAG), where I serve as museum director.[1] During one of our first exchanges, over the presentation of his work *Sandy Bay* (pp. 156–157, 222), we discussed how he—rather than me or the curator—knew the best way to present his work to audiences. This may seem obvious; however, it's also fundamental to my approach to and understanding of his art, and it is my responsibility as a museum director to honour the authority of the artist. These conversations have also taken place at a time when the WAG was responsive to his appeals—in the period following the Truth & Reconciliation Commission's calls to actions for museum and galleries. The gallery is located on Treaty One territory, on the traditional lands of the Anishinaabeg, Nêhiyawak, Oji-Cree, Dakota, and Dene peoples, and on the homeland of the Métis Nation. The WAG holds in trust the world's largest collection of contemporary Inuit art, now housed in Qaumajuq, an Inuit art centre that opened in the spring of 2021. As part of ongoing Indigenization efforts, the gallery is committed to working in partnership with the leadership and guidance of Inuit, who have worked to ensure the spirit of the art is upheld, and with the First Nations and Métis nations of this land. The interactions with Houle regarding the care and exhibition of his art at the WAG is very much part of the gallery's reconciliation work.

The WAG began collecting Houle's work in the early 1980s. That decade was highlighted by the acquisition of *Parfleches for the Last Supper* (1983) in 1986, followed by *Everything you ever wanted to know about Indians from A to Z* (1985) in 1989. *Parfleches* is comprised of thirteen paintings (acrylic on paper with porcupine quills), each one named for one of the twelve apostles and Jesus Christ. Parfleches (or medicine bags) were used as early as 1700 in New France to carry ceremonial objects or personal belongings. Usually made of elk or horse rawhide, they were painted with decorative designs employing natural dyes, and then folded into an envelope. In Houle's work, black and white quills appear affixed to or pressed into the paint layer, creating different configurations or patterns on the paintings, often in the places where the artist has built up the paint layer. The quills also form the quilting or stitching mechanism securing a folded flap back to the body of the paper, similar to a parfleche; quills are part of the structure and function of the container. For what is largely a two-dimensional work displayed as a painting, the parfleches have a distinct three-dimensional presence not unlike the receptacle they reference.

Shortly after my arrival as WAG director, I saw Houle's *Parfleches* stored on a painting rack in the gallery vaults. The colourfully and heavily painted sheets were mounted on white mats and framed behind glass in gilt wood frames; however, more than picture frames they were like glass containers holding other containers. The works themselves are tactile and portable, and I noticed that I had a desire to remove them from the decorative frames to better view them, even handle them. The individual sheets are fifty-six by fifty-six centimetres—larger than traditional parfleches but still accessible in their scale.

Many of Houle's parfleches are constructed from handmade paper, folded with a forward flap, and decorated with paint and quills. In *Parfleches for the Last Supper* (figs. 1 and 2) he folded the top portion over to resemble a parfleche, and after painting the surface he joined the fold with diagonal stitches of porcupine quills similar to those used by women in Blackfoot and Mi'kmaq communities to decorate clothing and containers. For this work, Houle researched the biographies of the thirteen men documented in the New Testament of the Bible and incorporated his interest in colour theory and ritualistic markings to bring together his two spiritual events, the Last Supper and the feasts held as a celebration in Saulteaux communities when children receive their names, creating a bicultural metaphor of the communal supper. The eldest of fifteen children, Houle was raised in the Anishnaabe Saulteaux culture and was fluent in Saulteaux at home; he recalled attending many of his younger sisters' naming ceremonies and sharing meals with spiritual guides.[2]

In 2016, I was reinstalling three of the WAG's collection galleries dedicated to European and North American art, and in the gallery featuring European paintings and sculptures from 1500 to 1700, I reserved one large wall for Houle's *Parfleches for the Last Supper*. The intersecting symbolism between the old master paintings, with their largely religious subject matter, and Houle's work referencing ceremony had prompted me to consider this arrangement. I hadn't spoken to the artist in advance of this plan, and it wasn't until we were finalizing the exhibition copyright that I finally discussed the installation with him. To my relief, he agreed with the plan, going as far to say he was not surprised with my interest in hanging the parfleches with the Northern Renaissance paintings depicting different Christian scenes. In fact, beyond the overlapping iconographies, one sensed a physical link between the wood panels, many of them fragments or separated altar panel sections, and Houle's painted parfleches. Originally the thirteen works were installed in a row, referencing the gathering or order of Christ's followers; however, in this instance I opted for a three-high grid of twelve with the painting representing Christ installed immediately to the lower right of the grid. Writing on the series in the WAG 1990 exhibition catalogue, Gerald McMaster states: "In a sense, *Parfleches* symbolizes the simultaneous death and rebirth of [Houle's] own [cultural] identity. Not a negative and reactionary statement, rather, *Parfleches* is autobiographical and a synthesis of both his [cultural] beliefs and those of Christianity."[3] A year later when we were removing the parfleches from the installation due to the light sensitivity of the works on paper, their absence was immediately felt in a profound way, and a material one—the thirteen works having left a permanent imprint on the gallery walls. Again, we understood Houle's desire to curate a physical and intellectual engagement with his art and the viewer, and it would impact on future showings of the work.

Everything you ever wanted to know about Indians from A to Z (fig. 3) consists of twenty-six linen and rawhide parfleches, each bearing a stencilled letter of the alphabet, and installed on a twenty-four-foot blue ledge attached to the wall. The installation, according to McMaster, resembles a library or church pew where reference or hymn books would be displayed.[4] The individual lettered parfleches represent an American Indian tribe beginning with the Aztec and ending with the Zuni, with the names of the extinct tribes recorded in the language of the people who ultimately vanquished them. The 1989 series builds upon the earlier *Parfleches for the Last Supper*; in the latter work the lettered sheets become three-dimensional, referencing further the physicality of the actual parfleche container. The prescribed installation for the WAG series marks a shift from the pieces being displayed as paintings to something more akin to objects or artifacts, which changes the viewer's access to and reading of the works.

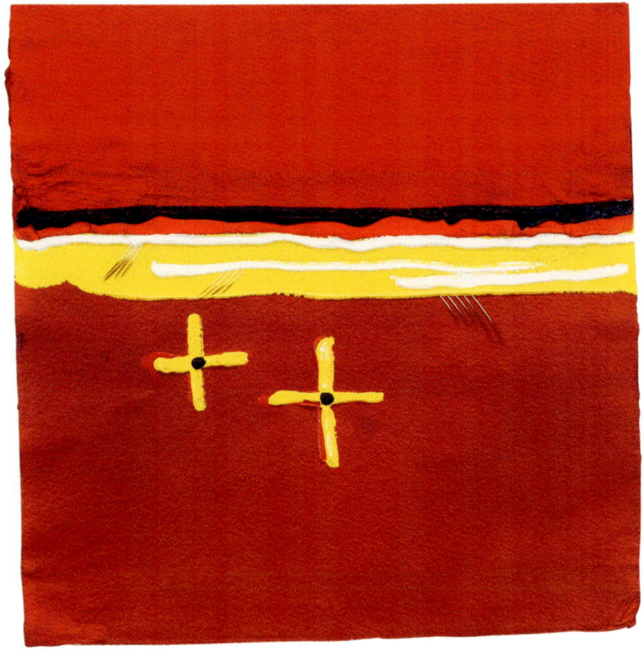

FIG. 1
Robert Houle, *Parfleche #5, Philip*, 1983, from *Parfleches for the Last Supper*. Acrylic and porcupine quills on paper, 56 × 56 cm. Collection of the Winnipeg Art Gallery, gift of Mr. Carl T. Grant, Artvest Inc., G-86-464.
Photo: Serge Gumenyuk courtesy of the Winnipeg Art Gallery.

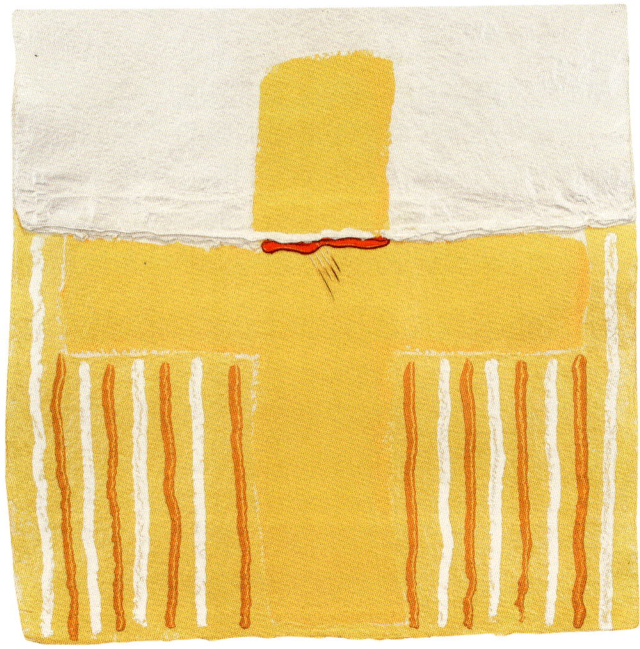

FIG. 2
Robert Houle, *Parfleche #12, Jesus*, 1983, from *Parfleches for the Last Supper*. Acrylic and porcupine quills on paper, 56 × 56 cm. Collection of the Winnipeg Art Gallery, gift of Mr. Carl T. Grant, Artvest Inc., G-86-471.
Photo: Serge Gumenyuk courtesy of the Winnipeg Art Gallery.

Following the acquisitions of Houle's work in the 1980s, the WAG became the first major gallery in Canada to organize, along with the McMichael Canadian Art Collection, a solo exhibition for the artist in 1989. This was the same year that Houle was appointed artist in residence at the WAG for a period of three months (figs. 4 and 5). During his residency he produced four large paintings in a celebratory response to his Manitoba roots and homeland. The series *Muhnedobe uhyahyuk [Where the gods are present] (Matthew, Philip, Bartholomew, Thomas)* (pages 76–77) offers insight into how the artist imagined the birth of his province as a cultural universe. In the mythology of the Saulteaux people, an island in the Narrows of Lake Manitoba is thought to be the dwelling place of God, Manitou. The place is called Manitowapah—and hence Manitoba.

Shirley Madill was the WAG curator of contemporary art and photography at the time of Robert's artist residency at the WAG. She went on to curate two exhibitions of his work along with two catalogues: *Indians from A to Z* in 1990 and *Sovereignty over Subjectivity* in 1999. The 1990 show included *Parfleches for the Last Supper* and *Everything you ever wanted to know about Indians from A to Z*, and it travelled to galleries in Thunder Bay, Banff, Calgary, and Ottawa after the Winnipeg presentation. Recalling her work on the first exhibition, Madill notes: "Meeting with Robert in his Toronto studio to prepare for his first solo exhibition, in Winnipeg, I was immediately struck and moved by his fearless determination to create awareness and make a difference in the treatment of Indigenous art and artists. His capacities as leader, catalyst, and committed agent of change are amplified by a subtle, empathetic, and

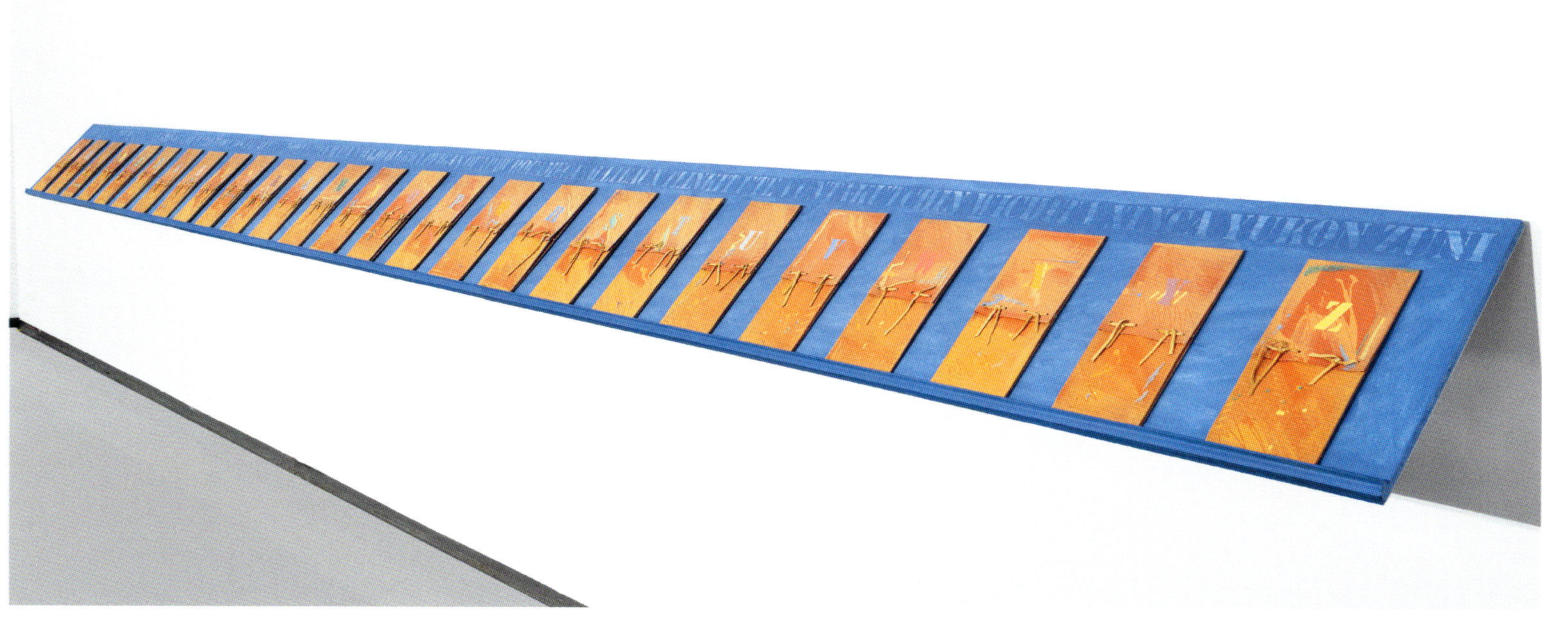

FIG. 3
Robert Houle, *Everything you ever wanted to know about Indians from A to Z*, 1985.
Acrylic, rawhide, wood, and linen, 45.3 × 735 cm. Collection of the Winnipeg Art Gallery, acquired with funds from The Winnipeg Art Gallery Foundation Inc., G-89-1501 a-cc.
Photo: Ernest Mayer, courtesy of the Winnipeg Art Gallery.

humanistic approach, both personal and political, seen in all that he does in his daily life."[5] These personal and artistic goals that stood out to Madill thirty years ago have remained a constant in Houle's artmaking and storytelling.

Almost precisely a decade after his WAG residency, Houle shifted his artistic focus to his formative years in Manitoba and the time he spent in residential schools, which spanned more than a decade. After attending the Sandy Bay school, he was enrolled in the co-ed Assiniboia Indian Residential School in Winnipeg for his high school years. Houle's return to this period in his life would result in the production of a number of seminal works, including the large multi-canvas work *Sandy Bay* (1998–1999), now in the WAG collection. The work was included in the 1999 show at the WAG, which later travelled to Toronto and Saskatoon.

Sandy Bay has been included in a number of exhibitions; however, one in particular stands out to me as a pivotal moment for the WAG and my directorship. The piece was featured in the 2016 WAG exhibition, *Qua'yuk tchi'gae'win: Making Good* (fig. 6), organized by the gallery's first permanent curator of Indigenous art, Jaimie Isaac. Joining the large *Sandy Bay* paintings were twenty-four oil stick drawings comprising the Sandy Bay Residential School series (2009), from the University of Manitoba's School of Art Gallery, which depict the site and circumstances around his abuse at the school. Writing on the series in *Robert Houle: Life & Work*, Madill states: "This highly personal work reclaims the artist's memories of the residential school experience—of physical, sexual, and spiritual abuse. Images of dormitory beds, crosses, and shadowy figures occupy the spaces in the drawings, with disturbing inscriptions written in his own hand, such as 'night predator,' 'I'm cornered,' 'outhouse abuse,' 'drive-in terror,' '*uhnuhmeahkazooh*—pretending to 'pray,' and 'fear.' The pieces are a powerful testament to a dark, shameful period of Canadian history."[6]

The exhibition title in Anishnaabemowin means the honour of righting a wrong. Over 150 years of the residential school system in Canada, the forcible separation from family and cultural traditions in ceremony, life ways, and language impacted more than seven generations of Indigenous peoples. In response to the Truth and Reconciliation Committee's calls to action, the WAG through its exhibitions and programs has begun to acknowledge the experiences of Indigenous survivors. Isaac's exhibition included works from the WAG collection, loans from other galleries, and the archival collections of the National Centre for Truth and Reconciliation.

I recall the email exchanges between the artist and curator, and then between myself and the artist, as we worked through the installation of *Sandy Bay* in the main entrance hall. The cavernous Eckhardt Hall, with its Tyndall-stone-clad floors and walls and twenty-one-foot-high ceiling, often dwarfs even large-scale paintings; consequently, artwork is often hung higher than normal in that space. An elevated hanging height is also a cautionary measure to protect the art due to the number of events held in the exhibition hall. Isaac opted for the higher hanging height for these reasons, but also so that visitors could view the work from the mezzanine level of the hall. However, upon learning of the plan, Houle asked that the large canvases be positioned as close as possible to the floor of the hall so that visitors could fully engage with the physicality and imagery of the narrative. Sensing some resistance from the WAG, Houle made his case by underlining the importance that the work be shown in the most accessible and impactful way. The negotiations with the artist went on, and at one point it became apparent that we might not be able to install the work. However, through an extended dialogue we reached an agreement. Coming to an understanding with the artist on issues that transcended the hanging height of the painting, it became clear to me the enormous emotional weight of this series on him, and the need for this story to be told and shared.

On May 4, 2017, I had a call in my office from the front desk at the WAG letting me know that Houle and three of his sisters had arrived in the gallery. Shortly after, I met them in our café, where the artist reminisced about his WAG residency, almost thirty years earlier, the solo exhibitions we organized, and the artwork that emerged from these periods. Then, over coffee, Robert turned his attention to the *Sandy Bay* paintings, and shared more about the genesis of this work. I anticipated this conversation might be a little awkward given the incident a year earlier when we had failed initially to hang the work as Robert had requested. The tone of our conversation shifted as he talked about his childhood and adolescent years in the residential school. With what seemed like little effort, he was able to recall the names of some of the teachers—the priests and nuns—and a few of his fellow students. When he paused, his sisters, who also attended the school with their brother, would add another detail or name to the story. When Robert had finished speaking, I suggested we all go down to the main art vault to look at the paintings in person—and they agreed. I hadn't really thought through the next few moments as we headed to the vault except that I knew it was an important step for me to take with Robert.

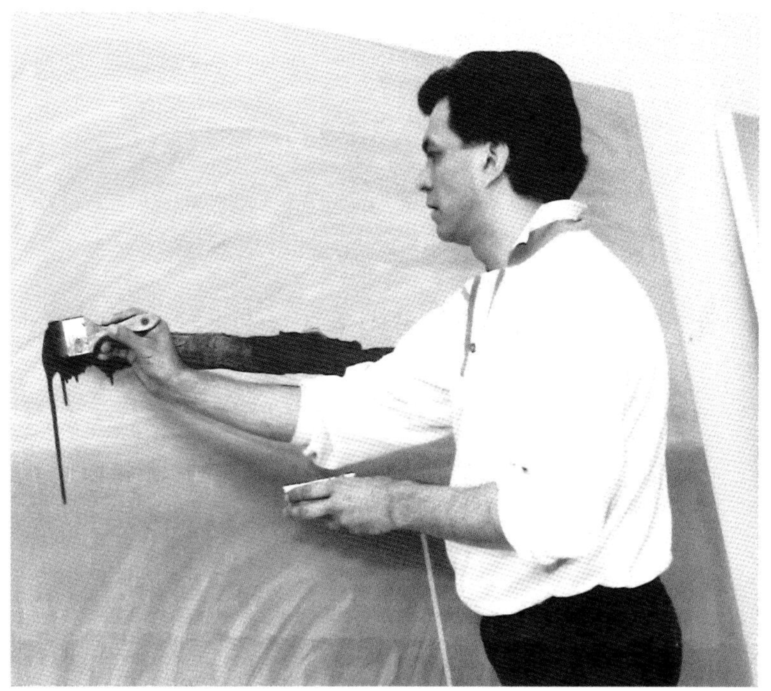

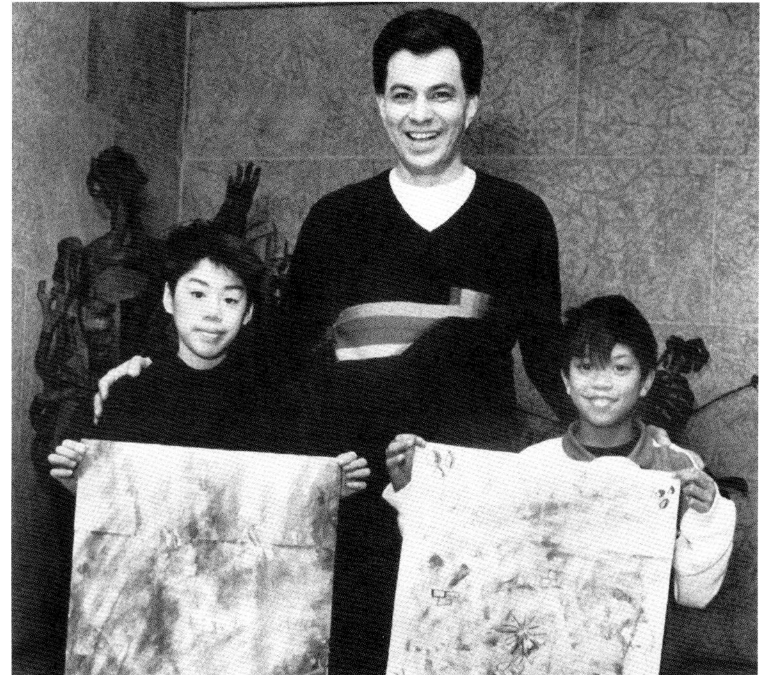

FIG. 4 (TOP)
Robert Houle painting in studio at the Winnipeg Art Gallery, as artist in residence, 1989. Image courtesy of the Winnipeg Art Gallery.

FIG. 5 (BOTTOM)
Robert Houle with two students at Winnipeg Art Gallery, as artist in residence, 1989. Image courtesy of the Winnipeg Art Gallery.

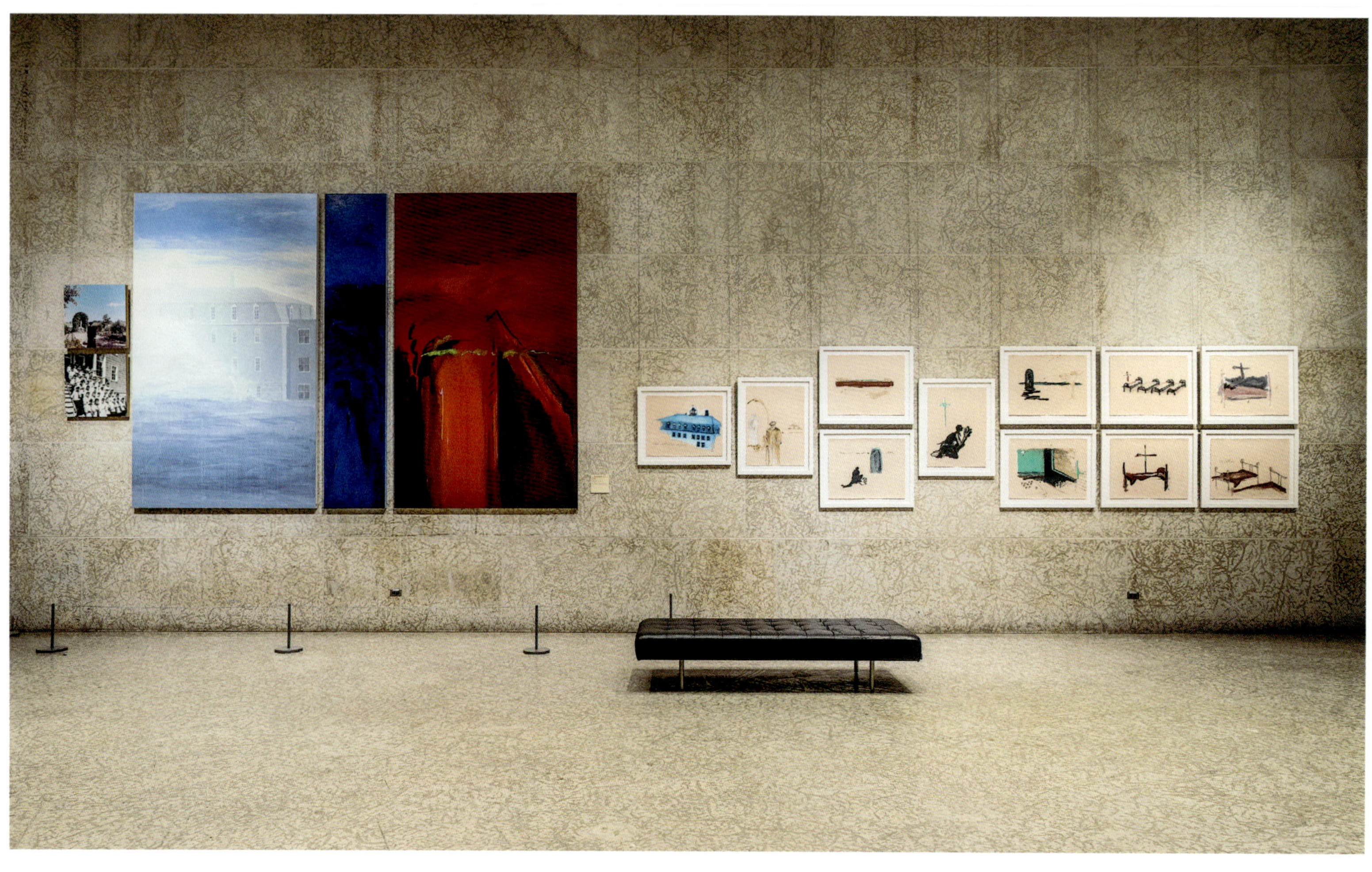

FIG. 6
Robert Houle, *Sandy Bay* (1998–1999) and *Sandy Bay Residential School Series* (2009). Installation view of *Qua'yuk tchi'gae'win: Making Good* at the Winnipeg Art Gallery, June 11 – October 9, 2016. Photo: Ernest Mayer, courtesy of the Winnipeg Art Gallery.

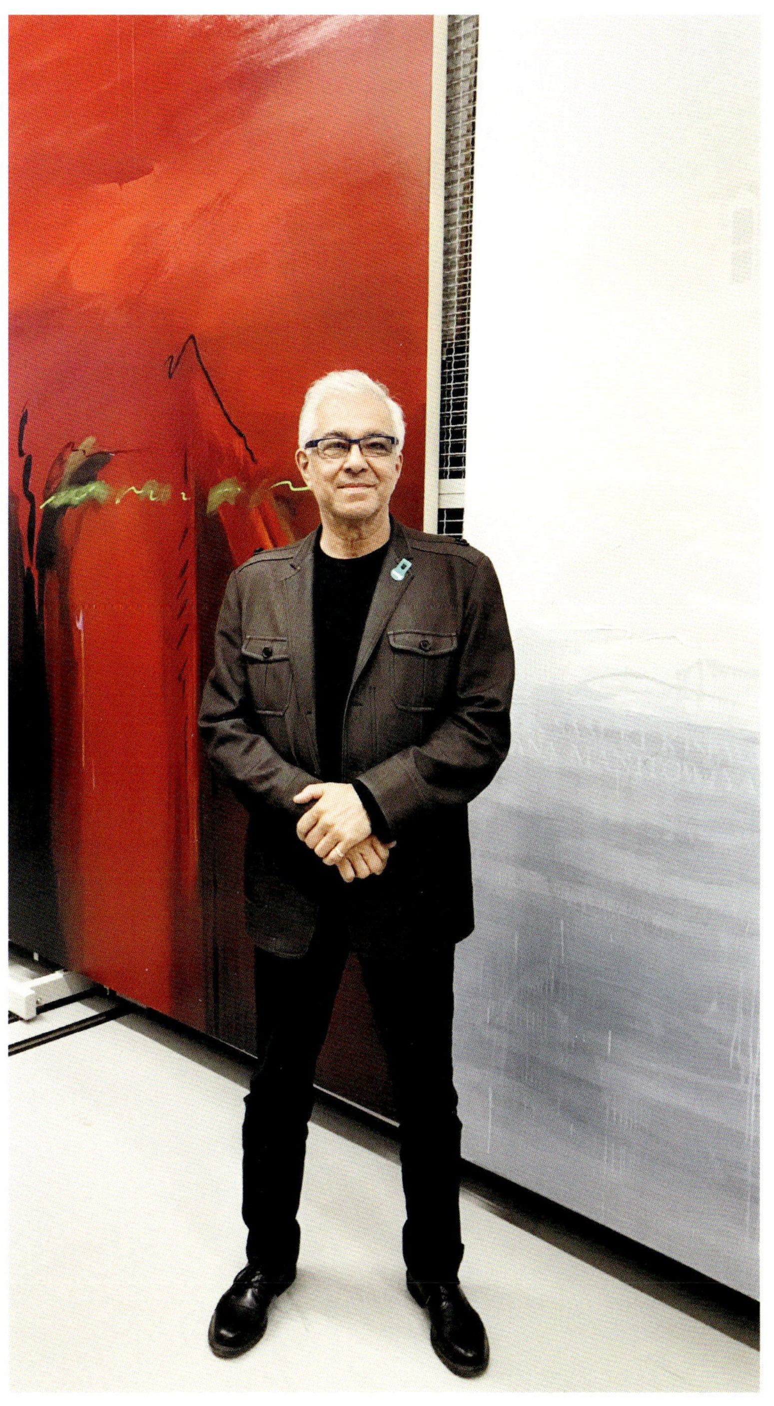

FIG. 7
Robert Houle standing in front of *Sandy Bay* (1998–1999), in the vault at the Winnipeg Art Gallery, May 4, 2017. Image courtesy of Stephen Borys.

Upon entering the vault, which comprises most of the basement level of the WAG building and rises up to gallery-height ceilings, we located the numbered racks containing *Sandy Bay*. Separating the large painting racks, we walked into the aisle and were encompassed by Robert's paintings. Taking up most of the rack space was *Sandy Bay*, which was stored in a different configuration than how they would be installed in the galleries (fig. 7). Robert quickly shared with us how they would hang, which reminded me of the conversations we had when they were installed in Eckhardt Hall. Robert's insistence on specific heights, physical adjacencies, and the need for people to see the images at eye level now made much more sense to me.

I recall the moment when, assembled in the WAG vault with Robert and his sisters that afternoon, everyone stopped speaking. It was silent as the four siblings, all of them former students at the Sandy Bay Indian Residential School, looked at the three towering canvases and the enlarged snapshots of one of the priests and a First Communion class. The silence went on for what seemed like minutes until Robert gestured to the large canvas on the left depicting the facade of the school, pointing to a window in the school building where he remembered he could look outside from the dormitory. Scanning the facade of the school building, painted in a pale, ghost-like grey, he made the point that there is no visible door—no entrance or exit. And if there had been a door, he had painted it out deliberately. Then he mentioned an interior door that separated the boys' dormitory from the girls' dormitory. Siblings were not permitted to see or visit with each other at the school except on special occasions, but every so often Robert would steal a glimpse of them. His sisters responded by naming off some of the girls in the First Communion photograph.

It was after Houle read Ruth Teichroeb's book *Flowers on My Grave: How an Ojibwa Boy's Death Helped Break the Silence on Child Abuse* (1998), the story of the suicide of a boy victimized by residential school violence on his own reserve, that he produced the *Sandy Bay* work, which took close to a year and a half to finish.[7] The work is composed of two photographs and three large canvases. The two photographs feature a priest standing in the cemetery on the reserve (where he was later interred) and a first communion class, which included Robert's sister Marilyn. Houle has said that physical and spiritual elements of the landscape are critical to understanding one's life. In Sandy Bay, the artist addresses the abuse he endured as a child at the residential school on the shores of Lake Manitoba. It was here in this series that he made the decision to engage memory as a path to healing. The memory begins with the two photographs, installed at the left, and then shifting to the right, three massive panels, each three metres in height, forming a triptych of white, blue, and red, the flag colours of the European colonizers. The final panel, at the right, is covered in a red ground, and represents Sister Clothilde, one of the individuals who abused Houle during his time at residential school. The paintings move from a representation of Houle's personal memory to an abstracted form, and together, the assembly of three canvases demonstrates a kind of healing power.

The residential school at Sandy Bay, run by the Roman Catholic Church through the Missionary Oblates of Mary Immaculate and Sisters of St. Joseph of St. Hyacinth, first opened in 1905 and occupied one hundred acres of land on the Sandy Bay Indian Reserve, as it was called, which was home to the Sandy Bay First Nation, near Marius, Manitoba, in the southwest part of the province. The school expanded as more children were institutionalized there, before being shut down in 1970. By 1976, the Sandy Bay First Nation was granted control of their own education system, along with three other large Manitoba communities: Peguis First Nation, Sagkeeng First Nation at Fort Alexander, and Nisichawayasihk Cree First Nation at Nelson House. Houle attended the school from grades one to eight, and then transferred in 1961 to the Assiniboia Residential High School for Indians in Winnipeg, run by the Oblates and the Grey Nuns.[8] According to the Roman Catholic Archdiocese of Winnipeg, the area around Marius, Manitoba, was visited by missionaries as early as 1861 and had a resident priest from 1904 when the Sandy Bay residential school opened. In 1968, the parish name was changed from Our Lady of Suffrage to Our Lady of Guadalupe.

A few weeks after my meeting with Robert and his sisters in May 2017, which concluded in the vault looking at the Sandy Bay paintings, I looked again at the 1999 WAG exhibition catalogue *Sovereignty over Subjectivity*. In artist and writer Bonnie Devine's text *Ways of Telling: Sandy Bay*, she weaves in her own family history with the residential school system. She recalls the story of her mother being sent to a school in Ontario at the age of six—and her insistence on telling her daughter that she was educated in a convent: "The subtle lie stood for years, disguising from us as it did perhaps from her, the ugliness and degradation inherent in the words "residential school."[9] Turning to Houle's own experience and trauma with the residential school system, Devine moves from "telling as loss" to "telling as painting." Aside from the works themselves and the artist's introduction, there is really nothing to add to Devine's statement on Robert Houle's return to Sandy Bay:

He painted the three large panels in white, blue, and red—the colours of the flags of European conquerors—to tell the story of a difficult time in his People's past. He tells of his vision of the residential school of his childhood, clothed in smoke or mist or time. He tells of the shoreline of Lake Manitoba at Sandy Bay, held in the sweet embrace of the land's strong arms. Finally, in a large, red panel alive with pain or ecstasy he tells of the body's connection to land, memory and self; of the peoples' connection.... No one can tell who has not healed. No one can heal who has not told. The process of telling contains the possibility of health and reconciliation. Not that healing or even reconciliation is the end or purpose of telling. The end of telling is story. The purpose of telling, history. [10]

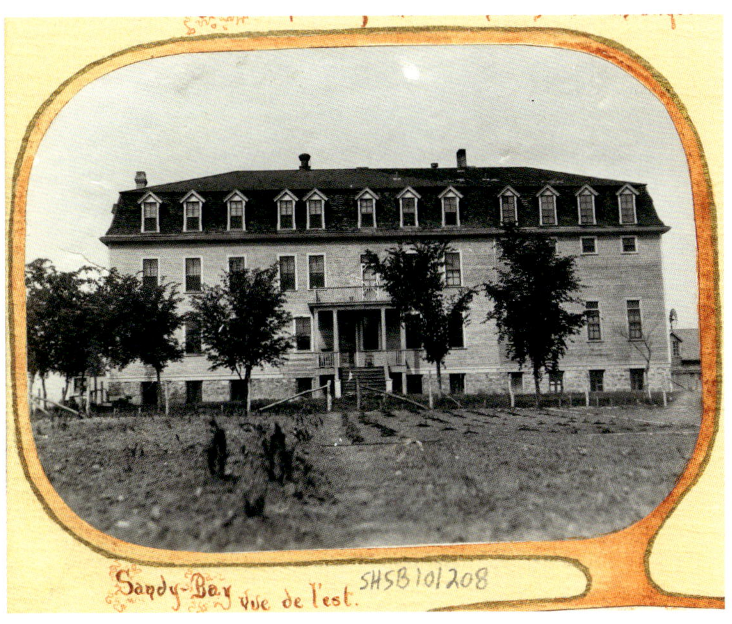

FIG. 8
Sandy Bay Residential School, 1914–1925. Archival photograph, pasted on beige cardboard, 8.5 × 11.5 cm. Société historique de Saint-Boniface, Sisters of Saint-Joseph of Saint-Hyacinthe Collection. SHSB 101208.

1 As I was preparing to write this essay, the news broke of the discovery of the remains of 215 children found interred in an unmarked burial site at the former Kamloops Indian Residential School located on Tk'emlúps te Secwépemc First Nation territory near Kamloops, British Columbia. Hundreds of children from neighbouring Indigenous communities were taken from their homes and placed in the institution, which was run by the Roman Catholic Church and operated from 1890 to 1969. This news was followed in subsequent weeks by similar discoveries at other former residential school sites. Aware that Robert had spent several years at residential schools in Sandy Bay, Manitoba, as well as in Winnipeg, and unsure about how I could contribute to the conversation going on across the country, I called Robert to get his input. In years previous, Robert and I had spoken about the place and significance of his paintings that deal with this subject, particularly the *Sandy Bay* piece, which I write about in this essay. In the end, he encouraged me to share my perspective as a settler and museum director responding to the Truth and Reconciliation Commission's calls to actions for museums. It was not the first time that Robert had helped me on my own journey.

2 Mary Lou Drieger, "Parfleches for the Last Supper," *What Next? Blog* (November 9, 2014), https://maryloudriedger2.wordpress.com/2014/11/09/parfleches-for-the-last-supper/; accessed October 18, 2021.

3 Gerald McMaster, *Robert Houle: Indians from A to Z.* (Winnipeg: Winnipeg Art Gallery, 1990), 40.

4 McMaster, *Robert Houle*, 40.

5 Shirley Madill, *Robert Houle: Life and Work* (Toronto: Art Canada Institute, 2018), https://www.aci-iac.ca/art-books/robert-houle/; accessed October 18, 2021.

6 Madill, *Robert Houle*, 48.

7 Madill, *Robert Houle*, 38.

8 Madill, *Robert Houle*, 5.

9 Bonnie Devine, *Robert Houle: Sovereignty over Subjectivity* (Winnipeg: Winnipeg Art Gallery, 1999), 43.

10 Devine, 47.

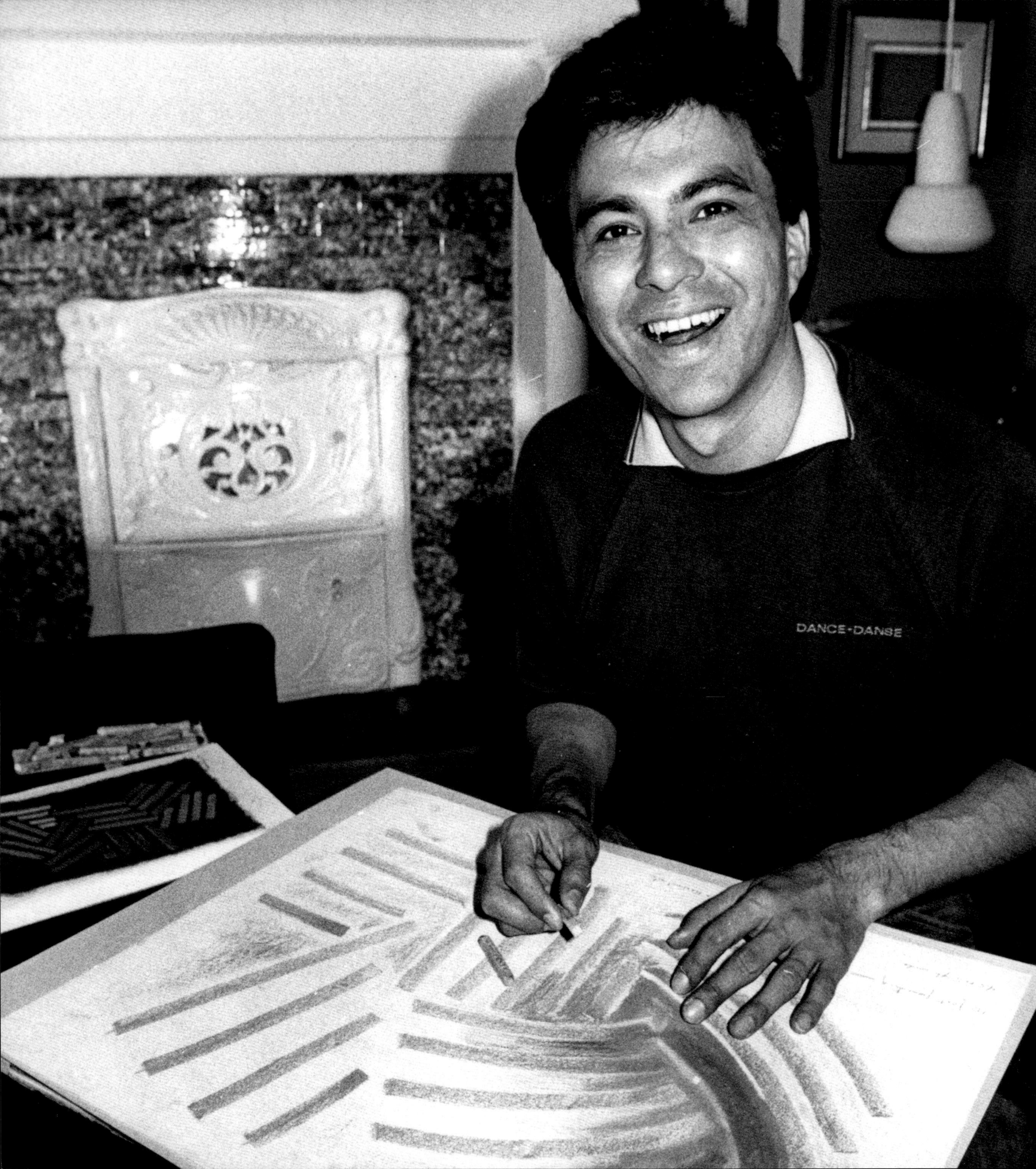
DANCE-DANSE

CRITICAL WRITING

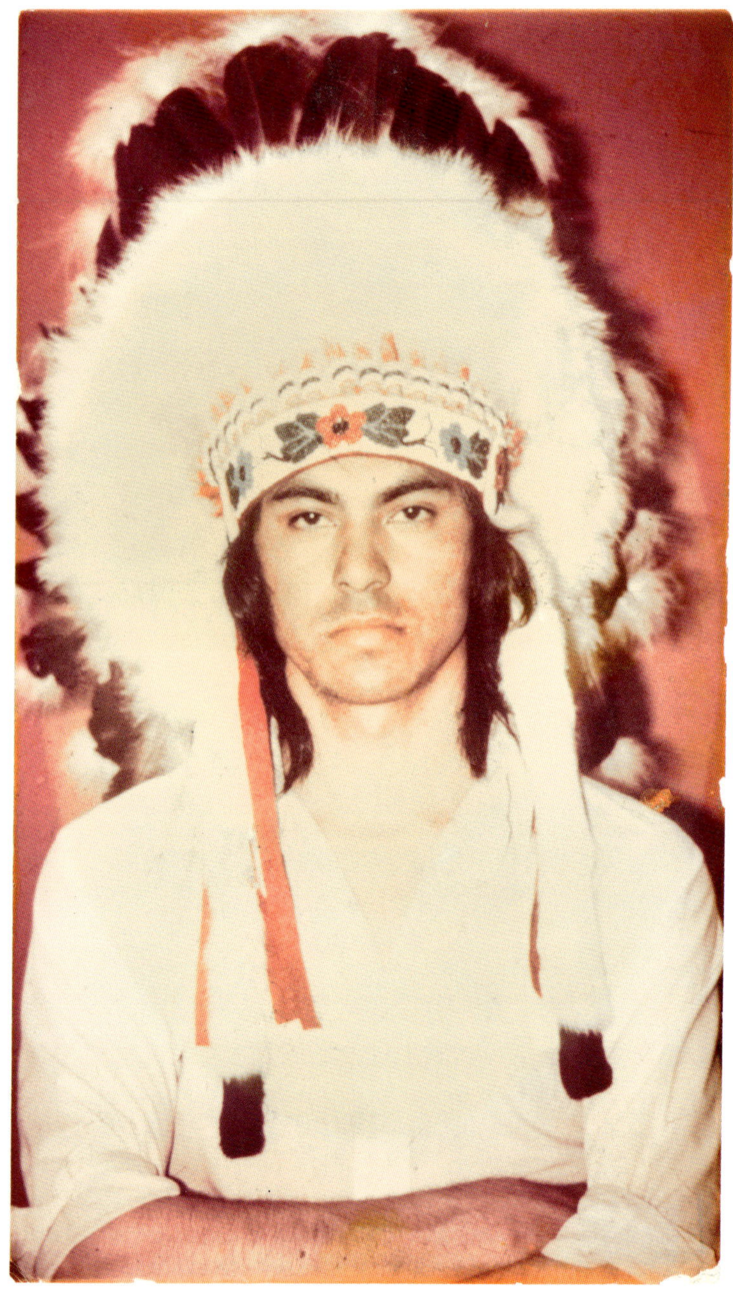

ABOVE:
Robert Houle wearing a headdress at the North American Indian Institute, Montreal, 1974. Image courtesy of the artist.

PAGE 226
Robert Houle practising his cross-hatching technique in his Wellesley Street East apartment, Toronto, 1981.
Photo by Edward Regan / The Globe and Mail.

The Symmetry of Time and Place

...

For assimilation would mean spiritual suicide.

Instead, we turn to the stories, premonitions, and prophecies that have been left by the first settlers of this hemisphere: whether they made their homes in the temperate cedar forest of the Northwest Coast, the subarctic tundra of the Mackenzie Lowlands, the high arid lands of the Columbia Plateau, the stark and monumental landscape of the Laurentian Shield, the mixed forests of deciduous and coniferous trees in the Appalachian Mountains, or the majestic open spaces of the Great Plains.[1] These stories and premonitions are the cultural capital, the inspirational source, that the artists in this exhibition invest into a new visual language. Theirs is a lexicon not just rich in historical forms and images, but one laced with the authentic vocabulary of a shamanic past, of a moment when humanity's indestructible dignity was in harmony with the symmetry of time and place.

...

The Indigenous "New" Art

...

Any rethinking of the history of modernism has to include the question of whether Western art now includes indigenous art, particularly the contemporary art in question. Another important question, perhaps more immediate, is whether postmodernism, to reiterate [Jimmie] Durham's cynicism, is just another fiction intended to exclude and protect: "There is no Western culture, but a power structure that pretends to be Western culture."[2] The real challenge facing these artists is to question all of that history; for one thing, they have never been part of it. They know why they have been excluded. The next question is, are they included in the current art discourse? Can they question a history they are not part of? Delacroix could express doubts about the growing academic tendencies of neo-classicism by looking back to antiquity. Why can't these artists seek the truth about who they are, where they came from, and where they are going, by looking back toward their own "antiquity" of "classic" native art? Is this exhibition the beginning of that dialogue? Do these artists who have been disinherited by history really have any room to manoeuvre?

Because, paradoxically, any refutation of this stance would be a denial of any history before 1492—the year of a historical/philosophical demarcation. The precarious dilemma is compounded by two factors: first, the use of revolutionary rhetoric, the need "to start from scratch," one of the fundamental tenets of modernism; and second, the conservative implications of an art based in believing in the traditional teachings left by the ancient ones, the "autochthonous."

No apologia is needed for any native aesthetics at work in the creative processes of these artists; that their indigenous inheritance is part of a continuum, especially within the context of the modernist heritage which informs all contemporary art, is unequivocal. Nevertheless, they straddle not only two cultures, but two histories; the first, the modern/postmodern dichotomy, and the second, that tension between the contemporary world and that of the ancient ones.

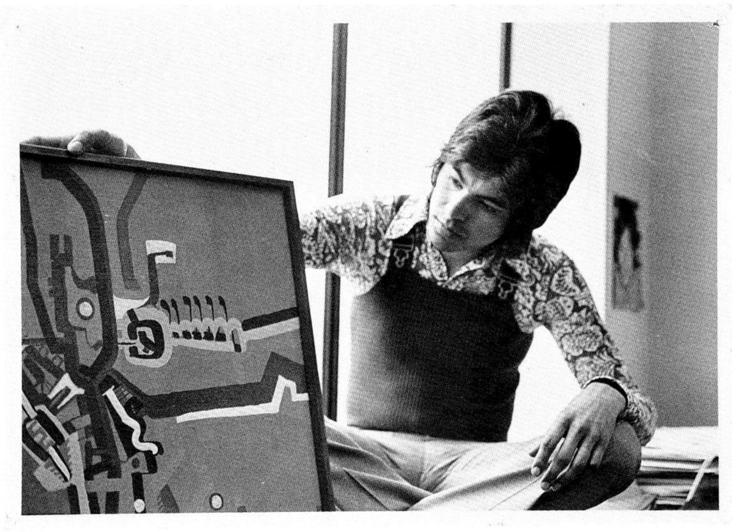

ABOVE:
Robert Houle, with a work by Alex Janvier, at the Department of Indian Affairs and Northern Development, Ottawa, 1969.
Photographed by Catherine Donnelly. Image courtesy of the artist.

1 See, for example, Peter Nabokov, ed., *Native American Testimony: A Chronicle of Indian-White Relations from Prophecy to the Present, 1492–1992* (New York: Viking, 1991).

2 Quote from Cherokee artist Jimmie Durham, in an article by Nancy Baele, *Ottawa Citizen*, December 2, 1991.

From "The Spiritual Legacy of the Ancient Ones," in Land, Spirit, Power: First Nations at the National Gallery of Canada, *exhibition catalogue, Susan McMaster and Claire Rochon, eds. (Ottawa: National Gallery of Canada, 1992) 44–73. © Robert Houle.*

Today, there is an emergence of a new art by a new generation of young artists. These artists have the distinction of having come from two different aesthetic traditions: North American and Western European. The former is deeply rooted in tribal ritual and symbolism; while the latter is an irreversible influence committed to change and personal development. This new art is rich in imagery and form that is both traditional and contemporary in source. Also, it is innovative and sophisticated in style and technique.

While putting to use contemporary styles, techniques and modes, the artists in this exhibition are still very much involved in leaving visual documents of their personal heritage. Nowhere is this more evident than in the diversity of creative expression found in the show. One is treated with an expression full of secular, sensuous counterpoints and mystical, existential visions. Each artist is invariably and intimately involved in recording personal experiences determined by tribal culture. This leaves the artist to create works of art traditionally inspired, but expressed through modern concepts and techniques. To deny the legitimacy of this inspirational source would be like refusing the Renaissance its Greco-Roman heritage; and to treat the validity of this creative process with deliberate reserve would be sanctimonious.

The artists in this exhibition have managed, sometimes at great odds, to straddle two not always compatible cultures. Not only must they refute the false representation as wagon train raiders, but they must avoid the excuse for paternalistic support as well. Regrettably, their artistic outpouring is still regulated as a cultural continuum of an anthropological past. Such

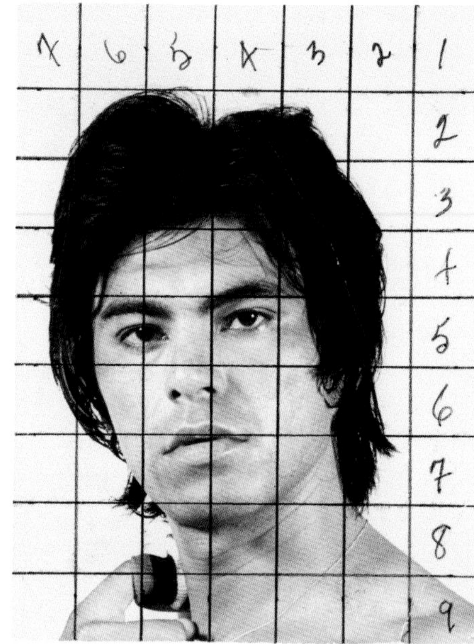

an intellectual approach only confines them as mere curiosities of a vanishing race whose art is a product of a fourth world often deemed highly insignificant by pontificating art historians.

This new generation of artists eloquently questions such short-sighted arguments through the seriousness and high quality of their work. The relegation of this new aesthetic to ethnological data by museums is to literally establish those cultural institutions as reservations of contemporary native art. Inevitably, the emergence of the artists, together with the understanding and use of the polemics of modern art, will lead to an appropriate environment, the art gallery.

From "The Emergence of a New Aesthetic Tradition," in New Work by a New Generation, *Exhibition catalogue (Regina: Norman Mackenzie Art Gallery, 1982) 2–5. © Robert Houle.*

ABOVE RIGHT:
Robert Houle, Study for *Self-Portrait*, c. 1970.
Image courtesy of the artist.

OPPOSITE PAGE:
Paul Gardner (left) and Robert Houle (right) with their cats, Simon and Windigo, in front of a series of paintings from Houle's installation *Zero Hour* (1988).
Photograph by André Leduc. Image courtesy of the artist.

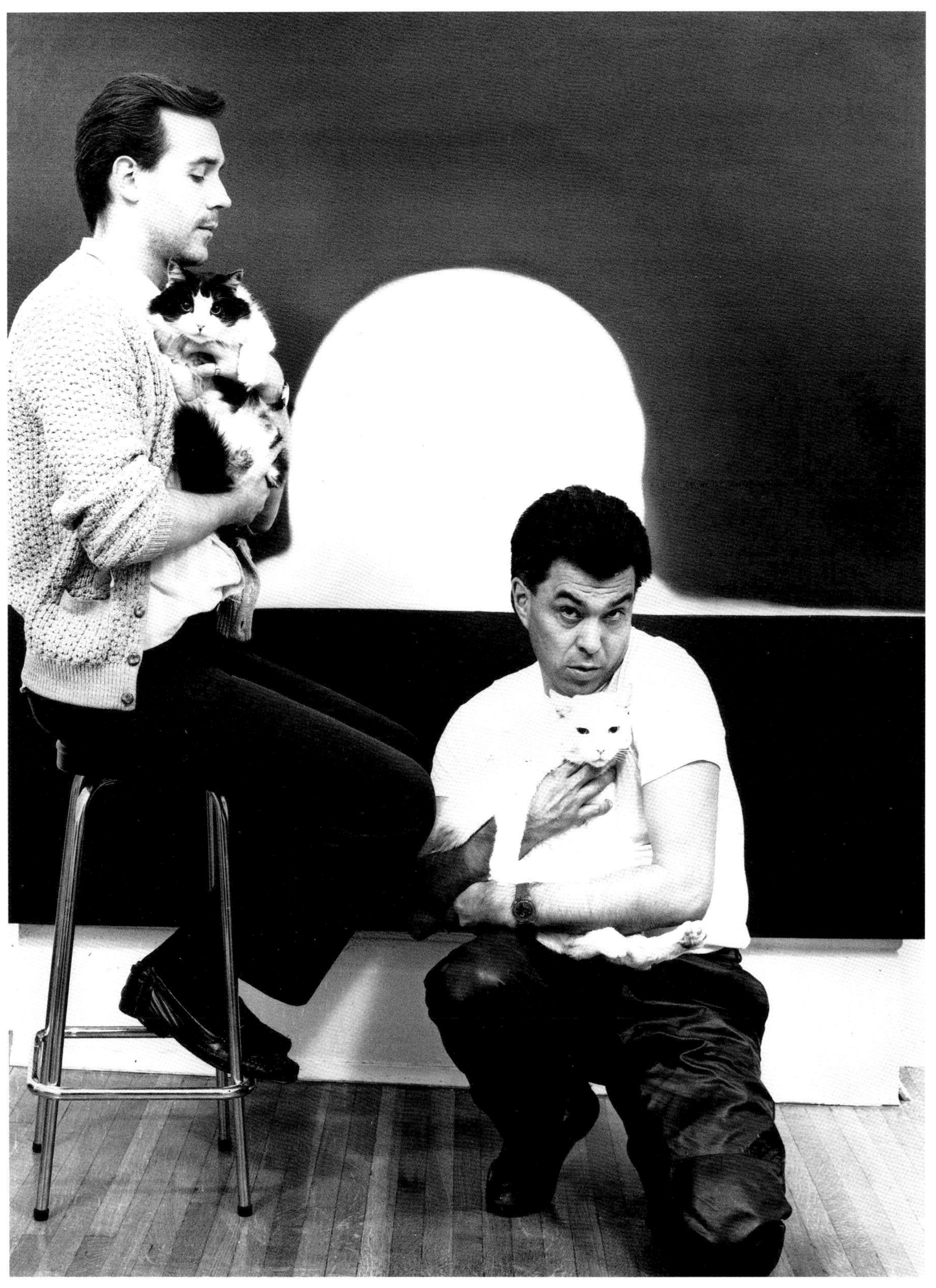

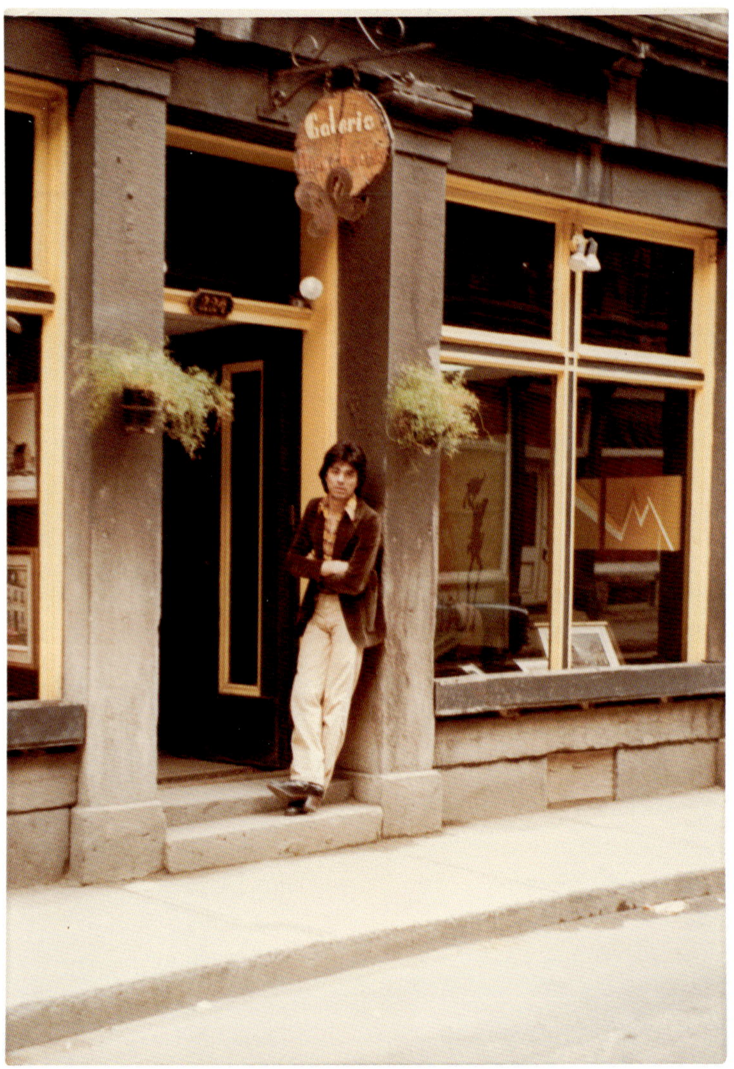

Viewing these looted Beothuk artifacts in the former bastion of European aesthetics—the National Gallery of Canada—the trivialization of a human tragedy was compounded by my knowledge that the sponsoring institution, the Canadian Museum of Civilization, was the depository of sacred and ceremonial regalia seized by the federal government in the early part of this century during the banning of potlatch. Here were fragments of the art of the First Nations, evidence of its subjectivity as well as of the denial of its ongoing construction and renewal.

Parallel to this cultural reality is a bitter political one, well-illustrated through a litany of native struggles: the Innu of Labrador working to decrease the impact of low-level flying over their ancestral lands; the Haida blockading loggers from cutting down centuries-old trees on South Moresby; the Mohawks of Kanesatake barricading access to land slated to become a golf course; and Elijah Harper effectively blocking the passage of a bill in the Manitoba legislature that would have brought Quebec into the Canadian political struggle over Indigenous title to land is central to discussing the aspirations of the First Nations artist.

...

I am convinced that art has the capacity to raise the spirit. My studio visits reaffirmed my belief that the place and process of creative activity, a place where the artist is at once powerful and vulnerable, is the site of political and cultural change.

From "Sovereignty over Subjectivity," C Magazine, *no. 30 (Summer 1991): 28–35. © Robert Houle.*

Above
Robert Houle standing on rue Maisonneuve in Montreal in the early 1970s. Image courtesy of the artist.

Modernity's rational perspective and the syntax of fractured reality proposed by surrealist art, with its incompatible aims of exploring and liberating the creative unconscious of formulating a policy of practical action for society, made this period of art history a radical time. The Indigenous perspective was one of sharing, a traditional tribal value that nurtured the Surrealists' desire for renewal and healing. The trauma in old Paris led to the shift to New York and, in that moment when Indigenous art traditions were about to change forever, North America's ancient cultures became the new frontier of creativity.

From Shape-shifting Images." in The Colour of My Dreams: The Surrealist Revolution in Art, *Exhibition catalogue, Dawn Ades, ed. (Vancouver: Vancouver Art Gallery, 2011). 271–275.*

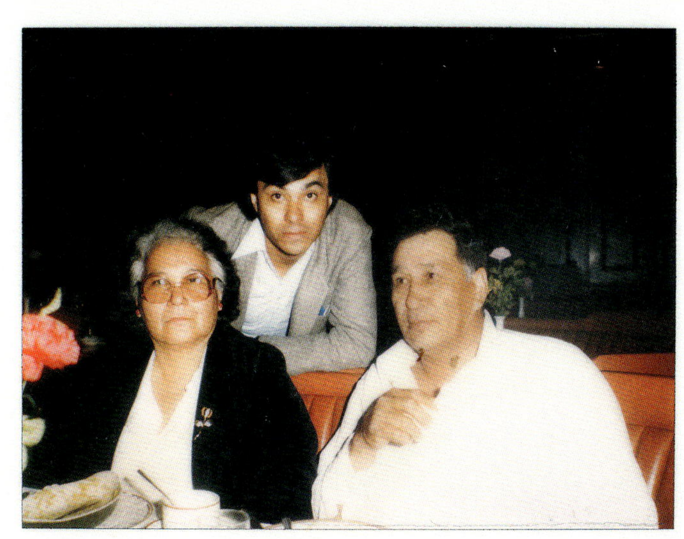

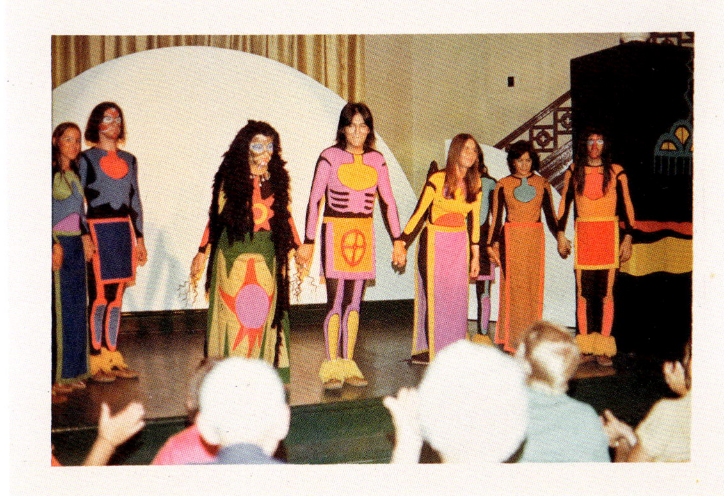

[Much] of HeavyShield's work in this exhibition also deals with other baggage from the "rez" memory. Throughout she becomes part of the medium, her body the site of political/spiritual struggle through which a radical deconstruction of an imposed Eurocentric language and god is achieved. This she does by exposing the veiled/denied eroticism of the nun's habit in *Heart, Hoof, Horn*, by revealing the *Spade* in the androgynous cruciform of the priest's Roman collar; and finally by celebrating the sensual and cultural values of native women as loving and maternal through the stiletto heels of her Sisters.

From "Heart, Hoof, Horn," pamphlet essay for Faye HeavyShield: Heart, Hoof, Horn *(Glenbow-Alberta Institute, Calgary, 1993).*

Top right
Robert Houle with his parents at the World Assembly of First Nations, Regina, 1982.
Image courtesy of the artist.

Bottom left
Cast of a play written by Duke Redbird with costumes, makeup, and sets designed by Robert Houle at Pendulum Theatre, Montreal, in the early 1970s.
Image courtesy of the artist.

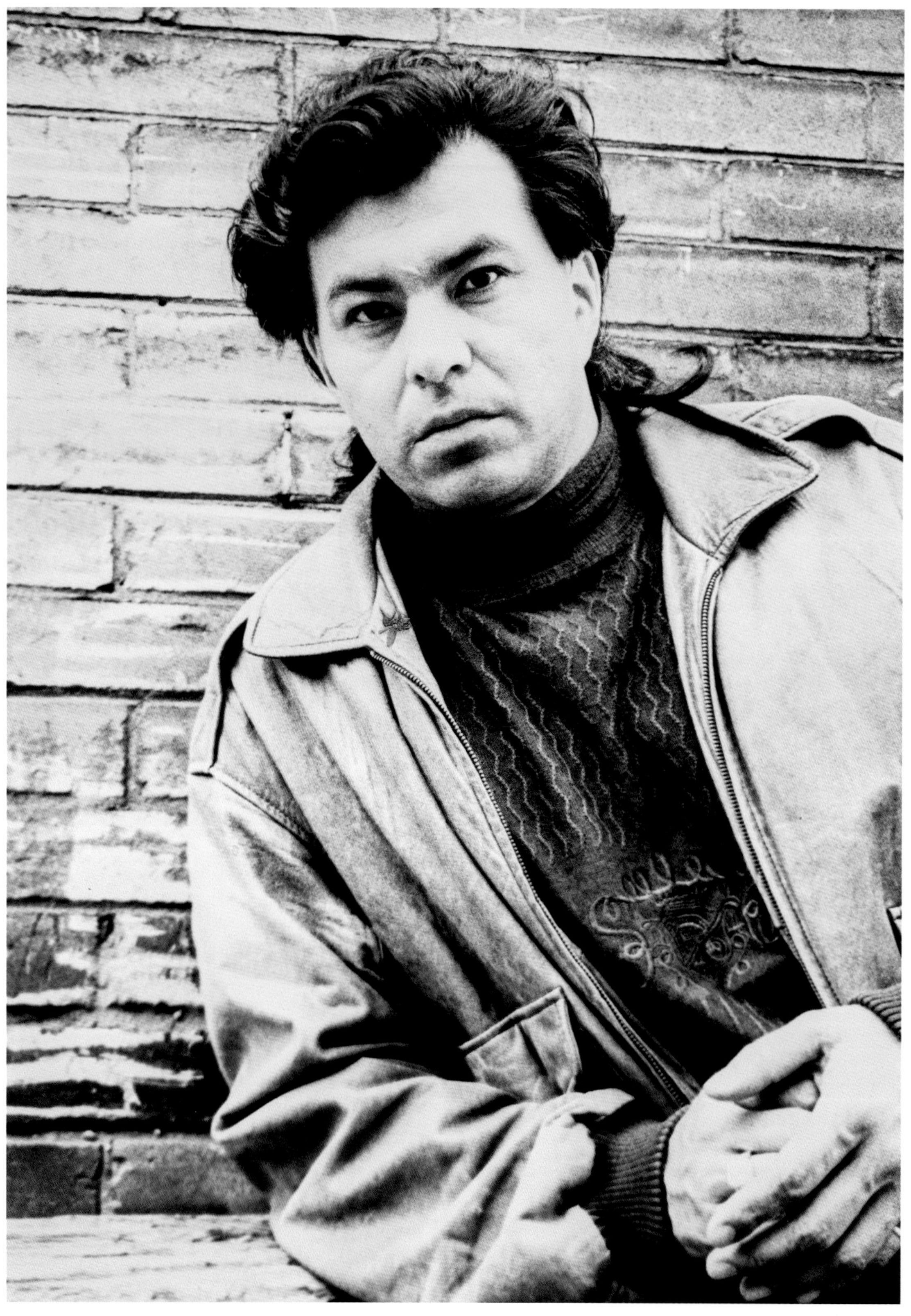

In an interview with Alex Coles, James Clifford speaks about his critique of Western institutions: "And I think there's no doubt that a globalizing system of cultural commodification is at work. But it's terribly inadequate to reduce the emerging subaltern and local productions that articulate with museums, cultural centres, and (inescapably) tourism to epiphenomenona of a late capitalist, postmodern, or "Americanized" world system of cultures." Artist interventions have helped both curators and the public learn vital lessons about the dilemma facing visual culture. Positioning Haida art within contemporary culture requires that the ovoids and formlines from regalia in static museum display cases can be seen as liberated. Raven, eagle, sea monster, and killer whale become the living symbols, the ethnography of contemporary culture. The irony is that the mythology implicit in [Robert] Davidson's abstracts would exclude them under colonial methodologies of classification.

Davidson's art is not in between art object and material culture; it is contemporary, and its modern hybridity is culturally specific with universal appeal. His untitled acrylic paintings, one on paper (1997) and the other on canvas (1999), are similar in their use of colour and form. Their primary colours recall the reductive look of a Mondrian painting without its right-angle geometry; their split forms have a simplicity that make them visually comfortable, their painterly qualities achieved with diluted paint. The two deerskin hand drums, *Eagle Looking at Eagle* (1990) and *Sea Monster* (2000), have a more condensed acrylic. Although they are also more representational, their radical contextualization as works of art comes from the fact that they may also be used in ceremonials. *Eagle Looking at Eagle* has a reflecting eagle image within a rhythmic circle, a symmetry established by its red reflection, in which a similar asymmetrical form is shared between its beaks. Framed within these drums are ideas paramount to understanding how art can transform from function. The handling and treatment of the acrylic on the deerskin brings out the experimental aspect of the contemporary; acrylic, a synthetic polymer of acrylic acid and acrylates, is seen as an opportunity for change, a time to develop the art and achieve greater excellence. Art can be transformed/translated by artist prerogative. The abstract works are eloquent; they are balanced with visual elements ranging from ideograph to expression.

As an art maverick, Davidson looks at Haida art on its own terms, away from the traditional museum. His synthetically produced palette is equally treated and contrasted with more traditional colours influenced by natural pigments. His drums mediate between ceremony and art, a concept affirmed during a conversation about *Eagle Looking at Eagle* in which he acknowledged its previous use. To him, framing had become an option: the drum had broken. Through distortion, abstraction, or repetition, Davidson shows in these five works that implicit images of mythology are not frozen in some momentous encounter between his ancestors and the pioneers: a juncture between purity and contamination. One hopes that contemporaneity in liberation.

From "A Context for Haida Abstraction," in Robert Davidson: The Abstract Edge, *Exhibition catalogue, Karen Duffek, ed. (Vancouver: Museum of Anthropology, University of British Columbia, 2004) 49–59.*

OPPOSITE PAGE
Robert Houle, 1991. Photographed by Mirella Mossanen. Image courtesy of the artist.

The United Nations Declaration on the Rights of Indigenous Peoples in 2007 changed the colonial cultural landscape. Today, independence is instantly affirmed through the frontier democracy of homogenizing cyberspace; we know what is happening in every corner of the planet and beyond but contemporary Indigenous cultures are still dominated by the vampiric nature of its centrifugal force. However, Indigenous art is finally appearing on the world map, flourishing among artists like Jeffrey Gibson, a Choctaw and Cherokee painter and installation artist who reveals a narrative of emergence of a utopia endangered by corruption and collapse. All continents have a history and a cultural capital steeped in colonization and Jeffrey salvages what remains, creating a new culture—globalized, cyberized, corporatized—a manifest Indigenous identity uncompromisingly troubled by exclusion. His art is inclusive of powwow and rave, traditional and pop culture, tribal and global.

From "Preface," in Jeffrey Gibson: Said the Pigeon to the Squirrel, *exhibition catalogue (New York: National Academy Museum, 2013) 12–13. © Robert Houle.*

Morrisseau paintings are like paradigms, viewpoints, methodologies, paradoxical complicities of potent critique, and resistance. Copper Thunderbird, a demi-god of the upper world, the place of the uhsokun, the place of the guardian, located his paintings outside the flawed matrix of context. They are somewhere between cultural salvage operation and romantic reconstruction. The baggage of destabilization, authenticity, and contamination are obscuring in understanding their creative source. It can get tangled in the complex postmodern literature on "otherness" and through the prism of cultural vulnerability, demise, and proclivities, the magic of contemporary shaman can still be felt.

It is an honour to have known him. As a fellow Nish artist, he was a warrior who led a coup on cultural apartheid; his dominance made him a true barometer of critical resistance and provided an excellent opportunity to have a dialogue about what kind of painting or sculpture to make and how to have them represented. Remaining aloof, Morrisseau's presence continued to be a catalyst for a conversation on the community's cry for justice and equality.

I want to acknowledge the Anishnabe people for having shared their son, a great soul, who in the words of an elder at the Native Canadian Centre the night a pipe was smoked to help him reach his destiny, was someone we see only every eight hundred years. I stand here, proud and inspired. Meegwetch. Thank you. Merci bien.

From "Anishnabe Supernova," in Copper Thunderbird: The Art of Norval Morrisseau, *Exhibition catalogue (Toronto: Westerkirk Works of Art, 2012), 98–102. The full text was originally read at Norval Morrisseau's memorial at the National Gallery of Canada. © Robert Houle.*

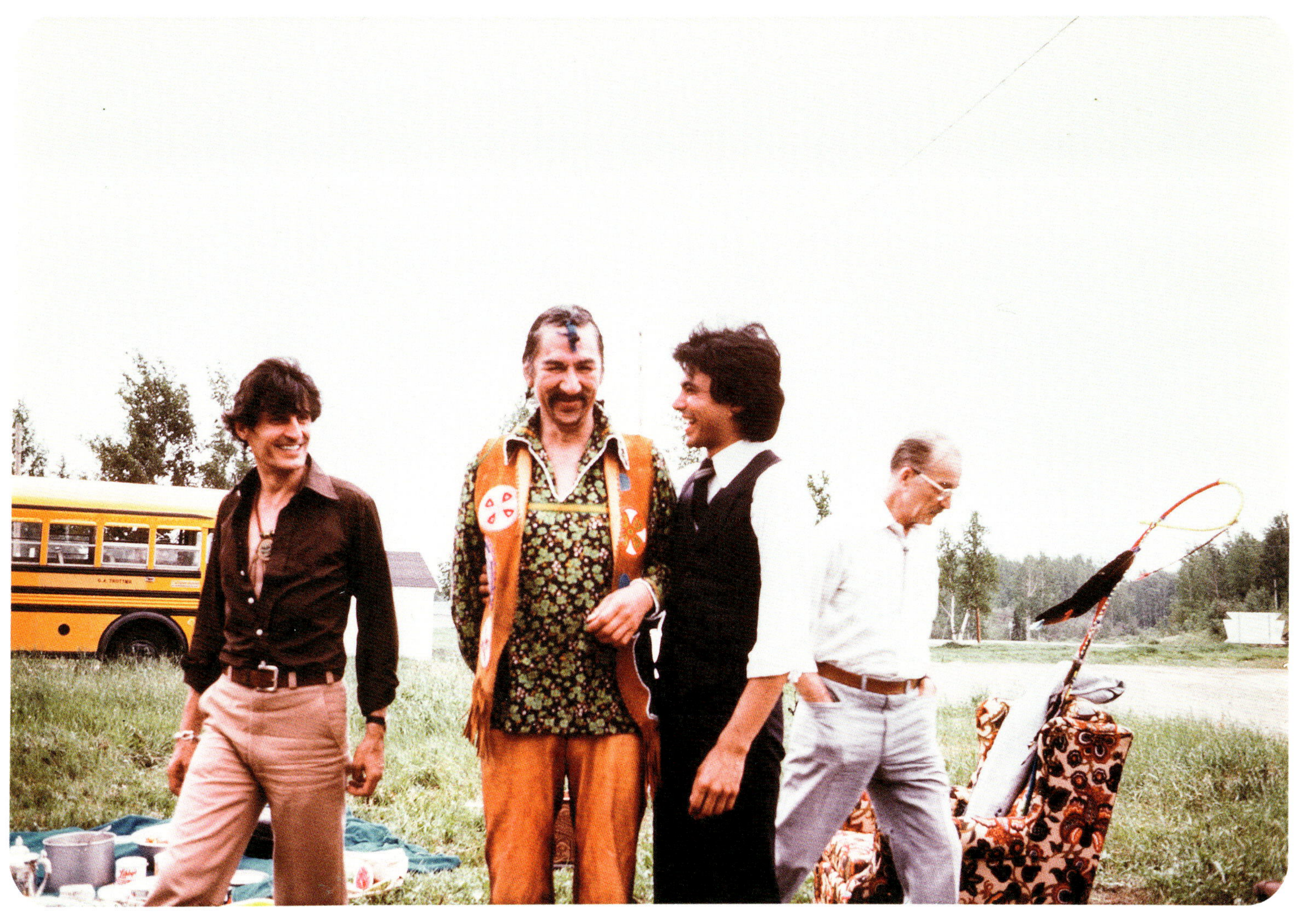

Jack Pollock, Norval Morrisseau, and Robert Houle in Beardmore, Ontario, 1978.
Photographed by Barbara Stimpson. Image courtesy of the artist.

Biography
Robert Houle

Robert Houle (b. 1947, St. Boniface, Manitoba) is an Anishinaabe Saulteaux contemporary artist, curator, writer, critic, and educator. For more than fifty years, he has worked to advocate for First Nations artistic representation and sovereignty and has established himself as an essential force within the artistic community in Canada and around the world. Houle studied at the University of Manitoba, McGill University, and the International Summer Academy of Fine Arts in Salzburg, Austria, and for many years taught Indigenous Studies at the Ontario College of Art and Design. From 1977 to 1981, he was Curator of Contemporary Aboriginal Art at the National Museum of Man (now the Canadian Museum of History). As a curator, he is also responsible for landmark exhibitions such as *Land, Spirit, Power: First Nations at the National Gallery of Canada* (1992).

Houle's various solo exhibitions include *Indians from A to Z and Sovereignty over Subjectivity*, Winnipeg Art Gallery (1990); *Lost Tribes*, Hood College, Maryland (1991); *Anishnabe Walker Court*, an intervention at the Art Gallery of Ontario, Toronto (1993); *Palisade*, Carleton University Art Gallery, Ottawa (2000–2001); *Paris/Ojibwa*, Canadian Cultural Centre, Paris, Peterborough, and Windsor (2010–2011); *Shaman Dream in Colour*, Kinsman Robinson Galleries, Toronto (2016); *Robert Houle: Pahgedenaun*, Carleton University Art Gallery, Ottawa (2018); and *Robert Houle: Histories*, McMichael Canadian Collection, Kleinburg, Ontario (2019–2020).

He has also participated in several important international group exhibitions, including *Recent Generations: Native American Art from 1950 to 1987*, Heard Museum, Phoenix (1987); *Traveling Theory*, Jordan National Gallery, Amman, Jordan (1992); *Notions of Conflict*, Stedelijk Museum, Amsterdam (1995); *Real Fictions: Four Canadian Artists*,

Museum of Contemporary Art, Sydney, Australia (1996); *Tout le temps/Every Time,* 2000 Montreal Biennale; *We Come in Peace...: Histories of the Americas,* Musée d'art Contemporain de Montréal (2004); *Sakahàn,* National Gallery of Canada, Ottawa (2013); *Before and After the Horizon: Anishinaabe Artists of the Great Lakes,* National Museum of the American Indian, Washington, and Art Gallery of Ontario, Toronto (2014); and *Toronto: Tributes + Tributaries,* 1971–1989 (2016) and *Every. Now. Then: Reframing Nationhood* (2017), both at the Art Gallery of Ontario.

Houle has been awarded two honorary doctorates—one in 2014 from his alma mater, the University of Manitoba, and one in 2016, from the University of Ontario Institute of Technology. His artistic achievements have garnered him numerous awards and accolades, including the 2001 Toronto Arts Award for the Visual Arts; the 2015 Governor General's Award in the Visual and Media Arts; and most recently, the 2020 Founder's Achievement Award from the Toronto Friends of the Visual Arts. Houle has also served on various boards and advisory committees, including those of the Art Gallery of Ontario, the Museum of Contemporary Art Toronto, The Indigenous Curatorial Collective, A Space, The Power Plant Contemporary Art Gallery, and the Native Canadian Centre of Toronto.

List of Works

All works © Robert Houle

1947
1996
Advertisement, colour photocopy, and plexiglass
78.8 × 61.6 × 6.6 cm
The Mendel Art Gallery Collection at Remai Modern. Purchased with support from the Canada Council's Acquisition Assistance Program, 1997
1997.28.1.a-e
Photo: Troy Mamer
Page 147

Aboriginal Title
1989–1990
Oil on canvas
228 × 167.6 cm
Art Gallery of Hamilton. Acquired with the assistance of the Alfred Wavell Peene and Susan Nottle Peene Memorial, 1992
Photo: Robert McNair
Page 181

Atomic Lacrosse
2005
Oil on board and gelatin silver prints
16 panels; stored and folded: 10 x 12.8 cm; expanded: 10 × 184 × 8 cm
Art Gallery of Ontario
Gift of Stephen B. Smart, 2020
2020/149
Photo: Art Gallery of Ontario
Page 194

B.N.A. Act 1867
1985
Acrylic on paper
102 × 64 cm
Indigenous Art Collection, Crown-Indigenous Relations and Northern Affairs Canada / Collection d'art autochtones, Relations Couronne-Autochtones et Affaires du Nord Canada
Photo: Lawrence Cook
Page 173

Blue Apache
2003
Oil on canvas, etched red slate
91.4 × 61 cm; 29.8 × 29.8 cm
Courtesy of the artist
Photo: Art Gallery of Ontario
Page 141

Cathedral
2016
Oil, graphite and porcelain skull on pine, vinyl text, and pine shelf
47 × 29.2 cm
Courtesy of the artist
Photo: Michael Cullen/TPG Digital Art Services, Courtesy Kinsman Robinson Galleries, Toronto
Page 159

Chief, the New Pontiac Big Six
c. 1997
Transfer chromolithograph with collage of vinyl letters, watercolour on paper, and quillwork laced through wood veneer support
Support: 43 × 56 cm; framed: 56.6 × 70 × 4.5 cm
Art Gallery of Ontario
Gift of Stephen B. Smart, 2018
2018/3729
Photo: Art Gallery of Ontario
Page 147

Constitution Act 1982
1985
Acrylic on paper
106 × 75 cm
Indigenous Art Collection, Crown-Indigenous Relations and Northern Affairs Canada / Collection d'art autochtones, Relations Couronne-Autochtones et Affaires du Nord Canada
Photo: Lawrence Cook
Page 170

Constitutional Wampum
1983
Conté crayon on paper
79.5 × 120 cm
Courtesy of the National Museum of the American Indian, Smithsonian Institution
Purchase, 2009
26/7195
Photo: Ernest Amoroso
Page 207
* exhibited at the NMAI only

Constitutional Wampum
1983
Conté crayon on paper
79.5 × 120 cm
Courtesy of the National Museum of the American Indian, Smithsonian Institution
Purchase, 2009
26/7196
Photo: Ernest Amoroso
Page 207
* exhibited at the NMAI only

Constitutional Wampum
1983
Conté crayon on paper
79.5 × 120 cm
Courtesy of the National Museum of the American Indian, Smithsonian Institution
Purchase, 2009
26/7197
Photo: Ernest Amoroso
Page 208
* exhibited at the NMAI only

Constitutional Wampum
1983
Conté crayon on paper
79.5 × 120 cm
Courtesy of the National Museum of the American Indian, Smithsonian Institution
Purchase, 2009
26/7198
Photo: Ernest Amoroso
Page 208
* exhibited at the NMAI only

Cryptogram No. 2
1981
Graphite on paper
Sheet (irregular): 51 × 67 cm
Art Gallery of Ontario
Purchase, with funds from the James Lahey Fund and the Estate of Penelope Glasser Fund, 2020
2020/64
Photo: Art Gallery of Ontario
Page 56

Dark Moses
2009
Oil on paper
112.5 × 76 cm
Indigenous Art Collection, Crown-Indigenous Relations and Northern Affairs Canada / Collection d'art autochtones, Relations Couronne-Autochtones et Affaires du Nord Canada
Photo: Lawrence Cook
Page 161

Demasduwit's Warrior #5
1988
Oil wash, ribbon, and porcupine quills on paper
28.5 × 19 cm
Royal Ontario Museum
989.116.1
Photo courtesy of the Royal Ontario Museum, © ROM
Page 182

Demasduwit's Warrior #13
1988
Oil wash, ribbon, and porcupine quills on paper
28.2 × 19.2 cm
Royal Ontario Museum
989.116.2
Photo courtesy of the Royal Ontario Museum, © ROM
Page 182

Diamond Composition
1980
Silkscreen on paper
Edition number 1/75
87 × 87 cm
Collection of Melvin Thompson & Harvey Bouchard
Photo: Art Gallery of Ontario
Page 54

Do Not Open Until You Get Home
2007
Installation: video, player, video projection, and vinyl lettering
Dimensions variable
Courtesy of the artist
Page 110

Epigram: A Visual Statement
1980–1983
Acrylic and quills on canvas
76.4 × 101.5 cm
McMichael Canadian Art Collection
Purchase 1985
1985.63
Page 47

Everything you ever wanted to know about Indians from A to Z
1985
Acrylic, rawhide, wood, and linen
45.3 × 735 cm
Collection of the Winnipeg Art Gallery. Acquired with funds from The Winnipeg Art Gallery Foundation Inc.,
G-89-1501 a-cc
Photo: Ernest Mayer, courtesy of the Winnipeg Art Gallery
Page 142–143

Falklands
1982
Acrylic on wood
147.2 × 3.5 cm
Art Gallery of Ontario
Gift of Tony Ryan in memory of Richard M. Barrett, 1992
92/30
Photo: Art Gallery of Ontario
Page 196

Grandmother (drum)
2015
Oil on canvas
30.5 cm diameter
Collection of Deborah Chansonneuve
Page 158

I Stand
1997
Oil, porcupine quills on canvas, etched brass plaque, vinyl text on large red wall, and 1947 Pontiac convertible
Dimensions variable
Courtesy of the artist and Norm Dumontier
Photo: Ernest Mayer, courtesy of the Winnipeg Art Gallery
Page 146

Idyllic Moments
1985
Acrylic on canvas
152 × 152 cm
Collection of the Thunder Bay Art Gallery. Purchased with the assistance of The Walter & Duncan L. Gordon Charitable Foundation Funding, 1986
Page 48

In Memoriam
1987
Oil, feathers, leather, and ribbon on plywood
137.2 × 151.9 × 9 cm
Art Gallery of Ontario
Gift of Vanessa, Britney, and Nelson Niedzielski, 2000
2000/1196
Photo: Art Gallery of Ontario
Page 6, 139

Indian Act 1876
1985
Acrylic on paper
102 × 64 cm
Indigenous Art Collection, Crown-Indigenous Relations and Northern Affairs Canada / Collection d'art autochtones, Relations Couronne-Autochtones et Affaires du Nord Canada
Photo: Lawrence Cook
Page 172

Innu Parfleche
1990
Oil, acrylic, iron, ink, metal, owl feather, and mammal leather
66.2 × 68 × 8 cm
Musée canadien de l'histoire / Canadian Museum of History
V-F-190
Image courtesy of McMaster Museum of Art, Hamilton
Page 197, 212

Ipperwash
2000–2001
Oil on canvas, digitized photograph mounted on masonite, and anodized aluminum
152.5 × 336.7 cm
Collection of Museum London (Ontario). Purchased in part with financial support of the Canada Council for the Arts and the Volunteer Committee and through a gift of the artist, 2006
006.A.064.1-.12
Photo: © Toni Hafkenscheid
Page 186

Kanata
1992
Acrylic and conté crayon on canvas
228.7 × 732 cm overall;
panels: 228.7 × 183 cm each
National Gallery of Canada, Ottawa. Purchased 1994
Acc. # 37479.1-4
Photo: NGC
Page 96

Kanehsatake
1990–1993
Oil on etched steel panels, and treated wood
221 × 122 cm
Art Gallery of Hamilton.
Gift of the artist, 1994
Photo: Robert McNair
Page 184

Kanehsatake X
2000
Oil on canvas, digital photo, and ionized steel
243.8 × 502.9 cm
Collection of Comsatec Inc.
Image courtesy of the lender
Page 185

Kekabishcoon Peenish Chipedahbung (I Will Stand in Your Path Till Dawn)
1997
Thirty-six third-generation advertisements on red latex background with vinyl lettering
63.8 × 550 cm
The Robert McLaughlin Gallery
Gift of Paul Gardner in memory of Donald Gardner, 2007
Photo: © Toni Hafkensheid
Page 148–149

Light Box
2011
Oil on canvas
91.4 × 61 cm
Collection of Christopher Varley + Sandra Shaul
Photo: Michael Cullen, TPG Digital Art Services, Courtesy of the Kinsman Robinson Galleries, Toronto
Page 90

Love Poems

Epigram for the Shortest Distance
1972
From *Love Poems*
Acrylic on canvas
Framed: 127.9 × 127.8 × 4.1 cm
Indigenous Art Collection, Crown-Indigenous Relations and Northern Affairs Canada / Collection d'art autochtones, Relations Couronne-Autochtones et Affaires du Nord Canada
Photo: Lawrence Cook
Page 51

Games
1972
From *Love Poems*
Acrylic on canvas
Framed: 127.5 × 127.5 × 3.5 cm
Indigenous Art Collection, Crown-Indigenous Relations and Northern Affairs Canada / Collection d'art autochtones, Relations Couronne-Autochtones et Affaires du Nord Canada
Photo: Lawrence Cook
Page 50

Parallel Lines
1972
From *Love Poems*
Acrylic on canvas
Framed: 62.2 × 52.1 × 3.5 cm
Indigenous Art Collection, Crown-Indigenous Relations and Northern Affairs Canada / Collection d'art autochtones, Relations Couronne-Autochtones et Affaires du Nord Canada
Photo: Lawrence Cook
Page 51

The First Step
1972
From *Love Poems*
Acrylic on canvas
152.2 × 61 cm
Indigenous Art Collection, Crown-Indigenous Relations and Northern Affairs Canada / Collection d'art autochtones, Relations Couronne-Autochtones et Affaires du Nord Canada
Photo: Lawrence Cook
Page 50

The Stuff of Which Dreams Are Made
1972
From *Love Poems*
Acrylic on canvas
63.5 × 155 cm
Indigenous Art Collection, Crown-Indigenous Relations and Northern Affairs Canada / Collection d'art autochtones, Relations Couronne-Autochtones et Affaires du Nord Canada
Photo: Lawrence Cook
Page 50

Wigwam
1972
From *Love Poems*
Acrylic on canvas
209 × 121 cm
Indigenous Art Collection, Crown-Indigenous Relations and Northern Affairs Canada / Collection d'art autochtones, Relations Couronne-Autochtones et Affaires du Nord Canada
Photo: Lawrence Cook
Page 51

Mississauga Portraits (Waubuddick, Maungwudaus, Hannah)
2012
3 panels, oil on canvas; oil on Masonite, each 172.7 × 121.9 cm
Art Gallery of Ontario
Gift of the artist, 2020
2020/113.1-.3
Image courtesy of the Art Gallery of Windsor, photographed by Frank Piccolo
Page 133

Mohawk Summer
1990
4 coloured cloth banners with vinyl text each 210.8 × 106.7 cm
Courtesy of the artist
Page 188

Mohawk Summer Collages
1991
Magazines, crayon, and paint
4 parts, 50.8 × 35.6 cm each
Collection of Amy Smart,
Squamish, BC
Photo: Art Gallery of Ontario
Page 188

Muhnedobe uhyahyuk
[Where the gods are present] (Matthew, Philip, Bartholomew, Thomas)
1989
Oil on canvas
4 parts, 244 × 182.4 × 5 cm each
National Gallery of Canada.
Purchased 1992
Acc. # 36168.1-4
Photo: NGC
Page 76–77

New Sentinel
1987
Oil on wood panel, ribbon, and encaustic on cow skull
244.3 × 45.5 × 3.5 cm
The Robert McLaughlin Gallery
Purchase, 1999
Photo: Lesli Michaelis Onusko
Page 138

O-ween du muh waun (We Were Told)
2017
Oil on canvas
triptych, 213.4 × 365.8 cm
Confederation Centre Art Gallery.
Commissioned with the A.G. and Eliza Jane Ramsden Endowment Fund, 2017
CAG 2017.1
Page 101

Ojibway Blanket
1983
Gouache and porcupine quills on paper
Framed: 74.8 × 93.2 × 4.1 cm
Indigenous Art Collection, Crown-Indigenous Relations and Northern Affairs Canada / Collection d'art autochtones, Relations Couronne-Autochtones et Affaires du Nord Canada
Photo: Lawrence Cook
Page 46

Ojibway Motif, #2, Purple Leaves Series
1972
Acrylic on canvas
91.4 × 61 cm
Collection of Carleton University Art Gallery, Gift of Raymonde Falardeau, 1998
1998.25.1
Photo: Justin Wonnacott, courtesy Carleton University Art Gallery
Page 49

Oka
1991
Oil on board
diptych, 243.84 × 91.44 cm per panel
Courtesy of the artist
Photo: Art Gallery of Ontario
Page 189

Palisade I
1999
Oil on canvas, watercolour on paper, and lithographic print
Installation dimensions variable, canvas panels: 244 × 61.2 cm each
Collection of the MacKenzie Art Gallery, purchased with the financial support of the Canada Council for the Arts Acquisition Assistance Program
2000-001
Photo: Don Hall, courtesy of the MacKenzie Art Gallery
Pages 104–105

Postscript
1999
Lithographic print on paper
121.9 × 163.2 cm
Collection of the MacKenzie Art Gallery, purchased with the financial support of the Canada Council for the Arts Acquisition Assistance Program
2000-001-001
Photo: Don Hall, courtesy of the MacKenzie Art Gallery
Page 109

Postscript
1999
Acrylic, graphite, ballpoint ink, computer printout from WWW site, photocopy, and mat board on paper
45.7 × 121.9 cm
Collection of the MacKenzie Art Gallery, purchased with the financial support of the Canada Council for the Arts Acquisition Assistance Program
2000-001-005
Photo: Don Hall, courtesy of the MacKenzie Art Gallery
Page 109

Postscript (study)
1999
Acrylic, ink, Xerox image, newsprint, vinyl lettering, and ballpoint pen ink on paper
45.5 × 60.7 cm
Collection of the MacKenzie Art Gallery, purchased with the financial support of the Canada Council for the Arts Acquisition Assistance Program
2000-001-002
Photo: Don Hall, courtesy of the MacKenzie Art Gallery
Page 109

Study for *Smallpox*
1999
Acrylic, collage, vinyl lettering, and graphite on paper
45.7 × 61 cm
Collection of the MacKenzie Art Gallery, purchased with the financial support of the Canada Council for the Arts Acquisition Assistance Program
2000-001-003
Photo: Don Hall, courtesy of the MacKenzie Art Gallery
Page 112

Vermine Virus
1999
Watercolour and graphite on paper
27.8 × 31 cm
Collection of the MacKenzie Art Gallery, purchased with the financial support of the Canada Council for the Arts Acquisition Assistance Program
2000-001-004
Photo: Don Hall, courtesy of the MacKenzie Art Gallery
Page 112

Parfleche
2011
Oil on canvas
91.4 × 61 cm
Collection of Christopher Varley + Sandra Shaul
Photo: Michael Cullen, TPG Digital Art Services, Courtesy of the Kinsman Robinson Galleries, Toronto
Page 91

Parfleche #14 Sitting Bull Sioux
1983
Mixed media on paper
54.5 × 54.5 cm
Collection of Barry Ace and Earl Truelove
Page 85

Parfleche #19 Chief Poundmaker
1983
Mixed media on paper
54.5 × 54.5 cm
Collection of Barry Ace and Earl Truelove
Page 85

Parfleche #20/Wovoka
1983
Acrylic and porcupine quills on paper
56.52 × 56.52 cm
Royal Ontario Museum
984.229.1
Photo: courtesy of the Royal Ontario Museum, © ROM
Page 84

Parfleche II
1985
Oil wash on paper
40.3 × 59.3 cm
Indigenous Art Collection, Crown-Indigenous Relations and Northern Affairs Canada / Collection d'art autochtones, Relations Couronne-Autochtones et Affaires du Nord Canada
Photo: Lawrence Cook
Page 72

Parfleche II – C
1984
Acrylic and porcupine quills on paper
Folded: 57 × 57 cm
McMichael Canadian Art Collection. Bequest of Anthony David Ryan
1995.23
Page 71

Parfleche II "H"
1984
Acrylic with porcupine quills on paper
Framed: 66.3 × 66.3 cm
Indigenous Art Collection, Crown-Indigenous Relations and Northern Affairs Canada / Collection d'art autochtones, Relations Couronne-Autochtones et Affaires du Nord Canada
Photo: Lawrence Cook
Page 70

Parfleche III "A"
1985
Acrylic on paper
77 × 97.4 cm
Indigenous Art Collection, Crown-Indigenous Relations and Northern Affairs Canada / Collection d'art autochtones, Relations Couronne-Autochtones et Affaires du Nord Canada
Photo: Lawrence Cook
Page 73

Parfleche for Alex Janvier
1999
Oil on canvas
101.6 × 50.8 cm
Courtesy of the artist
Photo: Michael Cullen, TPG Digital Art Services, Courtesy of the Kinsman Robinson Galleries, Toronto
Page 82

Parfleche for Edna Manitowabi
1999
Oil on canvas
101.6 × 50.8 cm
Courtesy of the artist
Image courtesy of McMaster Museum of Art, Hamilton; photo: Michael Cullen, TPG Digital Art Services
Page 82

Parfleche for Norval Morrisseau
1999
Oil on canvas, mounted to wood
51 × 101 × 6 cm
Courtesy of the National Museum of the American Indian, Smithsonian Institution
Purchase from the artist, 2012
26/9030
Photo: R.A. Whiteside
Page 83
* exhibited at the NMAI only

Parfleche for Rock Hudson
1985
Acrylic on canvas
111.8 × 90.2 cm
Courtesy of the artist
Photo: Art Gallery of Ontario
Page 200

Parfleches for the Last Supper
1983
Acrylic and porcupine quills on paper
56 × 56 cm each
Collection of the Winnipeg Art Gallery. Gift of Mr. Carl T. Grant, Artvest Inc., G-86-460 to G-86-472
Photo: Serge Gumenyuk, courtesy of the Winnipeg Art Gallery
Page 78–79

Parfleche #1, Matthew
1983
From *Parfleches for the Last Supper*
Acrylic and porcupine quills on paper
56 × 56 cm
Collection of the Winnipeg Art Gallery. Gift of Mr. Carl T. Grant, Artvest Inc., G-86-460
Photo: Serge Gumenyuk, courtesy of the Winnipeg Art Gallery
Page 78

Parfleche #2, James the Less
1983
From *Parfleches for the Last Supper*
Acrylic and porcupine quills on paper
56 × 56 cm
Collection of the Winnipeg Art Gallery. Gift of Mr. Carl T. Grant, Artvest Inc., G-86-461
Photo: Serge Gumenyuk, courtesy of the Winnipeg Art Gallery
Page 78

Parfleche #3, Jude
1983
From *Parfleches for the Last Supper*
Acrylic and porcupine quills on paper
56 × 56 cm
Collection of the Winnipeg Art Gallery. Gift of Mr. Carl T. Grant, Artvest Inc., G-86-462
Photo: Serge Gumenyuk, courtesy of the Winnipeg Art Gallery
Page 78

Parfleche #4, Simon
1983
From *Parfleches for the Last Supper*
Acrylic and porcupine quills on paper
56 × 56 cm
Collection of the Winnipeg Art Gallery. Gift of Mr. Carl T. Grant, Artvest Inc., G-86-463
Photo: Serge Gumenyuk, courtesy of the Winnipeg Art Gallery
Page 78

Parfleche #5, Philip
1983
From *Parfleches for the Last Supper*
Acrylic and porcupine quills on paper
56 × 56 cm
Collection of the Winnipeg Art Gallery. Gift of Mr. Carl T. Grant, Artvest Inc., G-86-464
Photo: Serge Gumenyuk, courtesy of the Winnipeg Art Gallery
Page 78

Parfleche #6, Andrew
1983
From *Parfleches for the Last Supper*
Acrylic and porcupine quills on paper
56 × 56 cm
Collection of the Winnipeg Art Gallery. Gift of Mr. Carl T. Grant, Artvest Inc., G-86-465
Photo: Serge Gumenyuk, courtesy of the Winnipeg Art Gallery
Page 78

Parfleche #7, Bartholomew
1983
From *Parfleches for the Last Supper*
Acrylic and porcupine quills on paper
56 × 56 cm
Collection of the Winnipeg Art Gallery. Gift of Mr. Carl T. Grant, Artvest Inc., G-86-466
Photo: Serge Gumenyuk, courtesy of the Winnipeg Art Gallery
Page 78

Parfleche #8, Thomas
1983
From *Parfleches for the Last Supper*
Acrylic and porcupine quills on paper
56 × 56 cm
Collection of the Winnipeg Art Gallery. Gift of Mr. Carl T. Grant, Artvest Inc., G-86-467
Photo: Serge Gumenyuk, courtesy of the Winnipeg Art Gallery
Page 78

Parfleche #9, James
1983
From *Parfleches for the Last Supper*
Acrylic and porcupine quills on paper
56 × 56 cm
Collection of the Winnipeg Art Gallery. Gift of Mr. Carl T. Grant, Artvest Inc., G-86-468
Photo: Serge Gumenyuk, courtesy of the Winnipeg Art Gallery
Page 78

Parfleche #10, John
1983
From *Parfleches for the Last Supper*
Acrylic and porcupine quills on paper
56 × 56 cm
Collection of the Winnipeg Art Gallery. Gift of Mr. Carl T. Grant, Artvest Inc., G-86-469
Photo: Serge Gumenyuk, courtesy of the Winnipeg Art Gallery
Page 79

Parfleche #11, Judas
1983
From *Parfleches for the Last Supper*
Acrylic and porcupine quills on paper
56 × 56 cm
Collection of the Winnipeg Art Gallery. Gift of Mr. Carl T. Grant, Artvest Inc., G-86-470
Photo: Serge Gumenyuk, courtesy of the Winnipeg Art Gallery
Page 79

Parfleche #12, Jesus
1983
From *Parfleches for the Last Supper*
Acrylic and porcupine quills on paper
56 × 56 cm
Collection of the Winnipeg Art Gallery. Gift of Mr. Carl T. Grant, Artvest Inc., G-86-471
Photo: Serge Gumenyuk, courtesy of the Winnipeg Art Gallery
Page 79

Parfleche #13, Peter
1983
From *Parfleches for the Last Supper*
Acrylic and porcupine quills on paper
56 × 56 cm
Collection of the Winnipeg Art Gallery. Gift of Mr. Carl T. Grant, Artvest Inc., G-86-472
Photo: Serge Gumenyuk, courtesy of the Winnipeg Art Gallery
Page 79

Paris/Ojibwa
2010
Multimedia installation: oil on wood, oil on canvas, video (colour, 3 min. 52 sec.), audio (6 min. 20 sec.), and gold lettering
Installed: 358 × 488 × 488 cm
Art Gallery of Ontario
Gift of Robert Houle, with funds by exchange from a gift in memory of J.G. Althouse from Isobel Althouse Wilkinson and John Provost Wilkinson, 2020
2020/3
Photo: Art Gallery of Ontario
Page 116-117

Pontiac
1996
Oil, porcupine quills, and varnish on canvas
30.5 × 30.5 cm
Collection of David McIntosh
Photo: Art Gallery of Ontario
Page 151

Premises for Self Rule: Constitution Act, 1982
1994
Oil on canvas, photo emulsion on canvas, and laser-cut vinyl
Painting: 152.4 × 152.4 cm; photograph on canvas: 50 × 80 cm; laser-cut vinyl: 152.4 × 152.4 cm
Art Gallery of Ontario
Purchased with funds from the Estate of Mary Eileen Ash, 2014
2014/1
Photo: Art Gallery of Ontario
Page 177

Premises for Self Rule: Indian Act, 1876
1994
Oil on canvas, photo emulsion on canvas, and laser-cut vinyl
Overall: 152.4 × 304.8 cm
Collection of the Canada Council Art Bank
94/5-0259
Photo: Brandon Clarida
Page 176

Premises for Self Rule: The British North America Act, 1867
1994
Oil on canvas, photo emulsion on canvas, and laser-cut vinyl
Overall: 152.4 × 304.8 cm
Collection of Osler, Hoskin & Harcourt LLP
Photo: Art Gallery of Ontario
Page 175

Premises for Self Rule: The Royal Proclamation, 1763
1994
Oil on canvas, photo emulsion on canvas, and laser-cut vinyl
Overall: 152.4 × 304.8 cm
City of Toronto Art Collection, MOCCA Collection
1994.002
Image courtesy of the City of Toronto
Page 174

Premises for Self Rule: Treaty No. 1
1994
Acrylic on canvas, photo emulsion on canvas, and laser-cut vinyl
Photographic panel: 38 × 64 × 5 cm; painting: 152 × 152 × 5 cm; laser-cut vinyl text: 152 × 152 cm
Collection of the Winnipeg Art Gallery. Acquired with funds from the Canada Council for the Arts Acquisition Assistance Program, G-96-11 abc
Photo: Ernest Mayer, courtesy of the Winnipeg Art Gallery
Page 178

Rainbow Woman
1982
Alkyd paint on wood
13.6 × 239 × 4.3 cm
Indigenous Art Collection, Crown-Indigenous Relations and Northern Affairs Canada / Collection d'art autochtones, Relations Couronne-Autochtones et Affaires du Nord Canada
Photo: Lawrence Cook
Page 68–69

Red is Beautiful
1970
Acrylic on canvas
45.5 × 61 cm
Musée canadien de l'histoire / Canadian Museum of History
V-F-174
Page 45

Return of the Red Man #1
1992
Polaroid photo, tape, paint, and magazine
45.72 × 76.2 cm
Collection of Stephen B. Smart
Photo: Art Gallery of Ontario
Page 14

Royal Proclamation 1763
1985
Acrylic on paper
106 × 75 cm
Indigenous Art Collection, Crown-Indigenous Relations and Northern Affairs Canada / Collection d'art autochtones, Relations Couronne-Autochtones et Affaires du Nord Canada
Photo: Lawrence Cook
Page 171

Sandy Bay
1998–1999
Oil, black and white photograph, colour photograph on canvas, and Masonite
300 × 548.4 cm
Collection of the Winnipeg Art Gallery. Acquired with funds from the President's Appeal 2000 and with the support of the Canada Council for the Arts Acquisition Assistance program
2000-87 a-e
Photo: Ernest Mayer, courtesy of the Winnipeg Art Gallery
Page 156–157

Sandy Bay
2007
Oil on Masonite
22.9 x 29.8 cm
Courtesy of the artist
Photo: Michael Cullen, TPG Digital Art Services
Page 124

Sandy Bay Indian Residential School I (schoolhouse, praying, sleeping, waiting, people, lake)
2010–2011
9 oil on canvas panels, watercolour, graphite and vinyl text on wall, and wainscoting
Each panel 30.5 × 22.9 × 1.9 cm; overall installation 195.6 × 337.8 cm
Courtesy of the artist
Installation photo: Keesic Douglas
Page 162

Sandy Bay Indian Residential School II (schoolhouse, praying, sleeping, waiting, people, lake)
2010–2011
9 oil on canvas panels, watercolour, graphite and vinyl text on wall, and wainscoting
7 panels each 30.5 × 22.9 × 1.9 cm, 2 panels each 35.6 × 27.9 cm × 1.9 cm; overall installation 195.6 × 337.8 cm
Courtesy of the artist
Installation photo: Keesic Douglas
Page 163

Sandy Bay Indian Residential School III (schoolhouse, praying, sleeping, people)
2012
4 oil on canvas panels, watercolour, and graphite and vinyl text on wall
Each panel 35.6 × 27.9 × 3.8 cm; overall installation 195.6 × 337.8 cm
Courtesy of the artist
Installation photo: Keesic Douglas
Page 164
* Not exhibited

Sandy Bay Indian Residential School IV (alizarin crimson, cobalt violet, winsor red deep, magenta, cadmium red light, cadmium red deep)
2012
6 oil on canvas panels, watercolour, graphite and vinyl text on wall, and wainscoting
Each panel 61 × 30.5 × 1.9 cm; overall installation 195.6 × 337.8 cm
Courtesy of the artist
Installation photo: Keesic Douglas
Page 165

Savage Love
c. 2003
Book covers and oil on canvas
30 × 80 × 2 cm
Collection of Grant Wedge and Bob Crouch
Photo: Art Gallery of Ontario
Page 202

Self Portraits
1990–1995
Graphite, polaroid prints, coloured pencil, Letraset, Krylon spray paint, and handmade paper
Overall closed: 27.1 × 24 × 1.5 cm
Art Gallery of Ontario
Gift of Stephen B. Smart, 2018
2018/3730
Photo: Art Gallery of Ontario
Pages 204–205

Seven Grandfathers

ma sah beh (transforming figure of the woodlands), quuh yu koo sá win (honesty)
2013
From *Seven Grandfathers*
Oil on canvas
20.3 cm diameter
Art Gallery of Ontario
Purchased with the assistance of the Martinsell Fund, 2016
2015/38.7
Photo: Art Gallery of Ontario
Page 89

mahéen gun (wolf), tah bus sá nin de zoo win (humility)
2013
From *Seven Grandfathers*
Oil on canvas
20.3 cm diameter
Art Gallery of Ontario
Purchased with the assistance of the Martinsell Fund, 2016
2015/38.4
Photo: Art Gallery of Ontario
Page 89

me ge zée (eagle), sah gee wá win (love)
2013
From *Seven Grandfathers*
Oil on canvas
20.3 cm diameter
Art Gallery of Ontario
Purchased with the assistance of the Martinsell Fund, 2016
2015/38.1
Photo: Art Gallery of Ontario
Page 88

muh quáh (bear), sóon ge daá win (courage)
2013
From *Seven Grandfathers*
Oil on canvas
20.3 cm diameter
Art Gallery of Ontario
Purchased with the assistance of the Martinsell Fund, 2016
2015/38.6
Photo: Art Gallery of Ontario
Page 89

músh kooda pezhéke (buffalo), me nah da ne mo win (respect)
2013
From *Seven Grandfathers*
Oil on canvas
20.3 cm diameter
Art Gallery of Ontario
Purchased with the assistance of the Martinsell Fund, 2016
2015/38.3
Photo: Art Gallery of Ontario
Page 89

shin gah dá me quaun (turtle), dah wa win (truth)
2013
From *Seven Grandfathers*
Oil on canvas
20.3 cm diameter
Art Gallery of Ontario
Purchased with the assistance of the Martinsell Fund, 2016
2015/38.5
Photo: Art Gallery of Ontario
Page 89

uh mik (beaver), neb wah káh win (wisdom)
2013
From *Seven Grandfathers*
Oil on canvas
20.3 cm diameter
Art Gallery of Ontario
Purchased with the assistance of the Martinsell Fund, 2016
2015/38.2
Photo: Art Gallery of Ontario
Page 89

Seven in Steel
1989
Oil on steel and maple
130.9 × 644 × 9.5 cm overall;
7 steel sections: 121.9 × 91.5 × .3 cm;
maple rail in 3 sections: 9.5 × 9.5 × 215 cm each (approx.)
National Gallery of Canada.
Gift of Norman Garnet, Toronto, 1996
Acc. # 38374.1-10
Photo: NGC
Page 136–137

Sketchbook for Paris/Ojibwa
2006
16 × 11.5 × 3 cm
Collection of Paul Gardner
* not illustrated

Shaman Dream in Colour
2015
Oil on canvas
44 × 60.96 cm
Collection of Sylvia and Michael Smith
Photo: Michael Cullen, TPG Digital Art Services, Courtesy of the Kinsman Robinson Galleries, Toronto
Page 166

Shaman Heals by Touching
2015
Oil on canvas
44 × 60.96 cm
Collection of Brian Norton
Photo: Michael Cullen, TPG Digital Art Services, Courtesy of the Kinsman Robinson Galleries, Toronto
Page 167

Shaman Never Die
2015
Oil on canvas
44 × 60.96 cm
Collection of Wanda Nanibush
Photo: Michael Cullen, TPG Digital Art Services, Courtesy of the Kinsman Robinson Galleries, Toronto
Page 167

Shaman Takes Away the Pain
2015
Oil on canvas
44 × 60.96 cm
Private collection
Photo: Michael Cullen, TPG Digital Art Services, Courtesy of the Kinsman Robinson Galleries, Toronto
Page 166

Shape Shifter
2009
Oil on paper
112.5 × 76 cm
Indigenous Art Collection, Crown-Indigenous Relations and Northern Affairs Canada / Collection d'art autochtones, Relations Couronne-Autochtones et Affaires du Nord Canada
Photo: Lawrence Cook
Page 161

Shield for Aboriginal Title
1990
Hide, human hair, oil paint, porcupine quill, and graphite on metal
67.4 cm diameter
Collection of David Andrew Welling
Photo: Art Gallery of Ontario
Page 180

Sister Clothilde
2009
Oil on paper
112.5 × 76 cm
Indigenous Art Collection, Crown-Indigenous Relations and Northern Affairs Canada / Collection d'art autochtones, Relations Couronne-Autochtones et Affaires du Nord Canada
Photo: Lawrence Cook
Page 160

Square 4
1980
Acrylic on canvas
Framed: 85.5 × 85.5 cm
Indigenous Art Collection, Crown-Indigenous Relations and Northern Affairs Canada / Collection d'art autochtones, Relations Couronne-Autochtones et Affaires du Nord Canada
Photo: Lawrence Cook
Page 67

Square Homage to Albers
1979
Acrylic on canvas
102.1 × 87 cm
Indigenous Art Collection, Crown-Indigenous Relations and Northern Affairs Canada / Collection d'art autochtones, Relations Couronne-Autochtones et Affaires du Nord Canada
Photo: Lawrence Cook
Page 66

Square No. 3
1978
Acrylic on canvas and on painted wooden mount
76 × 76 × 2.4 cm; mount: 85.2 × 85.2 cm
National Gallery of Canada.
Gift of Myron Laskin, Santa Monica, California, 1987
Acc. # 29856
Photo: NGC
Page 57

Study for *Premises for Self Rule*
1994
Assemblage of acrylic-painted, multi-ply boards in blue, dark red, green, red-brown, and yellow with graphite and blind inscriptions, photogravures with relief printed text, and acetate films with laser-printed text, mounted to white multi-ply board
Mount (support for assemblage): 75 × 138 × 2 cm; framed: 77.5 × 140.5 × 5 cm
Art Gallery of Ontario
Gift of Stephen B. Smart, 2020
2020/150
Photo: Art Gallery of Ontario
Page 179

Study for *These Apaches Are Not Helicopters*
1999
Collage: inkjet prints, vinyl letters, graphite, coloured pencil, ink, and oil paint on paper
Support: 48 × 64.4 × 0.2 cm; mount: 55.9 × 71.1 cm
Art Gallery of Ontario
Gift of Stephen B. Smart, 2018
2018/3728
Photo: Art Gallery of Ontario
Page 140

The Chief
1996
Oil on canvas
with Pontiac hood ornament
86.4 × 190.5 cm + ornament
Royal Bank of Canada Art Collection
Photo: Art Gallery of Ontario
Page 150

The Pines
2002–2004
Oil on canvas
Panel (centre): 91.4 × 121.9 cm; panel (side, each of two): 91.4 × 91.4 cm
Art Gallery of Ontario
Gift of Susan Whitney, 2017
2017/243
Photo: Art Gallery of Ontario
Page 187

Transforming BlueThunder
2021
Oil on mylar
222.25 × 106.68 cm
Courtesy of the artist
Photo: Art Gallery of Ontario
Page 10

Untitled (Male Nude)
2007
Conté on paper
182 × 127 cm
Collection of Barry Ace and Earl Truelove
Page 201

Untitled (Palisade colour bar)
2006
Oil on wood
25 × 183.5 × 4 cm
Collection of Grant Wedge & Bob Crouch
Photo: Art Gallery of Ontario
Page 113

Warrior à la Buren
2010
Oil stick on handmade paper
78.7 × 54.6 cm
Courtesy of the artist
Photo: Art Gallery of Ontario
Page 203

Warrior Lances for Temagami
1989
Mixed-media sculpture
Base: 5 × 76.2 cm diameter, overall: 152.5 × 76.2 cm diameter
Indigenous Art Collection, Crown-Indigenous Relations and Northern Affairs Canada / Collection d'art autochtones, Relations Couronne-Autochtones et Affaires du Nord Canada
Photo: Lawrence Cook
Page 183

Warrior Resting on Map of Lutetia
2010
Graphite on antique map
78.7 × 54.6 cm
Courtesy of the artist
Photo: Art Gallery of Ontario
Page 203

Working study for *Kanata*
1991–1992
Collage on paper board
Sheet: 21.5 × 27.8 cm
Art Gallery of Ontario
Gift of Lynn and Stephen Smart, 2004
2005/45
* not illustrated

Zero Hour
1988
Mixed media, oil on canvas, rocks, and sand
Dimensions vary by installation
Agnes Etherington Art Centre, Queen's University, Kingston. Purchase, Canada Council for the Arts Acquisition Assistance Program, 1998 (41-011)
Image courtesy of Agnes Etherington Art Centre, Queen's University
Pages 192–193

...

Apsáalooke (Crow) Artist once known
a miniature parfleche
1890–1910
Rawhide and natural dyes
30.5 × 30.5 cm
Courtesy of Robert Houle
Image courtesy of McMaster Museum of Art, Hamilton; photo: Michael Cullen, TPG Digital Art Services
Page 81

Photographer unknown
Robert Houle at the Assiniboia Residential High School dormitory in Winnipeg, preparing to go on the Centennial Train, which travelled across the country telling the story of "Canada," in 1967
Image courtesy of the artist
Page 155

THANK YOU

Supporting Sponsor

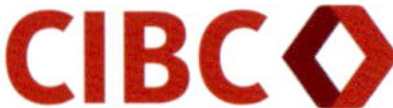

Contributing Sponsor

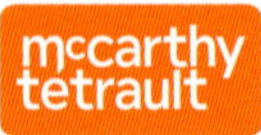

Generous Support

Cecily & Robert Bradshaw
The Delaney Family Foundation
Gerald Sheff & Shanitha Kachan
David Staines & Noreen Taylor

Media Partner

blogTO

The Art Gallery of Ontario is partially funded by the Ontario Ministry of Culture. Additional operating support is received from the City of Toronto, the Department of Canadian Heritage, and the Canada Council for the Arts. This publication is supported by the Sorel Etrog Publication Fund.

Contemporary programming at the Art Gallery of Ontario is supported by

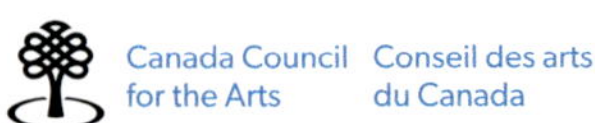

Library and Archives Canada Cataloguing in Publication

Title: Robert Houle : red is beautiful.
Other titles: Robert Houle (Toronto, Ont.) | Red is beautiful
Names: Container of (work): Houle, Robert. Works. Selections. | Art Gallery of Ontario, publisher.
Description: Essays by Kay WalkingStick, Stephen Borys, Jamelie Hassan and Ron Benner, Gerald Vizenor, Wanda Nanibush, Duke Redbird, Mark A. Cheetham, Alanaise Onischin Ferguson with Megan Davies, David Penney, Faye HeavyShield, Jessica L. Horton, and Michael Bell; edited by Wanda Nanibush.
Identifiers: Canadiana 20210329297 | ISBN 9781636810379 (hardcover)
Subjects: LCSH: Houle, Robert. | LCSH: Indigenous art—Canada.
Classification: LCC N6549.H67 A4 2021 | DDC 709.2—dc23

This book was published on the occasion of the exhibition *Robert Houle: Red is Beautiful*, organized by the Art Gallery of Ontario from December 3, 2021 to April 18, 2022.

Contemporary Calgary
Calgary, Alberta, Canada
June 2022 – September 2022

Winnipeg Art Gallery
Winnipeg, Manitoba, Canada
October 2022 – March 2023

National Museum of the American Indian
Washington, DC, United States
May 2023 – May 2024

Published in 2021 by the Art Gallery of Ontario and DelMonico Books • D.A.P.

Art Gallery of Ontario
317 Dundas Street West
Toronto, Ontario M5T 1G4
Canada
www.ago.ca

DelMonico Books
available through ARTBOOK | D.A.P.
75 Broad Street, Suite 630
New York, NY 10004
artbook.com
delmonicobooks.com

Printed and bound in Belgium
ISBN: 978-1-63681-037-9

10 9 8 7 6 5 4 3 2 1

PUBLICATION

Editor: Wanda Nanibush
Managing Editor: Jim Shedden
Production and Copy Editors: Gina Badger, Nives Hajdin, Sarah Liss
Publishing Coordinator: Kathryn Yuen
Proofreader: Judy Phillips
Designer: Sébastien Aubin
Typeset: Allen's Cruz
Photographers: Craig Boyko, Sean Weaver
Pre-Press: Type A Print Inc.
Printing: Type A Print Inc.

AGO EXHIBITION

Deputy Director and Chief Curator: Julian Cox
Curator: Wanda Nanibush
Project Manager: Katarina Veljovic
Administrative Assistant: Chloé Wittes
Interpretive Planner: Nadia Abraham
Editors: Nives Hajdin, Sarah Liss
Exhibition Design: Theodora Doulamis
Graphic Design: Aleksandra Grzywaczewska
Production: Malene Hjørngaard, Evelyn Quinn

EXHIBITIONS AND COLLECTIONS

Chief, Exhibitions, Collections, & Conservation: Jessica Bright
Associate Director, Exhibitions: Laura Comerford
Registration: Alison Beckett, Cindy Brouse, Jerry Drozdowsky, Joel Herman, Dale Mahar, Sabine Schaefer, Curtis Strilchuk
Collection Information: Alexandra Cousins, Tracy Mallon-Jensen, Liana Radvak, Joe Venturella, Olga Zotova
Conservators: Maureen del Degan, Shu-Wen Lin, Christina McLean, Meaghan Monaghan, Sherry Phillips, Brent Roe, Fiona Rutka, Maria Sullivan, Sjoukje van der Laan, Joan Weir, Katharine Whitman, John Williams

LOGISTICS AND ART SERVICES

Gregory Baszun, Scott Cameron, Colin Campbell, Meagan Christou, Patric Colosimo, Brian Davis, Randal Fedje, Tina Giovinazzo, Brian Groombridge, Roland Hardy, Iain Hoadley, Matthew Janisse, Ruth Jones, David Kinsman, Jason Laudadio, Alison Lindsay, Paul Mathiesen, Jacques Oulé, Angelo Pedari, Craig Spence, Manny Trinh, Craig Whiteside, Darin Yorston, Tanya Zhilinsky

EDUCATION & PROGRAMMING

Richard & Elizabeth Currie Chief, Education & Programming: Audrey Hudson

Director, Engagement & Learning: Paola Poletto

Education & Programming: Danah Abusido, Elizabeth Adams, Lesley Ashton, Madelyne Beckles, Samantha Benjamin, Erica Chan, Maureen DaSilva, Sarah Febbraro, Nathan Huisman, Idalette Martins, Kathleen McLean, Deborah Nolan, Zavette Quadros-Evangelista, Annie Roper, Melissa Smith

MEDIA PRODUCTION

Matthew Scott

Front cover designed by Sébastien Aubin, based on a weaving bands motif that inspired Robert Houle's *Red is Beautiful* (1970).

Page 252:
Robert Houle with Simon the cat in the living room of his Parliament Street apartment in the 1980s. Photographed by Paul Gardner.
Image courtesy of the artist.

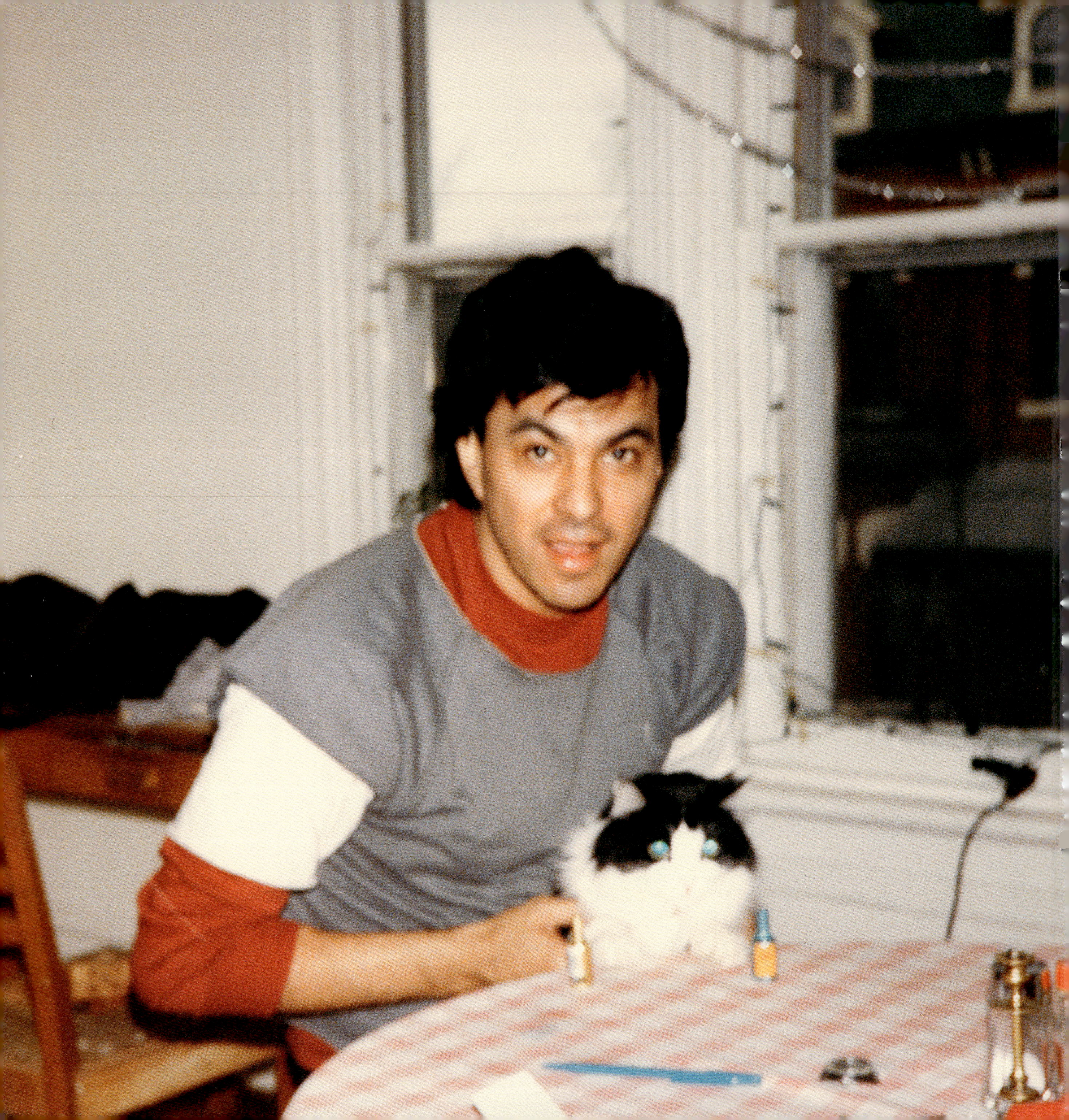